For my wife, Nancy, and son, Austin. You are both my true north.
— Mike

This is dedicated to my parents, and my sister, Margaret, who have always been there for me.
— Austin

For my family: Bruno, Nina, Lucca, Vicente, Pilar.
—Nelson

For Meg.
—Zach

LOGO DESIGN BY
J.R. ROBINSON AND **RIKYO**
WILD BLUE YONDER CREATED BY
RAICHT, HOWARD, AND **HARRISON**

COVER
ZACH HOWARD
COLLECTION EDITORS
JUSTIN EISINGER AND ALONZO SIMON
COLLECTION DESIGN
JEFF POWELL

Special thanks to Savannah Ervin.

ISBN: 978-1-61377-863-0

18 17 16 15   2 3 4 5

Ted Adams, CEO & Publisher
Greg Goldstein, President & COO
Robbie Robbins, EVP/Sr. Graphic Artist
Chris Ryall, Chief Creative Officer/Editor-in-Chief
Matthew Ruzicka, CPA, Chief Financial Officer
Alan Payne, VP of Sales
Dirk Wood, VP of Marketing
Lorelei Bunjes, VP of Digital Services
Jeff Webber, VP of Digital Publishing & Business Development

www.IDWPUBLISHING.com
IDW founded by Ted Adams, Alex Garner, Kris Oprisko, and Robbie Robbins

Facebook: **facebook.com/idwpublishing**
Twitter: **@idwpublishing**
YouTube: **youtube.com/idwpublishing**
Instagram: **instagram.com/idwpublishing**
deviantART: **idwpublishing.deviantart.com**
Pinterest: **pinterest.com/idwpublishing/idw-staff-faves**

STORY & WRITER
MIKE RAICHT
STORY & ART
ZACH HOWARD
STORY
AUSTIN HARRISON
COLOR
NELSON DANIEL
INK ASSIST
JOLYON YATES
LETTERS
THOMPSON KNOX
SERIES EDITOR
BOBBY CURNOW

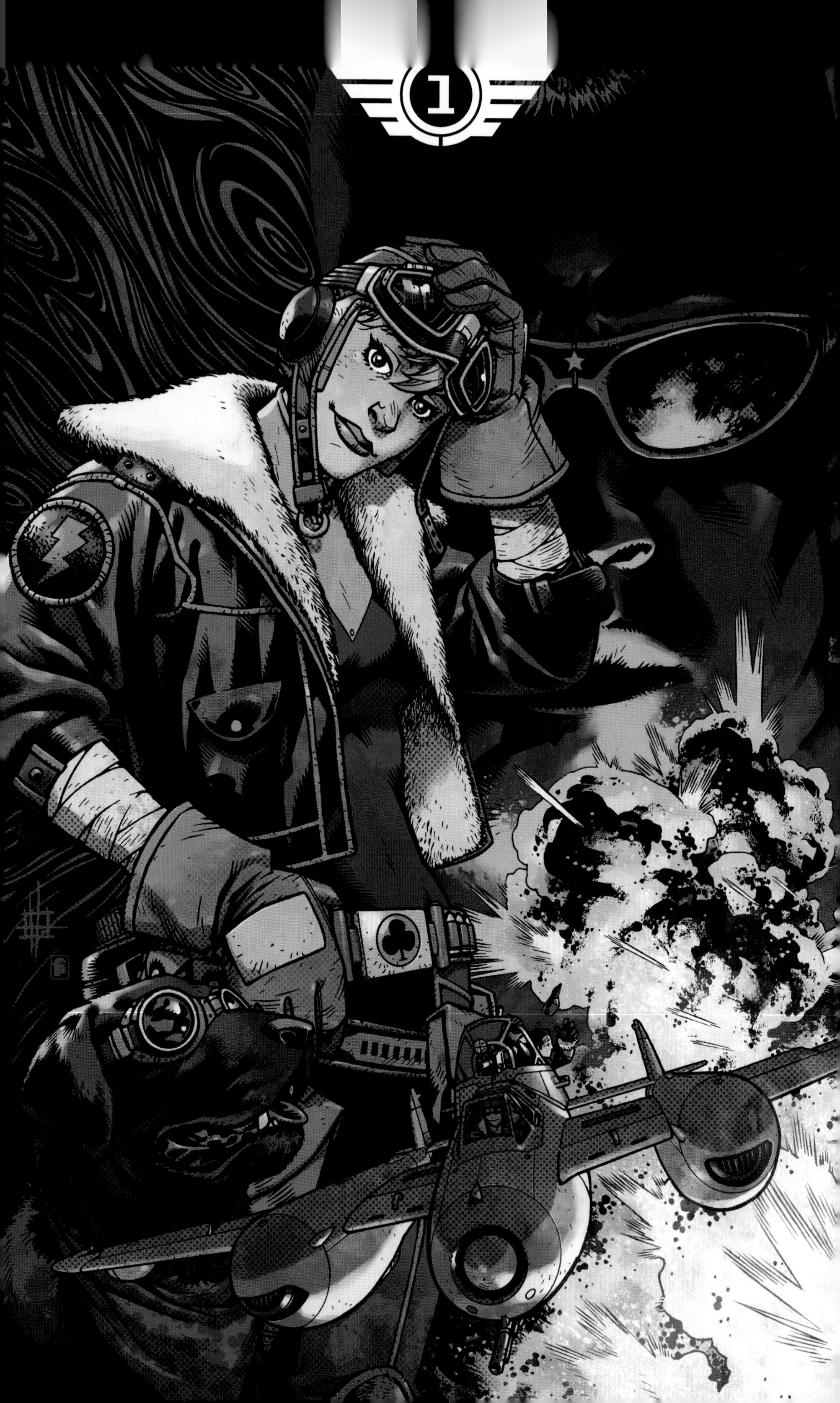

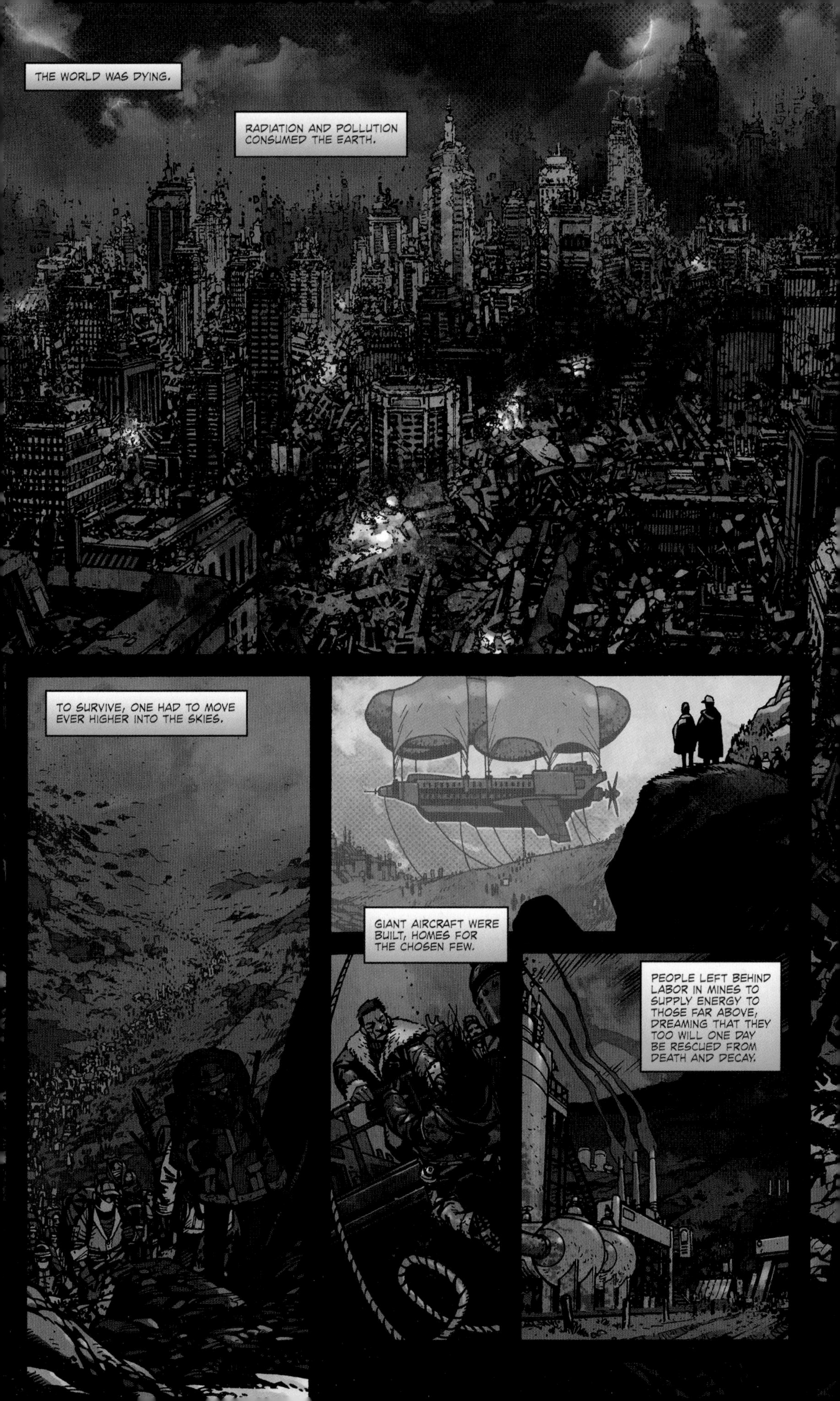
THE WORLD WAS DYING.
RADIATION AND POLLUTION CONSUMED THE EARTH.
TO SURVIVE, ONE HAD TO MOVE EVER HIGHER INTO THE SKIES.
GIANT AIRCRAFT WERE BUILT, HOMES FOR THE CHOSEN FEW.
PEOPLE LEFT BEHIND LABOR IN MINES TO SUPPLY ENERGY TO THOSE FAR ABOVE, DREAMING THAT THEY TOO WILL ONE DAY BE RESCUED FROM DEATH AND DECAY.

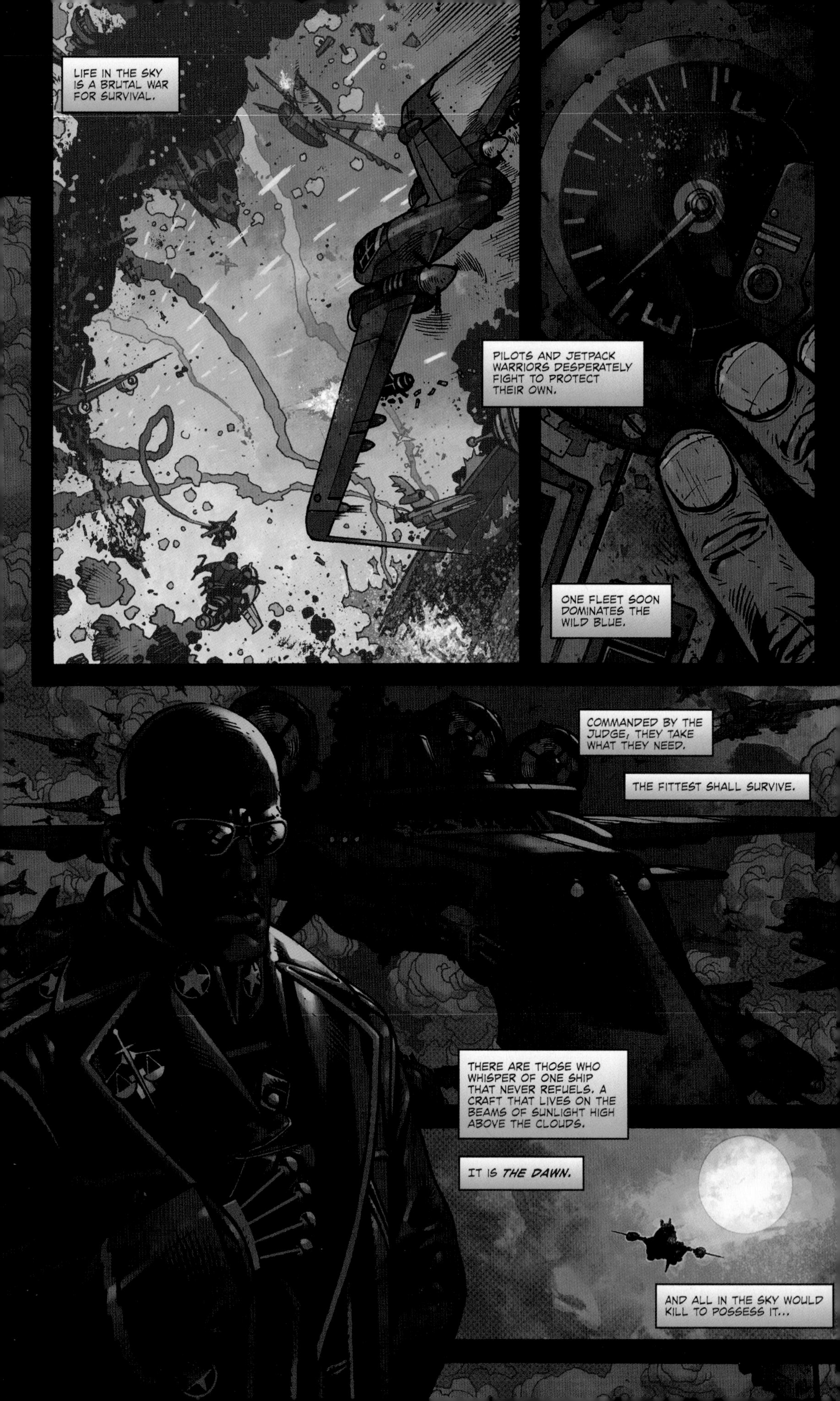

LIFE IN THE SKY IS A BRUTAL WAR FOR SURVIVAL.
PILOTS AND JETPACK WARRIORS DESPERATELY FIGHT TO PROTECT THEIR OWN.
ONE FLEET SOON DOMINATES THE WILD BLUE.
COMMANDED BY THE JUDGE, THEY TAKE WHAT THEY NEED.
THE FITTEST SHALL SURVIVE.
THERE ARE THOSE WHO WHISPER OF ONE SHIP THAT NEVER REFUELS. A CRAFT THAT LIVES ON THE BEAMS OF SUNLIGHT HIGH ABOVE THE CLOUDS.
IT IS THE DAWN.
AND ALL IN THE SKY WOULD KILL TO POSSESS IT...

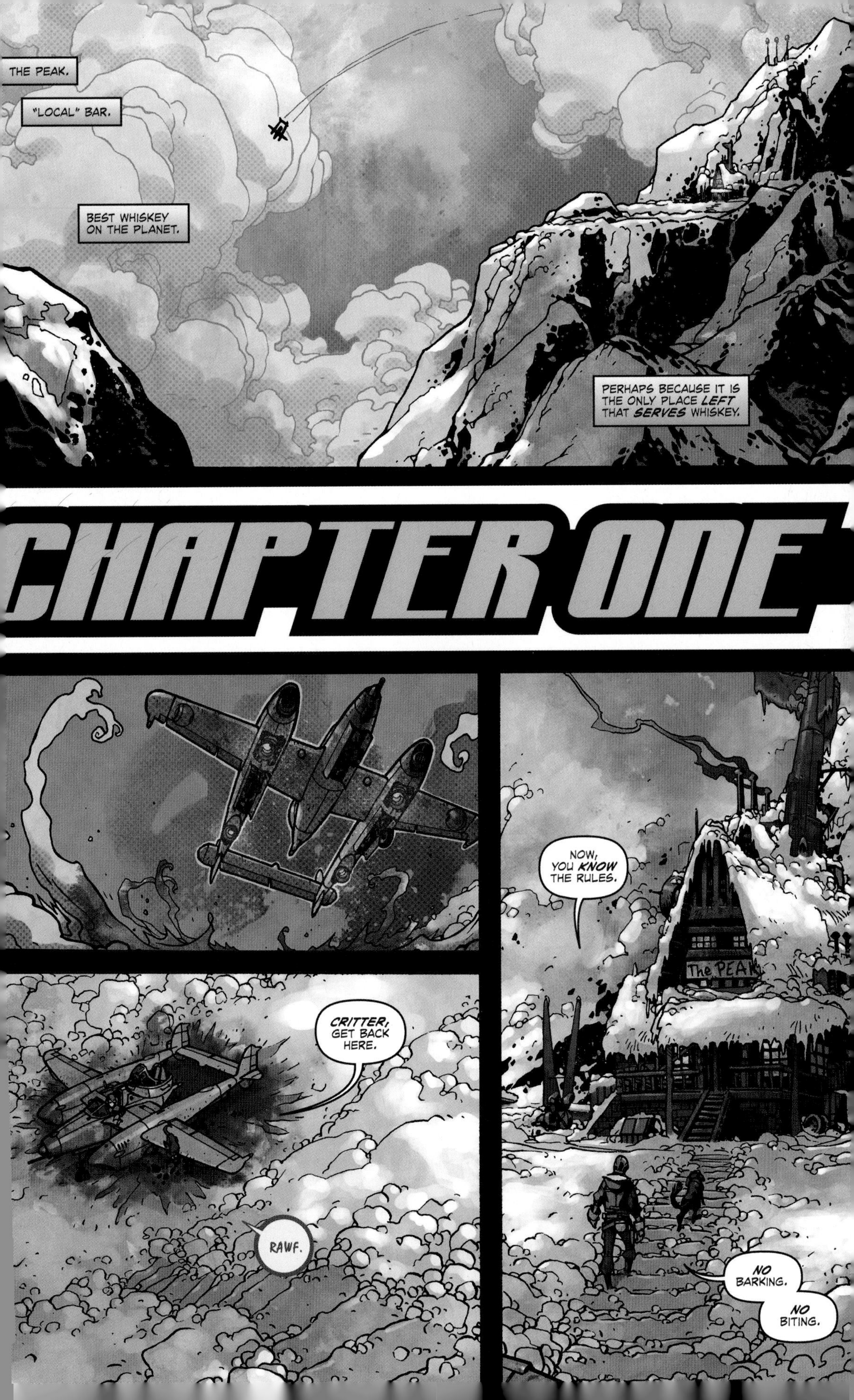
THE PEAK.
"LOCAL" BAR.
BEST WHISKEY ON THE PLANET.
PERHAPS BECAUSE IT IS THE ONLY PLACE *LEFT* THAT *SERVES* WHISKEY.
CHAPTER ONE
NOW, YOU *KNOW* THE RULES.
The PEAK
CRITTER, GET BACK HERE.
RAWF.
NO BARKING.
NO BITING.

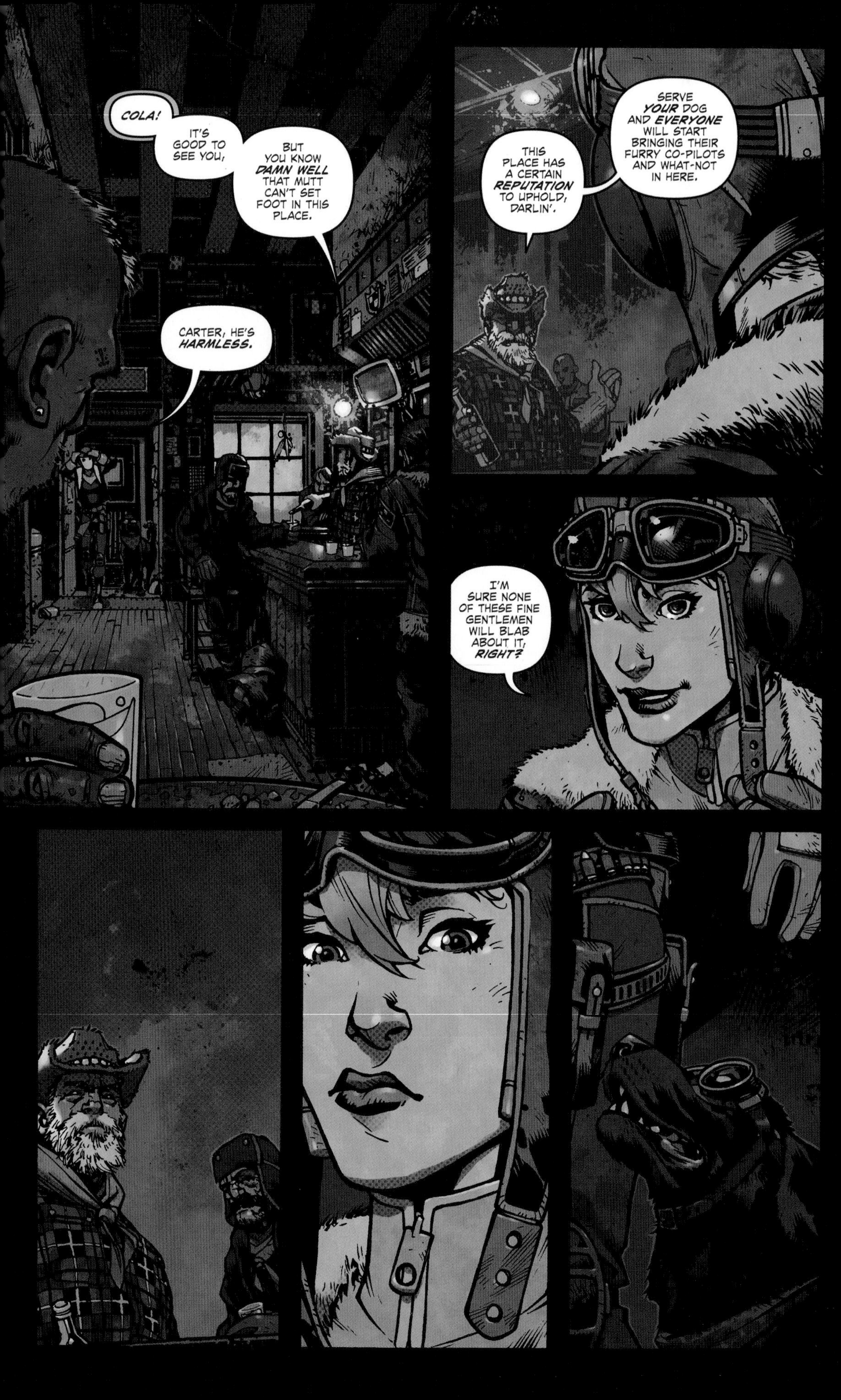
COLA!
IT'S GOOD TO SEE YOU,
BUT YOU KNOW DAMN WELL THAT MUTT CAN'T SET FOOT IN THIS PLACE.
CARTER, HE'S HARMLESS.
THIS PLACE HAS A CERTAIN REPUTATION TO UPHOLD, DARLIN'.
SERVE YOUR DOG AND EVERYONE WILL START BRINGING THEIR FURRY CO-PILOTS AND WHAT-NOT IN HERE.
I'M SURE NONE OF THESE FINE GENTLEMEN WILL BLAB ABOUT IT, RIGHT?

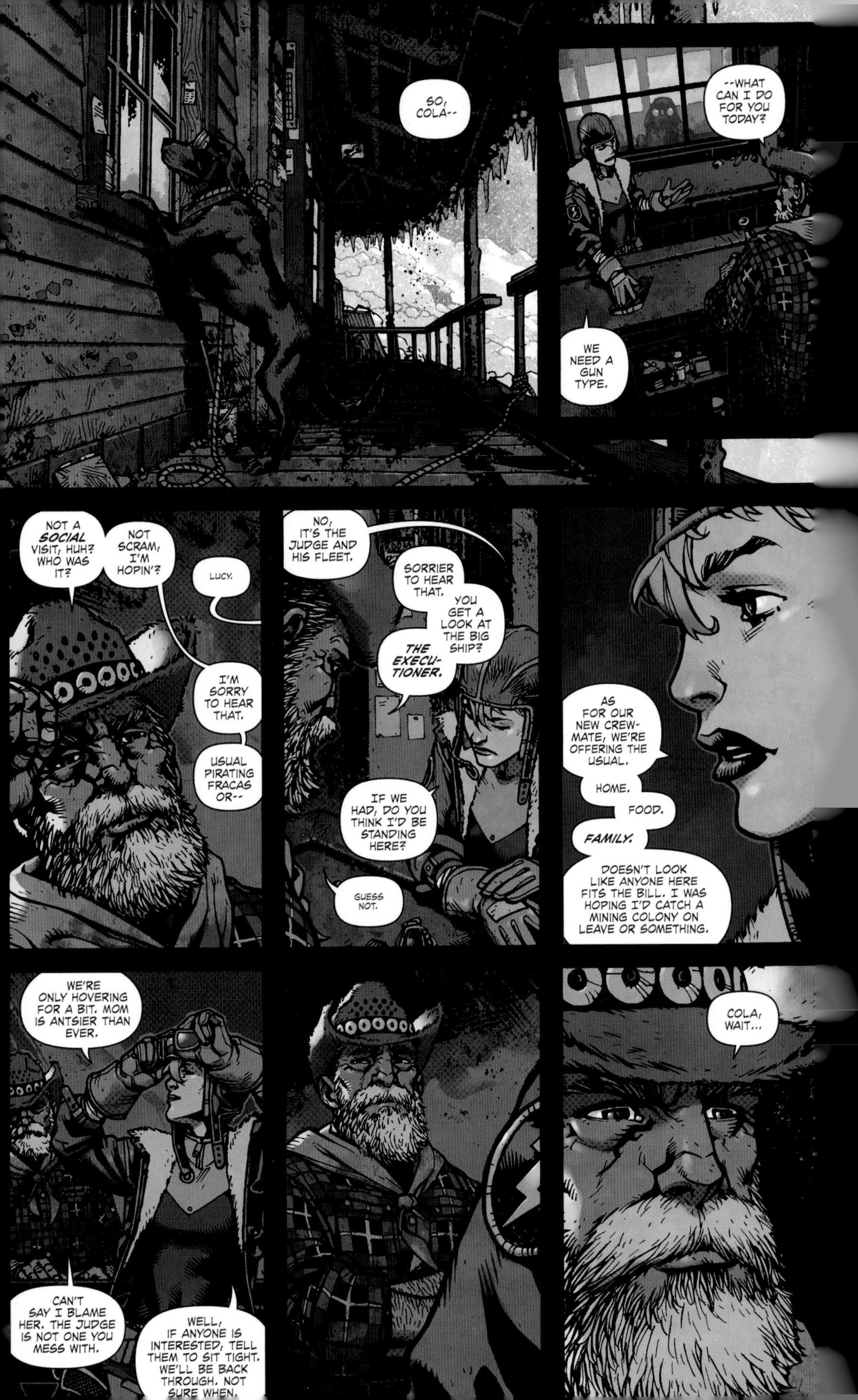
SO, COLA--
--WHAT CAN I DO FOR YOU TODAY?
WE NEED A GUN TYPE.
NOT A SOCIAL VISIT, HUH? WHO WAS IT?
NOT SCRAM, I'M HOPIN'?
LUCY.
I'M SORRY TO HEAR THAT.
USUAL PIRATING FRACAS OR--
NO, IT'S THE JUDGE AND HIS FLEET.
SORRIER TO HEAR THAT.
YOU GET A LOOK AT THE BIG SHIP?
THE EXECUTIONER.
IF WE HAD, DO YOU THINK I'D BE STANDING HERE?
GUESS NOT.
AS FOR OUR NEW CREWMATE, WE'RE OFFERING THE USUAL.
HOME.
FOOD.
FAMILY.
DOESN'T LOOK LIKE ANYONE HERE FITS THE BILL. I WAS HOPING I'D CATCH A MINING COLONY ON LEAVE OR SOMETHING.
WE'RE ONLY HOVERING FOR A BIT. MOM IS ANTSIER THAN EVER.
CAN'T SAY I BLAME HER. THE JUDGE IS NOT ONE YOU MESS WITH.
WELL, IF ANYONE IS INTERESTED, TELL THEM TO SIT TIGHT. WE'LL BE BACK THROUGH. NOT SURE WHEN.
COLA, WAIT...

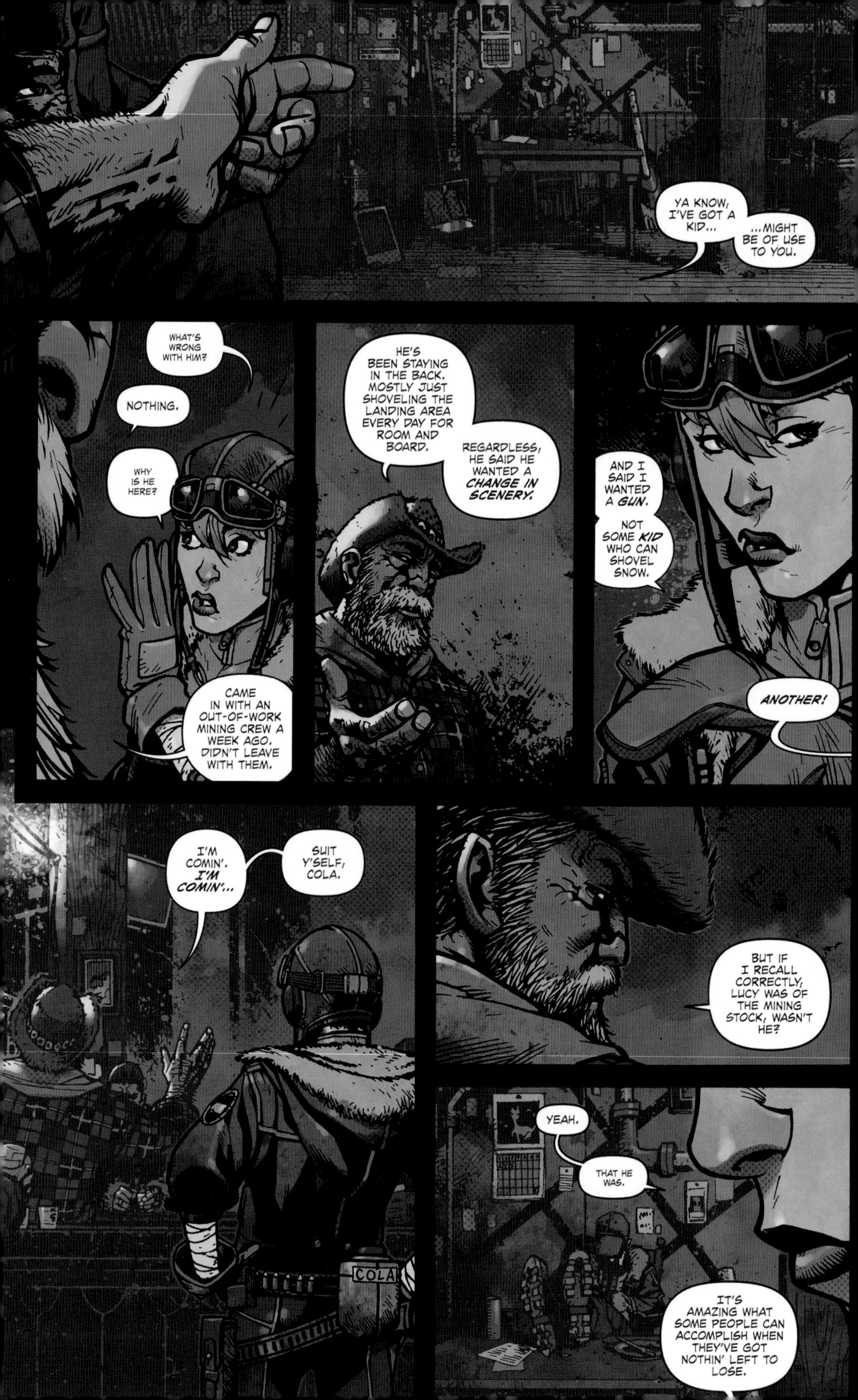

YA KNOW, I'VE GOT A KID...
...MIGHT BE OF USE TO YOU.
WHAT'S WRONG WITH HIM?
NOTHING.
WHY IS HE HERE?
CAME IN WITH AN OUT-OF-WORK MINING CREW A WEEK AGO. DIDN'T LEAVE WITH THEM.
HE'S BEEN STAYING IN THE BACK. MOSTLY JUST SHOVELING THE LANDING AREA EVERY DAY FOR ROOM AND BOARD.
REGARDLESS, HE SAID HE WANTED A CHANGE IN SCENERY.
AND I SAID I WANTED A GUN.
NOT SOME KID WHO CAN SHOVEL SNOW.
ANOTHER!
I'M COMIN'. I'M COMIN'...
SUIT Y'SELF, COLA.
COLA
BUT IF I RECALL CORRECTLY, LUCY WAS OF THE MINING STOCK, WASN'T HE?
YEAH.
THAT HE WAS.
IT'S AMAZING WHAT SOME PEOPLE CAN ACCOMPLISH WHEN THEY'VE GOT NOTHIN' LEFT TO LOSE.

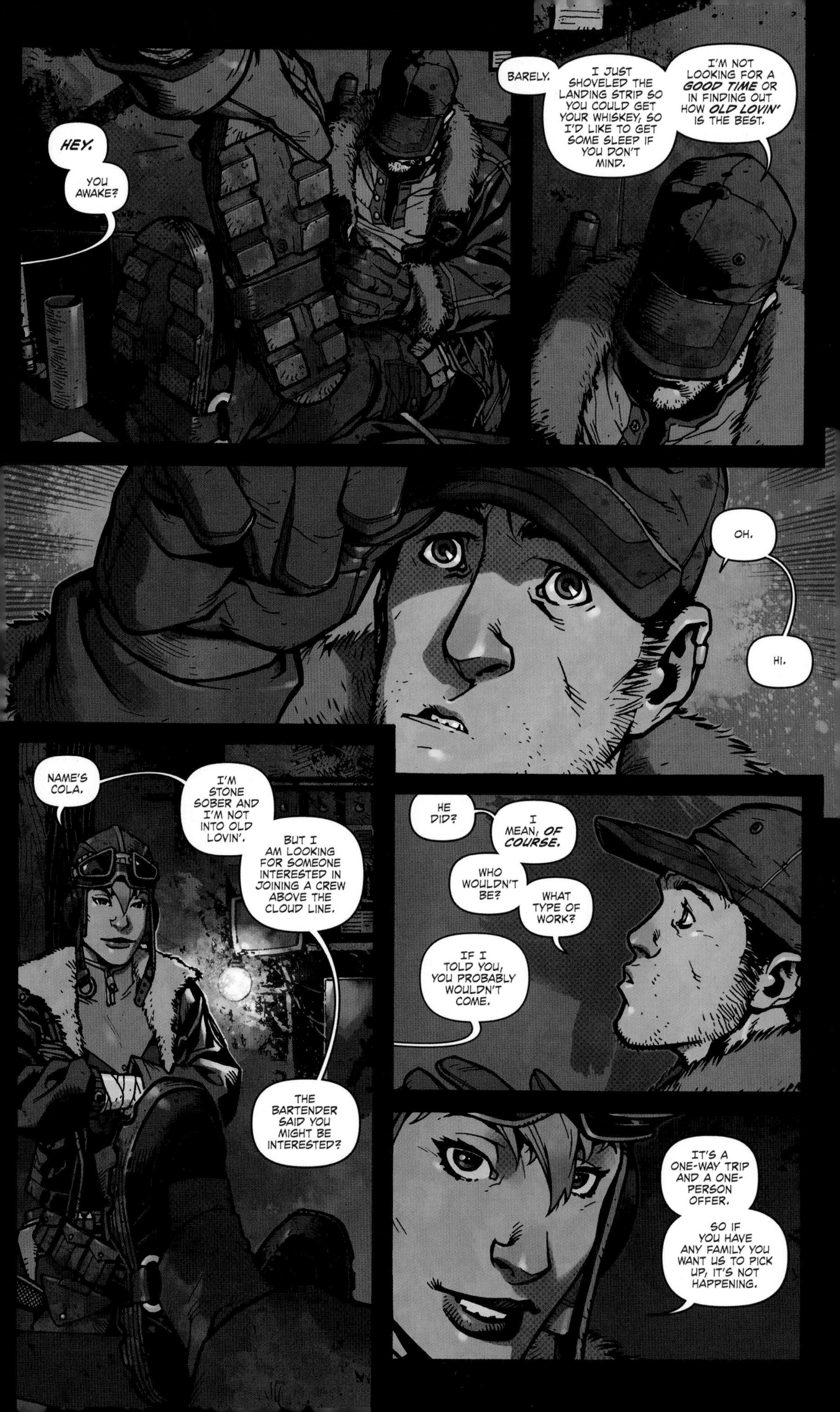
HEY.
YOU AWAKE?
BARELY.
I JUST SHOVELED THE LANDING STRIP SO YOU COULD GET YOUR WHISKEY, SO I'D LIKE TO GET SOME SLEEP IF YOU DON'T MIND.
I'M NOT LOOKING FOR A GOOD TIME OR IN FINDING OUT HOW OLD LOVIN' IS THE BEST.
OH.
HI.
NAME'S COLA.
I'M STONE SOBER AND I'M NOT INTO OLD LOVIN'.
BUT I AM LOOKING FOR SOMEONE INTERESTED IN JOINING A CREW ABOVE THE CLOUD LINE.
THE BARTENDER SAID YOU MIGHT BE INTERESTED?
HE DID?
I MEAN, OF COURSE.
WHO WOULDN'T BE?
WHAT TYPE OF WORK?
IF I TOLD YOU, YOU PROBABLY WOULDN'T COME.
IT'S A ONE-WAY TRIP AND A ONE-PERSON OFFER.
SO IF YOU HAVE ANY FAMILY YOU WANT US TO PICK UP, IT'S NOT HAPPENING.

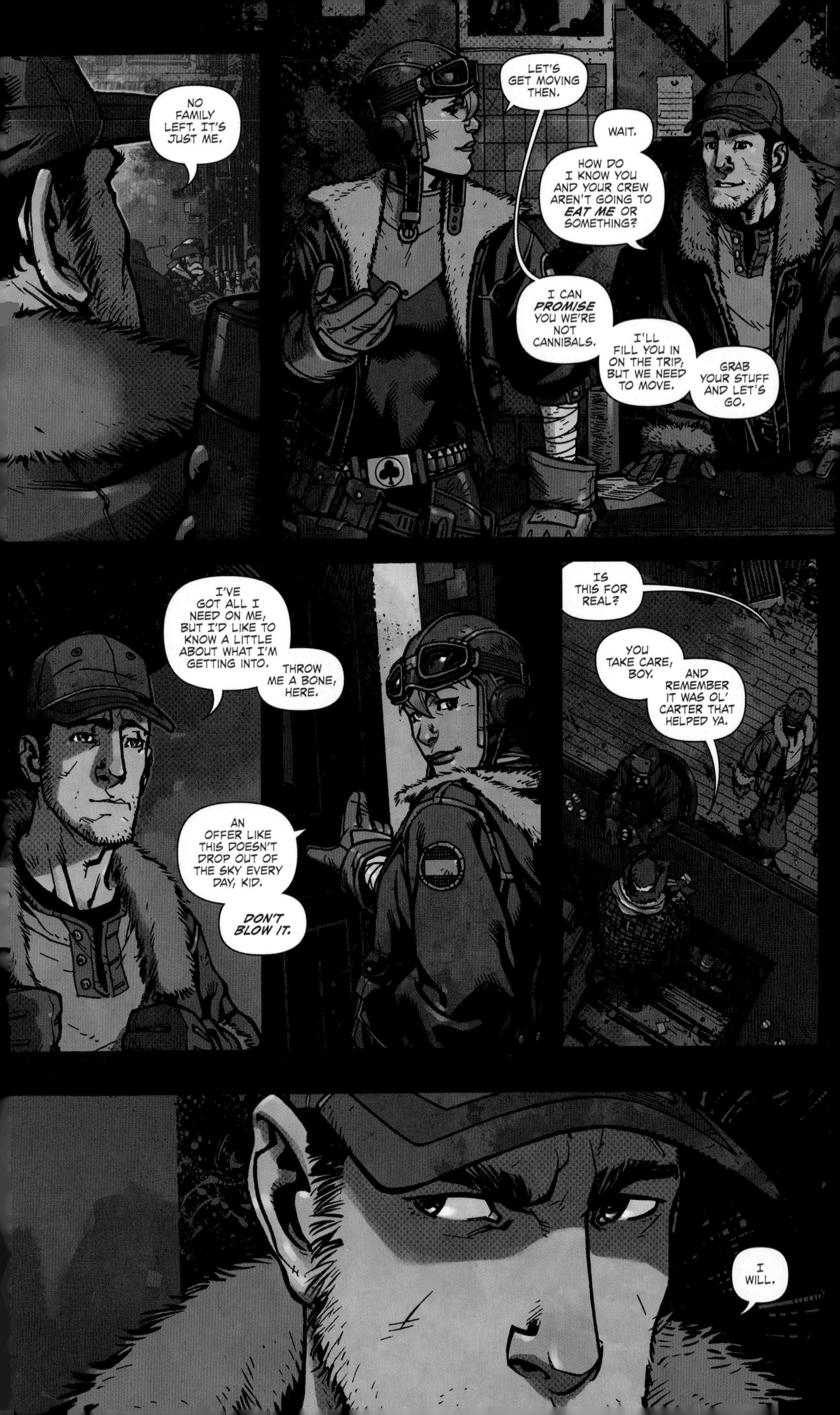
NO FAMILY LEFT. IT'S JUST ME.
LET'S GET MOVING THEN.
WAIT.
HOW DO I KNOW YOU AND YOUR CREW AREN'T GOING TO *EAT ME* OR SOMETHING?
I CAN **PROMISE** YOU WE'RE NOT CANNIBALS.
I'LL FILL YOU IN ON THE TRIP, BUT WE NEED TO MOVE.
GRAB YOUR STUFF AND LET'S GO.
I'VE GOT ALL I NEED ON ME, BUT I'D LIKE TO KNOW A LITTLE ABOUT WHAT I'M GETTING INTO.
THROW ME A BONE, HERE.
AN OFFER LIKE THIS DOESN'T DROP OUT OF THE SKY EVERY DAY, KID.
DON'T BLOW IT.
IS THIS FOR REAL?
YOU TAKE CARE, BOY.
AND REMEMBER IT WAS OL' CARTER THAT HELPED YA.
I WILL.

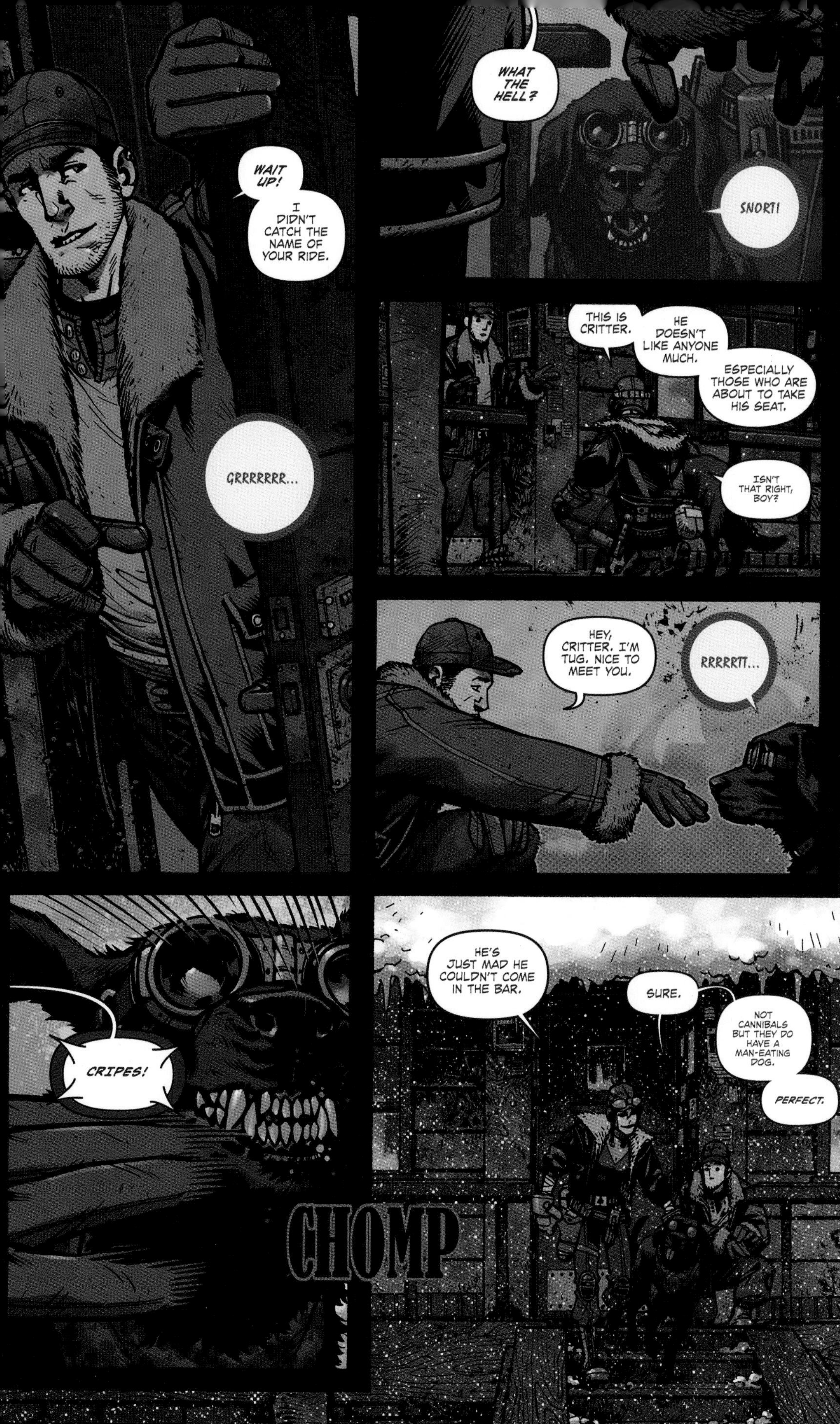
WAIT UP!
I DIDN'T CATCH THE NAME OF YOUR RIDE.
GRRRRRRR...
WHAT THE HELL?
SNORT!
THIS IS CRITTER.
HE DOESN'T LIKE ANYONE MUCH.
ESPECIALLY THOSE WHO ARE ABOUT TO TAKE HIS SEAT.
ISN'T THAT RIGHT, BOY?
HEY, CRITTER. I'M TUG. NICE TO MEET YOU.
RRRRRTT...
CRIPES!
CHOMP
HE'S JUST MAD HE COULDN'T COME IN THE BAR.
SURE.
NOT CANNIBALS BUT THEY DO HAVE A MAN-EATING DOG.
PERFECT.

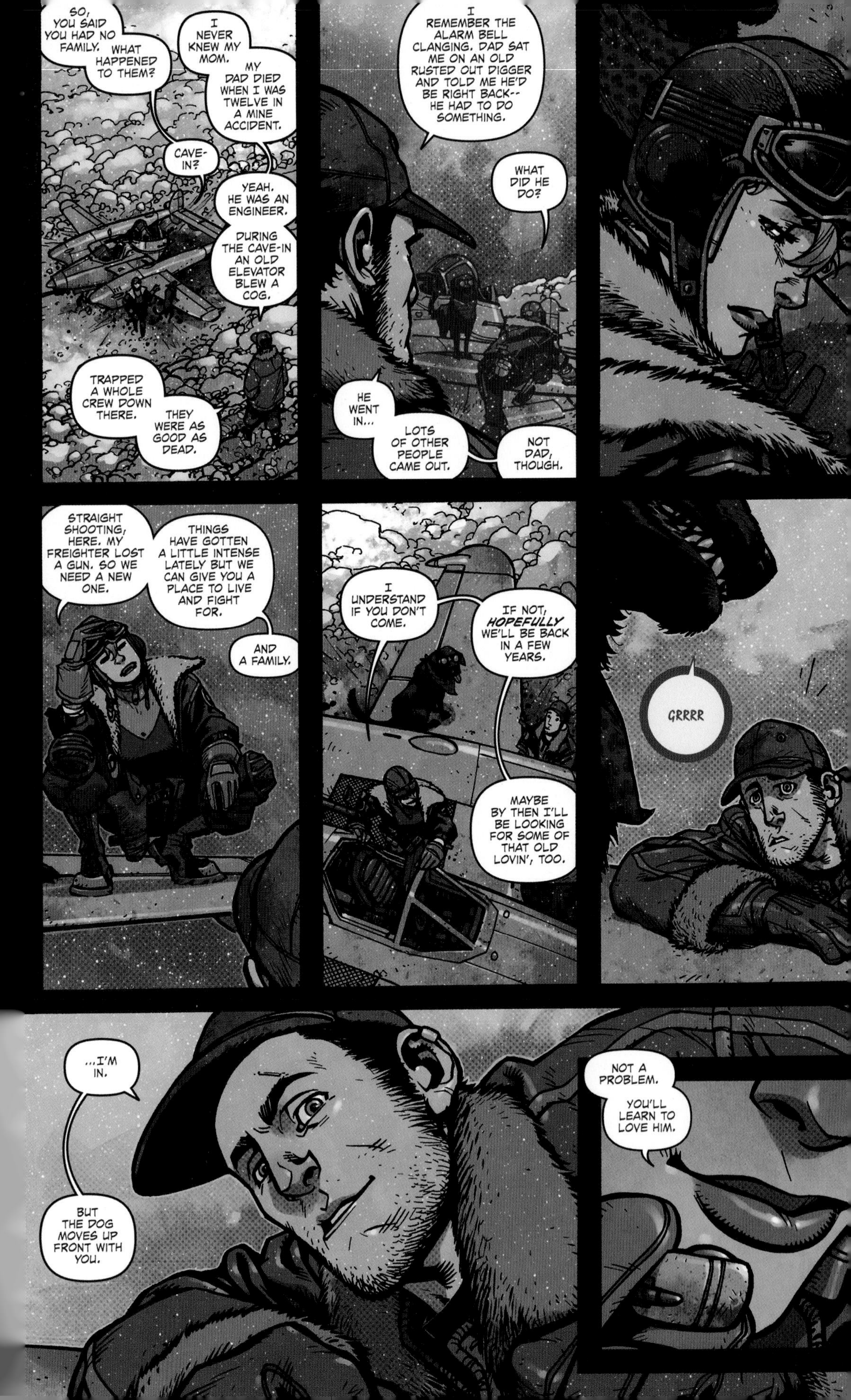
SO, YOU SAID YOU HAD NO FAMILY.
WHAT HAPPENED TO THEM?
I NEVER KNEW MY MOM.
MY DAD DIED WHEN I WAS TWELVE IN A MINE ACCIDENT.
CAVE-IN?
YEAH. HE WAS AN ENGINEER.
DURING THE CAVE-IN AN OLD ELEVATOR BLEW A COG.
TRAPPED A WHOLE CREW DOWN THERE.
THEY WERE AS GOOD AS DEAD.
I REMEMBER THE ALARM BELL CLANGING. DAD SAT ME ON AN OLD RUSTED OUT DIGGER AND TOLD ME HE'D BE RIGHT BACK--HE HAD TO DO SOMETHING.
WHAT DID HE DO?
HE WENT IN...
LOTS OF OTHER PEOPLE CAME OUT.
NOT DAD, THOUGH.
STRAIGHT SHOOTING, HERE. MY FREIGHTER LOST A GUN. SO WE NEED A NEW ONE.
THINGS HAVE GOTTEN A LITTLE INTENSE LATELY BUT WE CAN GIVE YOU A PLACE TO LIVE AND FIGHT FOR.
AND A FAMILY.
I UNDERSTAND IF YOU DON'T COME.
IF NOT, *HOPEFULLY* WE'LL BE BACK IN A FEW YEARS.
MAYBE BY THEN I'LL BE LOOKING FOR SOME OF THAT OLD LOVIN', TOO.
GRRRR
...I'M IN.
BUT THE DOG MOVES UP FRONT WITH YOU.
NOT A PROBLEM.
YOU'LL LEARN TO LOVE HIM.

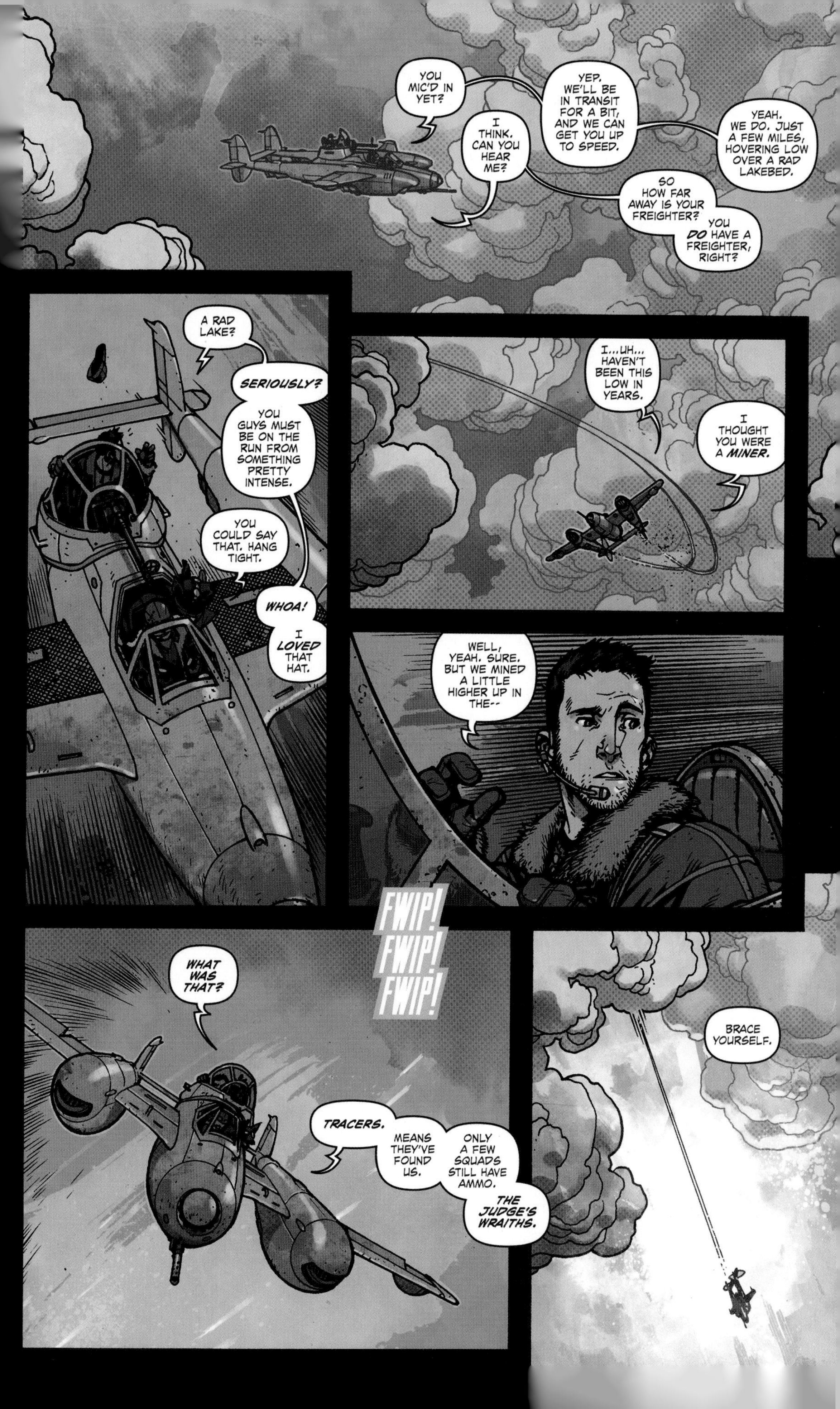

YOU MIC'D IN YET?
I THINK. CAN YOU HEAR ME?
YEP. WE'LL BE IN TRANSIT FOR A BIT, AND WE CAN GET YOU UP TO SPEED.
SO HOW FAR AWAY IS YOUR FREIGHTER?
YOU *DO* HAVE A FREIGHTER, RIGHT?
YEAH. WE DO. JUST A FEW MILES, HOVERING LOW OVER A RAD LAKEBED.
A RAD LAKE?
SERIOUSLY?
YOU GUYS MUST BE ON THE RUN FROM SOMETHING PRETTY INTENSE.
YOU COULD SAY THAT. HANG TIGHT.
WHOA!
I *LOVED* THAT HAT.
I...UH... HAVEN'T BEEN THIS LOW IN YEARS.
I THOUGHT YOU WERE A *MINER.*
WELL, YEAH. SURE. BUT WE MINED A LITTLE HIGHER UP IN THE--
FWIP! FWIP! FWIP!
WHAT WAS THAT?
TRACERS.
MEANS THEY'VE FOUND US.
ONLY A FEW SQUADS STILL HAVE AMMO.
THE JUDGE'S WRAITHS.
BRACE YOURSELF.

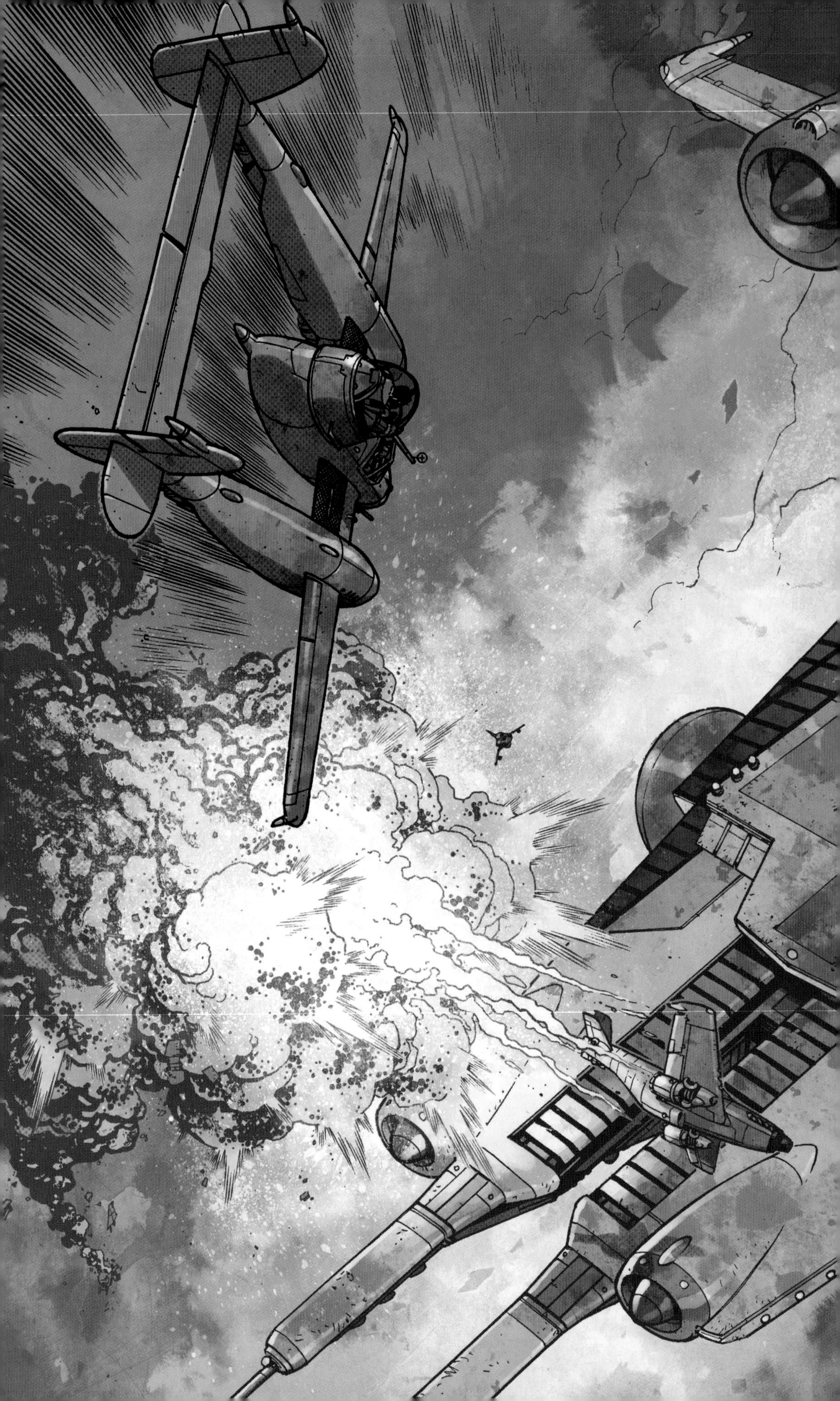

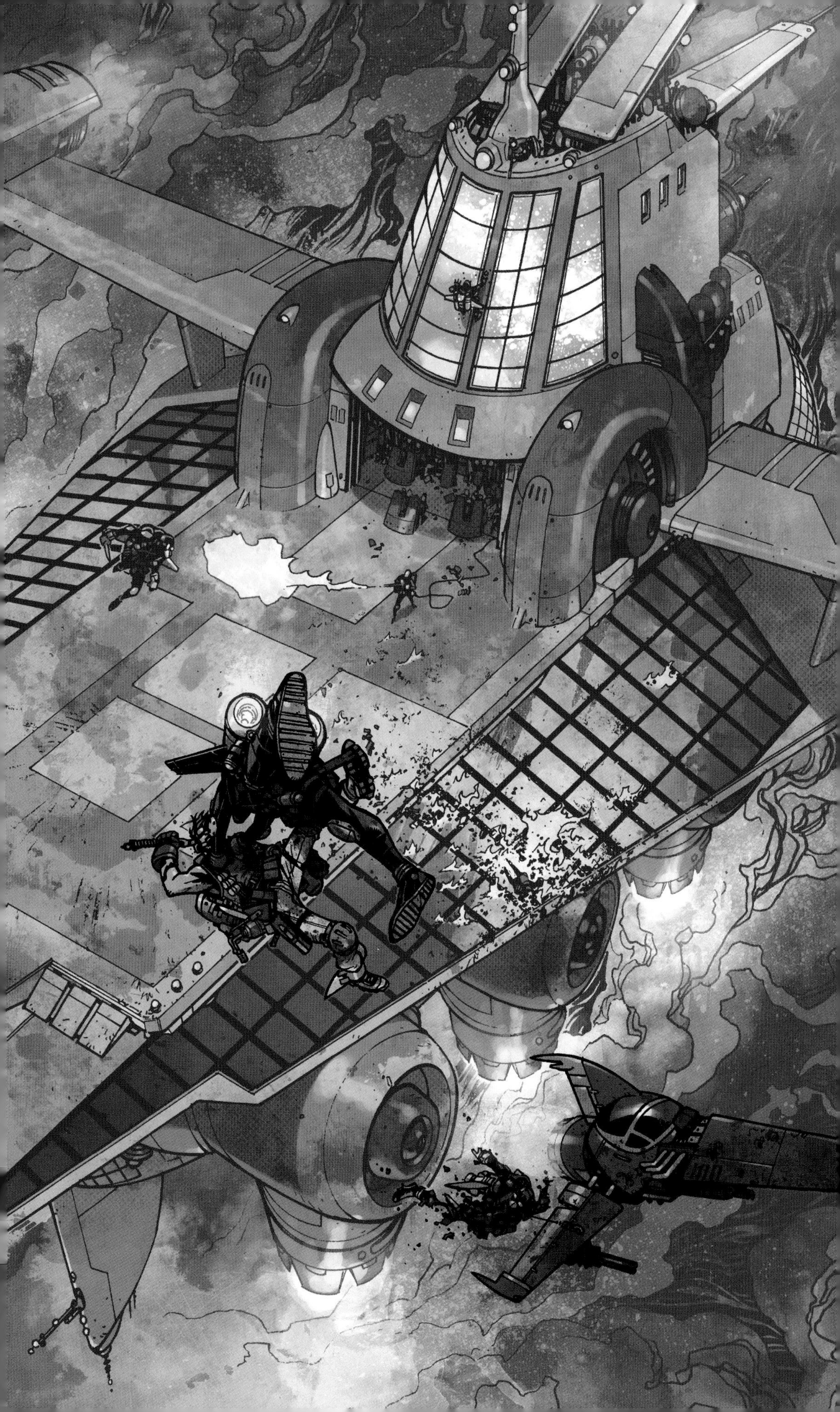

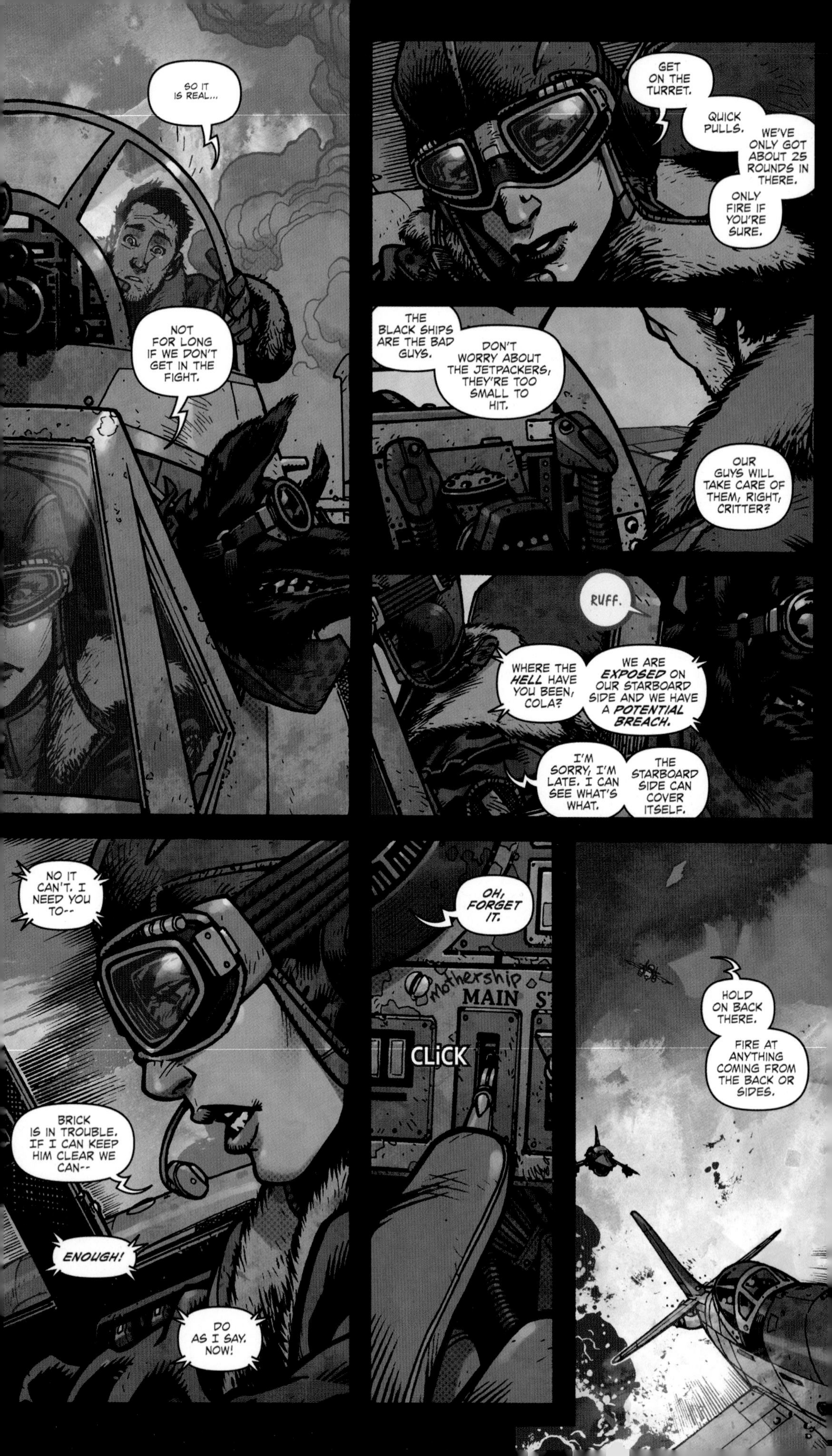
SO IT IS REAL...
NOT FOR LONG IF WE DON'T GET IN THE FIGHT.
GET ON THE TURRET.
QUICK PULLS.
WE'VE ONLY GOT ABOUT 25 ROUNDS IN THERE.
ONLY FIRE IF YOU'RE SURE.
THE BLACK SHIPS ARE THE BAD GUYS.
DON'T WORRY ABOUT THE JETPACKERS, THEY'RE TOO SMALL TO HIT.
OUR GUYS WILL TAKE CARE OF THEM, RIGHT, CRITTER?
RUFF.
WHERE THE HELL HAVE YOU BEEN, COLA?
WE ARE EXPOSED ON OUR STARBOARD SIDE AND WE HAVE A POTENTIAL BREACH.
I'M SORRY, I'M LATE. I CAN SEE WHAT'S WHAT.
THE STARBOARD SIDE CAN COVER ITSELF.
NO IT CAN'T. I NEED YOU TO--
BRICK IS IN TROUBLE. IF I CAN KEEP HIM CLEAR WE CAN--
ENOUGH!
DO AS I SAY. NOW!
OH, FORGET IT.
Mothership
MAIN ST
CLiCK
HOLD ON BACK THERE.
FIRE AT ANYTHING COMING FROM THE BACK OR SIDES.

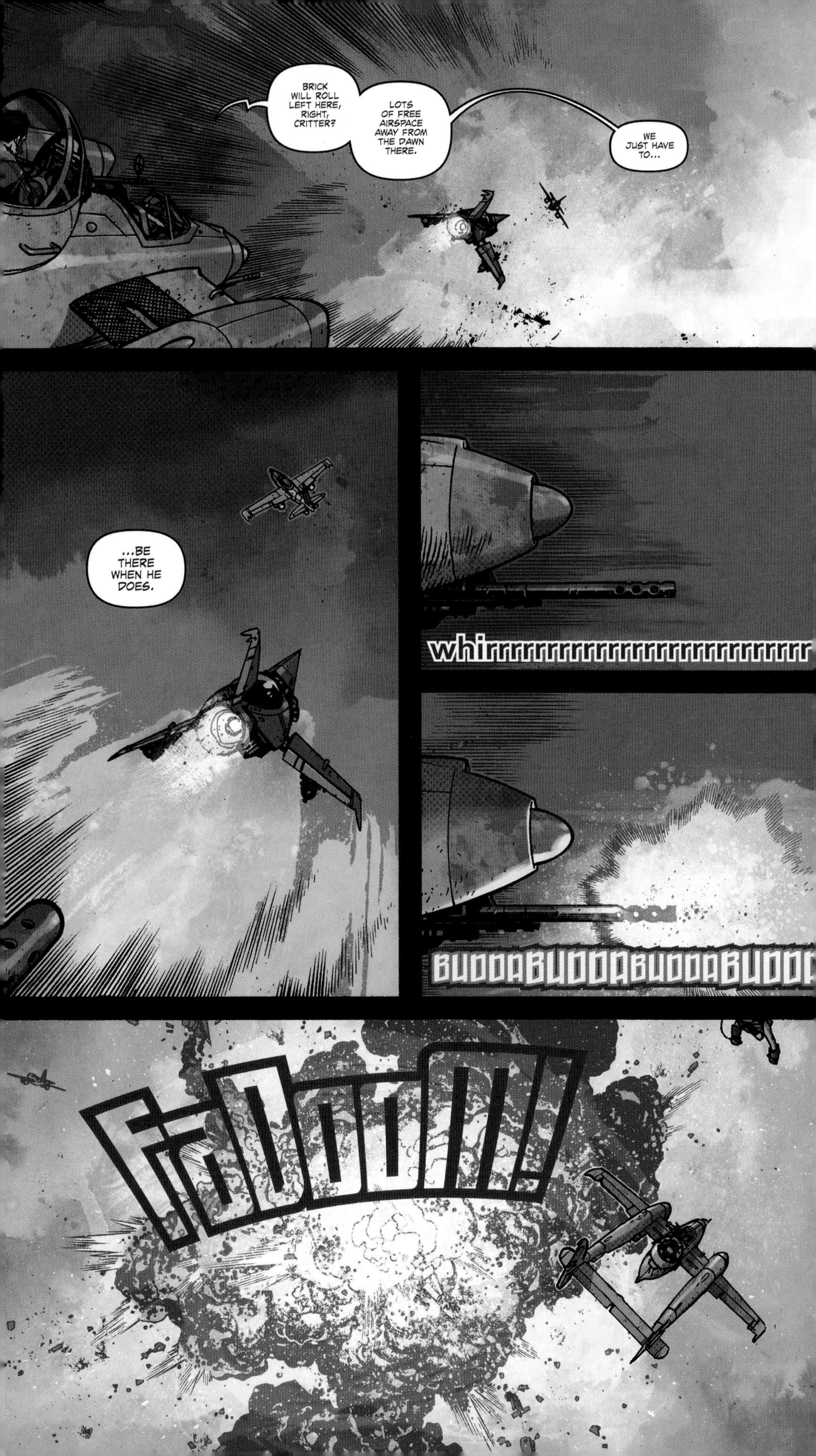
BRICK WILL ROLL LEFT HERE, RIGHT, CRITTER?
LOTS OF FREE AIRSPACE AWAY FROM THE DAWN THERE.
WE JUST HAVE TO...
...BE THERE WHEN HE DOES.
whirrrrrrrrrrrrrrrrrrrrrrrrrr
BUDDABUDDABUDDABUDD
FOOOOM!

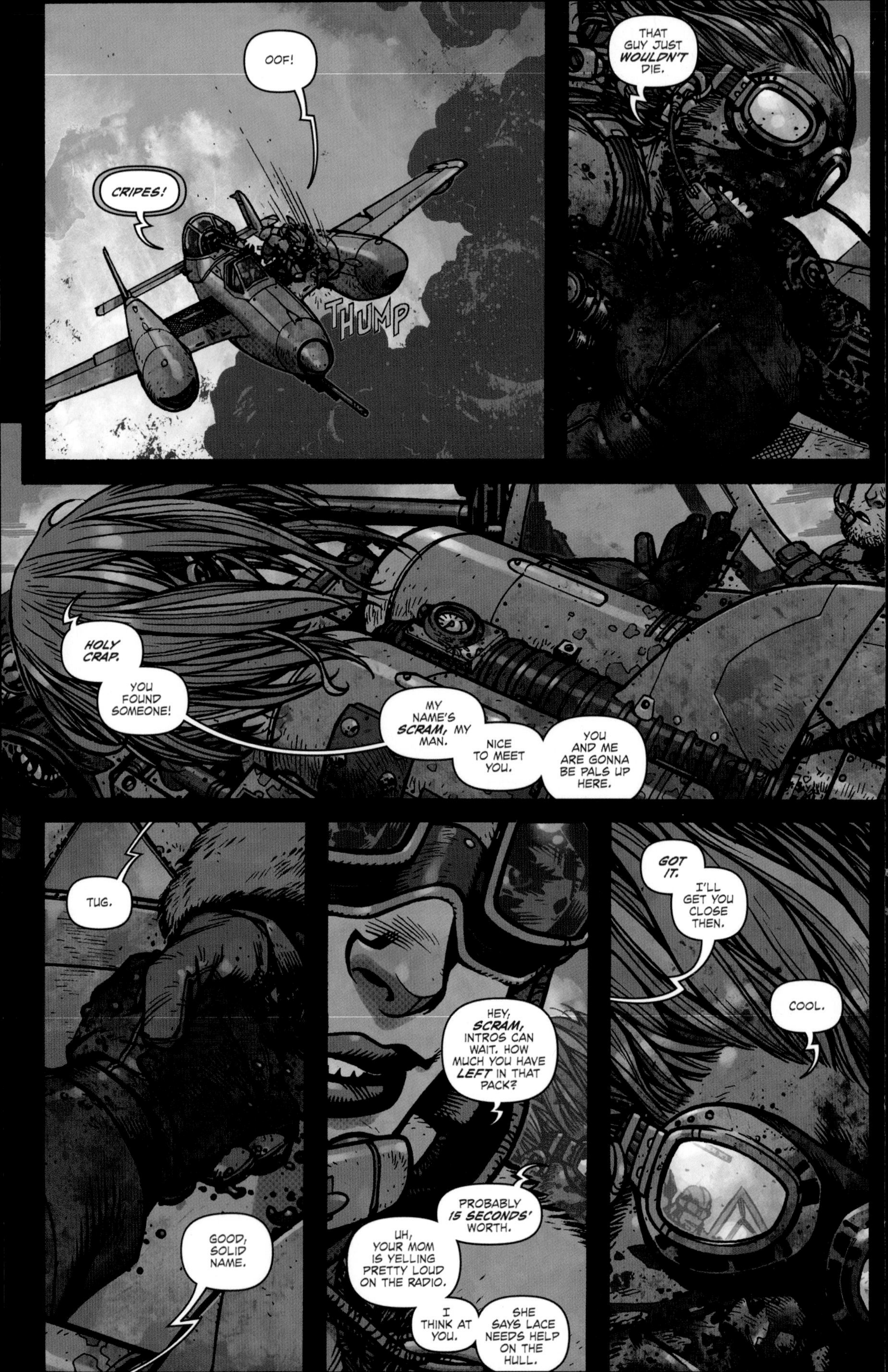
OOF!
CRIPES!
THUMP
THAT GUY JUST WOULDN'T DIE.
HOLY CRAP.
YOU FOUND SOMEONE!
MY NAME'S SCRAM, MY MAN.
NICE TO MEET YOU.
YOU AND ME ARE GONNA BE PALS UP HERE.
TUG.
GOOD, SOLID NAME.
HEY, SCRAM, INTROS CAN WAIT. HOW MUCH YOU HAVE LEFT IN THAT PACK?
PROBABLY 15 SECONDS' WORTH.
UH, YOUR MOM IS YELLING PRETTY LOUD ON THE RADIO.
I THINK AT YOU.
SHE SAYS LACE NEEDS HELP ON THE HULL.
GOT IT.
I'LL GET YOU CLOSE THEN.
COOL.

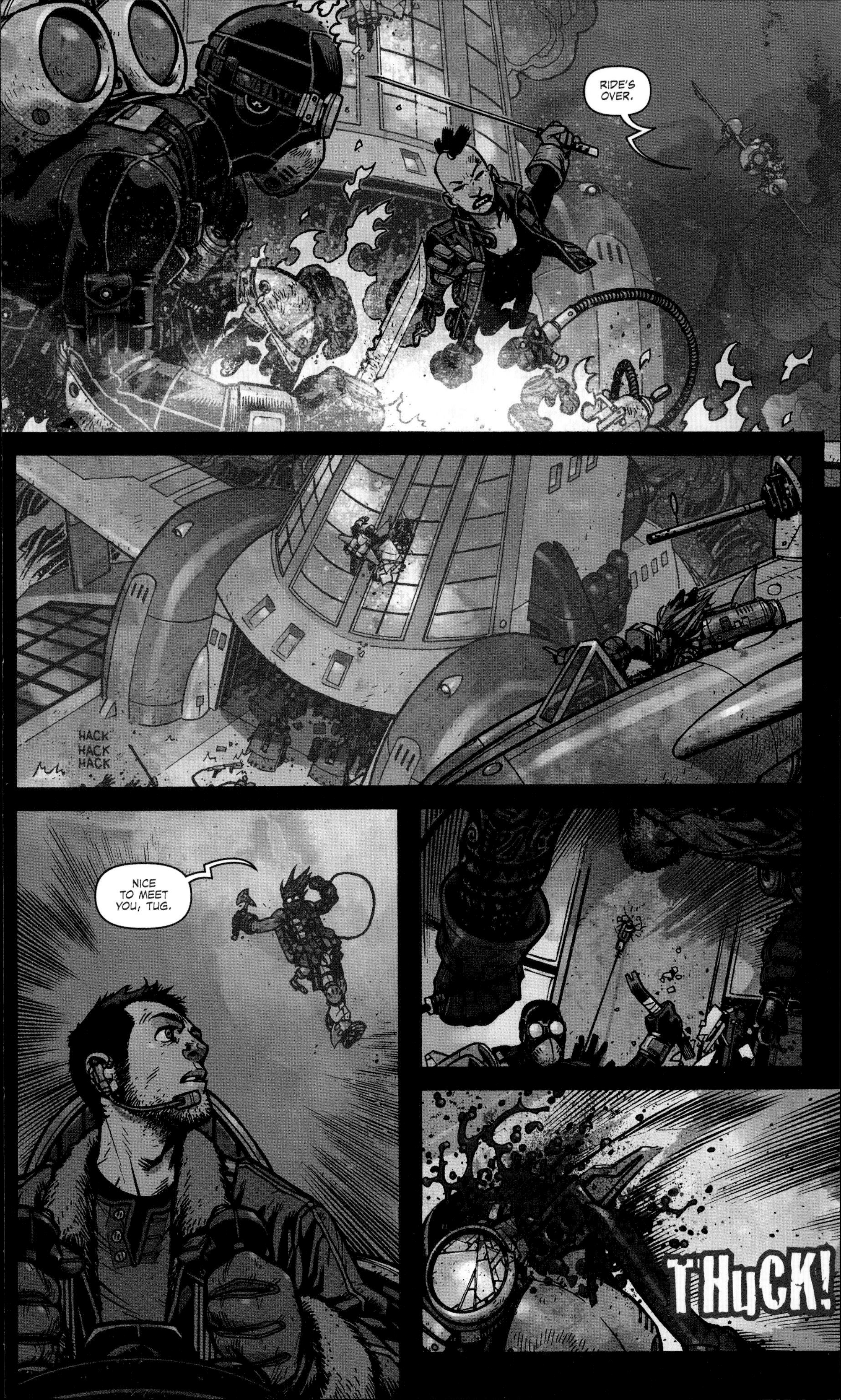

RIDE'S OVER.
HACK
HACK
HACK
NICE TO MEET YOU, TUG.
T'HUCK!

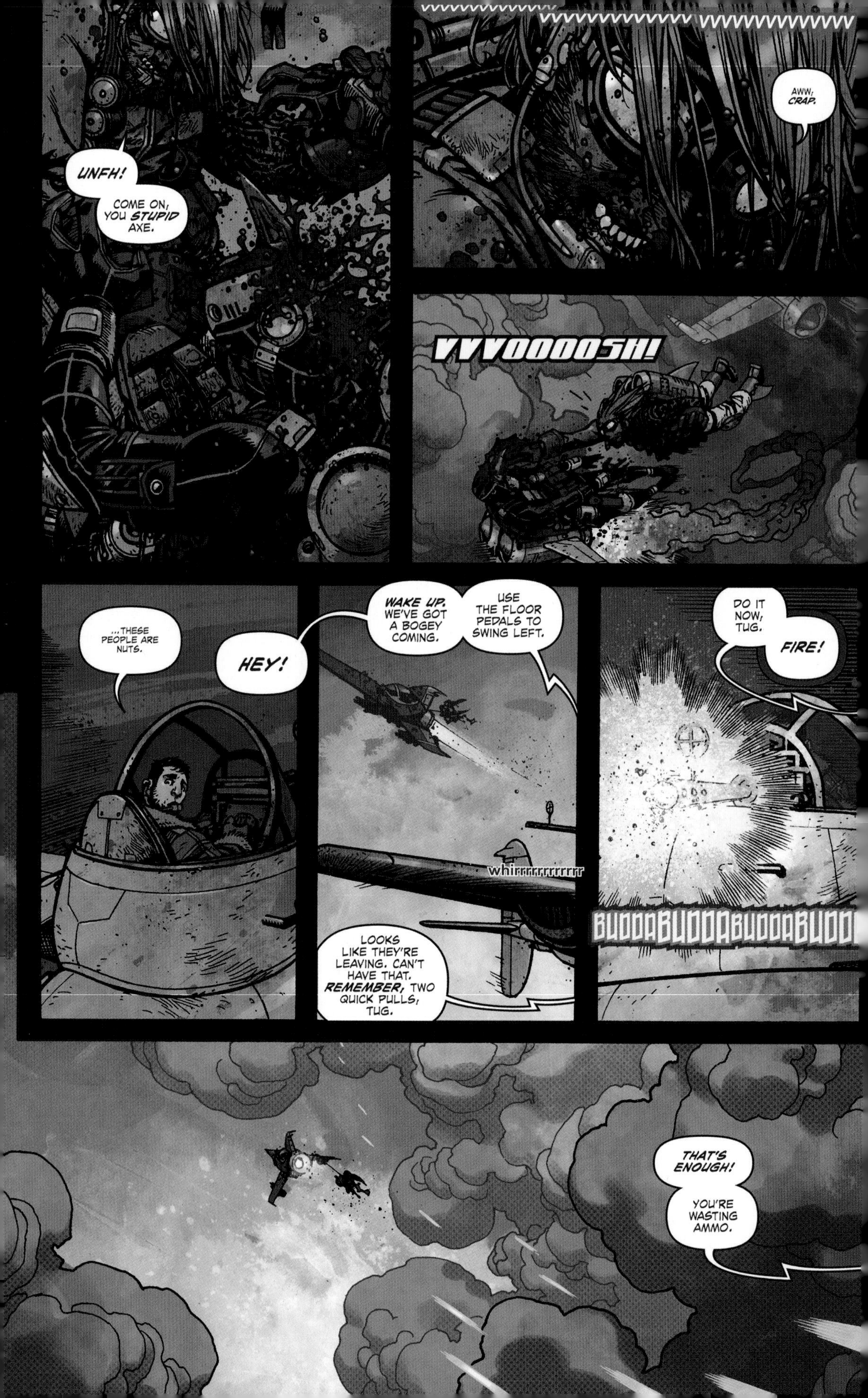
VVVVVVVVVVVVVVVVVVVVVVVVVVVVVVVVVVVVVVVVV
UNFH!
COME ON, YOU STUPID AXE.
AWW, CRAP.
VVVOOOOSH!
...THESE PEOPLE ARE NUTS.
HEY!
WAKE UP. WE'VE GOT A BOGEY COMING.
USE THE FLOOR PEDALS TO SWING LEFT.
whirrrrrrrrrrrr
LOOKS LIKE THEY'RE LEAVING. CAN'T HAVE THAT. REMEMBER, TWO QUICK PULLS, TUG.
DO IT NOW, TUG.
FIRE!
BUDDABUDDABUDDABUDD
THAT'S ENOUGH!
YOU'RE WASTING AMMO.

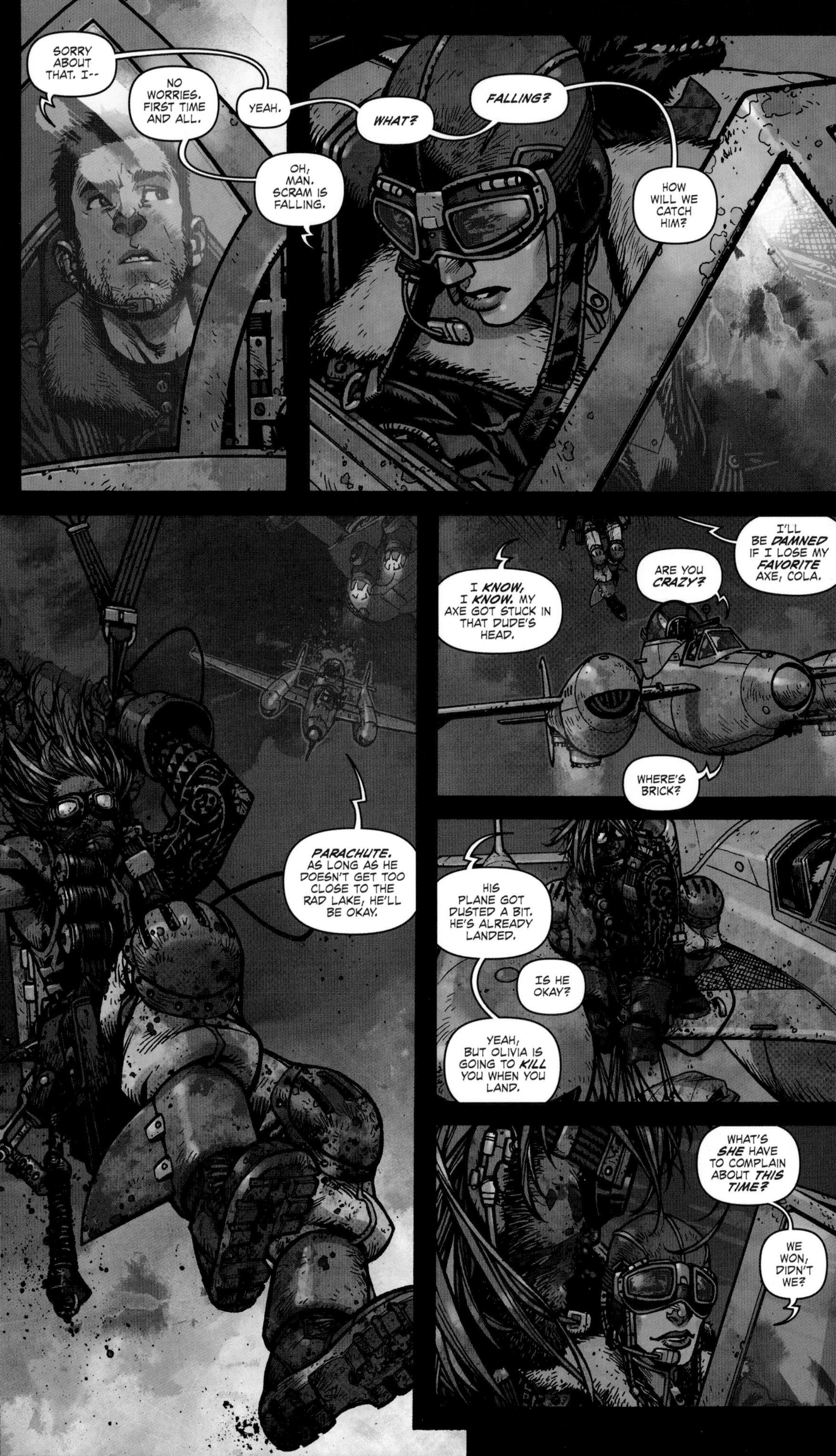
SORRY ABOUT THAT. I--
NO WORRIES. FIRST TIME AND ALL.
YEAH.
WHAT?
FALLING?
OH, MAN. SCRAM IS FALLING.
HOW WILL WE CATCH HIM?
PARACHUTE. AS LONG AS HE DOESN'T GET TOO CLOSE TO THE RAD LAKE, HE'LL BE OKAY.
I'LL BE DAMNED IF I LOSE MY FAVORITE AXE, COLA.
ARE YOU CRAZY?
I KNOW, I KNOW. MY AXE GOT STUCK IN THAT DUDE'S HEAD.
WHERE'S BRICK?
HIS PLANE GOT DUSTED A BIT. HE'S ALREADY LANDED.
IS HE OKAY?
YEAH, BUT OLIVIA IS GOING TO KILL YOU WHEN YOU LAND.
WHAT'S SHE HAVE TO COMPLAIN ABOUT THIS TIME?
WE WON, DIDN'T WE?

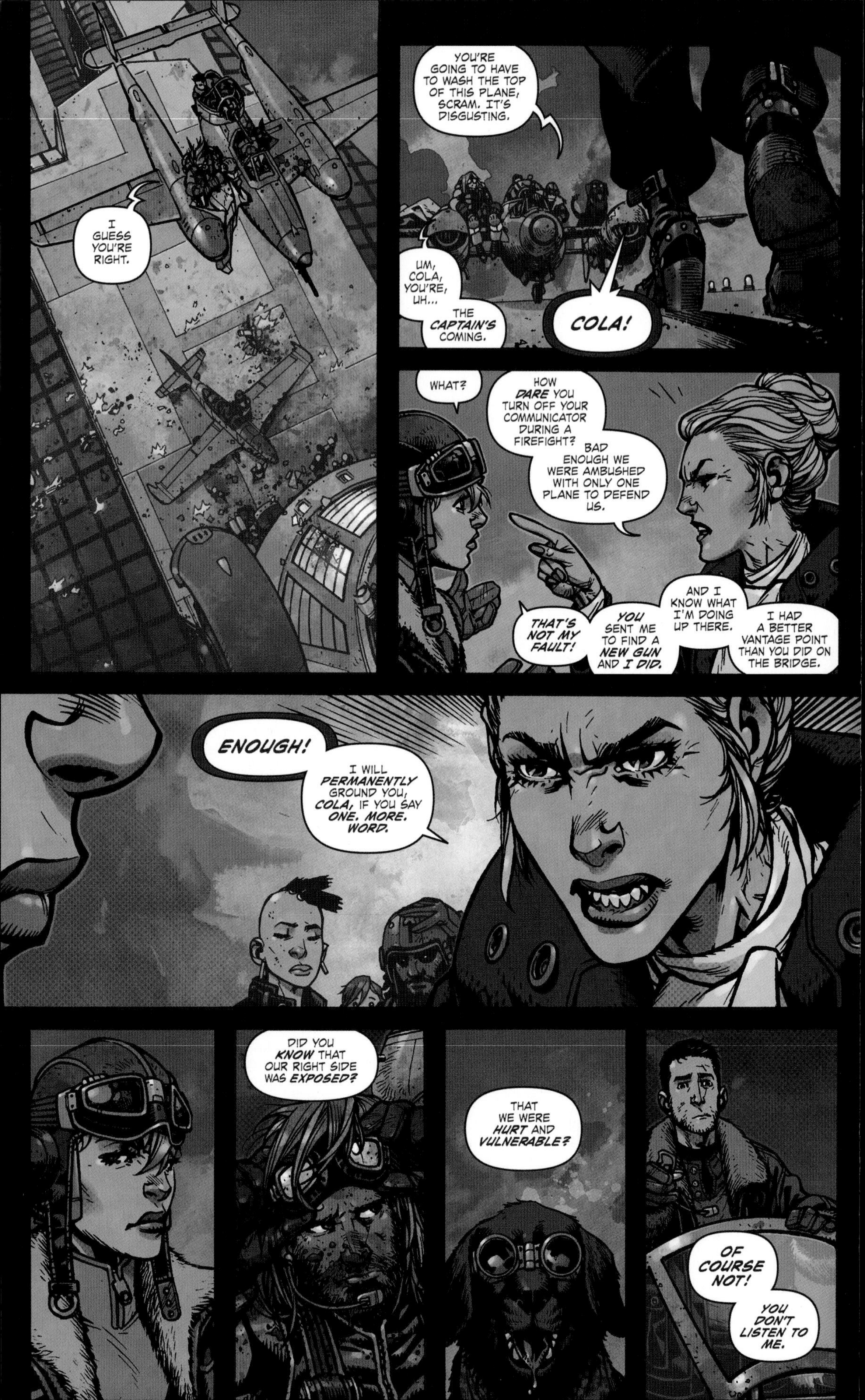

I GUESS YOU'RE RIGHT.
YOU'RE GOING TO HAVE TO WASH THE TOP OF THIS PLANE, SCRAM. IT'S DISGUSTING.
UM, COLA, YOU'RE, UH...
THE CAPTAIN'S COMING.
COLA!
WHAT?
HOW DARE YOU TURN OFF YOUR COMMUNICATOR DURING A FIREFIGHT?
BAD ENOUGH WE WERE AMBUSHED WITH ONLY ONE PLANE TO DEFEND US.
THAT'S NOT MY FAULT!
YOU SENT ME TO FIND A NEW GUN AND I DID.
AND I KNOW WHAT I'M DOING UP THERE.
I HAD A BETTER VANTAGE POINT THAN YOU DID ON THE BRIDGE.
ENOUGH!
I WILL PERMANENTLY GROUND YOU, COLA, IF YOU SAY ONE. MORE. WORD.
DID YOU KNOW THAT OUR RIGHT SIDE WAS EXPOSED?
THAT WE WERE HURT AND VULNERABLE?
OF COURSE NOT!
YOU DON'T LISTEN TO ME.

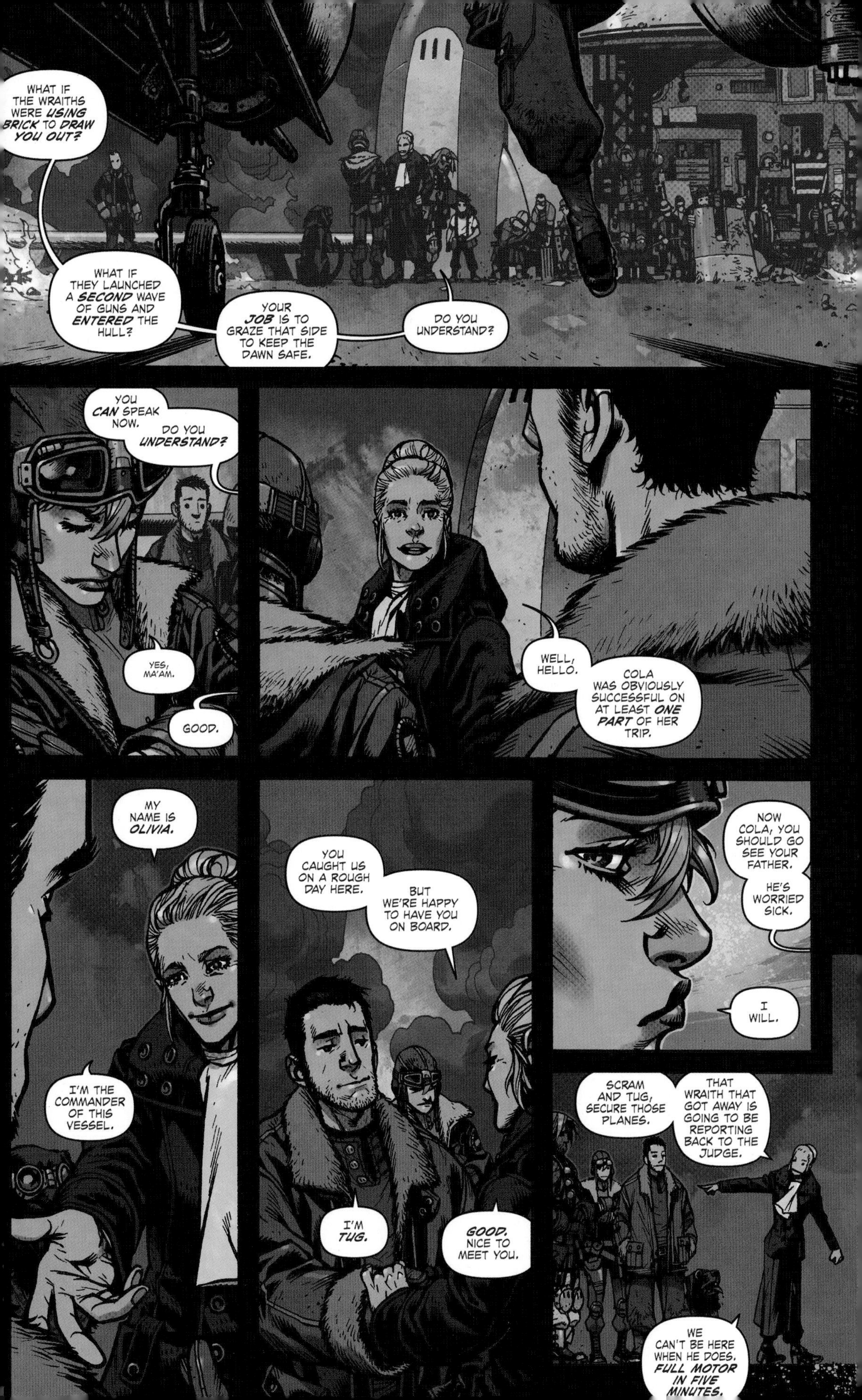
WHAT IF THE WRAITHS WERE USING BRICK TO DRAW YOU OUT?
WHAT IF THEY LAUNCHED A SECOND WAVE OF GUNS AND ENTERED THE HULL?
YOUR JOB IS TO GRAZE THAT SIDE TO KEEP THE DAWN SAFE.
DO YOU UNDERSTAND?
YOU CAN SPEAK NOW.
DO YOU UNDERSTAND?
YES, MA'AM.
GOOD.
WELL, HELLO.
COLA WAS OBVIOUSLY SUCCESSFUL ON AT LEAST ONE PART OF HER TRIP.
MY NAME IS OLIVIA.
I'M THE COMMANDER OF THIS VESSEL.
YOU CAUGHT US ON A ROUGH DAY HERE.
BUT WE'RE HAPPY TO HAVE YOU ON BOARD.
I'M TUG.
GOOD. NICE TO MEET YOU.
NOW COLA, YOU SHOULD GO SEE YOUR FATHER.
HE'S WORRIED SICK.
I WILL.
SCRAM AND TUG, SECURE THOSE PLANES.
THAT WRAITH THAT GOT AWAY IS GOING TO BE REPORTING BACK TO THE JUDGE.
WE CAN'T BE HERE WHEN HE DOES. FULL MOTOR IN FIVE MINUTES.

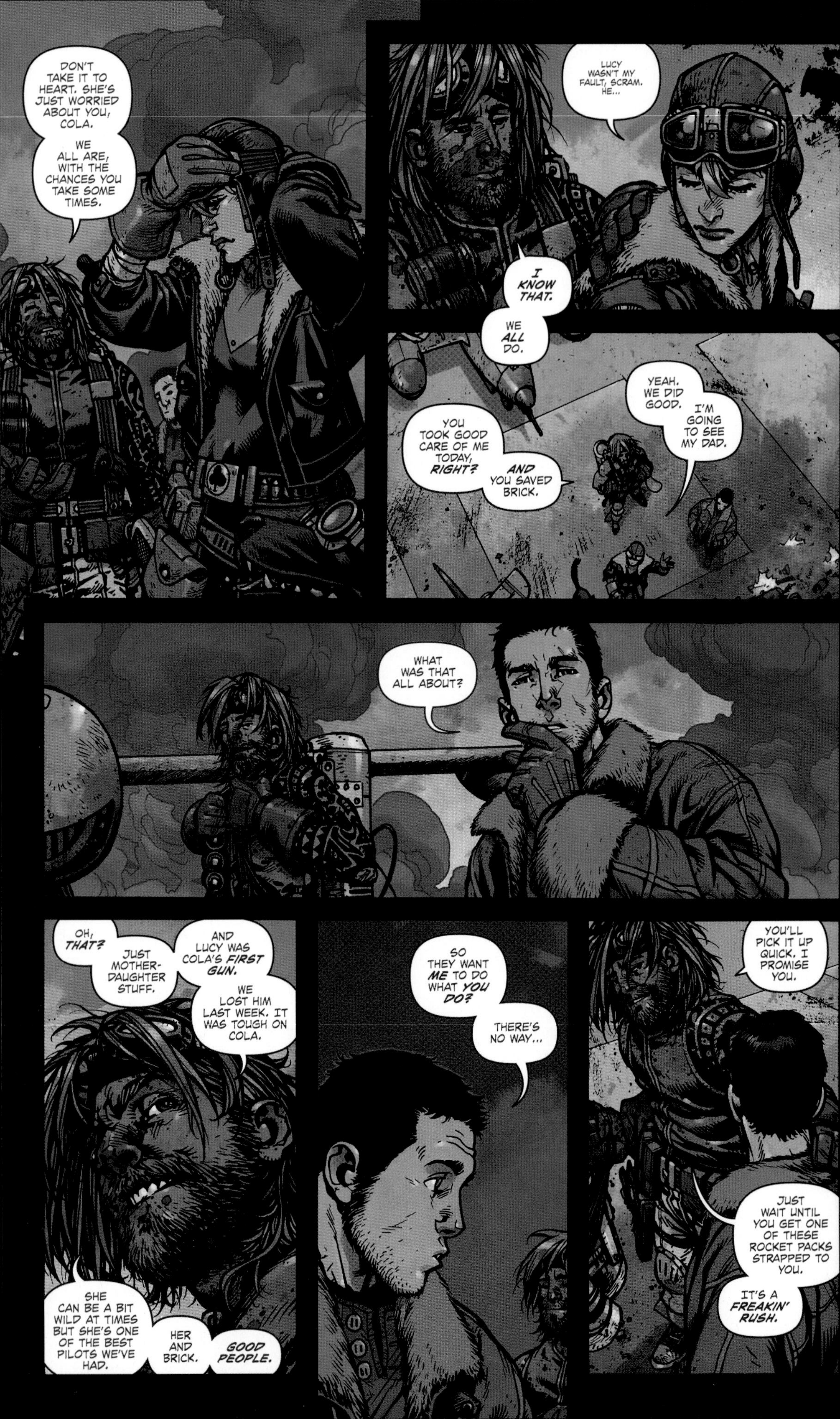
DON'T TAKE IT TO HEART. SHE'S JUST WORRIED ABOUT YOU, COLA.
WE ALL ARE, WITH THE CHANCES YOU TAKE SOME TIMES.
LUCY WASN'T MY FAULT, SCRAM. HE...
I KNOW THAT.
WE *ALL* DO.
YOU TOOK GOOD CARE OF ME TODAY, *RIGHT?*
AND YOU SAVED BRICK.
YEAH. WE DID GOOD.
I'M GOING TO SEE MY DAD.
WHAT WAS THAT ALL ABOUT?
OH, *THAT?*
JUST MOTHER-DAUGHTER STUFF.
AND LUCY WAS COLA'S *FIRST GUN.*
WE LOST HIM LAST WEEK. IT WAS TOUGH ON COLA.
SHE CAN BE A BIT WILD AT TIMES BUT SHE'S ONE OF THE BEST PILOTS WE'VE HAD.
HER AND BRICK.
GOOD PEOPLE.
SO THEY WANT *ME* TO DO WHAT *YOU DO?*
THERE'S NO WAY...
YOU'LL PICK IT UP QUICK. I PROMISE YOU.
JUST WAIT UNTIL YOU GET ONE OF THESE ROCKET PACKS STRAPPED TO YOU.
IT'S A *FREAKIN' RUSH.*

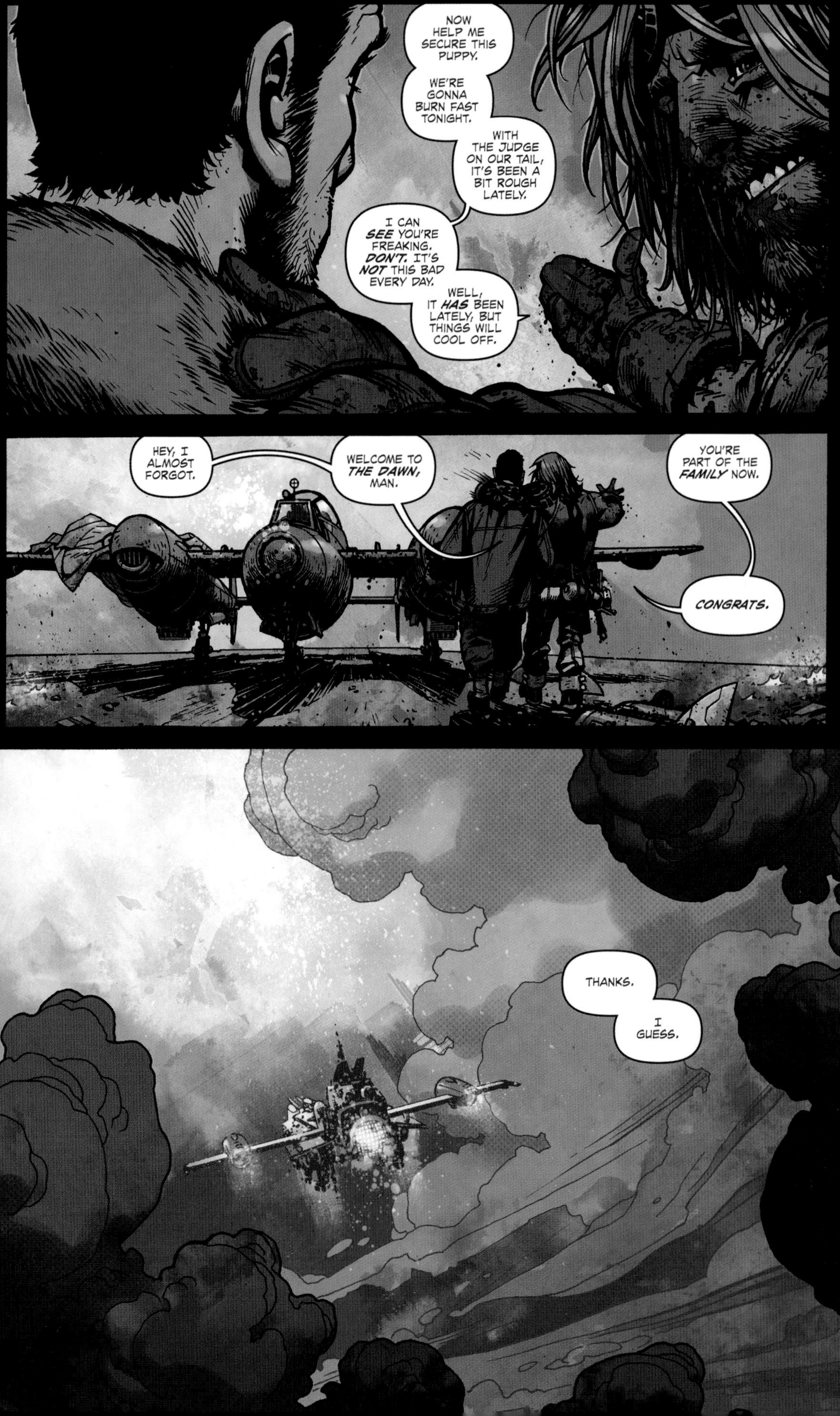
NOW HELP ME SECURE THIS PUPPY.
WE'RE GONNA BURN FAST TONIGHT.
WITH THE JUDGE ON OUR TAIL, IT'S BEEN A BIT ROUGH LATELY.
I CAN *SEE* YOU'RE FREAKING. *DON'T.* IT'S *NOT* THIS BAD EVERY DAY.
WELL, IT *HAS* BEEN LATELY, BUT THINGS WILL COOL OFF.
HEY, I ALMOST FORGOT.
WELCOME TO *THE DAWN,* MAN.
YOU'RE PART OF THE *FAMILY* NOW.
CONGRATS.
THANKS.
I GUESS.

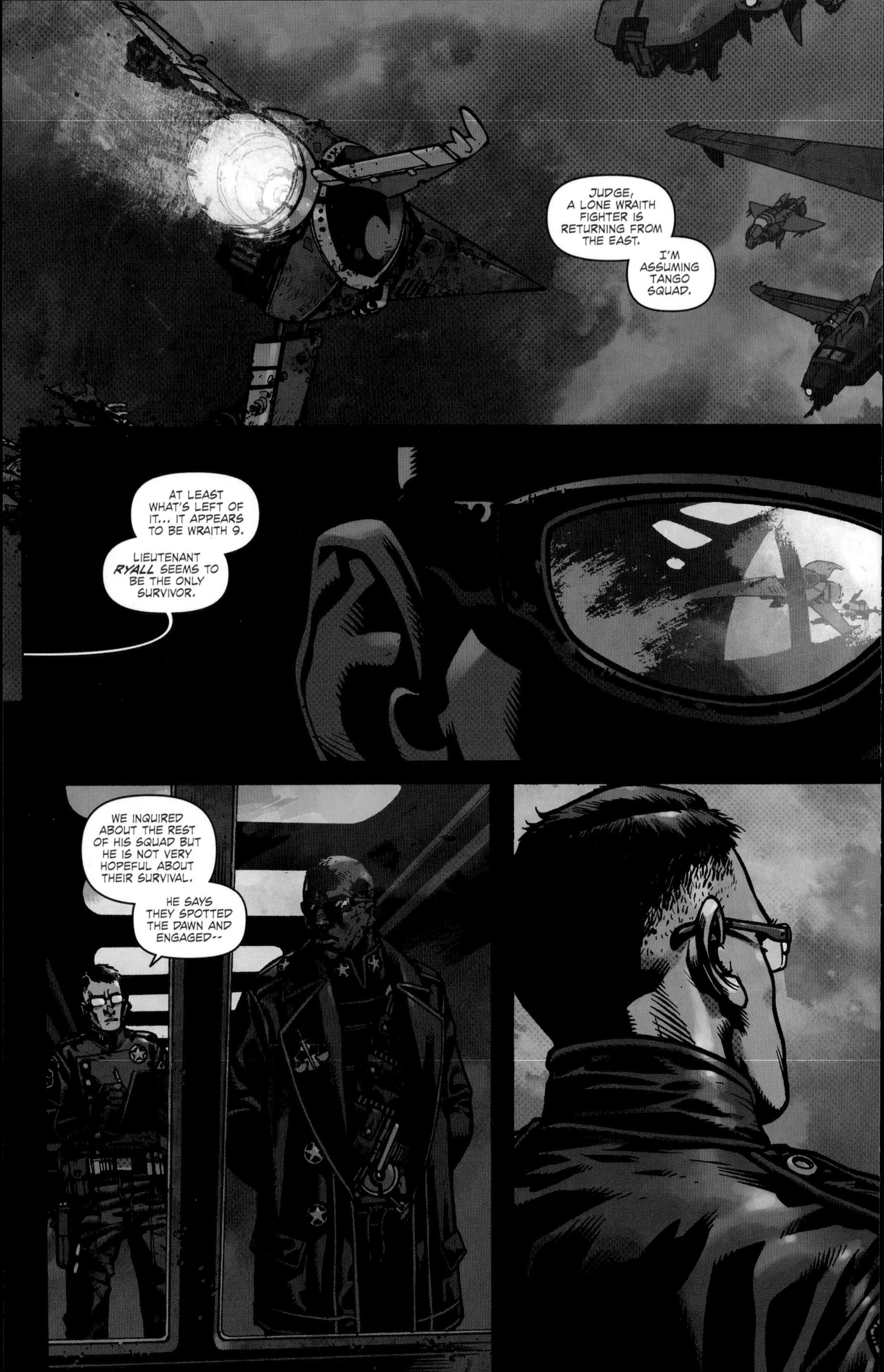
JUDGE, A LONE WRAITH FIGHTER IS RETURNING FROM THE EAST.
I'M ASSUMING TANGO SQUAD.
AT LEAST WHAT'S LEFT OF IT... IT APPEARS TO BE WRAITH 9.
LIEUTENANT RYALL SEEMS TO BE THE ONLY SURVIVOR.
WE INQUIRED ABOUT THE REST OF HIS SQUAD BUT HE IS NOT VERY HOPEFUL ABOUT THEIR SURVIVAL.
HE SAYS THEY SPOTTED THE DAWN AND ENGAGED--

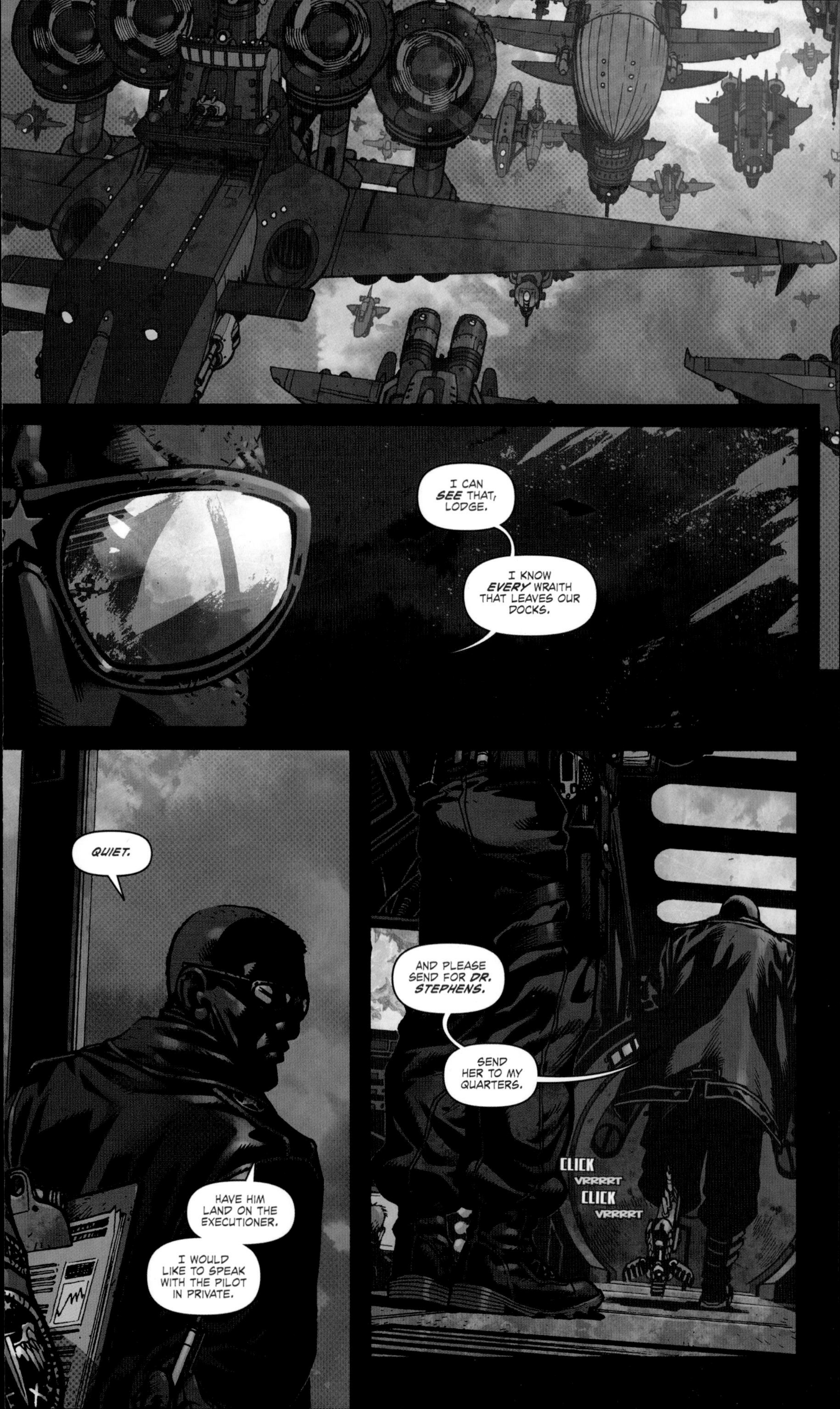
I CAN SEE THAT, LODGE.
I KNOW EVERY WRAITH THAT LEAVES OUR DOCKS.
QUIET.
HAVE HIM LAND ON THE EXECUTIONER.
I WOULD LIKE TO SPEAK WITH THE PILOT IN PRIVATE.
AND PLEASE SEND FOR DR. STEPHENS.
SEND HER TO MY QUARTERS.
CLICK
VRRRRT
CLICK
VRRRRT

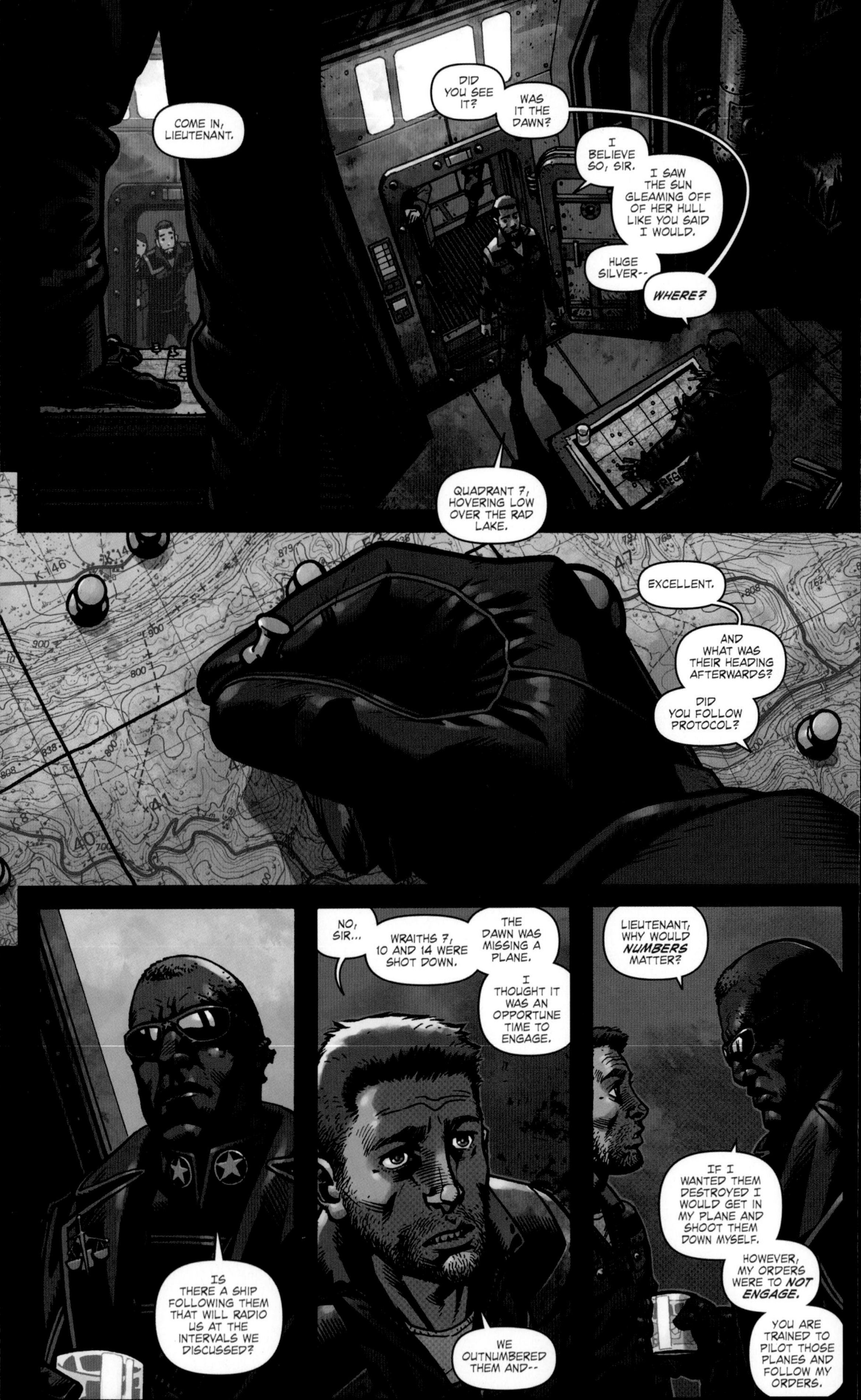

COME IN, LIEUTENANT.
DID YOU SEE IT?
WAS IT THE DAWN?
I BELIEVE SO, SIR.
I SAW THE SUN GLEAMING OFF OF HER HULL LIKE YOU SAID I WOULD.
HUGE SILVER--
WHERE?
QUADRANT 7, HOVERING LOW OVER THE RAD LAKE.
EXCELLENT.
AND WHAT WAS THEIR HEADING AFTERWARDS?
DID YOU FOLLOW PROTOCOL?
NO, SIR...
WRAITHS 7, 10 AND 14 WERE SHOT DOWN.
THE DAWN WAS MISSING A PLANE.
I THOUGHT IT WAS AN OPPORTUNE TIME TO ENGAGE.
IS THERE A SHIP FOLLOWING THEM THAT WILL RADIO US AT THE INTERVALS WE DISCUSSED?
WE OUTNUMBERED THEM AND--
LIEUTENANT, WHY WOULD NUMBERS MATTER?
IF I WANTED THEM DESTROYED I WOULD GET IN MY PLANE AND SHOOT THEM DOWN MYSELF.
HOWEVER, MY ORDERS WERE TO NOT ENGAGE.
YOU ARE TRAINED TO PILOT THOSE PLANES AND FOLLOW MY ORDERS.

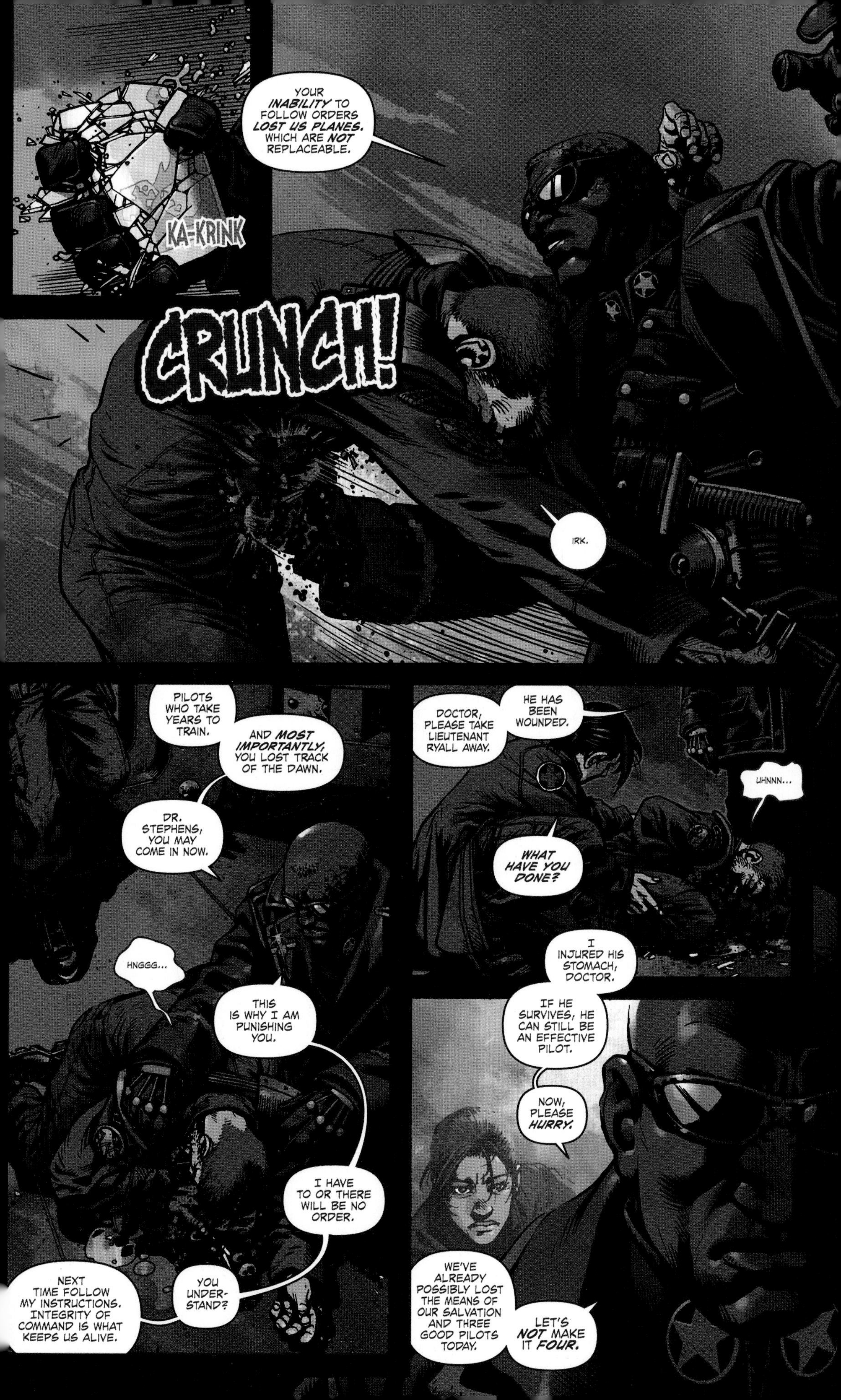

KA-KRINK
YOUR INABILITY TO FOLLOW ORDERS LOST US PLANES. WHICH ARE NOT REPLACEABLE.
CRUNCH!
IRK.
PILOTS WHO TAKE YEARS TO TRAIN.
AND MOST IMPORTANTLY, YOU LOST TRACK OF THE DAWN.
DR. STEPHENS, YOU MAY COME IN NOW.
HNGGG...
THIS IS WHY I AM PUNISHING YOU.
I HAVE TO OR THERE WILL BE NO ORDER.
YOU UNDER-STAND?
NEXT TIME FOLLOW MY INSTRUCTIONS. INTEGRITY OF COMMAND IS WHAT KEEPS US ALIVE.
DOCTOR, PLEASE TAKE LIEUTENANT RYALL AWAY.
HE HAS BEEN WOUNDED.
UHNNN...
WHAT HAVE YOU DONE?
I INJURED HIS STOMACH, DOCTOR.
IF HE SURVIVES, HE CAN STILL BE AN EFFECTIVE PILOT.
NOW, PLEASE HURRY.
WE'VE ALREADY POSSIBLY LOST THE MEANS OF OUR SALVATION AND THREE GOOD PILOTS TODAY.
LET'S NOT MAKE IT FOUR.

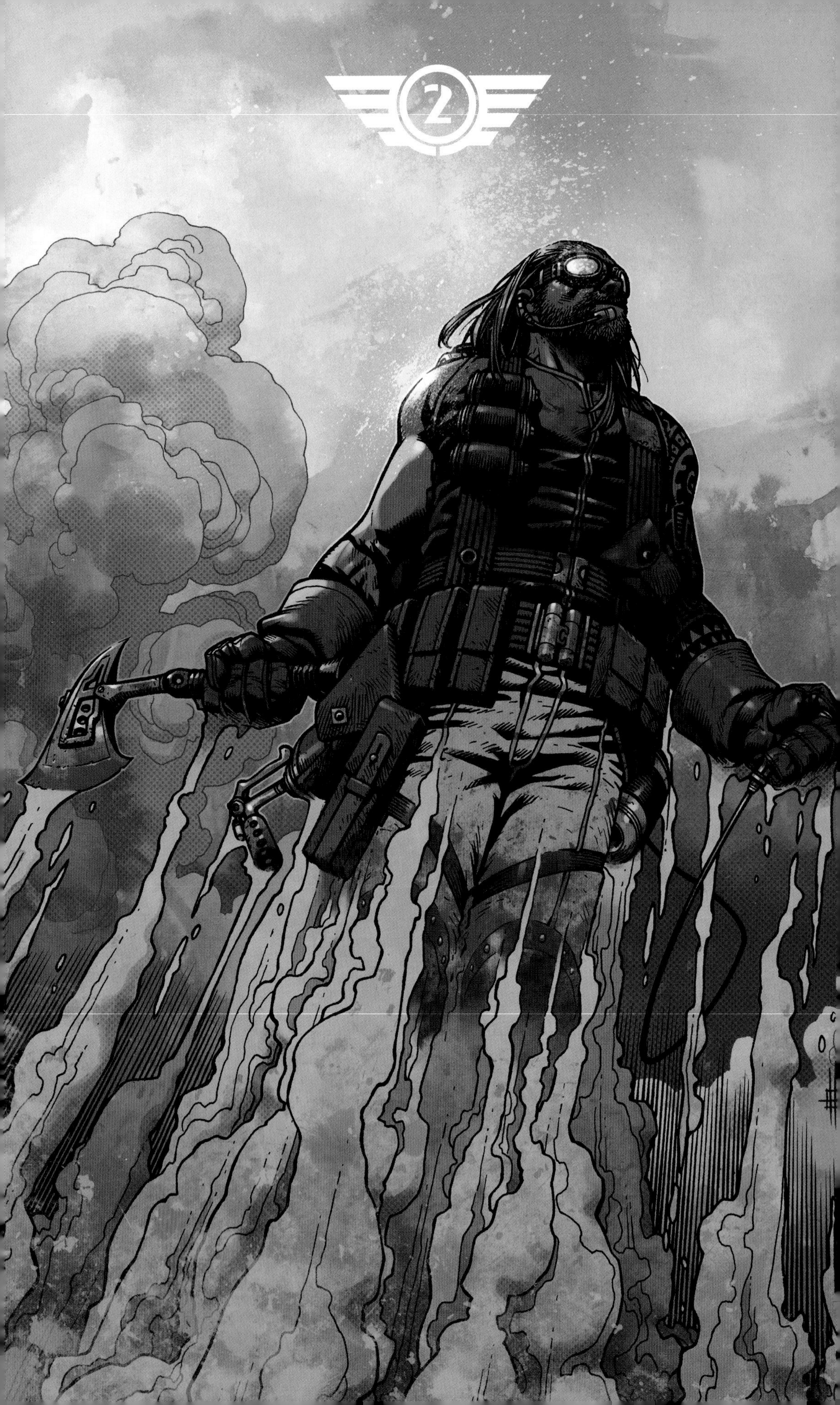
2

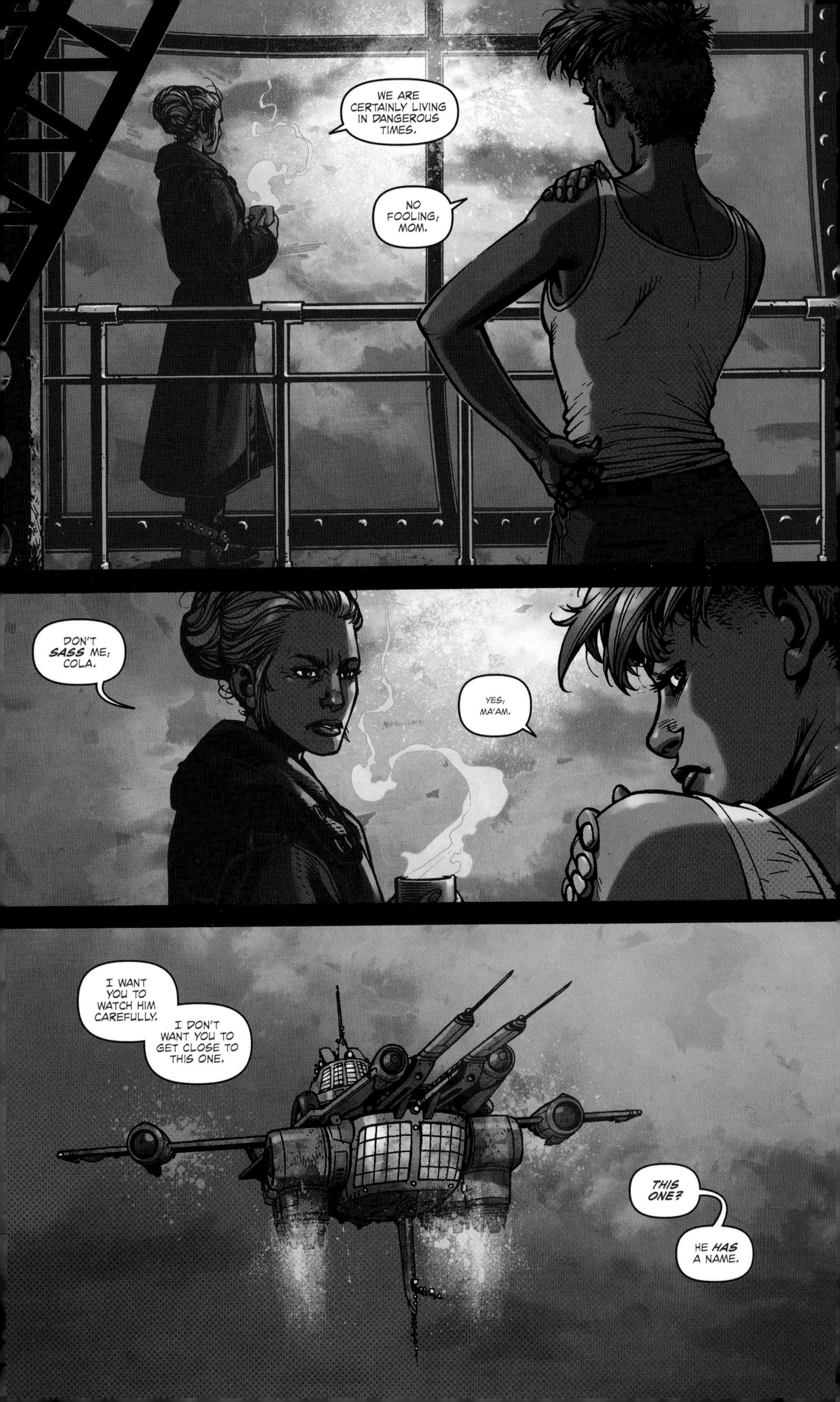
WE ARE CERTAINLY LIVING IN DANGEROUS TIMES.
NO FOOLING, MOM.
DON'T SASS ME, COLA.
YES, MA'AM.
I WANT YOU TO WATCH HIM CAREFULLY.
I DON'T WANT YOU TO GET CLOSE TO THIS ONE.
THIS ONE?
HE HAS A NAME.

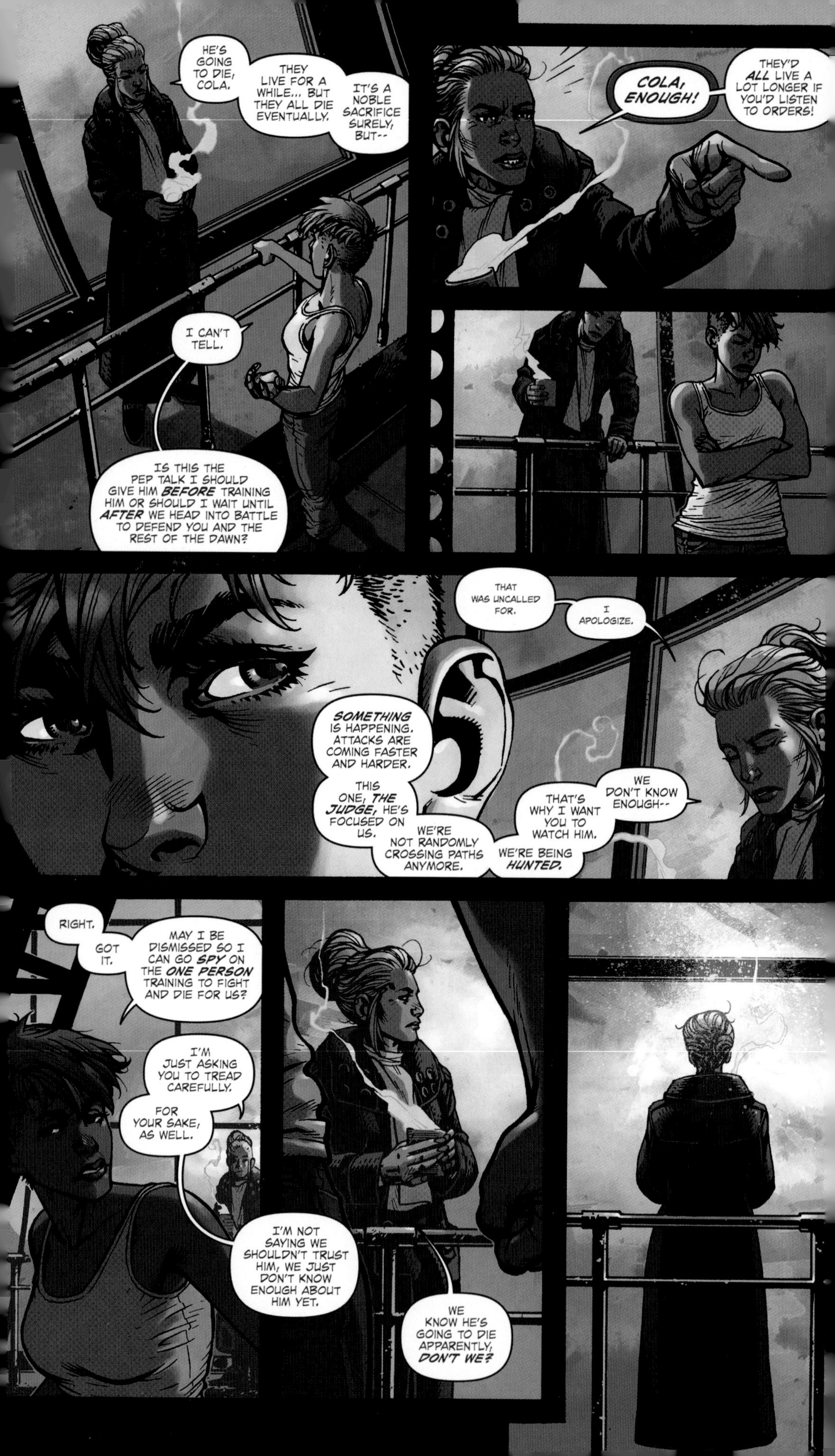

HE'S GOING TO DIE, COLA.
THEY LIVE FOR A WHILE... BUT THEY ALL DIE EVENTUALLY.
IT'S A NOBLE SACRIFICE SURELY, BUT--
COLA, ENOUGH!
THEY'D ALL LIVE A LOT LONGER IF YOU'D LISTEN TO ORDERS!
I CAN'T TELL.
IS THIS THE PEP TALK I SHOULD GIVE HIM BEFORE TRAINING HIM OR SHOULD I WAIT UNTIL AFTER WE HEAD INTO BATTLE TO DEFEND YOU AND THE REST OF THE DAWN?
THAT WAS UNCALLED FOR.
I APOLOGIZE.
SOMETHING IS HAPPENING. ATTACKS ARE COMING FASTER AND HARDER.
THIS ONE, THE JUDGE, HE'S FOCUSED ON US.
WE'RE NOT RANDOMLY CROSSING PATHS ANYMORE.
WE'RE BEING HUNTED.
WE DON'T KNOW ENOUGH--
THAT'S WHY I WANT YOU TO WATCH HIM.
RIGHT.
GOT IT.
MAY I BE DISMISSED SO I CAN GO SPY ON THE ONE PERSON TRAINING TO FIGHT AND DIE FOR US?
I'M JUST ASKING YOU TO TREAD CAREFULLY.
FOR YOUR SAKE, AS WELL.
I'M NOT SAYING WE SHOULDN'T TRUST HIM, WE JUST DON'T KNOW ENOUGH ABOUT HIM YET.
WE KNOW HE'S GOING TO DIE APPARENTLY, DON'T WE?

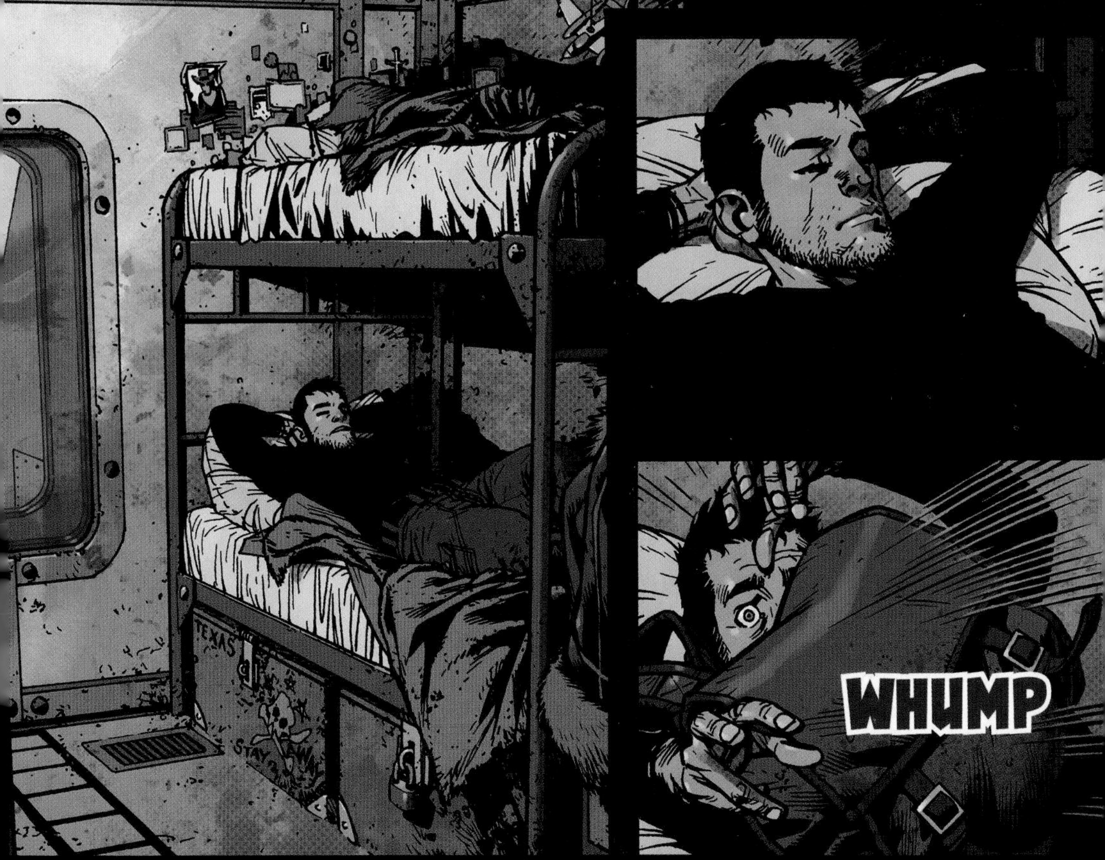
WHUMP

CHAPTER TWO

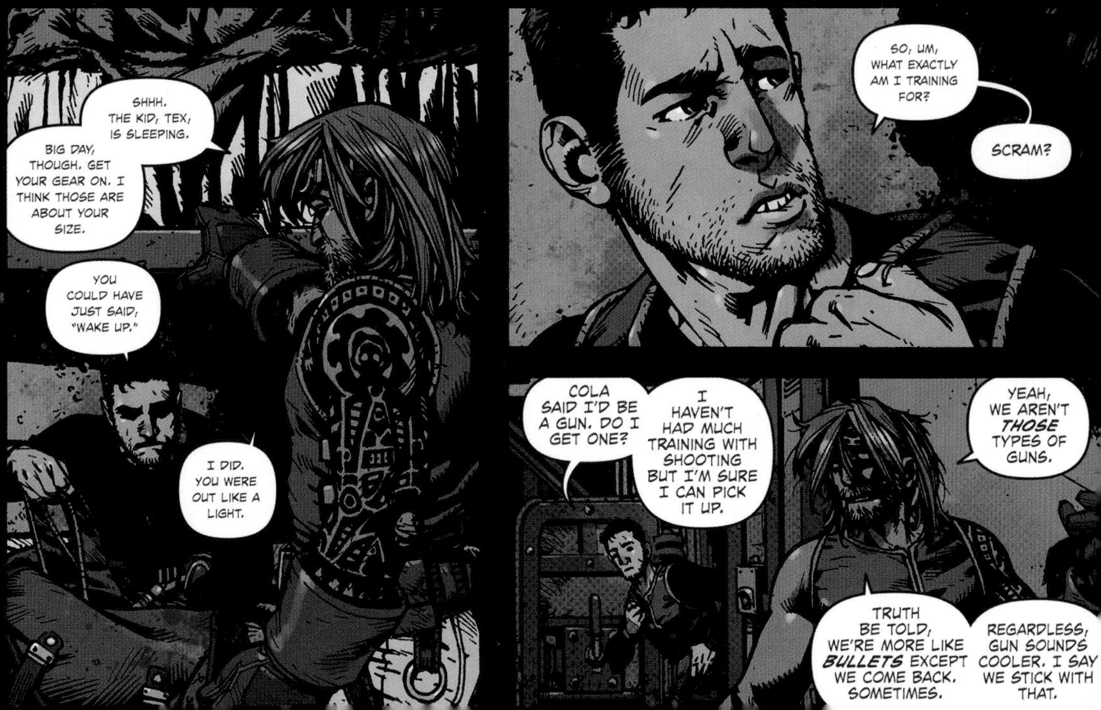
SHHH. THE KID, TEX, IS SLEEPING.
BIG DAY, THOUGH. GET YOUR GEAR ON. I THINK THOSE ARE ABOUT YOUR SIZE.
YOU COULD HAVE JUST SAID, "WAKE UP."
I DID. YOU WERE OUT LIKE A LIGHT.
SO, UM, WHAT EXACTLY AM I TRAINING FOR?
SCRAM?
COLA SAID I'D BE A GUN. DO I GET ONE?
I HAVEN'T HAD MUCH TRAINING WITH SHOOTING BUT I'M SURE I CAN PICK IT UP.
YEAH, WE AREN'T *THOSE* TYPES OF GUNS.
TRUTH BE TOLD, WE'RE MORE LIKE ***BULLETS*** EXCEPT WE COME BACK. SOMETIMES.
REGARDLESS, GUN SOUNDS COOLER. I SAY WE STICK WITH THAT.

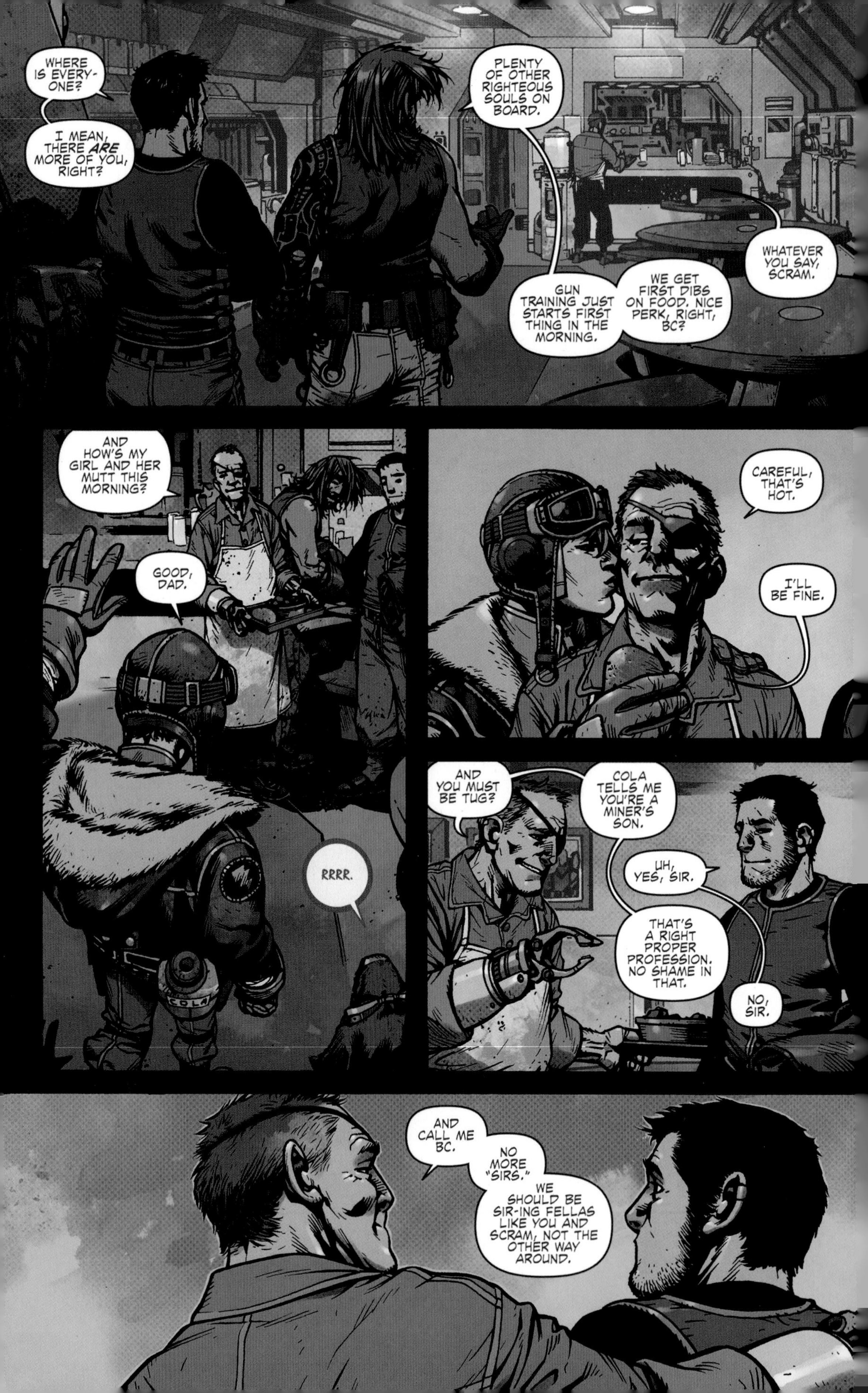
WHERE IS EVERY-ONE?
I MEAN, THERE ARE MORE OF YOU, RIGHT?
PLENTY OF OTHER RIGHTEOUS SOULS ON BOARD.
GUN TRAINING JUST STARTS FIRST THING IN THE MORNING.
WE GET FIRST DIBS ON FOOD. NICE PERK, RIGHT, BC?
WHATEVER YOU SAY, SCRAM.
AND HOW'S MY GIRL AND HER MUTT THIS MORNING?
GOOD, DAD.
RRRR.
CAREFUL, THAT'S HOT.
I'LL BE FINE.
AND YOU MUST BE TUG?
COLA TELLS ME YOU'RE A MINER'S SON.
UH, YES, SIR.
THAT'S A RIGHT PROPER PROFESSION. NO SHAME IN THAT.
NO, SIR.
AND CALL ME BC.
NO MORE "SIRS."
WE SHOULD BE SIR-ING FELLAS LIKE YOU AND SCRAM, NOT THE OTHER WAY AROUND.

EAT UP, CRITTER.

UM, SIR, YOU FORGOT MINE.

FEEDING YOU WOULD BE A WASTE OF FOOD TODAY, SON.

DOUBT YOU'D KEEP IT DOWN.

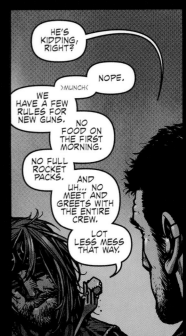

HE'S KIDDING, RIGHT?

NOPE.

>MUNCH<

WE HAVE A FEW RULES FOR NEW GUNS.

NO FOOD ON THE FIRST MORNING.

NO FULL ROCKET PACKS.

AND UH... NO MEET AND GREETS WITH THE ENTIRE CREW.

LOT LESS MESS THAT WAY.

WHAT THE HELL IS HE TALKING ABOUT?

>CHOMP<

WE'VE HAD A FEW MISHAPS. PUKING IN THE SKY. SMACKED SKULLS.

WE LIKE TO HOLD OFF ON INTRODUCING YOU TO EVERYONE UNTIL WE'RE SURE YOU'RE NOT GOING TO...

...YOU KNOW...

...TSEEEE!

SEE YOU OUTSIDE.

MAKE SURE YOU TIE HIM TIGHT, SCRAM.

WE DON'T WANT ANY ACCIDENTS.

THIS ONE MIGHT TAKE A WHILE.

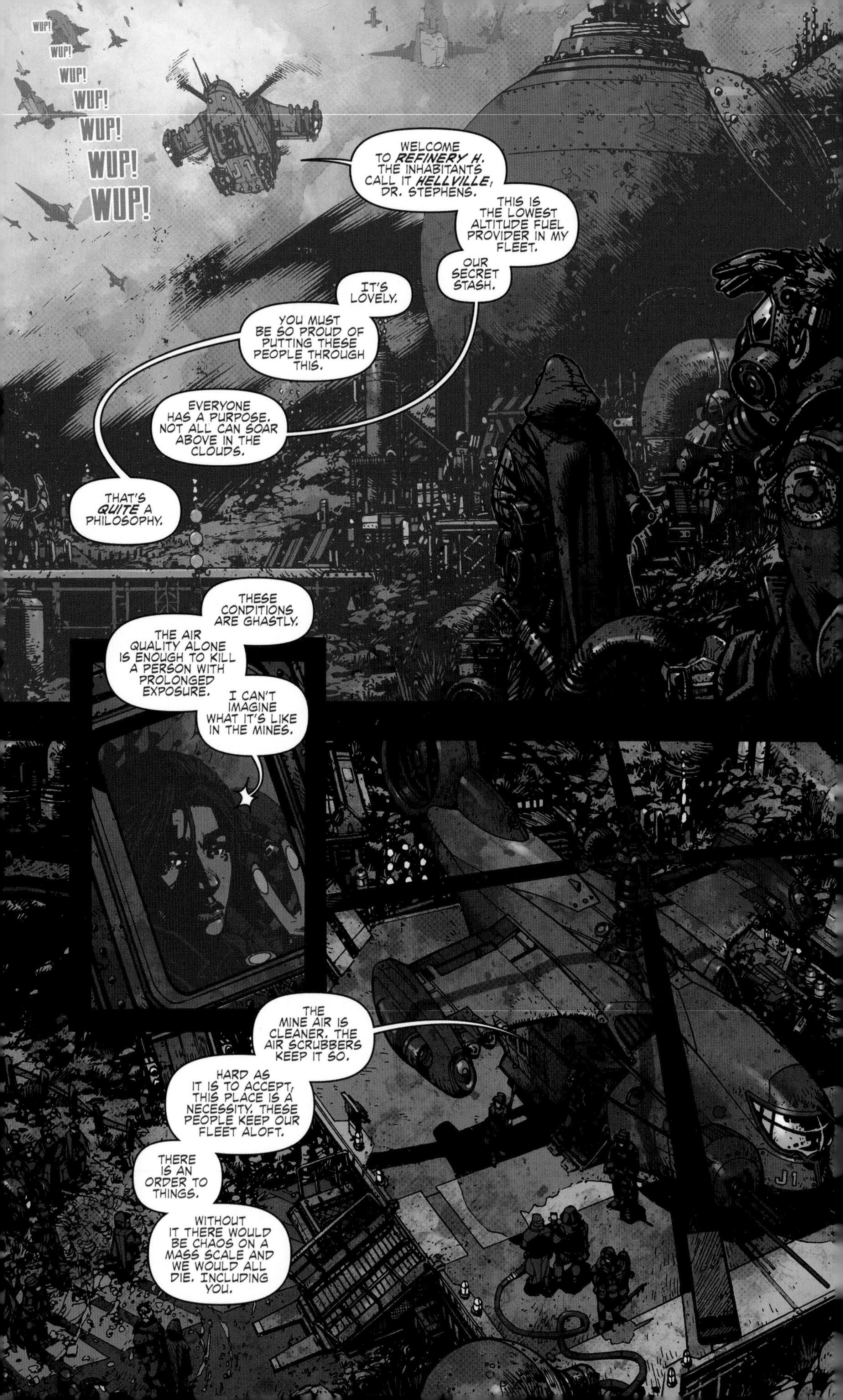

WUP!
WUP!
WUP!
WUP!
WUP!
WUP!
WUP!
WELCOME TO *REFINERY H.* THE INHABITANTS CALL IT *HELLVILLE*, DR. STEPHENS.
THIS IS THE LOWEST ALTITUDE FUEL PROVIDER IN MY FLEET.
OUR SECRET STASH.
IT'S LOVELY.
YOU MUST BE SO PROUD OF PUTTING THESE PEOPLE THROUGH THIS.
EVERYONE HAS A PURPOSE. NOT ALL CAN SOAR ABOVE IN THE CLOUDS.
THAT'S *QUITE* A PHILOSOPHY.
THESE CONDITIONS ARE GHASTLY.
THE AIR QUALITY ALONE IS ENOUGH TO KILL A PERSON WITH PROLONGED EXPOSURE.
I CAN'T IMAGINE WHAT IT'S LIKE IN THE MINES.
THE MINE AIR IS CLEANER. THE AIR SCRUBBERS KEEP IT SO.
HARD AS IT IS TO ACCEPT, THIS PLACE IS A NECESSITY. THESE PEOPLE KEEP OUR FLEET ALOFT.
THERE IS AN ORDER TO THINGS.
WITHOUT IT THERE WOULD BE CHAOS ON A MASS SCALE AND WE WOULD ALL DIE. INCLUDING YOU.

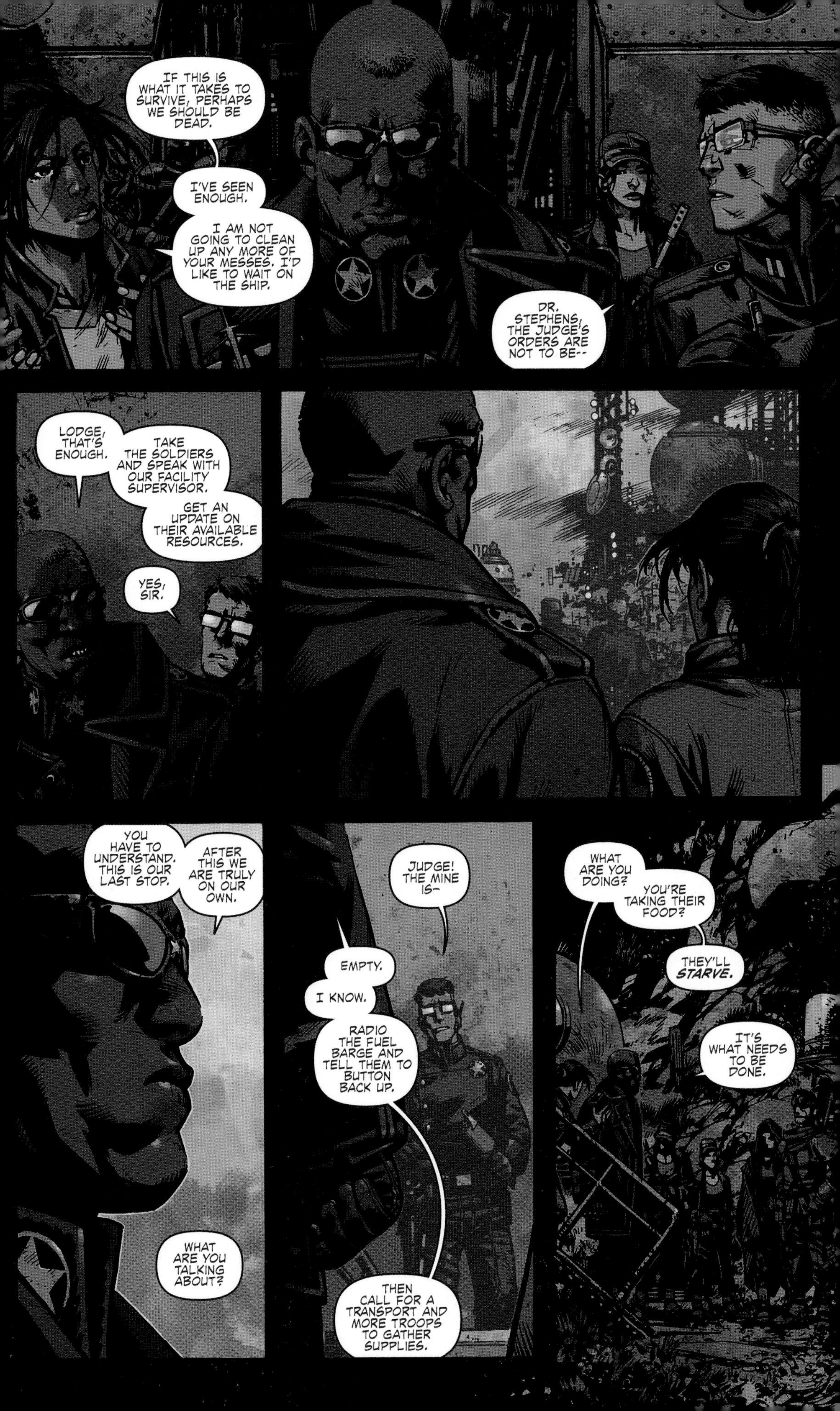
IF THIS IS WHAT IT TAKES TO SURVIVE, PERHAPS WE SHOULD BE DEAD.
I'VE SEEN ENOUGH.
I AM NOT GOING TO CLEAN UP ANY MORE OF YOUR MESSES. I'D LIKE TO WAIT ON THE SHIP.
DR. STEPHENS, THE JUDGE'S ORDERS ARE NOT TO BE--
LODGE, THAT'S ENOUGH.
TAKE THE SOLDIERS AND SPEAK WITH OUR FACILITY SUPERVISOR.
GET AN UPDATE ON THEIR AVAILABLE RESOURCES.
YES, SIR.
YOU HAVE TO UNDERSTAND. THIS IS OUR LAST STOP.
AFTER THIS WE ARE TRULY ON OUR OWN.
WHAT ARE YOU TALKING ABOUT?
JUDGE! THE MINE IS-
EMPTY.
I KNOW.
RADIO THE FUEL BARGE AND TELL THEM TO BUTTON BACK UP.
THEN CALL FOR A TRANSPORT AND MORE TROOPS TO GATHER SUPPLIES.
WHAT ARE YOU DOING?
YOU'RE TAKING THEIR FOOD?
THEY'LL *STARVE.*
IT'S WHAT NEEDS TO BE DONE.

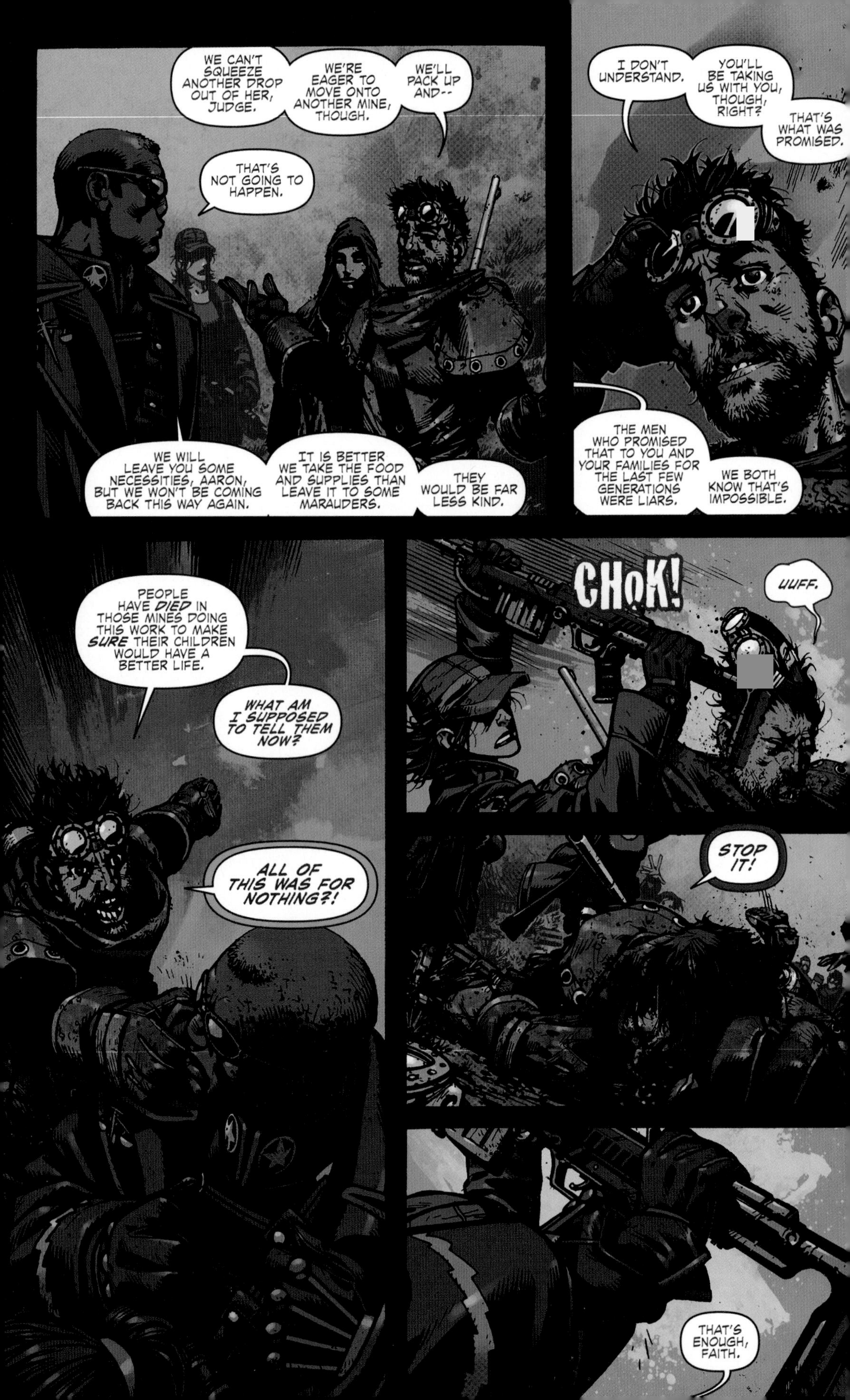
WE CAN'T SQUEEZE ANOTHER DROP OUT OF HER, JUDGE.
WE'RE EAGER TO MOVE ONTO ANOTHER MINE, THOUGH.
WE'LL PACK UP AND--
THAT'S NOT GOING TO HAPPEN.
WE WILL LEAVE YOU SOME NECESSITIES, AARON, BUT WE WON'T BE COMING BACK THIS WAY AGAIN.
IT IS BETTER WE TAKE THE FOOD AND SUPPLIES THAN LEAVE IT TO SOME MARAUDERS.
THEY WOULD BE FAR LESS KIND.
I DON'T UNDERSTAND.
YOU'LL BE TAKING US WITH YOU, THOUGH, RIGHT?
THAT'S WHAT WAS PROMISED.
THE MEN WHO PROMISED THAT TO YOU AND YOUR FAMILIES FOR THE LAST FEW GENERATIONS WERE LIARS.
WE BOTH KNOW THAT'S IMPOSSIBLE.
PEOPLE HAVE DIED IN THOSE MINES DOING THIS WORK TO MAKE SURE THEIR CHILDREN WOULD HAVE A BETTER LIFE.
WHAT AM I SUPPOSED TO TELL THEM NOW?
ALL OF THIS WAS FOR NOTHING?!
CHOK!
UUFF.
STOP IT!
THAT'S ENOUGH, FAITH.

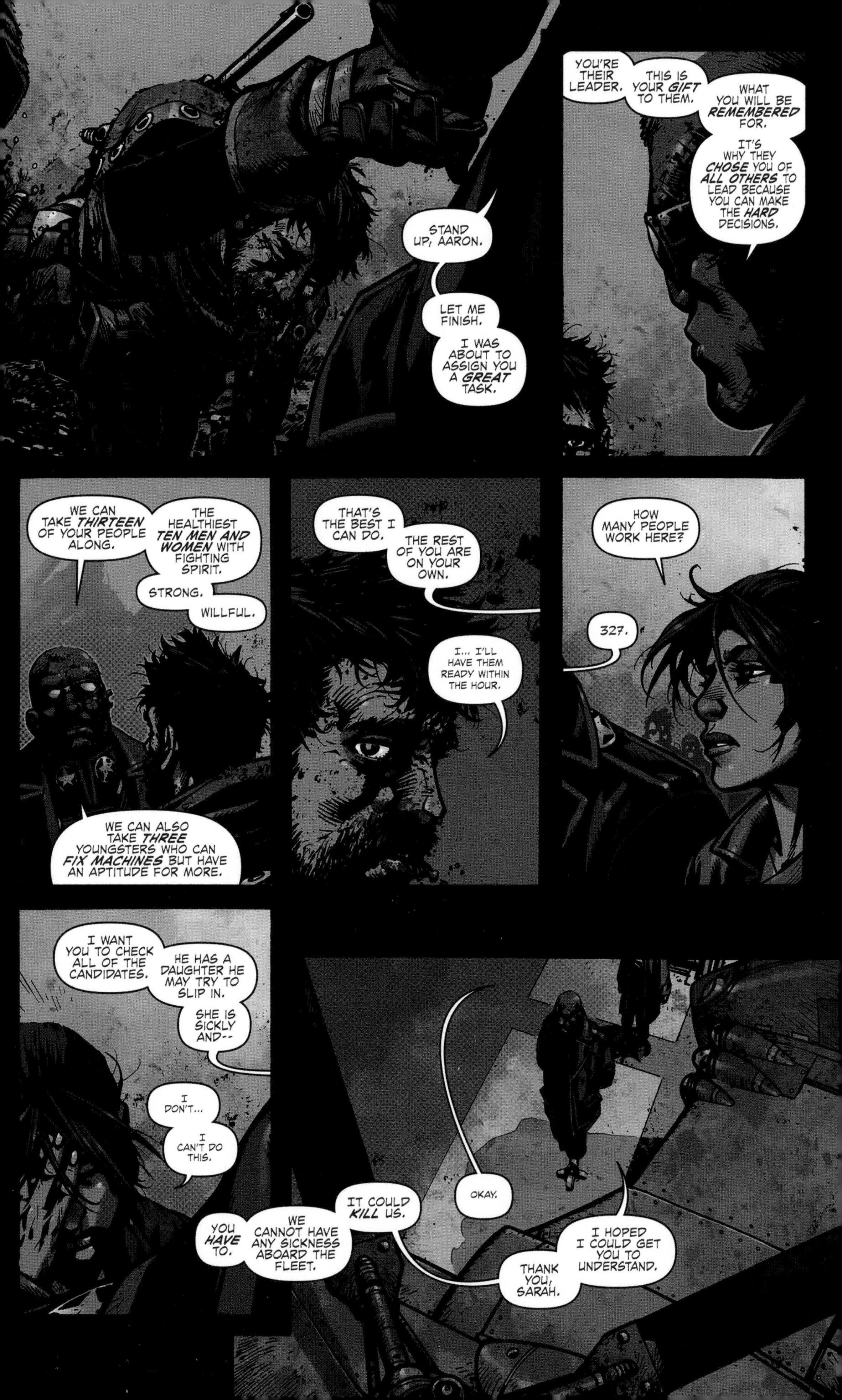
STAND UP, AARON.
LET ME FINISH.
I WAS ABOUT TO ASSIGN YOU A GREAT TASK.
YOU'RE THEIR LEADER.
THIS IS YOUR GIFT TO THEM.
WHAT YOU WILL BE REMEMBERED FOR.
IT'S WHY THEY CHOSE YOU OF ALL OTHERS TO LEAD BECAUSE YOU CAN MAKE THE HARD DECISIONS.
WE CAN TAKE THIRTEEN OF YOUR PEOPLE ALONG.
THE HEALTHIEST TEN MEN AND WOMEN WITH FIGHTING SPIRIT.
STRONG.
WILLFUL.
WE CAN ALSO TAKE THREE YOUNGSTERS WHO CAN FIX MACHINES BUT HAVE AN APTITUDE FOR MORE.
THAT'S THE BEST I CAN DO.
THE REST OF YOU ARE ON YOUR OWN.
I... I'LL HAVE THEM READY WITHIN THE HOUR.
HOW MANY PEOPLE WORK HERE?
327.
I WANT YOU TO CHECK ALL OF THE CANDIDATES.
HE HAS A DAUGHTER HE MAY TRY TO SLIP IN.
SHE IS SICKLY AND--
I DON'T...
I CAN'T DO THIS.
YOU HAVE TO.
WE CANNOT HAVE ANY SICKNESS ABOARD THE FLEET.
IT COULD KILL US.
OKAY.
THANK YOU, SARAH.
I HOPED I COULD GET YOU TO UNDERSTAND.

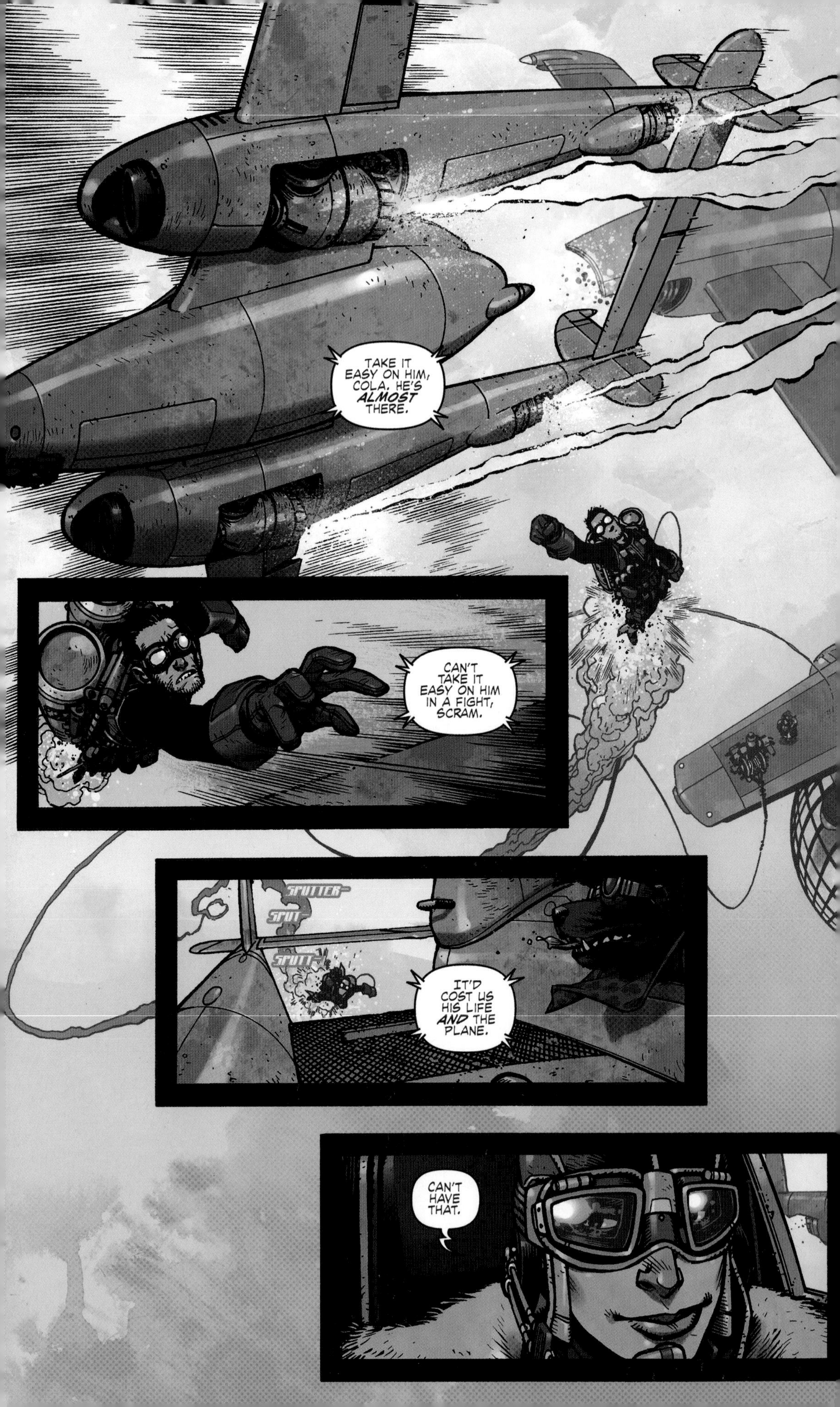
TAKE IT EASY ON HIM, COLA. HE'S ALMOST THERE.
CAN'T TAKE IT EASY ON HIM IN A FIGHT, SCRAM.
SPUTTER-
SPUT-
SPUTT-
IT'D COST US HIS LIFE AND THE PLANE.
CAN'T HAVE THAT.

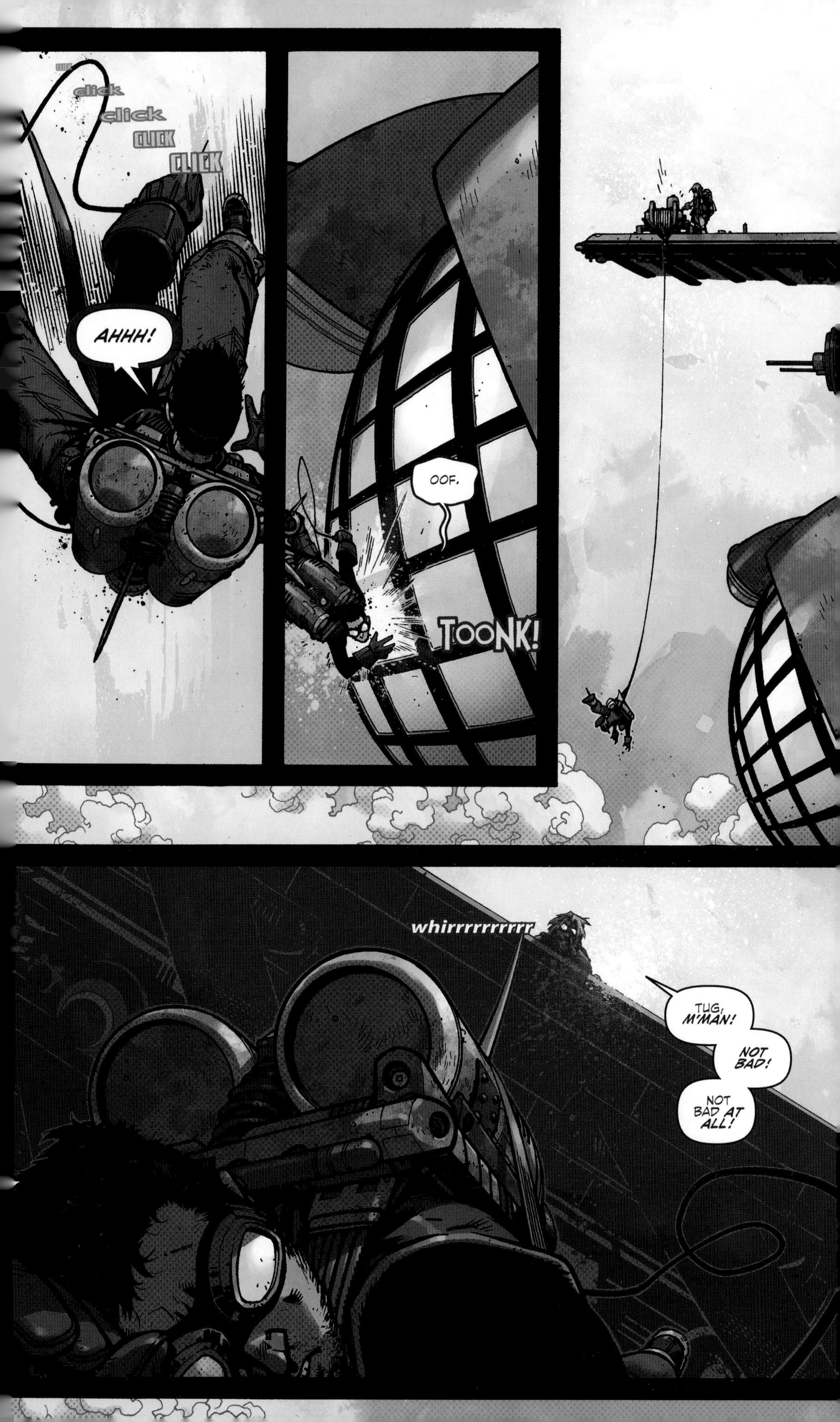
click
click
CLICK
CLICK
AHHH!
OOF.
TOONK!
whirrrrrrrrrr
TUG, M'MAN!
NOT BAD!
NOT BAD AT ALL!

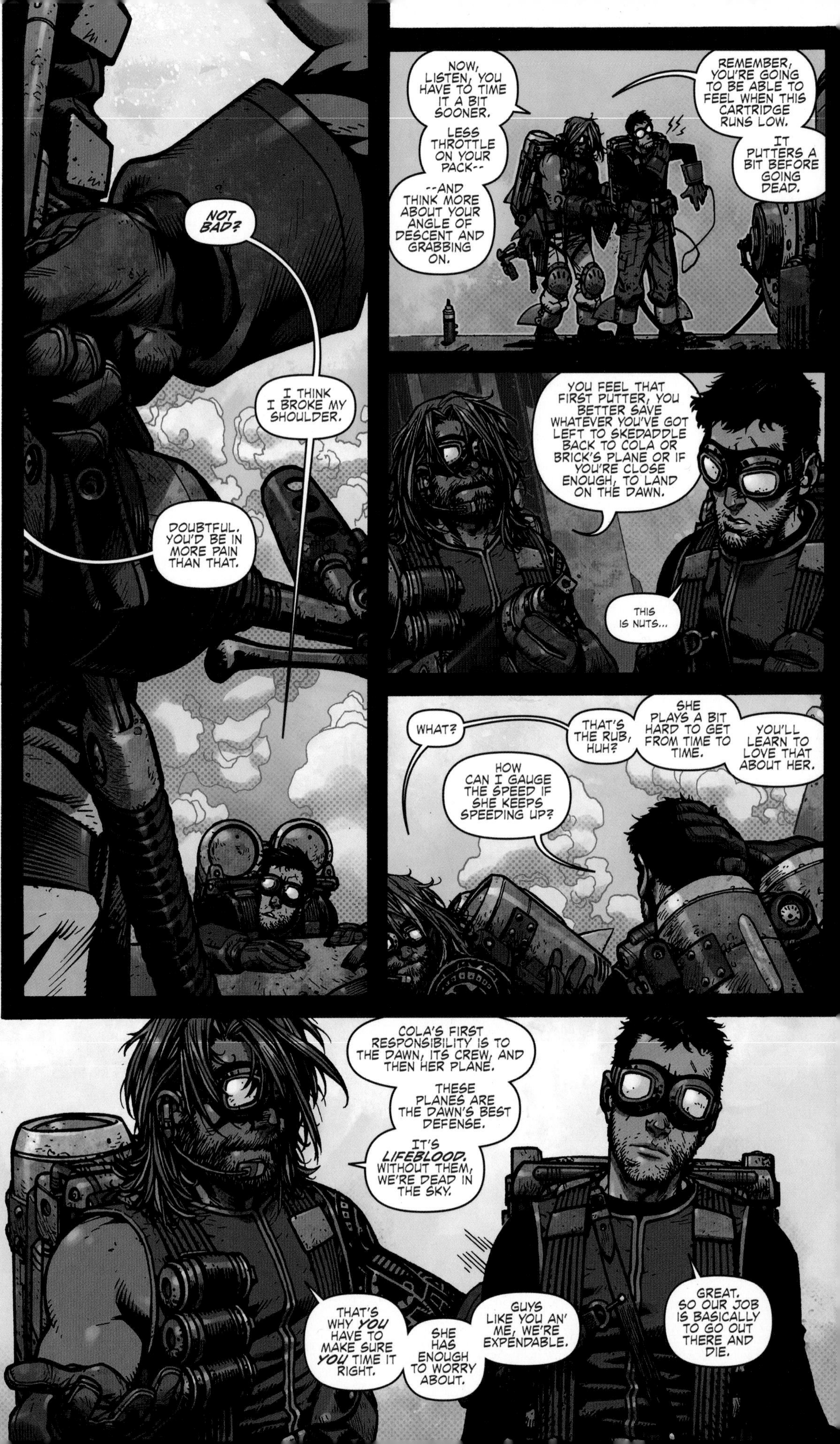
NOT BAD?
I THINK I BROKE MY SHOULDER.
DOUBTFUL. YOU'D BE IN MORE PAIN THAN THAT.
NOW, LISTEN, YOU HAVE TO TIME IT A BIT SOONER.
LESS THROTTLE ON YOUR PACK--
--AND THINK MORE ABOUT YOUR ANGLE OF DESCENT AND GRABBING ON.
REMEMBER, YOU'RE GOING TO BE ABLE TO FEEL WHEN THIS CARTRIDGE RUNS LOW.
IT PUTTERS A BIT BEFORE GOING DEAD.
YOU FEEL THAT FIRST PUTTER, YOU BETTER SAVE WHATEVER YOU'VE GOT LEFT TO SKEDADDLE BACK TO COLA OR BRICK'S PLANE OR IF YOU'RE CLOSE ENOUGH, TO LAND ON THE DAWN.
THIS IS NUTS...
WHAT?
HOW CAN I GAUGE THE SPEED IF SHE KEEPS SPEEDING UP?
THAT'S THE RUB, HUH?
SHE PLAYS A BIT HARD TO GET FROM TIME TO TIME.
YOU'LL LEARN TO LOVE THAT ABOUT HER.
COLA'S FIRST RESPONSIBILITY IS TO THE DAWN, ITS CREW, AND THEN HER PLANE.
THESE PLANES ARE THE DAWN'S BEST DEFENSE.
IT'S LIFEBLOOD. WITHOUT THEM, WE'RE DEAD IN THE SKY.
THAT'S WHY YOU HAVE TO MAKE SURE YOU TIME IT RIGHT.
SHE HAS ENOUGH TO WORRY ABOUT.
GUYS LIKE YOU AN' ME, WE'RE EXPENDABLE.
GREAT. SO OUR JOB IS BASICALLY TO GO OUT THERE AND DIE.

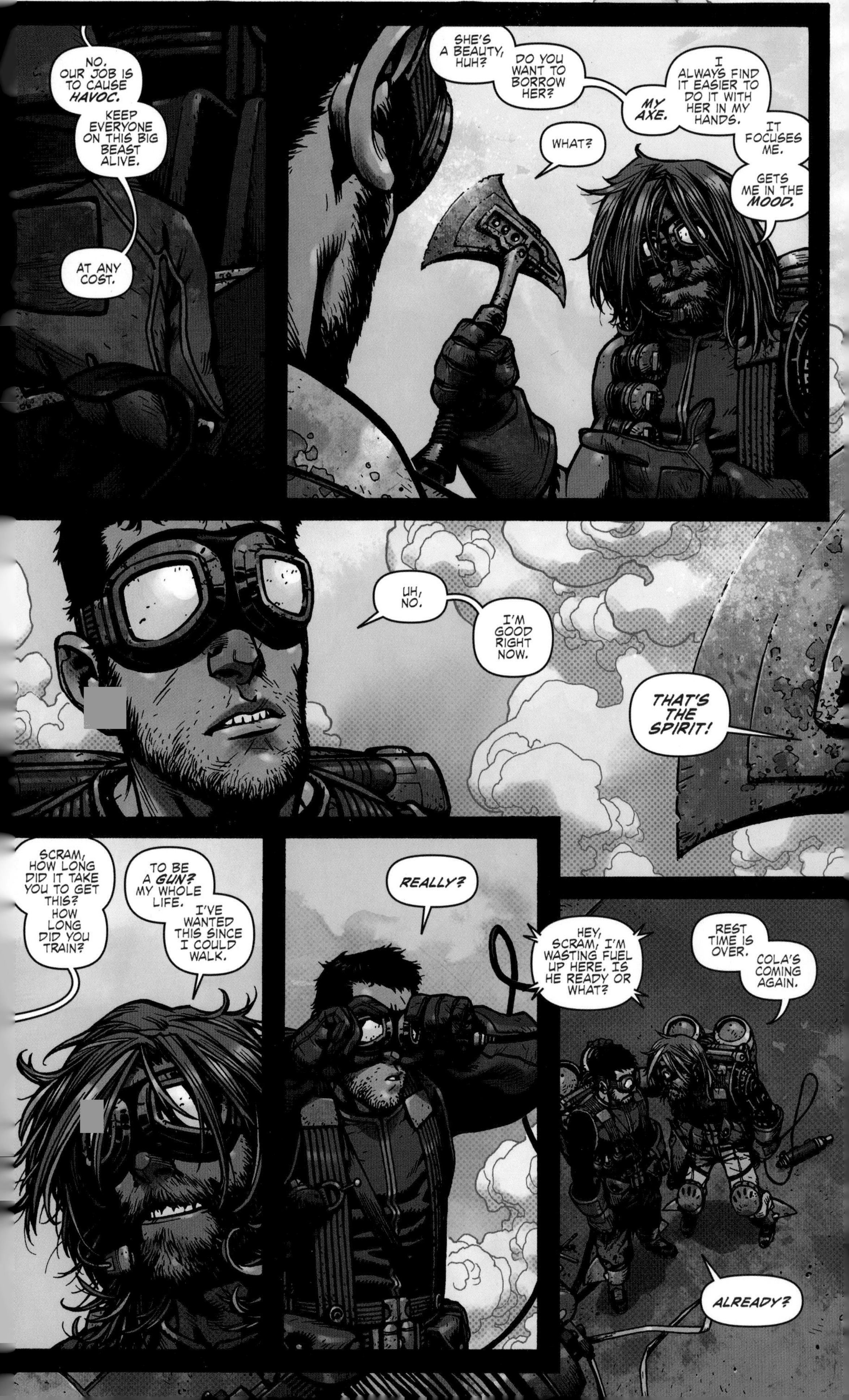
NO. OUR JOB IS TO CAUSE *HAVOC.*
KEEP EVERYONE ON THIS BIG BEAST ALIVE.
AT ANY COST.
SHE'S A BEAUTY, HUH?
DO YOU WANT TO BORROW HER?
WHAT?
MY AXE.
I ALWAYS FIND IT EASIER TO DO IT WITH HER IN MY HANDS.
IT FOCUSES ME.
GETS ME IN THE *MOOD.*
UH, NO.
I'M GOOD RIGHT NOW.
THAT'S THE SPIRIT!
SCRAM, HOW LONG DID IT TAKE YOU TO GET THIS? HOW LONG DID YOU TRAIN?
TO BE A *GUN?* MY WHOLE LIFE.
I'VE WANTED THIS SINCE I COULD WALK.
REALLY?
HEY, SCRAM, I'M WASTING FUEL UP HERE. IS HE READY OR WHAT?
REST TIME IS OVER.
COLA'S COMING AGAIN.
ALREADY?

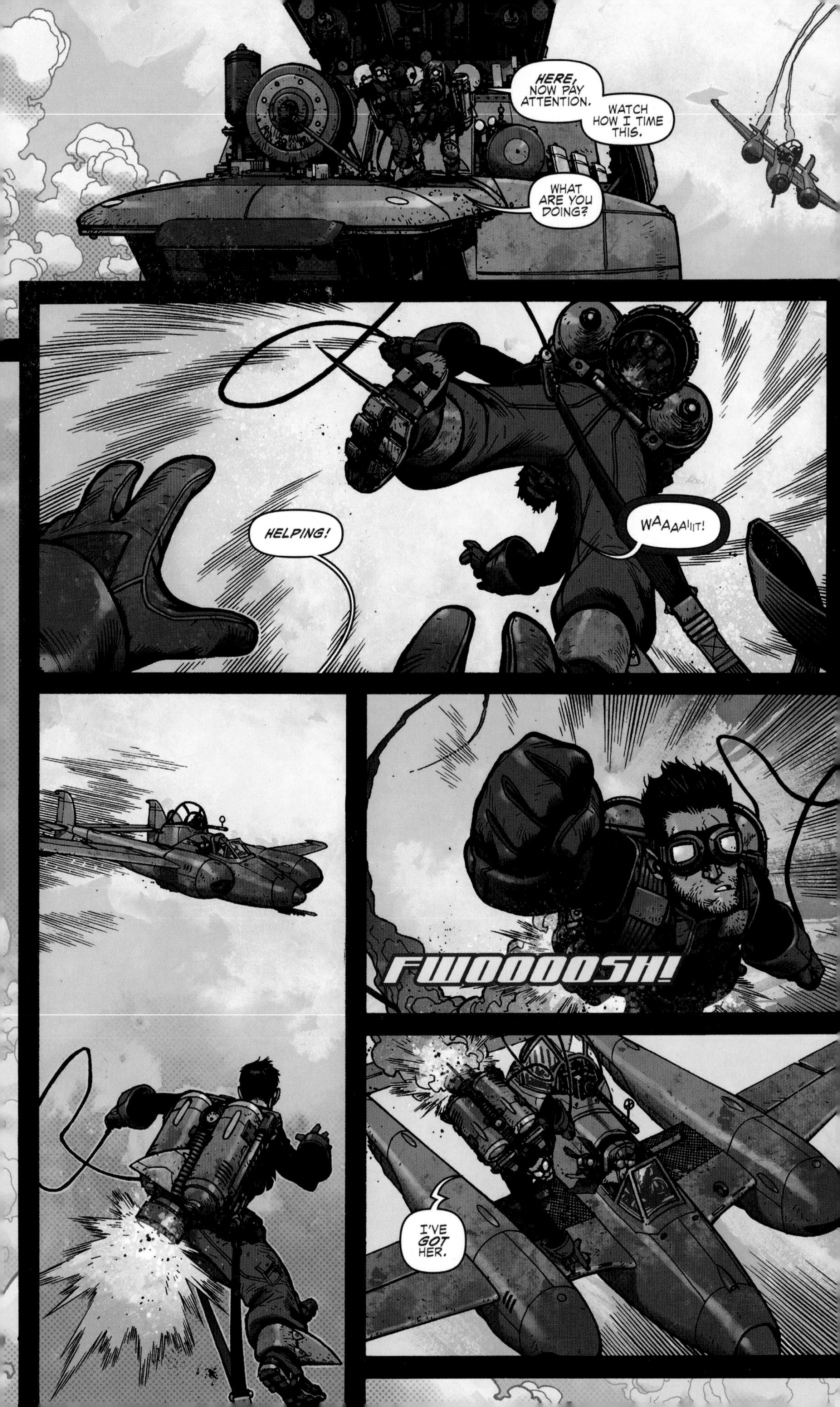
HERE, NOW PAY ATTENTION.
WATCH HOW I TIME THIS.
WHAT ARE YOU DOING?
HELPING!
WAAAAIIIT!
FWOOOOOSH!
I'VE GOT HER.

DAMMIT!

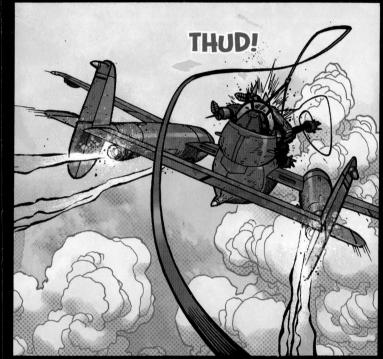

THUD!

OUCH.

WHAT THE HELL ARE YOU DOING?

SORRY. MISTIMED IT.

BUT TO BE CONSTRUCTIVE, YOU OVER-THROTTLED.

YOU THREW ME OFF THE DAWN.

YEAH, WELL, AT LEAST YOU TOUCHED THE PLANE THAT TIME.

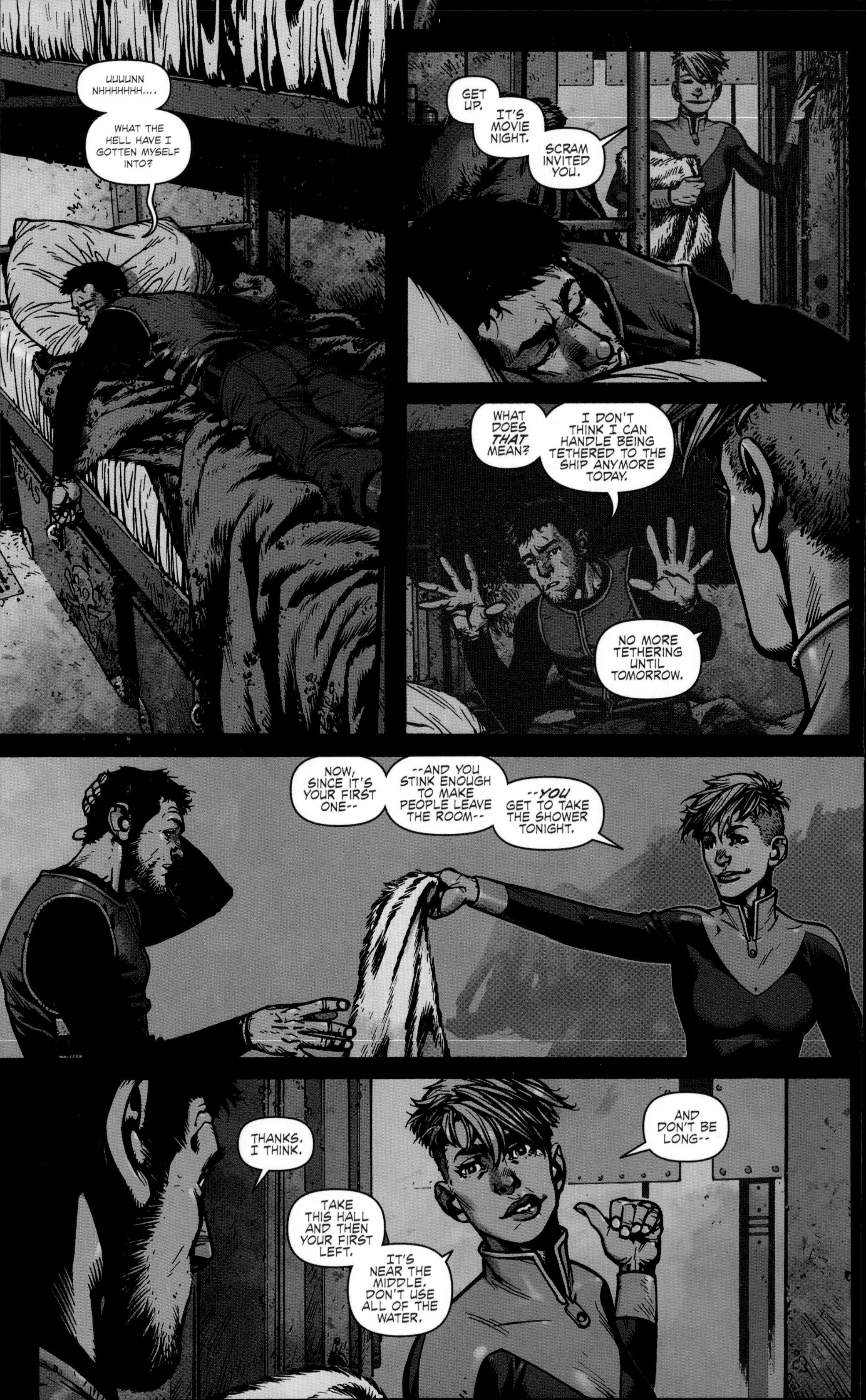
UUUUNN NHHHHHHH....
WHAT THE HELL HAVE I GOTTEN MYSELF INTO?
GET UP.
IT'S MOVIE NIGHT.
SCRAM INVITED YOU.
WHAT DOES THAT MEAN?
I DON'T THINK I CAN HANDLE BEING TETHERED TO THE SHIP ANYMORE TODAY.
NO MORE TETHERING UNTIL TOMORROW.
NOW, SINCE IT'S YOUR FIRST ONE--
--AND YOU STINK ENOUGH TO MAKE PEOPLE LEAVE THE ROOM--
--YOU GET TO TAKE THE SHOWER TONIGHT.
THANKS. I THINK.
AND DON'T BE LONG--
TAKE THIS HALL AND THEN YOUR FIRST LEFT.
IT'S NEAR THE MIDDLE. DON'T USE ALL OF THE WATER.

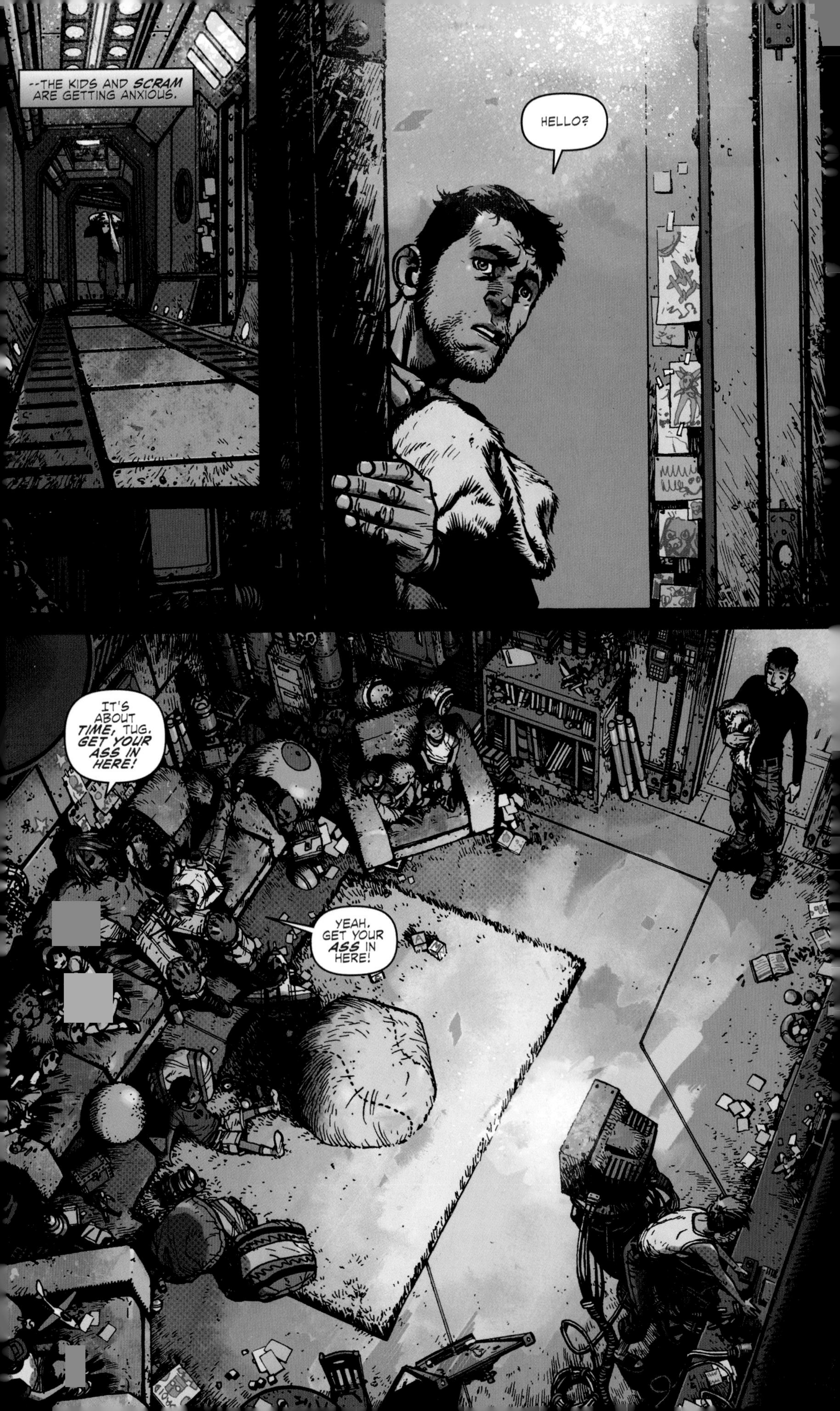
--THE KIDS AND SCRAM ARE GETTING ANXIOUS.
HELLO?
IT'S ABOUT TIME, TUG. GET YOUR ASS IN HERE!
YEAH. GET YOUR ASS IN HERE!

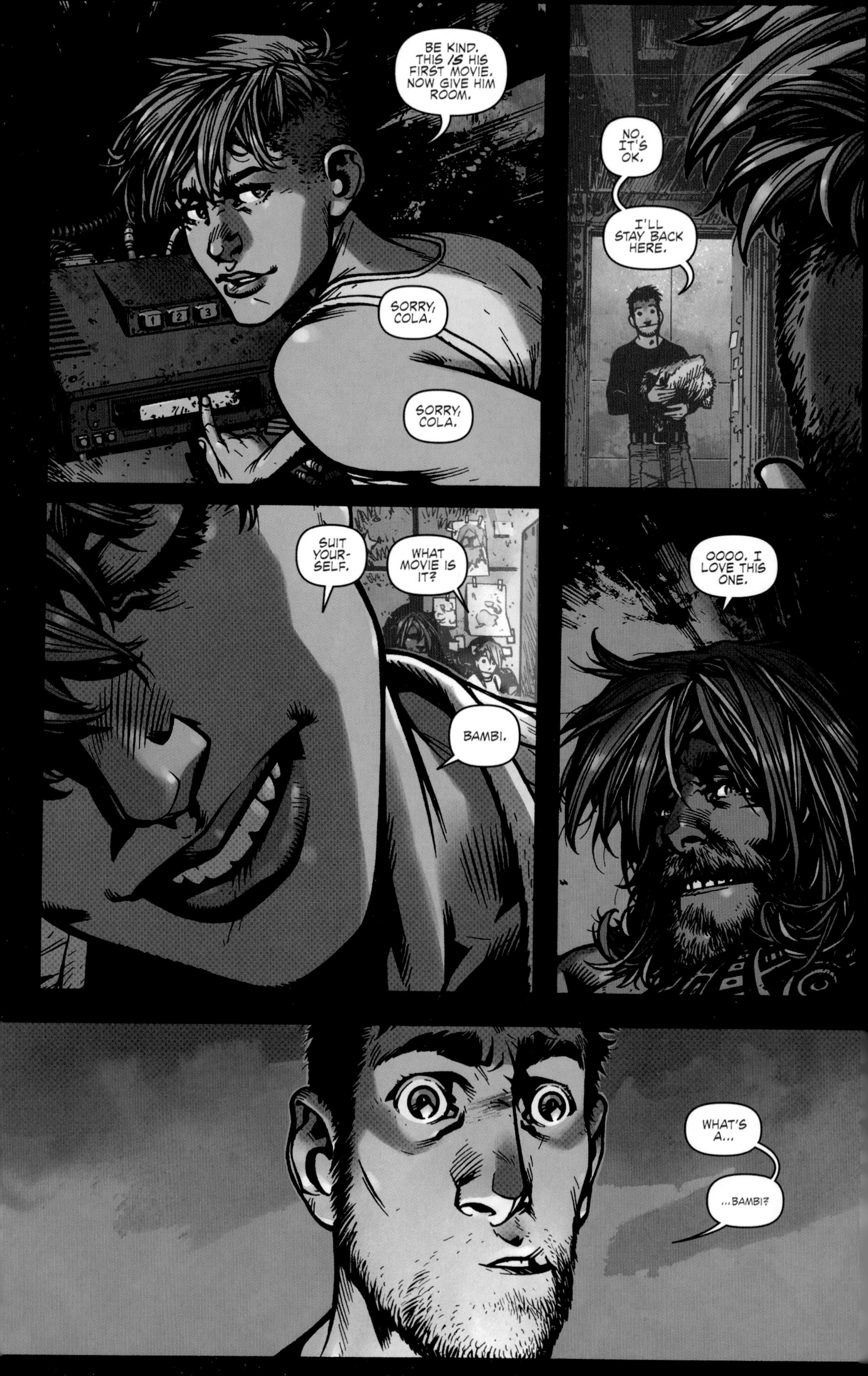
BE KIND. THIS IS HIS FIRST MOVIE. NOW GIVE HIM ROOM.
SORRY, COLA.
SORRY, COLA.
NO. IT'S OK.
I'LL STAY BACK HERE.
SUIT YOUR-SELF.
WHAT MOVIE IS IT?
BAMBI.
OOOO. I LOVE THIS ONE.
WHAT'S A...
...BAMBI?

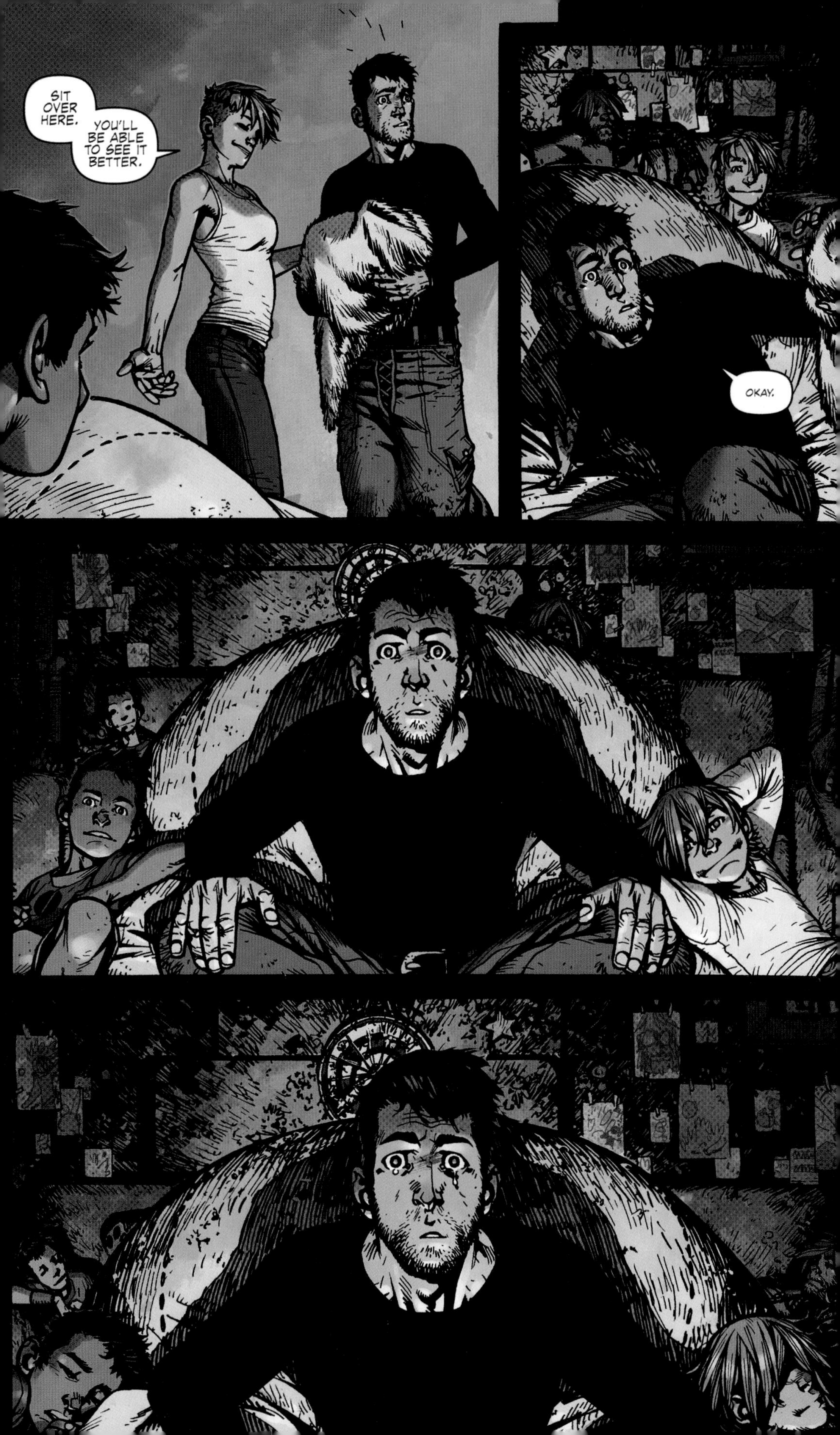
SIT OVER HERE.
YOU'LL BE ABLE TO SEE IT BETTER.
OKAY.

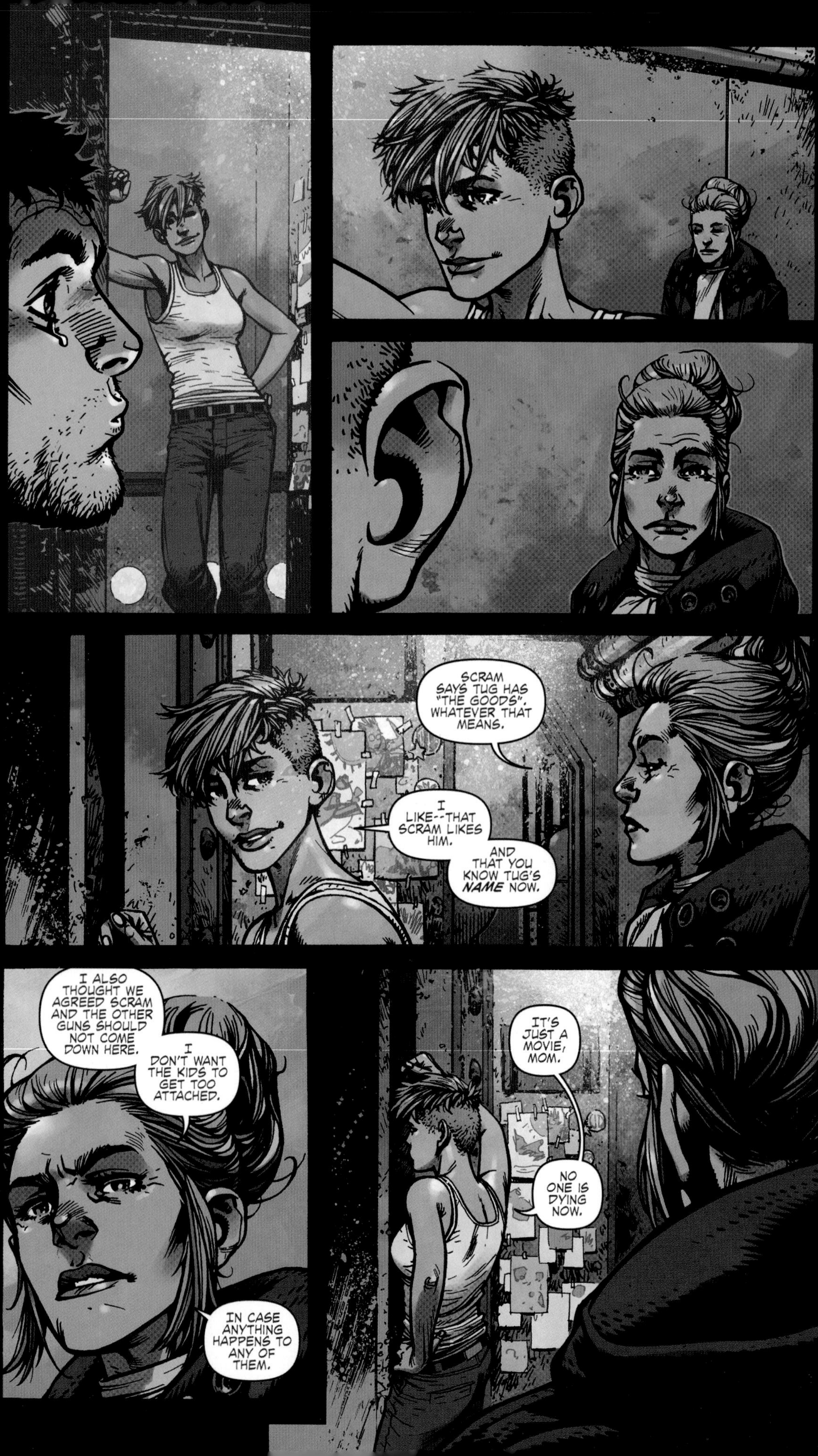
SCRAM SAYS TUG HAS "THE GOODS". WHATEVER THAT MEANS.
I LIKE--THAT SCRAM LIKES HIM.
AND THAT YOU KNOW TUG'S ***NAME*** NOW.
I ALSO THOUGHT WE AGREED SCRAM AND THE OTHER GUNS SHOULD NOT COME DOWN HERE.
I DON'T WANT THE KIDS TO GET TOO ATTACHED.
IN CASE ANYTHING HAPPENS TO ANY OF THEM.
IT'S JUST A MOVIE, MOM.
NO ONE IS DYING NOW.

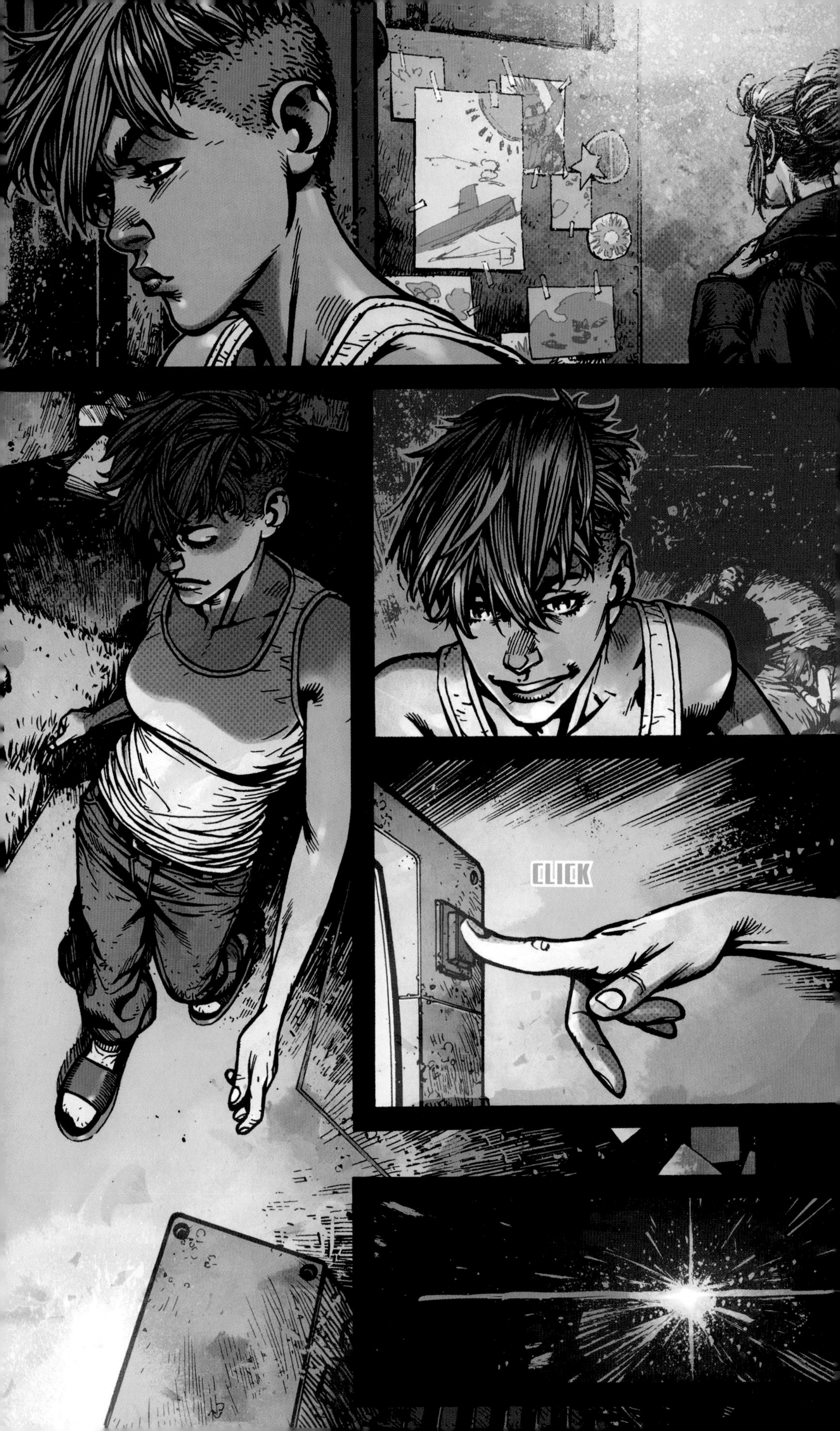
CLICK

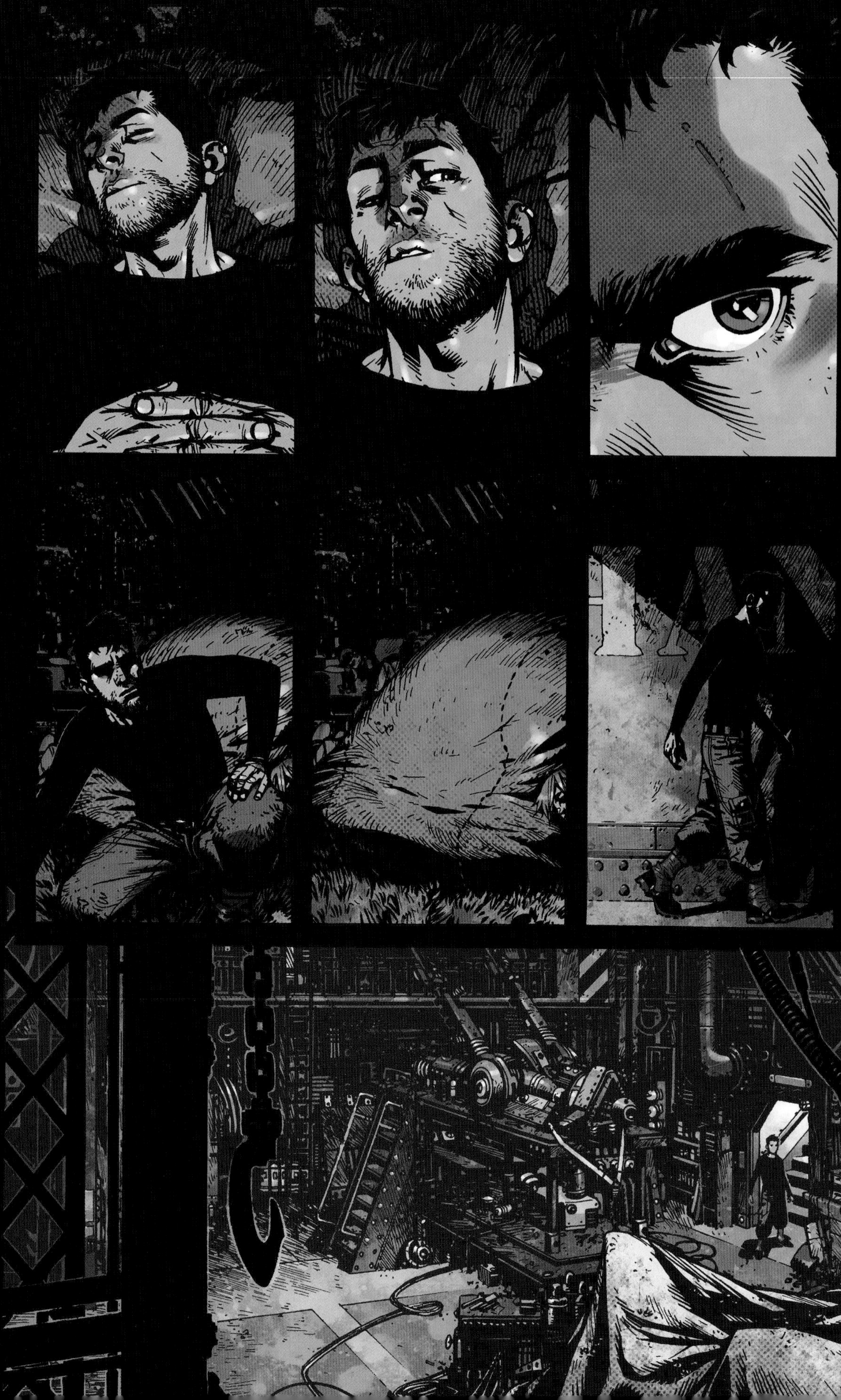

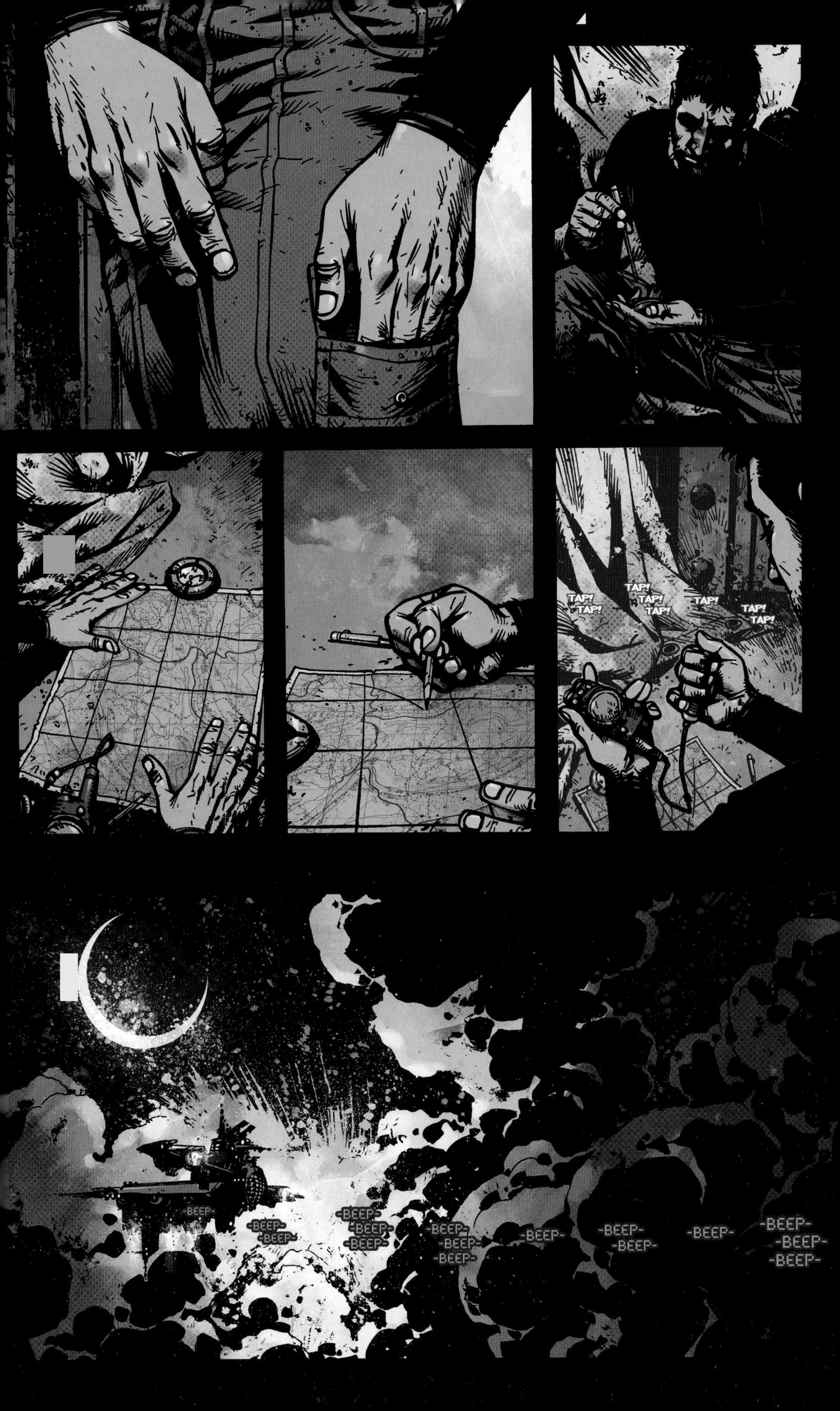
TAP!
TAP!
TAP!
TAP!
TAP!
TAP!
TAP!
TAP!
-BEEP-
-BEEP-
-BEEP-
-BEEP-
-BEEP-
-BEEP-
-BEEP-
-BEEP-
-BEEP-
-BEEP-
-BEEP-
-BEEP-
-BEEP-
-BEEP-
-BEEP-
-BEEP-

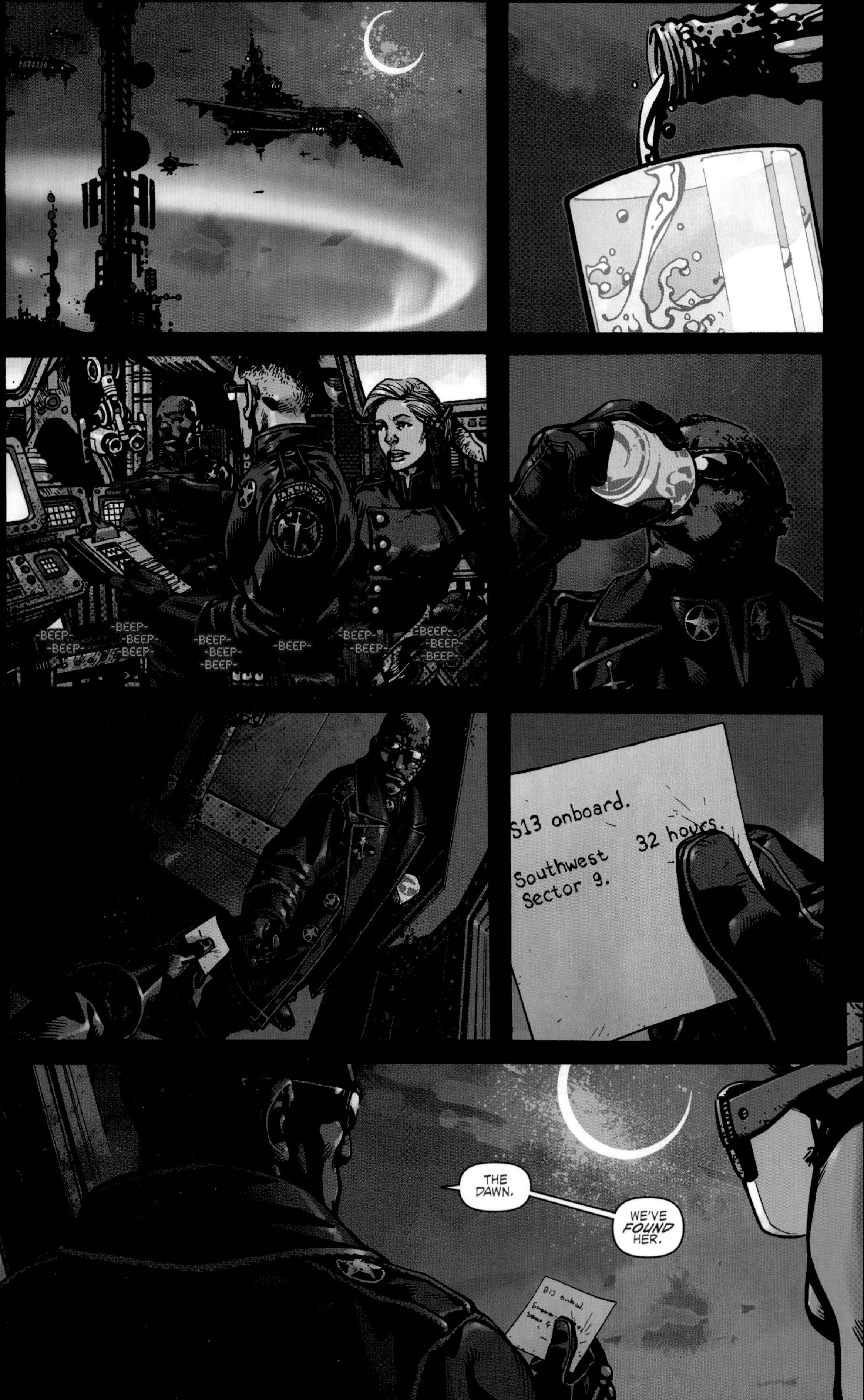
-BEEP-
-BEEP-
-BEEP-
-BEEP-
-BEEP-
-BEEP-
-BEEP-
-BEEP-
-BEEP-
-BEEP-
-BEEP-
-BEEP-
-BEEP-
-BEEP-
S13 onboard.
32 hours.
Southwest
Sector 9.
THE DAWN.
WE'VE *FOUND* HER.

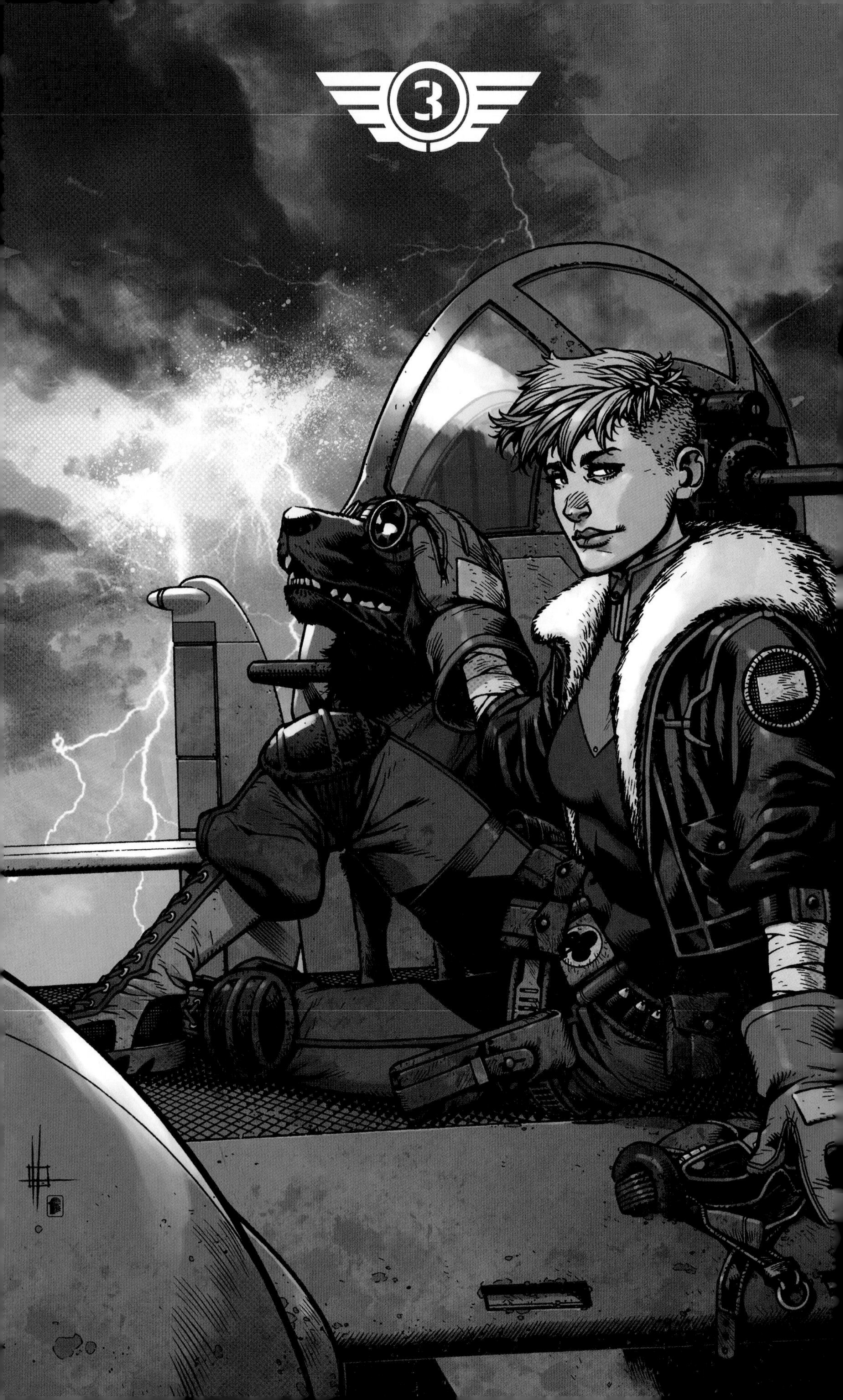
3

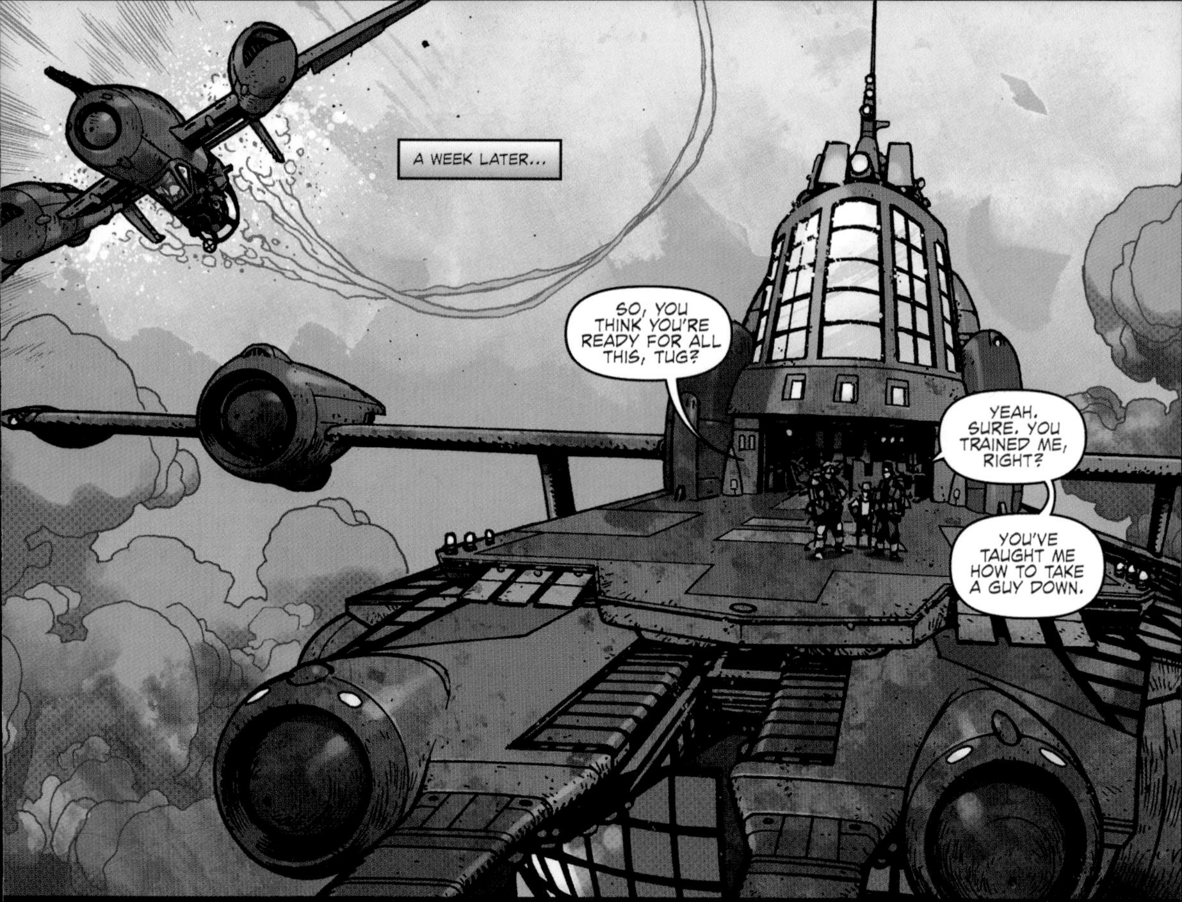
A WEEK LATER...
SO, YOU THINK YOU'RE READY FOR ALL THIS, TUG?
YEAH. SURE. YOU TRAINED ME, RIGHT?
YOU'VE TAUGHT ME HOW TO TAKE A GUY DOWN.

CHAPTER THREE

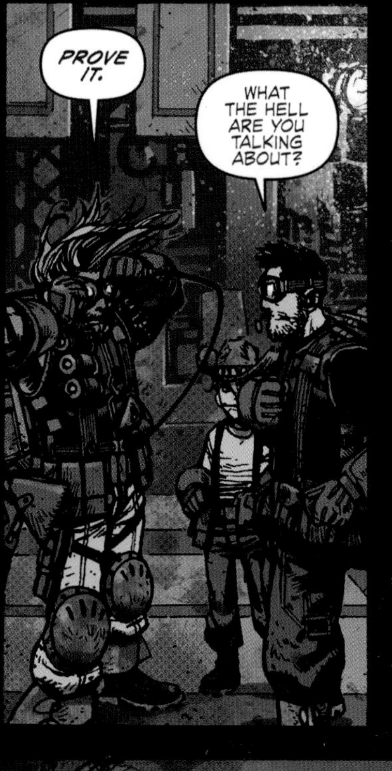
PROVE IT.
WHAT THE HELL ARE YOU TALKING ABOUT?

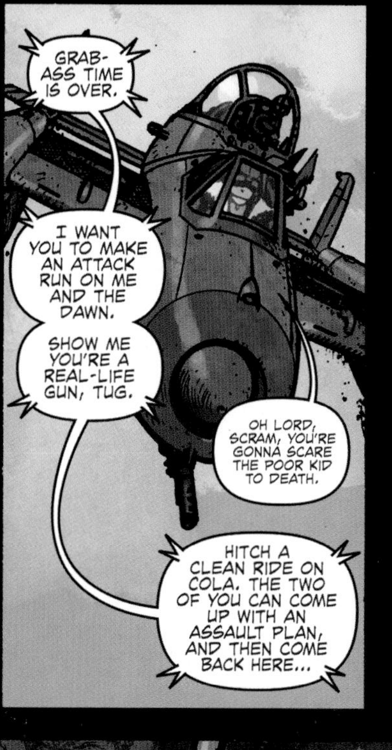
GRAB-ASS TIME IS OVER.
I WANT YOU TO MAKE AN ATTACK RUN ON ME AND THE DAWN.
SHOW ME YOU'RE A REAL-LIFE GUN, TUG.
OH LORD, SCRAM, YOU'RE GONNA SCARE THE POOR KID TO DEATH.
HITCH A CLEAN RIDE ON COLA. THE TWO OF YOU CAN COME UP WITH AN ASSAULT PLAN, AND THEN COME BACK HERE...

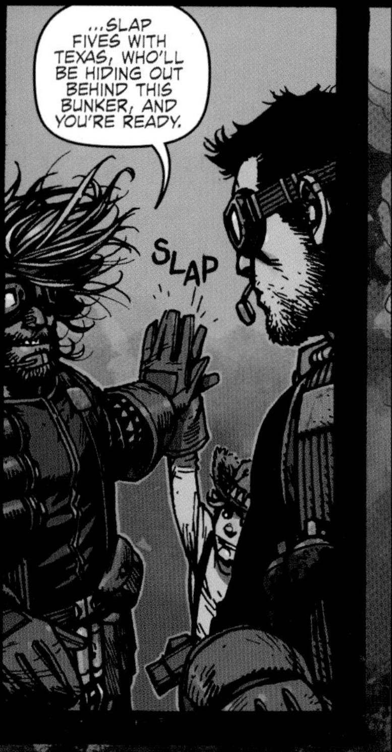
...SLAP FIVES WITH TEXAS, WHO'LL BE HIDING OUT BEHIND THIS BUNKER, AND YOU'RE READY.
SLAP

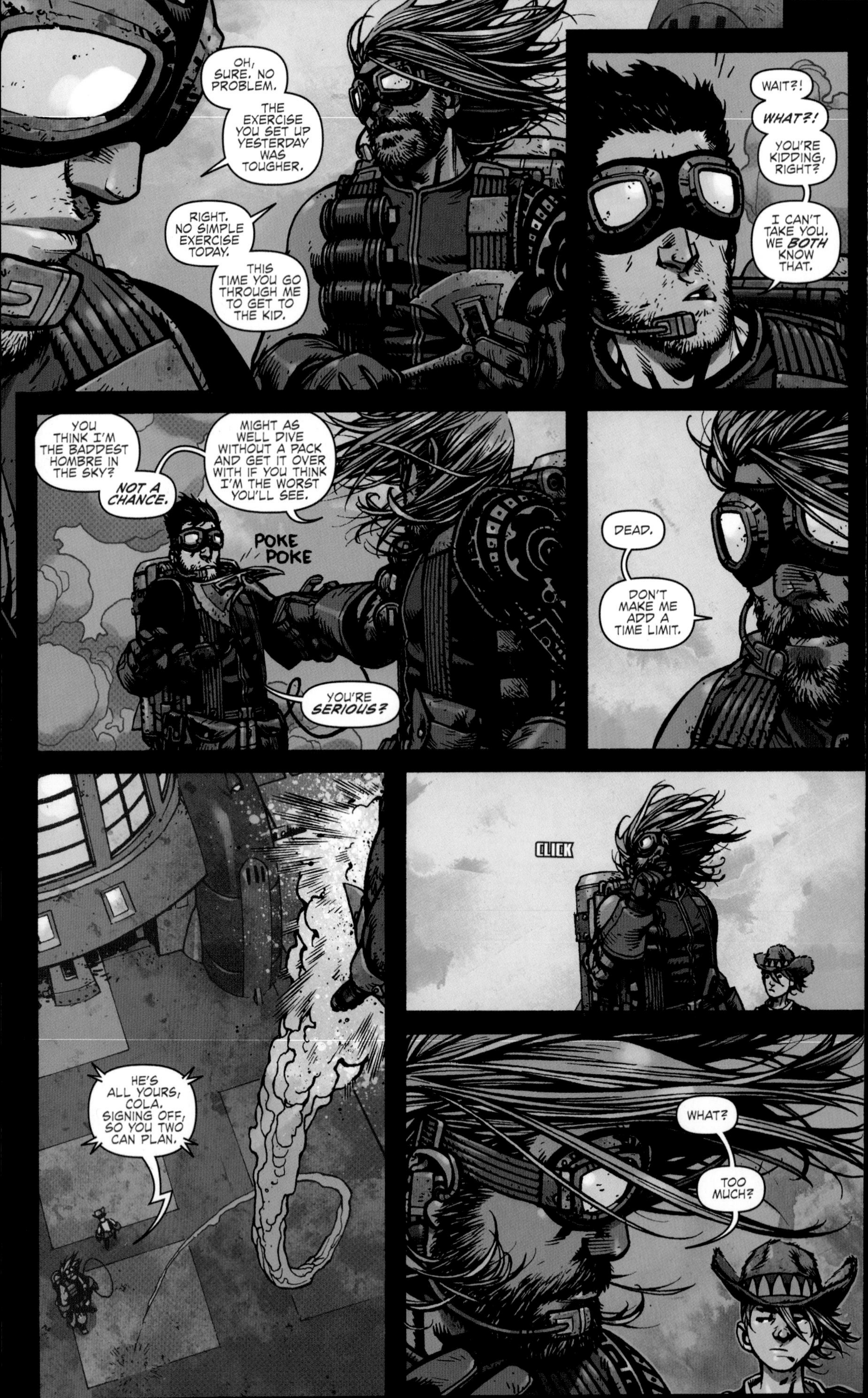
OH, SURE. NO PROBLEM.
THE EXERCISE YOU SET UP YESTERDAY WAS TOUGHER.
RIGHT. NO SIMPLE EXERCISE TODAY.
THIS TIME YOU GO THROUGH ME TO GET TO THE KID.
WAIT?!
WHAT?!
YOU'RE KIDDING, RIGHT?
I CAN'T TAKE YOU. WE BOTH KNOW THAT.
YOU THINK I'M THE BADDEST HOMBRE IN THE SKY?
NOT A CHANCE.
MIGHT AS WELL DIVE WITHOUT A PACK AND GET IT OVER WITH IF YOU THINK I'M THE WORST YOU'LL SEE.
POKE POKE
YOU'RE SERIOUS?
DEAD.
DON'T MAKE ME ADD A TIME LIMIT.
HE'S ALL YOURS, COLA. SIGNING OFF, SO YOU TWO CAN PLAN.
CLICK
WHAT?
TOO MUCH?

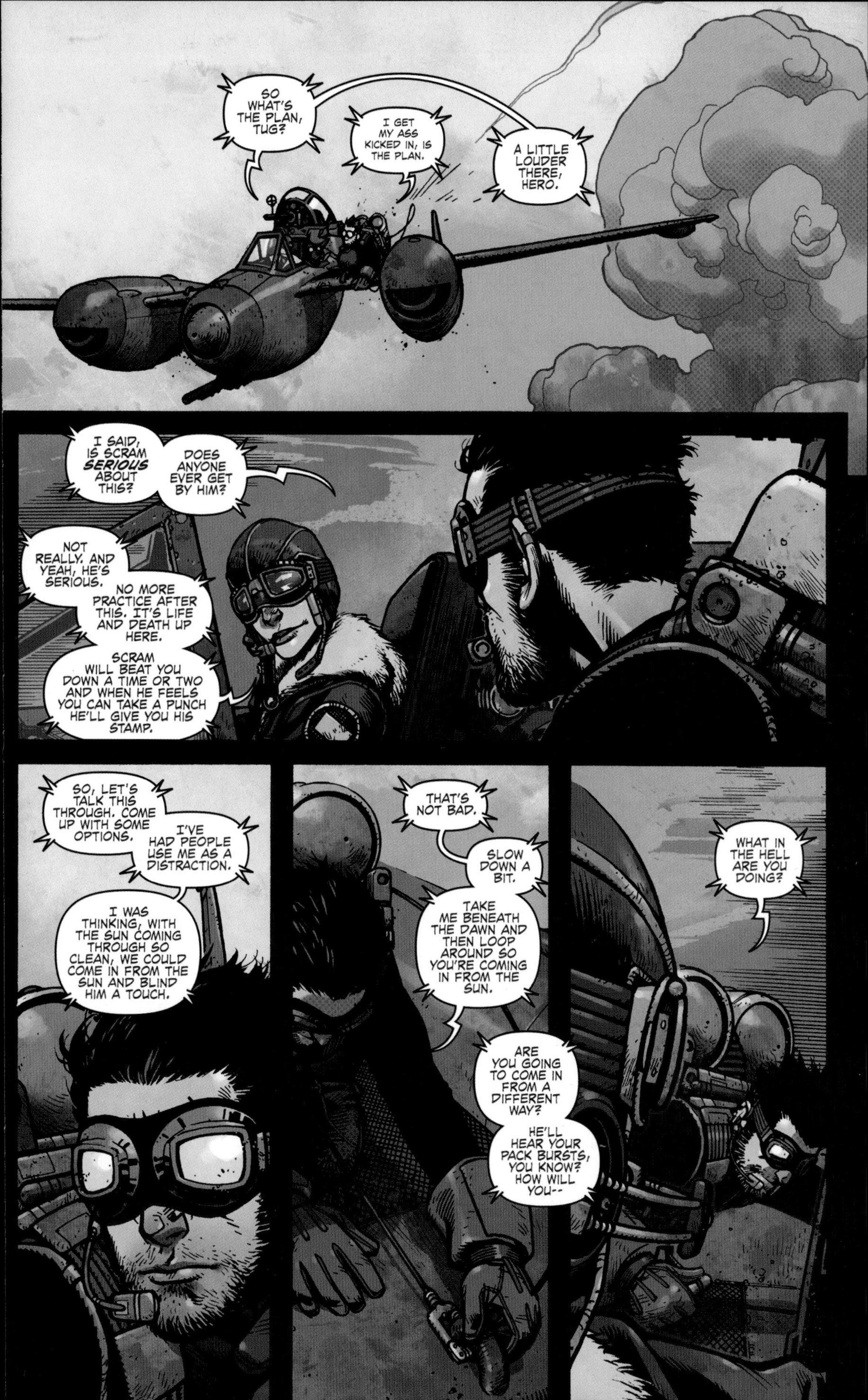
SO WHAT'S THE PLAN, TUG?
I GET MY ASS KICKED IN, IS THE PLAN.
A LITTLE LOUDER THERE, HERO.
I SAID, IS SCRAM SERIOUS ABOUT THIS?
DOES ANYONE EVER GET BY HIM?
NOT REALLY. AND YEAH, HE'S SERIOUS.
NO MORE PRACTICE AFTER THIS. IT'S LIFE AND DEATH UP HERE.
SCRAM WILL BEAT YOU DOWN A TIME OR TWO AND WHEN HE FEELS YOU CAN TAKE A PUNCH HE'LL GIVE YOU HIS STAMP.
SO, LET'S TALK THIS THROUGH. COME UP WITH SOME OPTIONS.
I'VE HAD PEOPLE USE ME AS A DISTRACTION.
I WAS THINKING, WITH THE SUN COMING THROUGH SO CLEAN, WE COULD COME IN FROM THE SUN AND BLIND HIM A TOUCH.
THAT'S NOT BAD.
SLOW DOWN A BIT.
TAKE ME BENEATH THE DAWN AND THEN LOOP AROUND SO YOU'RE COMING IN FROM THE SUN.
ARE YOU GOING TO COME IN FROM A DIFFERENT WAY?
HE'LL HEAR YOUR PACK BURSTS, YOU KNOW? HOW WILL YOU--
WHAT IN THE HELL ARE YOU DOING?

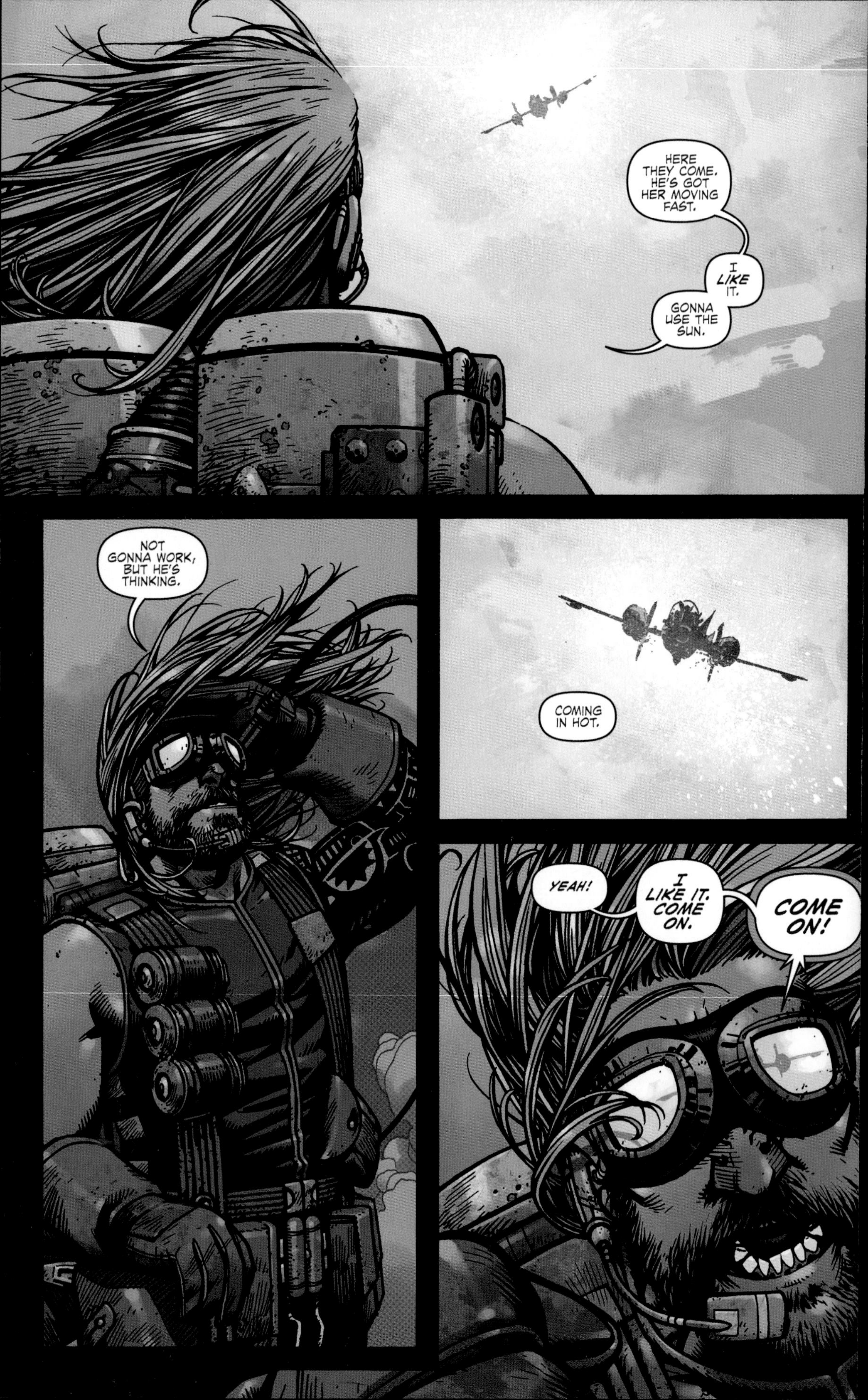
HERE THEY COME. HE'S GOT HER MOVING FAST.
I *LIKE* IT.
GONNA USE THE SUN.
NOT GONNA WORK, BUT HE'S THINKING.
COMING IN HOT.
YEAH!
I LIKE IT. COME ON.
COME ON!

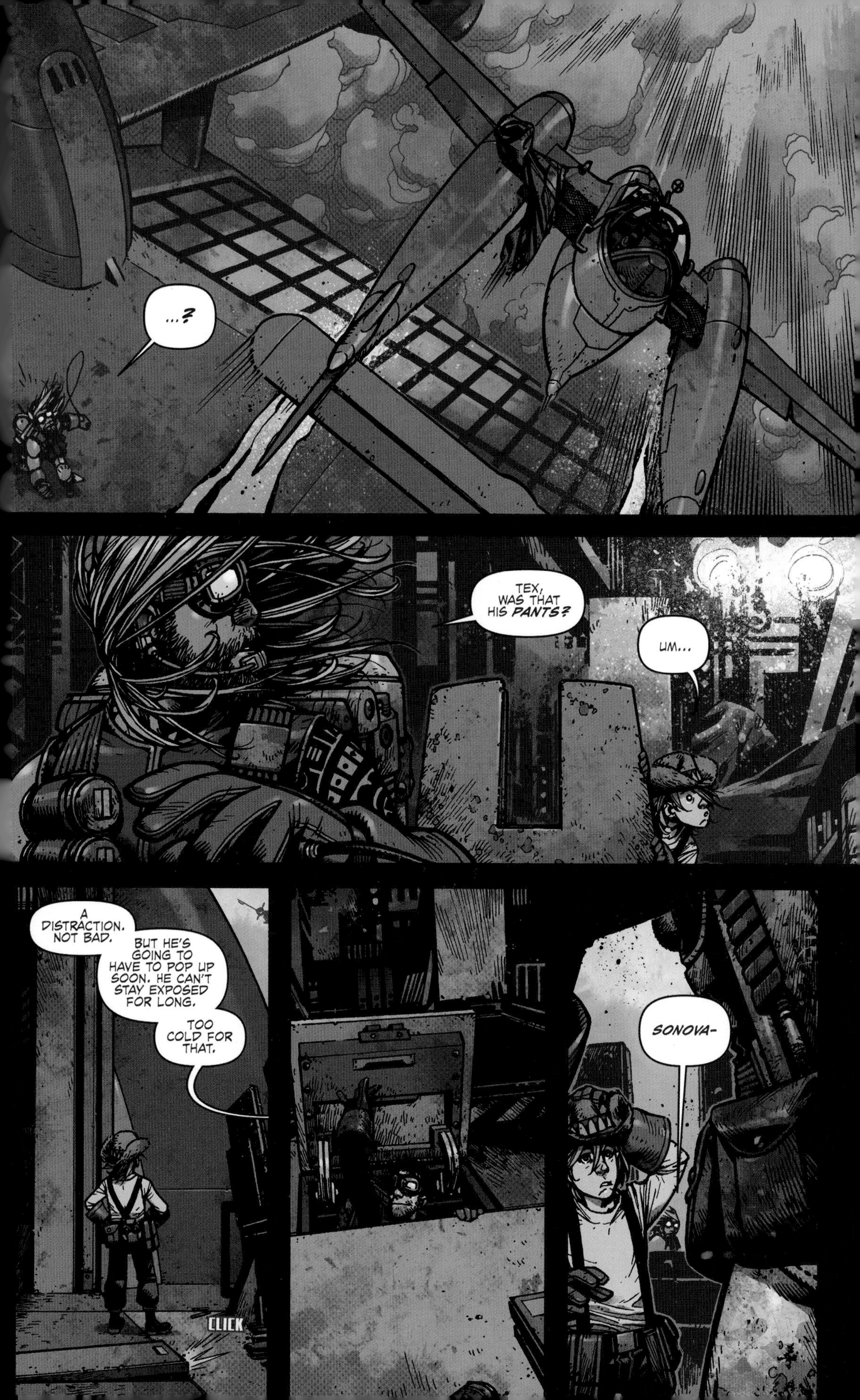
...?
TEX, WAS THAT HIS PANTS?
UM...
A DISTRACTION. NOT BAD.
BUT HE'S GOING TO HAVE TO POP UP SOON. HE CAN'T STAY EXPOSED FOR LONG.
TOO COLD FOR THAT.
CLICK
SONOVA-

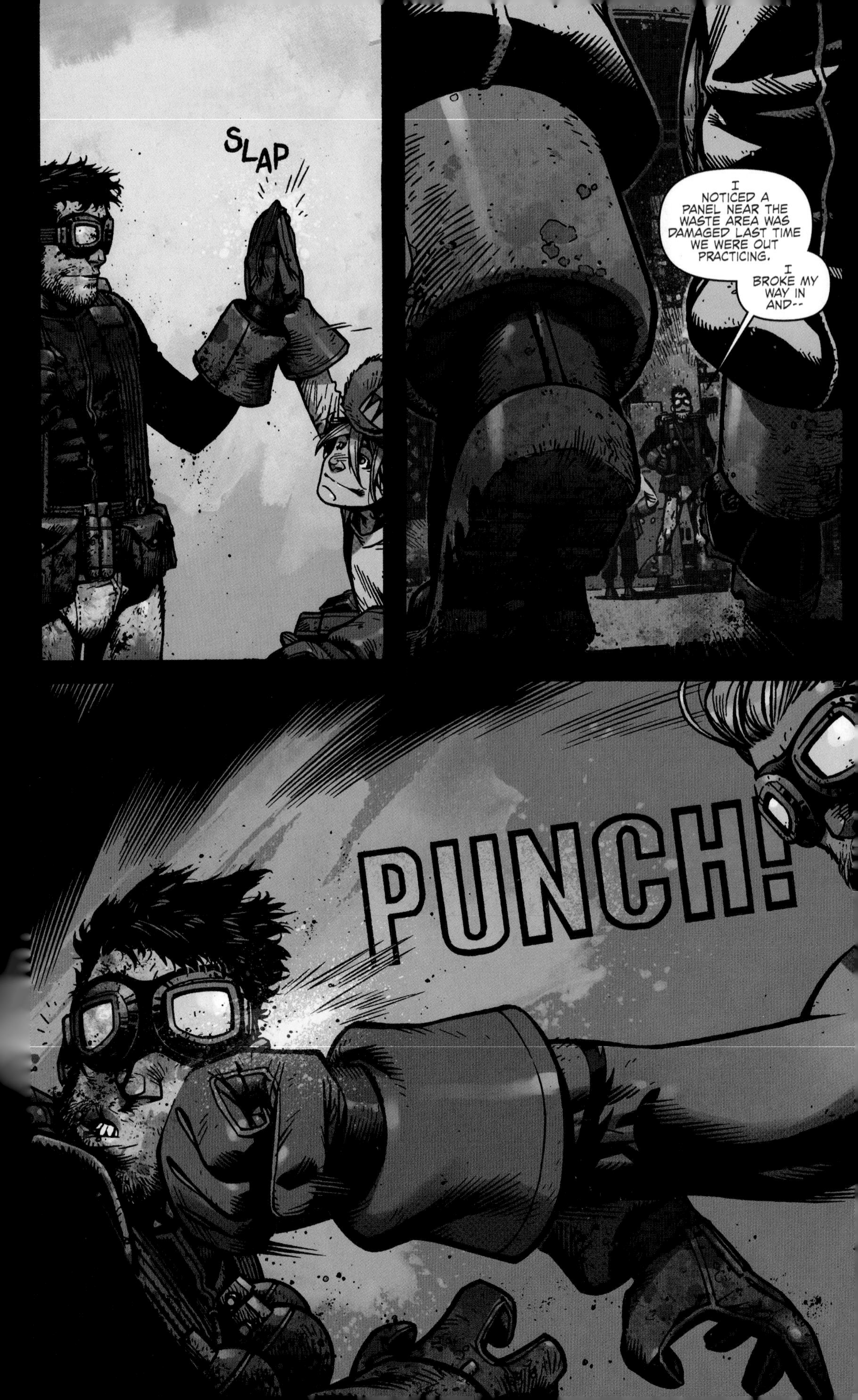
SLAP
I NOTICED A PANEL NEAR THE WASTE AREA WAS DAMAGED LAST TIME WE WERE OUT PRACTICING.
I BROKE MY WAY IN AND--
PUNCH!

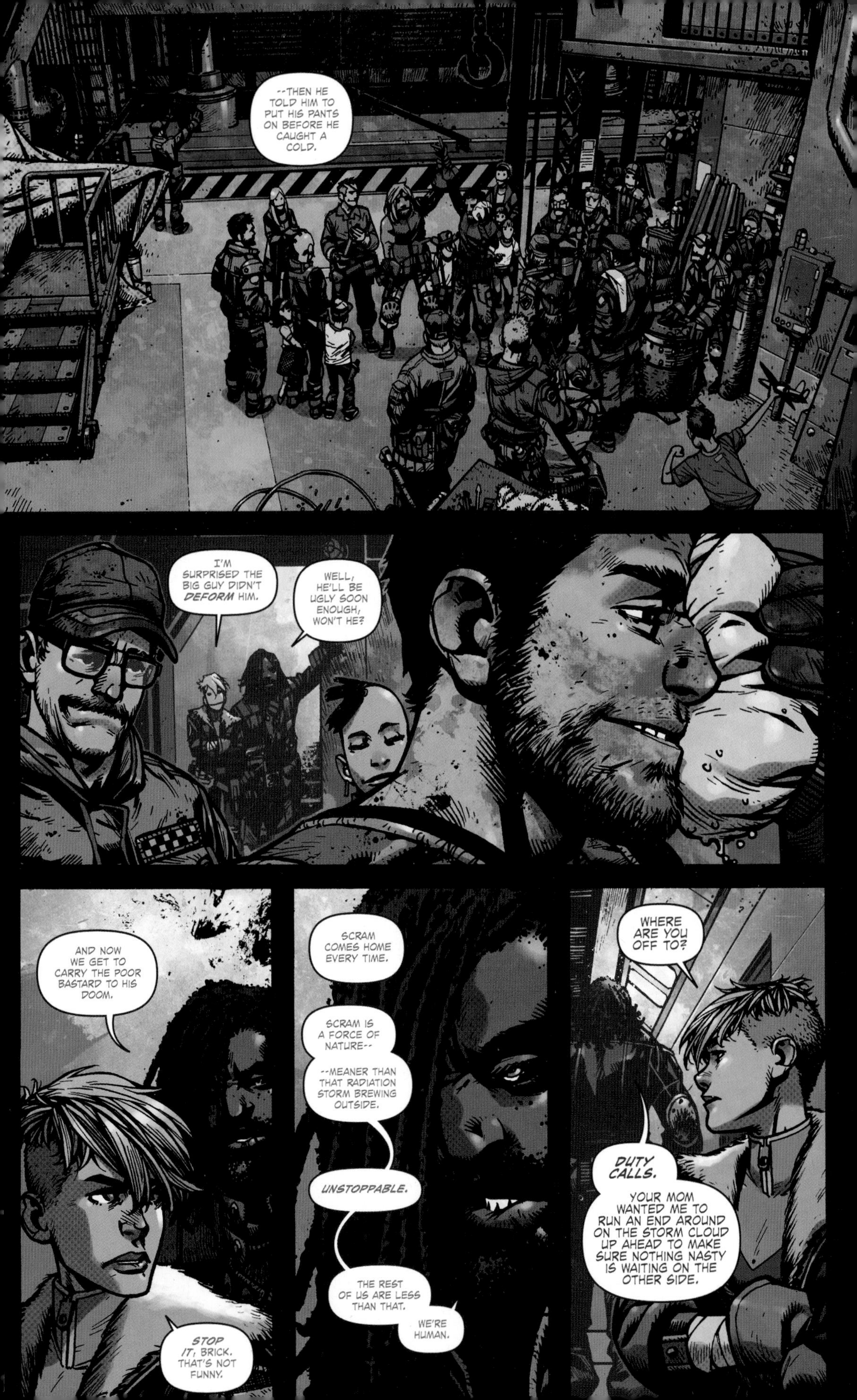
--THEN HE TOLD HIM TO PUT HIS PANTS ON BEFORE HE CAUGHT A COLD.
I'M SURPRISED THE BIG GUY DIDN'T DEFORM HIM.
WELL, HE'LL BE UGLY SOON ENOUGH, WON'T HE?
AND NOW WE GET TO CARRY THE POOR BASTARD TO HIS DOOM.
STOP IT, BRICK. THAT'S NOT FUNNY.
SCRAM COMES HOME EVERY TIME.
SCRAM IS A FORCE OF NATURE--
--MEANER THAN THAT RADIATION STORM BREWING OUTSIDE.
UNSTOPPABLE.
THE REST OF US ARE LESS THAN THAT.
WE'RE HUMAN.
WHERE ARE YOU OFF TO?
DUTY CALLS.
YOUR MOM WANTED ME TO RUN AN END AROUND ON THE STORM CLOUD UP AHEAD TO MAKE SURE NOTHING NASTY IS WAITING ON THE OTHER SIDE.

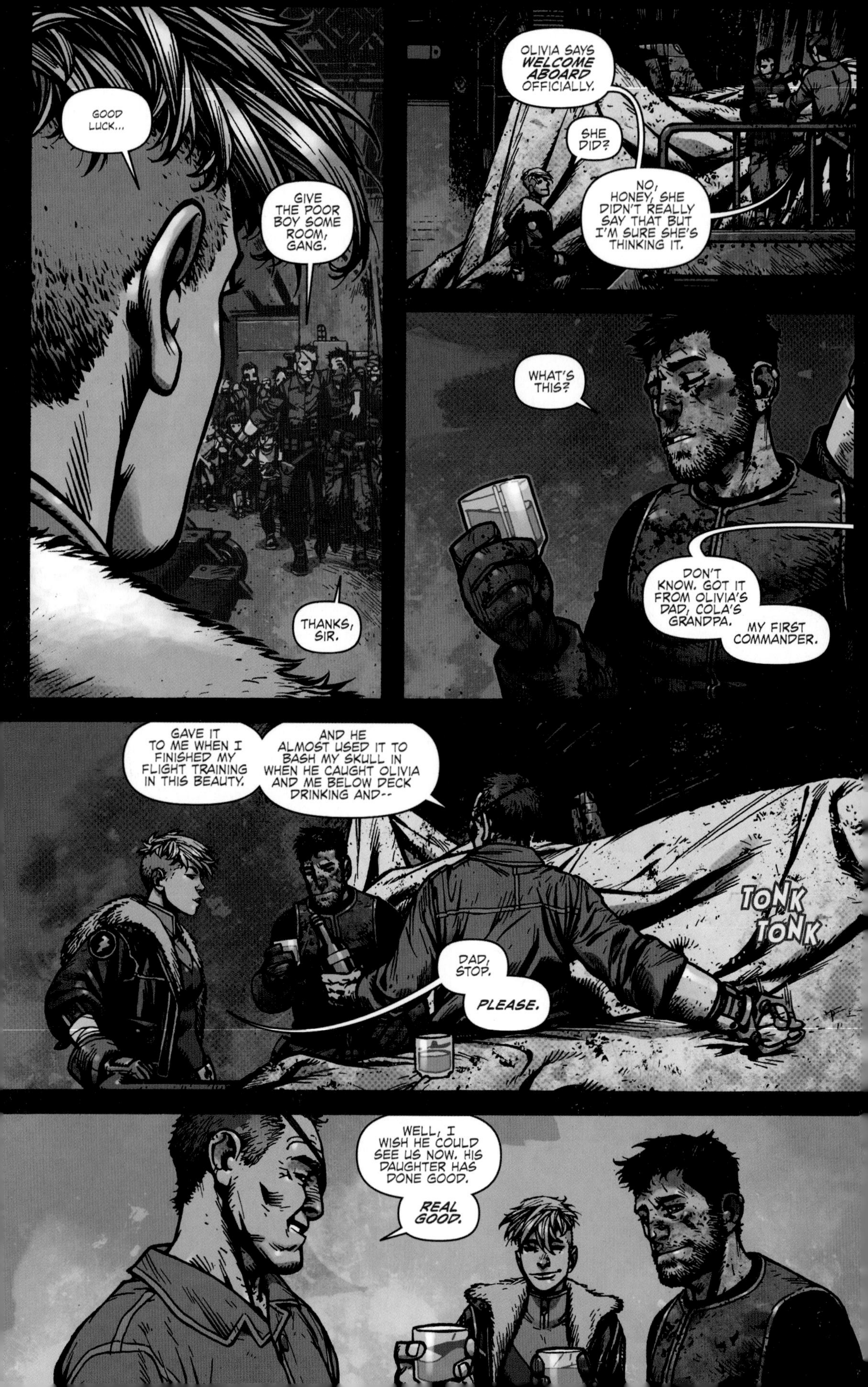
GOOD LUCK...
GIVE THE POOR BOY SOME ROOM, GANG.
THANKS, SIR.
OLIVIA SAYS *WELCOME ABOARD* OFFICIALLY.
SHE DID?
NO, HONEY, SHE DIDN'T REALLY SAY THAT BUT I'M SURE SHE'S THINKING IT.
WHAT'S THIS?
DON'T KNOW. GOT IT FROM OLIVIA'S DAD, COLA'S GRANDPA.
MY FIRST COMMANDER.
GAVE IT TO ME WHEN I FINISHED MY FLIGHT TRAINING IN THIS BEAUTY.
AND HE ALMOST USED IT TO BASH MY SKULL IN WHEN HE CAUGHT OLIVIA AND ME BELOW DECK DRINKING AND--
TONK TONK
DAD, STOP.
PLEASE.
WELL, I WISH HE COULD SEE US NOW. HIS DAUGHTER HAS DONE GOOD.
REAL GOOD.

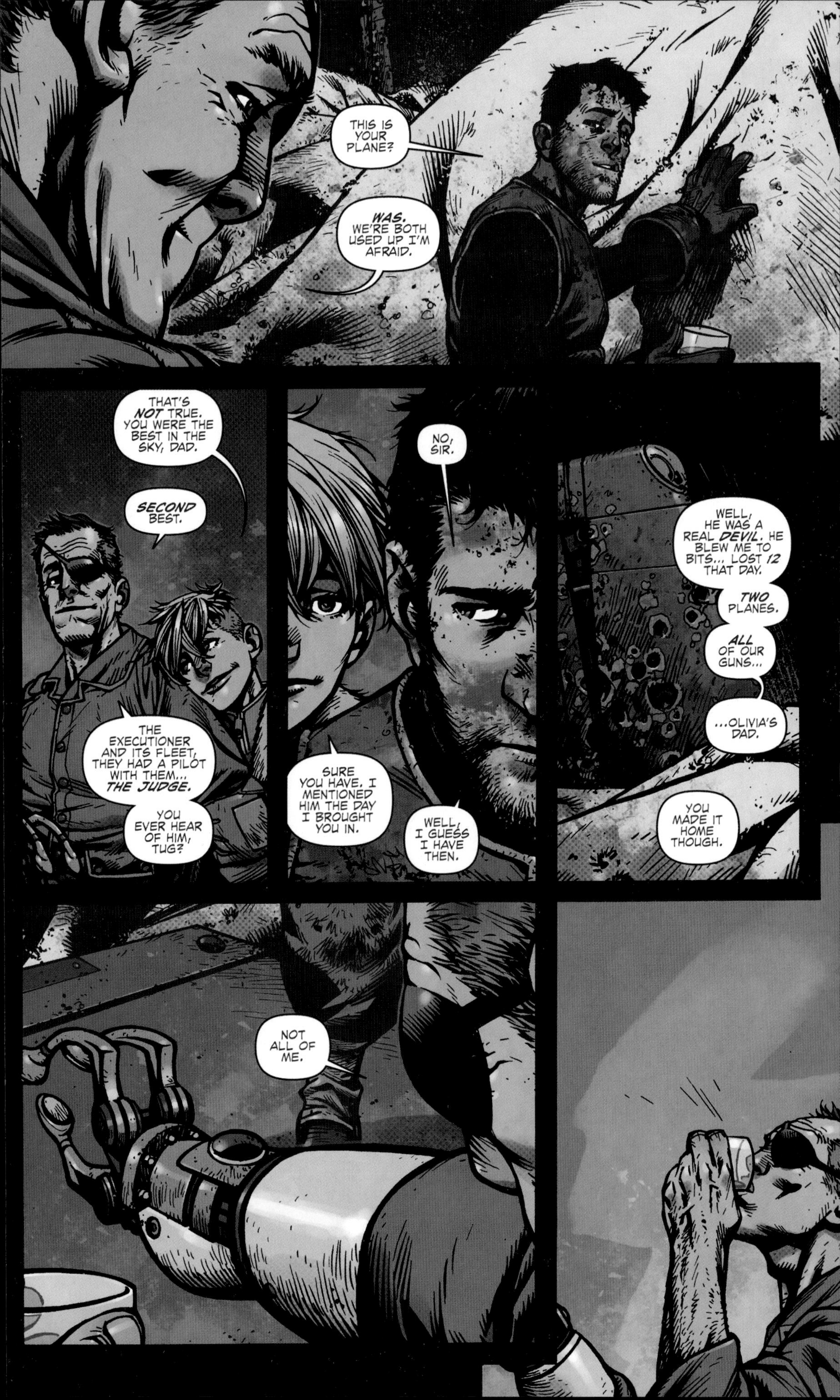
THIS IS YOUR PLANE?
WAS. WE'RE BOTH USED UP I'M AFRAID.
THAT'S NOT TRUE. YOU WERE THE BEST IN THE SKY, DAD.
SECOND BEST.
THE EXECUTIONER AND ITS FLEET, THEY HAD A PILOT WITH THEM... THE JUDGE.
YOU EVER HEAR OF HIM, TUG?
NO, SIR.
SURE YOU HAVE. I MENTIONED HIM THE DAY I BROUGHT YOU IN.
WELL, I GUESS I HAVE THEN.
WELL, HE WAS A REAL DEVIL. HE BLEW ME TO BITS... LOST 12 THAT DAY.
TWO PLANES.
ALL OF OUR GUNS...
...OLIVIA'S DAD.
YOU MADE IT HOME THOUGH.
NOT ALL OF ME.

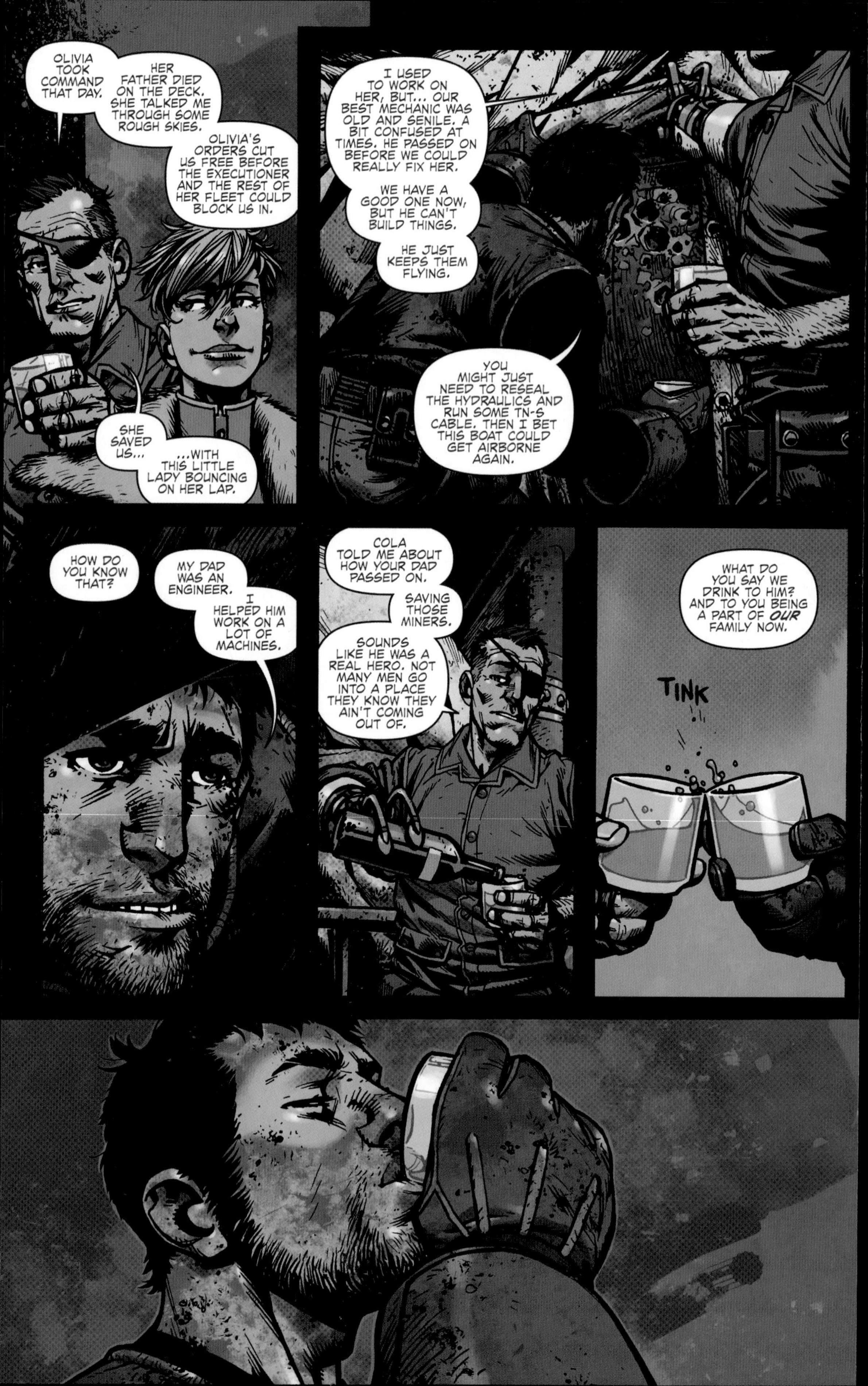
OLIVIA TOOK COMMAND THAT DAY.
HER FATHER DIED ON THE DECK. SHE TALKED ME THROUGH SOME ROUGH SKIES.
OLIVIA'S ORDERS CUT US FREE BEFORE THE EXECUTIONER AND THE REST OF HER FLEET COULD BLOCK US IN.
SHE SAVED US...
...WITH THIS LITTLE LADY BOUNCING ON HER LAP.
I USED TO WORK ON HER, BUT... OUR BEST MECHANIC WAS OLD AND SENILE. A BIT CONFUSED AT TIMES. HE PASSED ON BEFORE WE COULD REALLY FIX HER.
WE HAVE A GOOD ONE NOW, BUT HE CAN'T BUILD THINGS.
HE JUST KEEPS THEM FLYING.
YOU MIGHT JUST NEED TO RESEAL THE HYDRAULICS AND RUN SOME TN-S CABLE. THEN I BET THIS BOAT COULD GET AIRBORNE AGAIN.
HOW DO YOU KNOW THAT?
MY DAD WAS AN ENGINEER.
I HELPED HIM WORK ON A LOT OF MACHINES.
COLA TOLD ME ABOUT HOW YOUR DAD PASSED ON.
SAVING THOSE MINERS.
SOUNDS LIKE HE WAS A REAL HERO. NOT MANY MEN GO INTO A PLACE THEY KNOW THEY AIN'T COMING OUT OF.
WHAT DO YOU SAY WE DRINK TO HIM? AND TO YOU BEING A PART OF *OUR* FAMILY NOW.
TINK

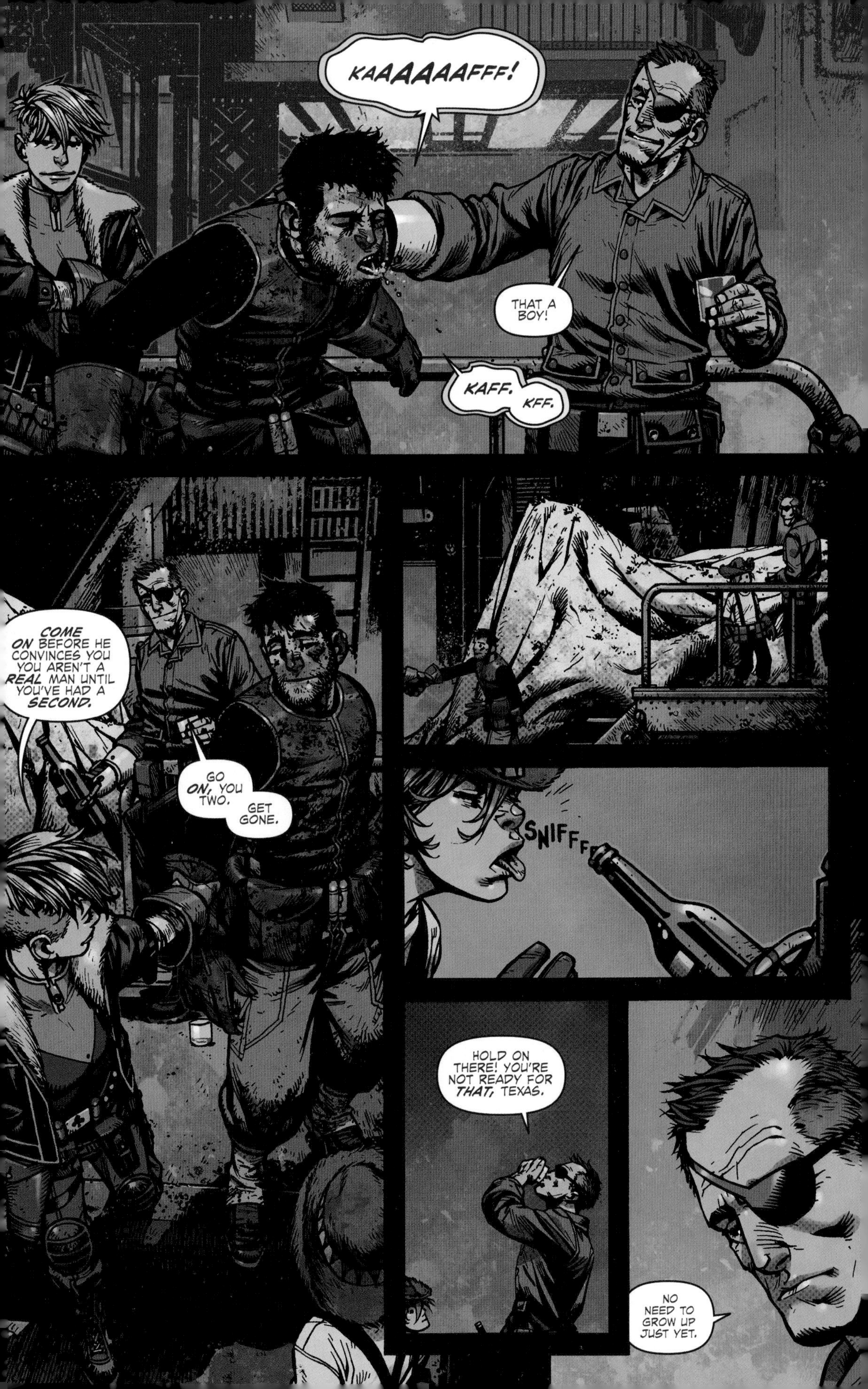
KAAAAAAFFF!
THAT A BOY!
KAFF. KFF.
COME ON BEFORE HE CONVINCES YOU YOU AREN'T A REAL MAN UNTIL YOU'VE HAD A SECOND.
GO ON, YOU TWO.
GET GONE.
SNIFFFF
HOLD ON THERE! YOU'RE NOT READY FOR THAT, TEXAS.
NO NEED TO GROW UP JUST YET.

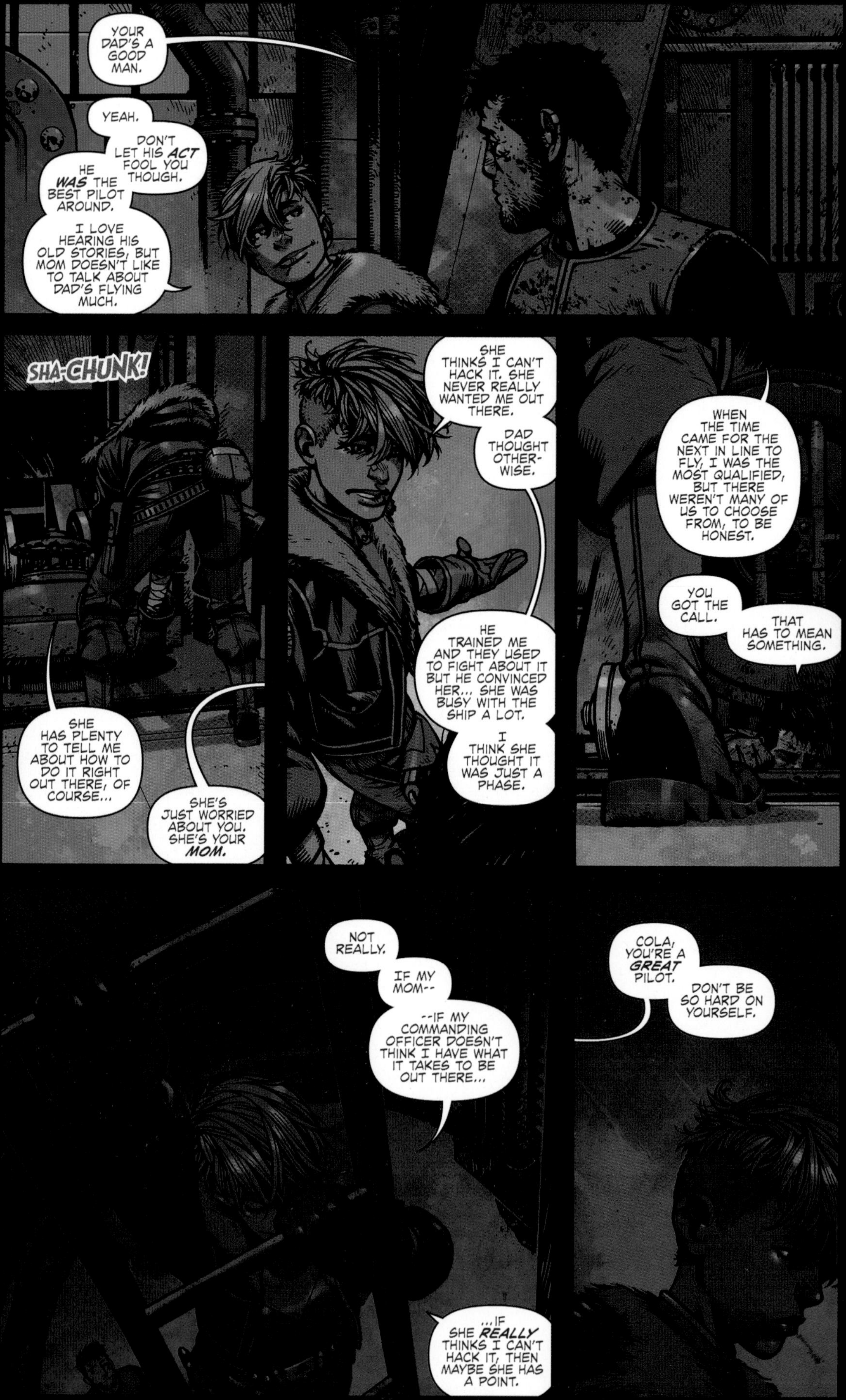
YOUR DAD'S A GOOD MAN.
YEAH.
DON'T LET HIS ACT FOOL YOU THOUGH.
HE WAS THE BEST PILOT AROUND.
I LOVE HEARING HIS OLD STORIES, BUT MOM DOESN'T LIKE TO TALK ABOUT DAD'S FLYING MUCH.
SHA-CHUNK!
SHE HAS PLENTY TO TELL ME ABOUT HOW TO DO IT RIGHT OUT THERE, OF COURSE...
SHE'S JUST WORRIED ABOUT YOU. SHE'S YOUR MOM.
SHE THINKS I CAN'T HACK IT. SHE NEVER REALLY WANTED ME OUT THERE.
DAD THOUGHT OTHER-WISE.
HE TRAINED ME AND THEY USED TO FIGHT ABOUT IT BUT HE CONVINCED HER... SHE WAS BUSY WITH THE SHIP A LOT.
I THINK SHE THOUGHT IT WAS JUST A PHASE.
WHEN THE TIME CAME FOR THE NEXT IN LINE TO FLY, I WAS THE MOST QUALIFIED, BUT THERE WEREN'T MANY OF US TO CHOOSE FROM, TO BE HONEST.
YOU GOT THE CALL.
THAT HAS TO MEAN SOMETHING.
NOT REALLY.
IF MY MOM--
--IF MY COMMANDING OFFICER DOESN'T THINK I HAVE WHAT IT TAKES TO BE OUT THERE...
...IF SHE REALLY THINKS I CAN'T HACK IT, THEN MAYBE SHE HAS A POINT.
COLA, YOU'RE A GREAT PILOT.
DON'T BE SO HARD ON YOURSELF.

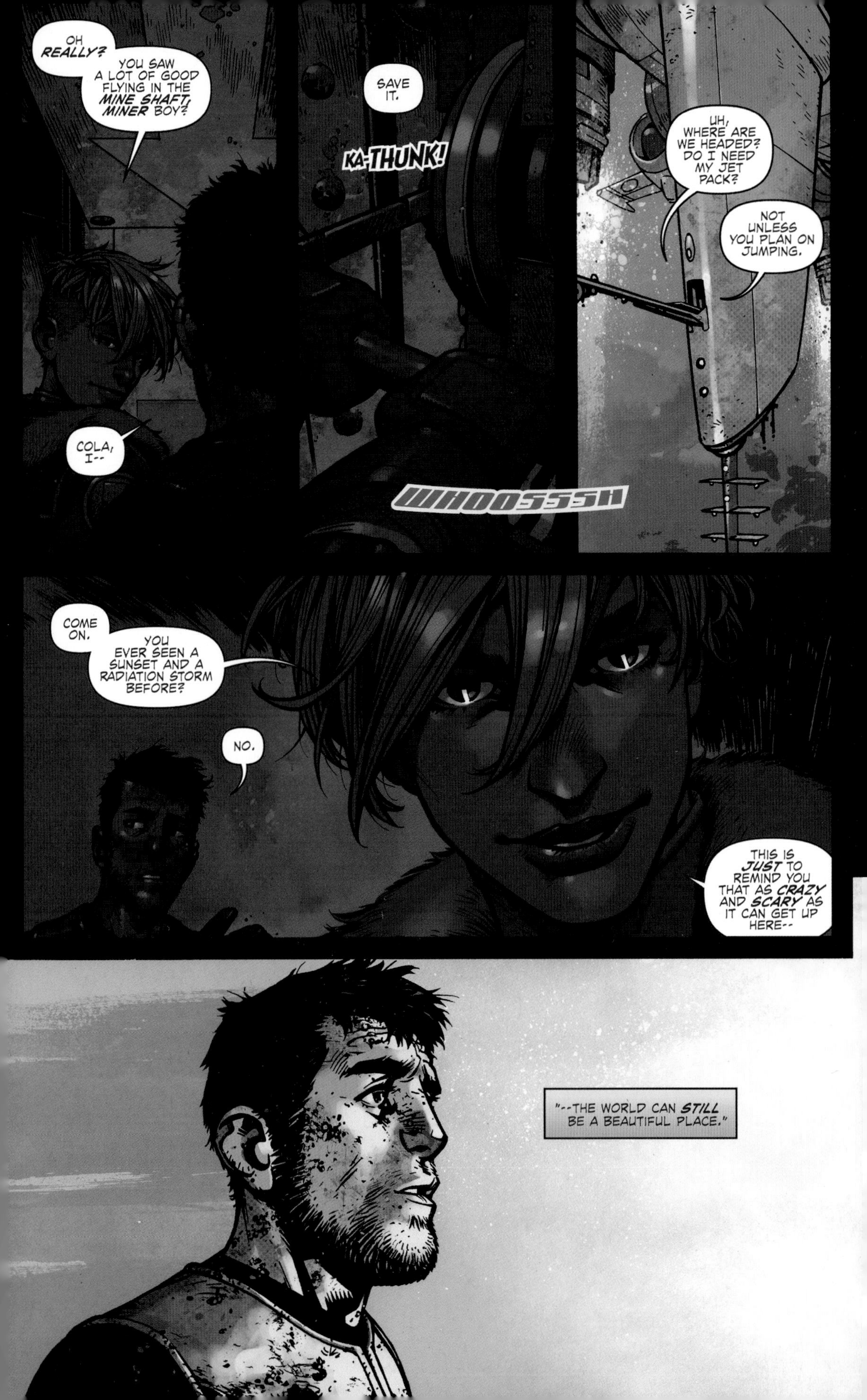
OH REALLY? YOU SAW A LOT OF GOOD FLYING IN THE MINE SHAFT, MINER BOY?
COLA, I--
SAVE IT.
KA-THUNK!
UH, WHERE ARE WE HEADED? DO I NEED MY JET PACK?
NOT UNLESS YOU PLAN ON JUMPING.
WHOOSSSSH
COME ON.
YOU EVER SEEN A SUNSET AND A RADIATION STORM BEFORE?
NO.
THIS IS JUST TO REMIND YOU THAT AS CRAZY AND SCARY AS IT CAN GET UP HERE--
"--THE WORLD CAN STILL BE A BEAUTIFUL PLACE."

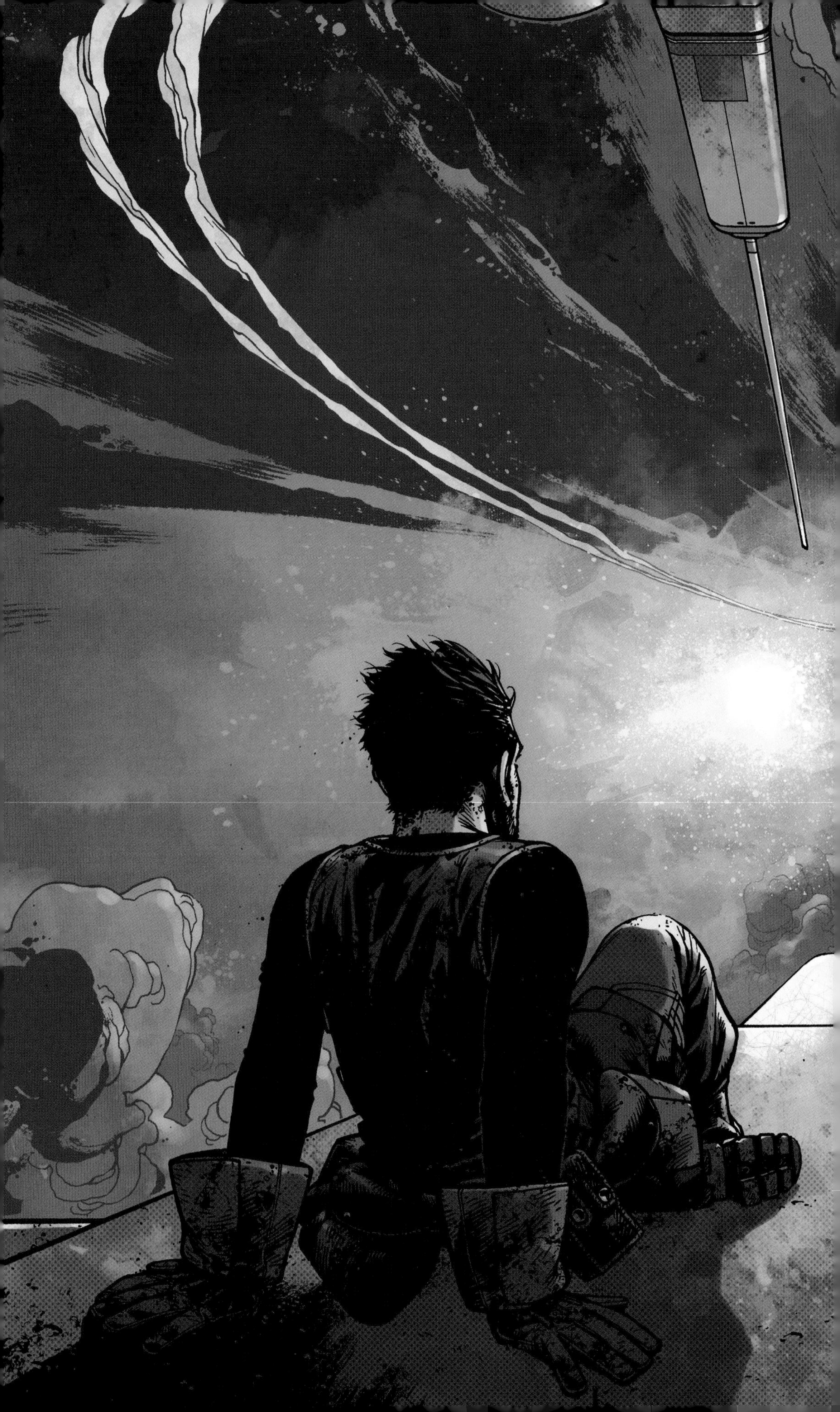

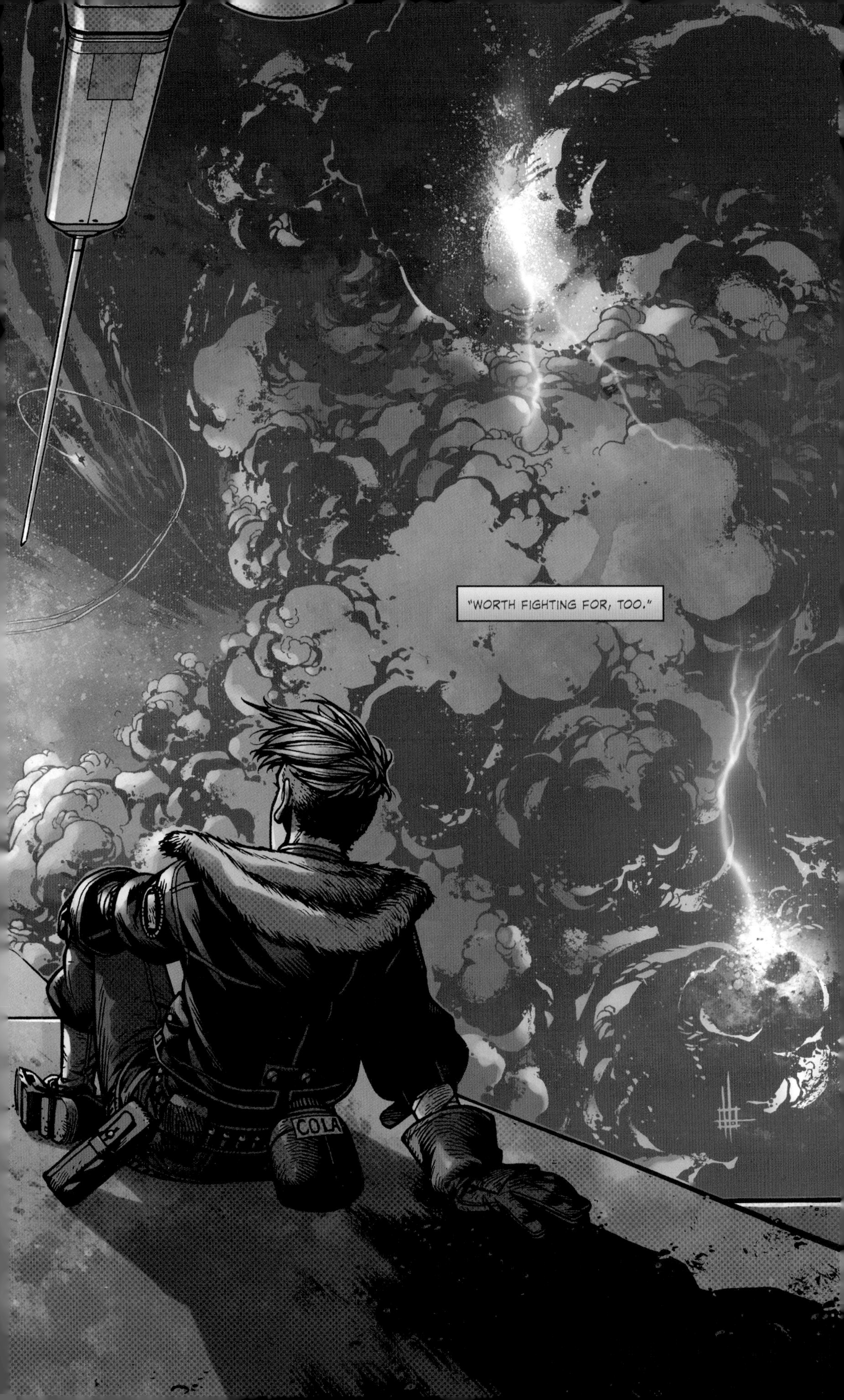
"WORTH FIGHTING FOR, TOO."
COLA

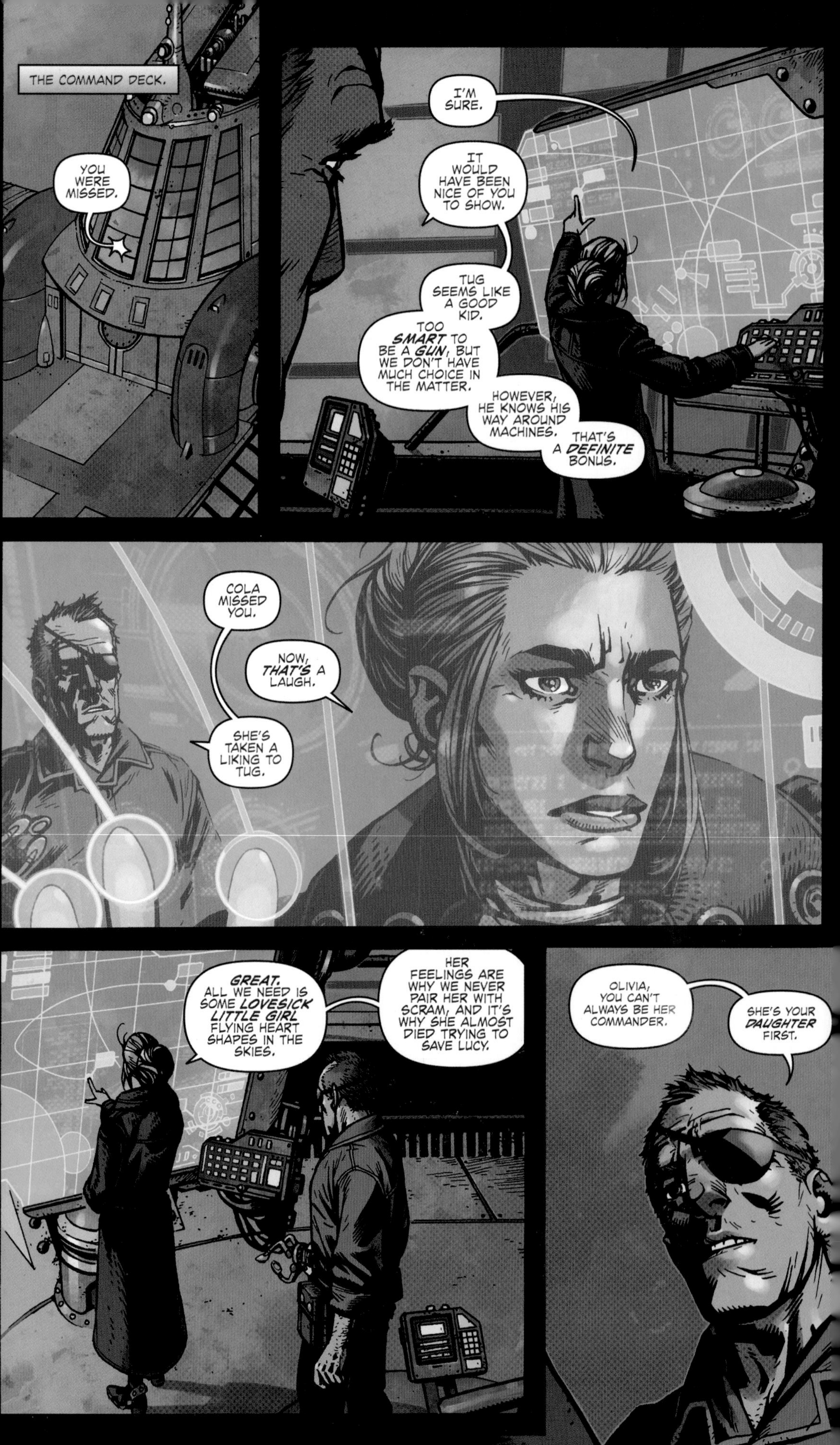
THE COMMAND DECK.
YOU WERE MISSED.
I'M SURE.
IT WOULD HAVE BEEN NICE OF YOU TO SHOW.
TUG SEEMS LIKE A GOOD KID.
TOO SMART TO BE A GUN, BUT WE DON'T HAVE MUCH CHOICE IN THE MATTER.
HOWEVER, HE KNOWS HIS WAY AROUND MACHINES.
THAT'S A DEFINITE BONUS.
COLA MISSED YOU.
NOW, THAT'S A LAUGH.
SHE'S TAKEN A LIKING TO TUG.
GREAT. ALL WE NEED IS SOME LOVESICK LITTLE GIRL FLYING HEART SHAPES IN THE SKIES.
HER FEELINGS ARE WHY WE NEVER PAIR HER WITH SCRAM, AND IT'S WHY SHE ALMOST DIED TRYING TO SAVE LUCY.
OLIVIA, YOU CAN'T ALWAYS BE HER COMMANDER.
SHE'S YOUR DAUGHTER FIRST.

YOU MADE IT THIS WAY. SHE SHOULD HAVE BEEN UP HERE WITH ME.

LEARNING TO LEAD.

NOT OUT THERE FLYING. SHE'S NOT GOOD ENOUGH TO--

SHE IS, OLIVIA.

YOU WON'T LET YOURSELF SEE IT.

YOU NEVER TAUGHT HER TO RESPECT COMMAND.

IF SHE WOULD HAVE LISTENED TO ME IN THE FIRST PLACE WE COULD HAVE SAVED LUCY TOGETHER.

INSTEAD I'M--WE'RE ALL REACTING TO HER RECKLESSNESS.

YOU DON'T KNOW WHAT IT'S LIKE OUT THERE. THERE'S NO TIME TO THINK.

YOU HAVE TO REACT. IT'S THE ONLY WAY TO STAY ALIVE.

WE NEED TO BE IN SYNC OR WE WILL DIE.

IF SHE CAN'T HACK IT OUT THERE, IF ANYONE ELSE DIES BECAUSE OF HER, SHE WILL BE DONE.

YOU'RE WRONG.

THE TRUTH IS SHE MIGHT HAVE SAVED LUCY IF YOUR ORDERS HADN'T MADE HER PAUSE FOR A SPLIT SECOND.

YOU CAN'T MESS WITH A PILOT'S INTUITION. THEY HAVE TO--

SHE'S A CHILD. SHE'S JOYRIDING OUT THERE.

THAT'S HOW YOU RAISED HER. IT'S GOING TO GET HER KILLED.

OLIVIA, I--

WE'RE DONE HERE.

NOW, GO ON BACK TO YOUR PARTY.

I DON'T HAVE TIME FOR THIS. I HAVE TO FIND A SAFE ZONE FOR US.

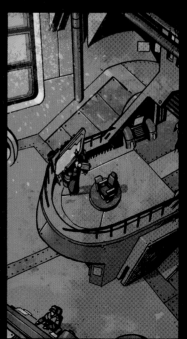

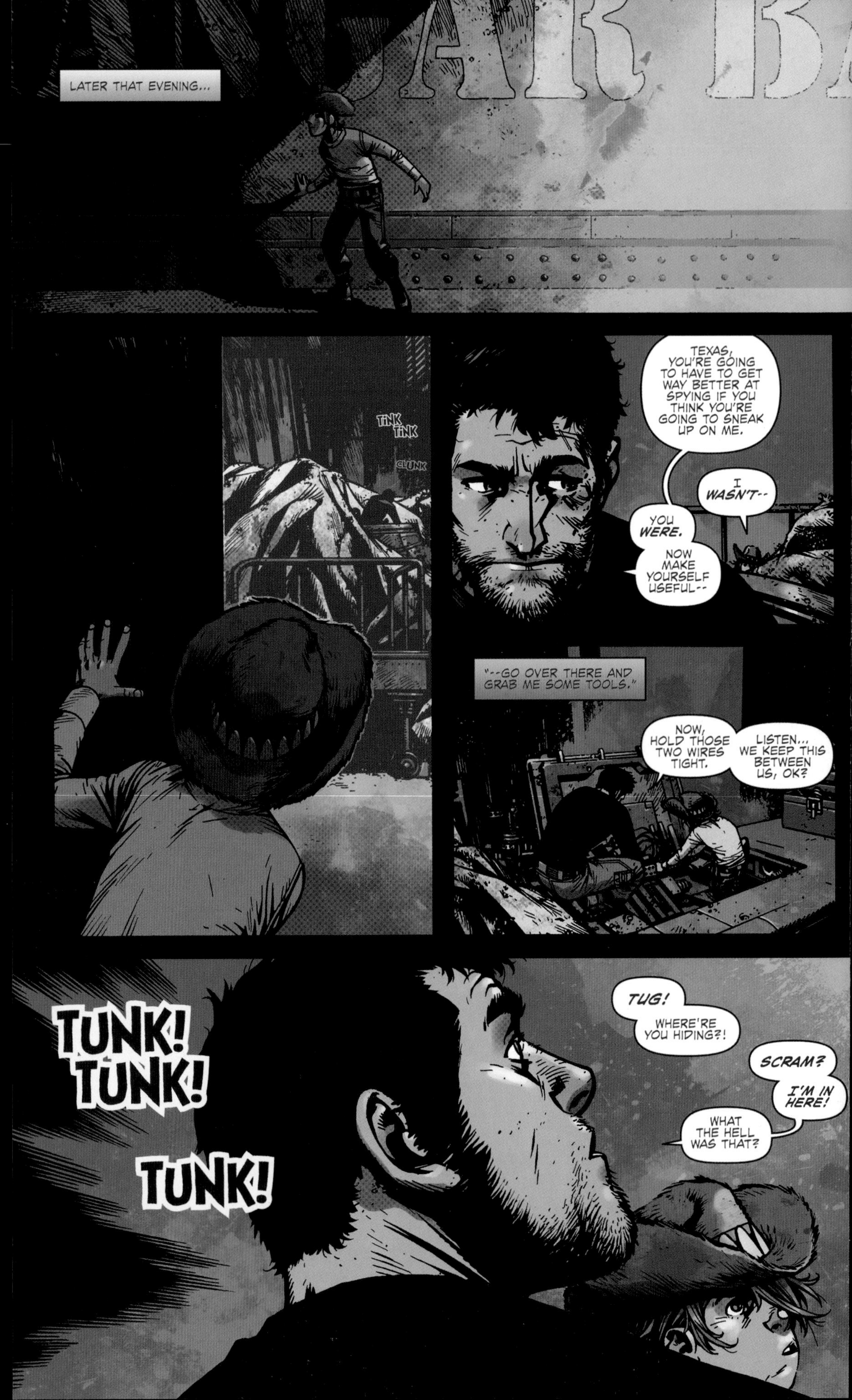

LATER THAT EVENING...
TiNK TiNK
CLUNK
TEXAS, YOU'RE GOING TO HAVE TO GET WAY BETTER AT SPYING IF YOU THINK YOU'RE GOING TO SNEAK UP ON ME.
I WASN'T--
YOU WERE.
NOW MAKE YOURSELF USEFUL--
"--GO OVER THERE AND GRAB ME SOME TOOLS."
NOW, HOLD THOSE TWO WIRES TIGHT.
LISTEN... WE KEEP THIS BETWEEN US, OK?
TUNK! TUNK!
TUNK!
TUG!
WHERE'RE YOU HIDING?!
SCRAM?
I'M IN HERE!
WHAT THE HELL WAS THAT?

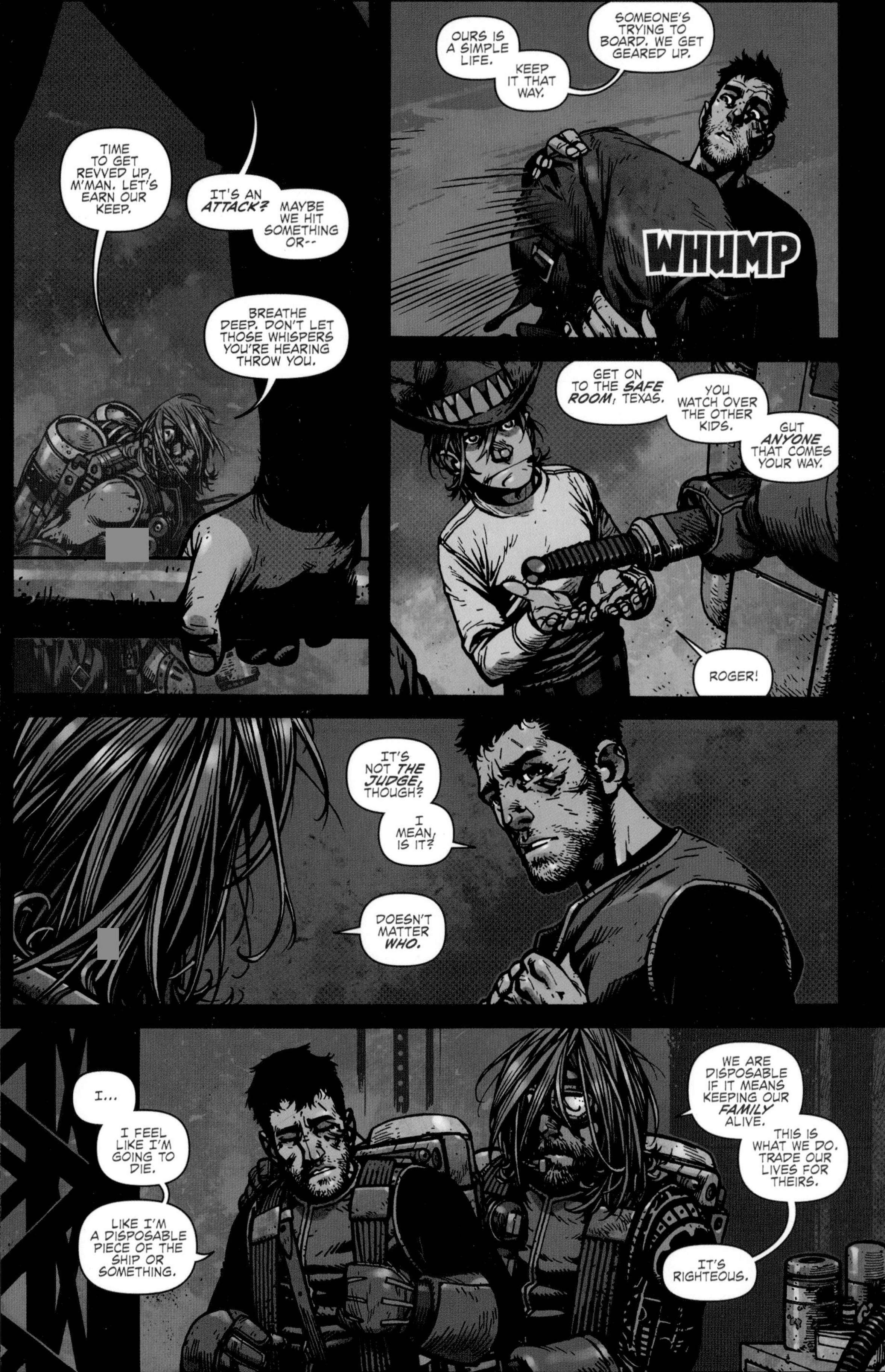

TIME TO GET REVVED UP, M'MAN. LET'S EARN OUR KEEP.
IT'S AN ATTACK?
MAYBE WE HIT SOMETHING OR--
BREATHE DEEP. DON'T LET THOSE WHISPERS YOU'RE HEARING THROW YOU.
OURS IS A SIMPLE LIFE.
KEEP IT THAT WAY.
SOMEONE'S TRYING TO BOARD. WE GET GEARED UP.
WHUMP
GET ON TO THE SAFE ROOM, TEXAS.
YOU WATCH OVER THE OTHER KIDS.
GUT ANYONE THAT COMES YOUR WAY.
ROGER!
IT'S NOT THE JUDGE, THOUGH?
I MEAN, IS IT?
DOESN'T MATTER WHO.
I...
I FEEL LIKE I'M GOING TO DIE.
LIKE I'M A DISPOSABLE PIECE OF THE SHIP OR SOMETHING.
WE ARE DISPOSABLE IF IT MEANS KEEPING OUR FAMILY ALIVE.
THIS IS WHAT WE DO. TRADE OUR LIVES FOR THEIRS.
IT'S RIGHTEOUS.

"NOW, LET'S GET TOPSIDE AND DO OUR THING."

THIS RIG FLEW RIGHT OUT OF THE *RAD CLOUD* BEHIND US AND STARTED BOARDING.

BRICK'S OFF SCOUTING.

OLIVIA'S HAILING HIM, BUT IT'S JUST YOU TWO AND COLA FOR NOW.

COLA DOESN'T HAVE ENOUGH ROUNDS TO TAKE THEM ALL DOWN.

IT'S UP TO YOU TWO TO STEM THE TIDE.

SCRAM!

LACE NEEDS--

NOTHING. THE ONLY THING SHE NEEDS IS FOR US TO STOP ANY MORE FROM BOARDING.

GET HIGH.

FIND COLA.

SHE'LL GIVE YOU THE SITUATION.

THWOOOM!

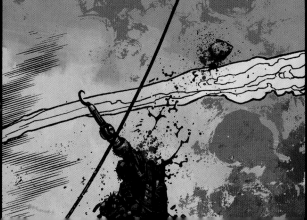

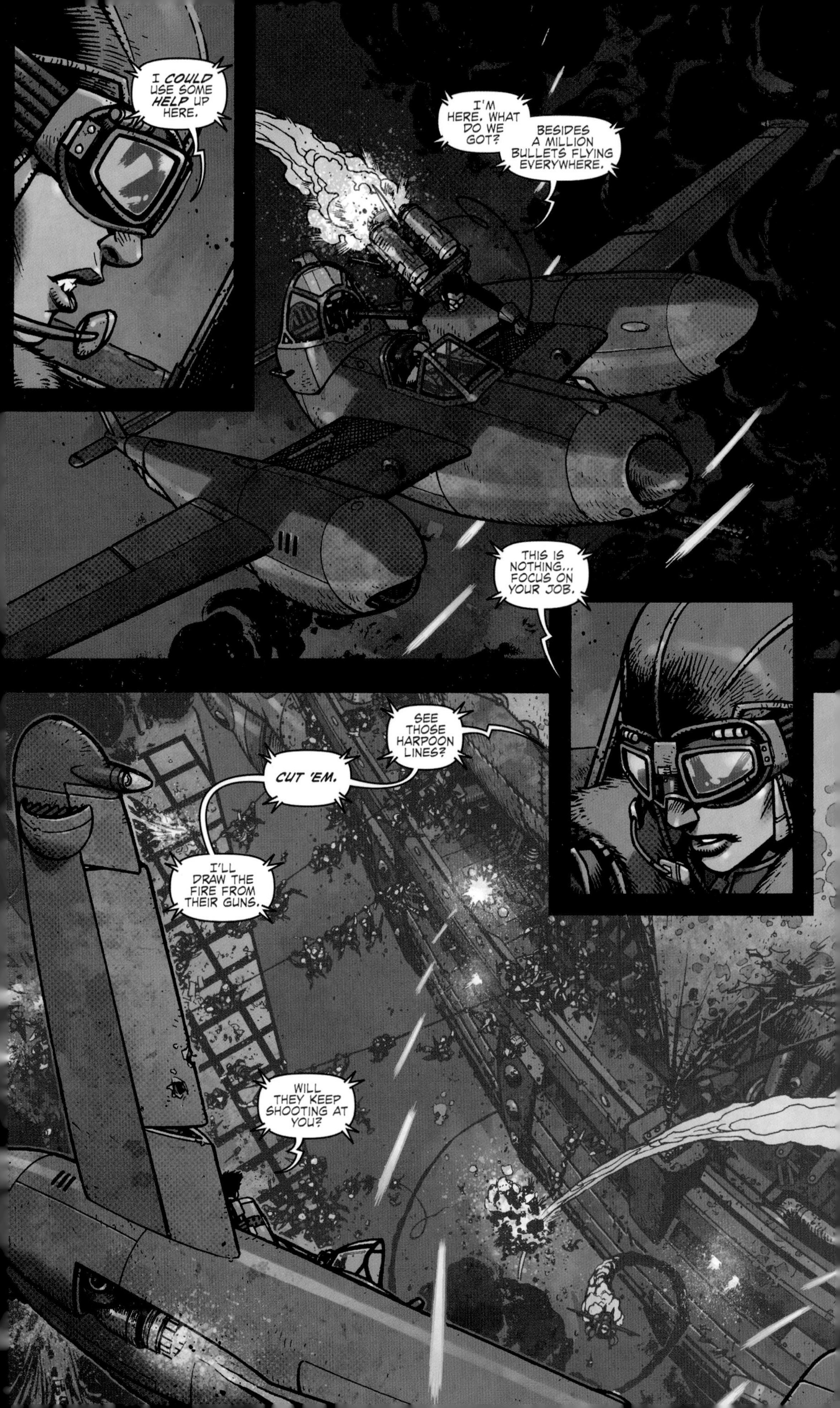
I COULD USE SOME HELP UP HERE.
I'M HERE. WHAT DO WE GOT?
BESIDES A MILLION BULLETS FLYING EVERYWHERE.
THIS IS NOTHING... FOCUS ON YOUR JOB.
SEE THOSE HARPOON LINES?
CUT 'EM.
I'LL DRAW THE FIRE FROM THEIR GUNS.
WILL THEY KEEP SHOOTING AT YOU?

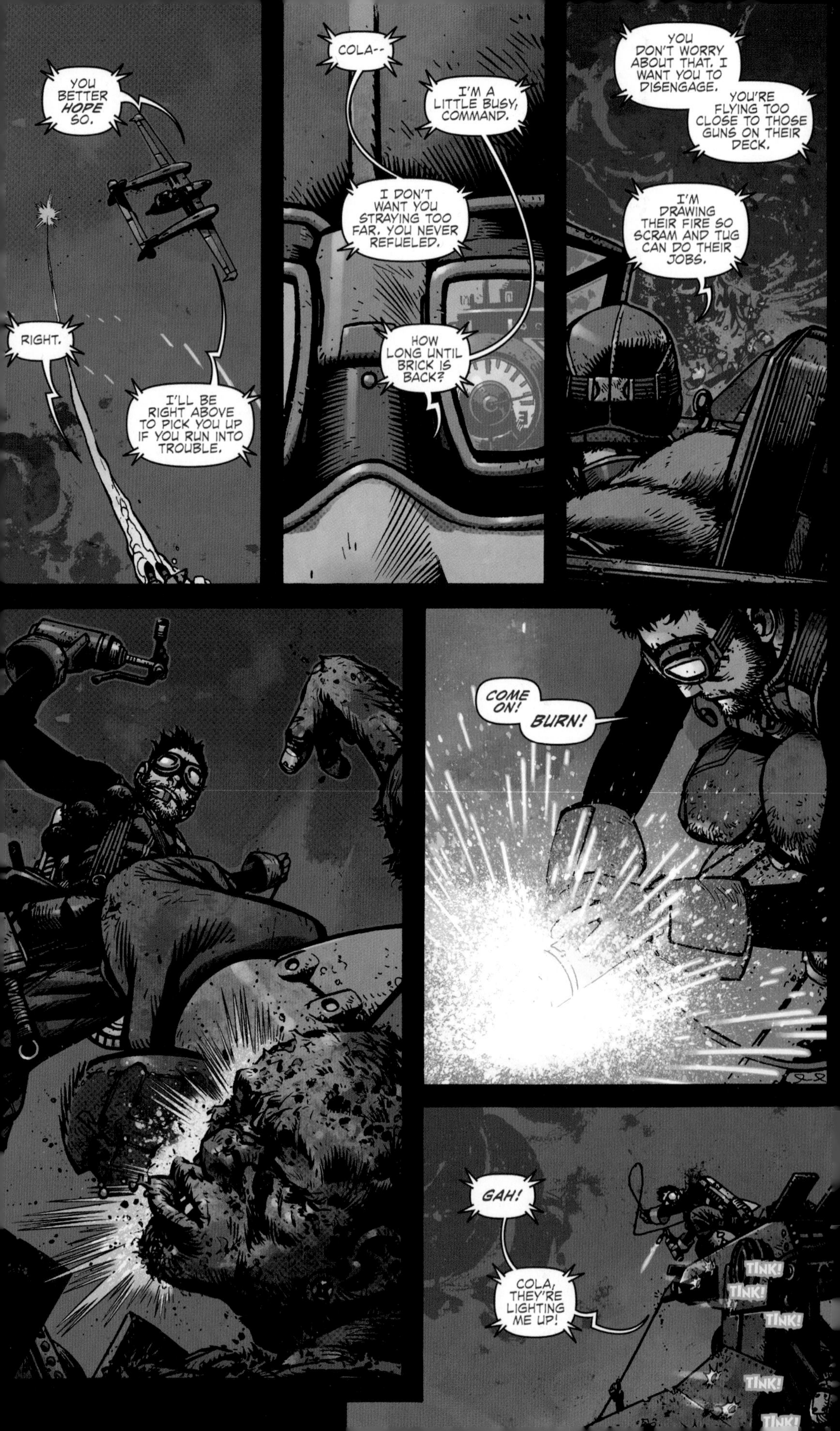
YOU BETTER HOPE SO.
RIGHT.
I'LL BE RIGHT ABOVE TO PICK YOU UP IF YOU RUN INTO TROUBLE.
COLA--
I'M A LITTLE BUSY, COMMAND.
I DON'T WANT YOU STRAYING TOO FAR. YOU NEVER REFUELED.
HOW LONG UNTIL BRICK IS BACK?
YOU DON'T WORRY ABOUT THAT. I WANT YOU TO DISENGAGE.
YOU'RE FLYING TOO CLOSE TO THOSE GUNS ON THEIR DECK.
I'M DRAWING THEIR FIRE SO SCRAM AND TUG CAN DO THEIR JOBS.
COME ON! BURN!
GAH!
COLA, THEY'RE LIGHTING ME UP!
TINK!
TINK!
TINK!
TINK!
TINK!

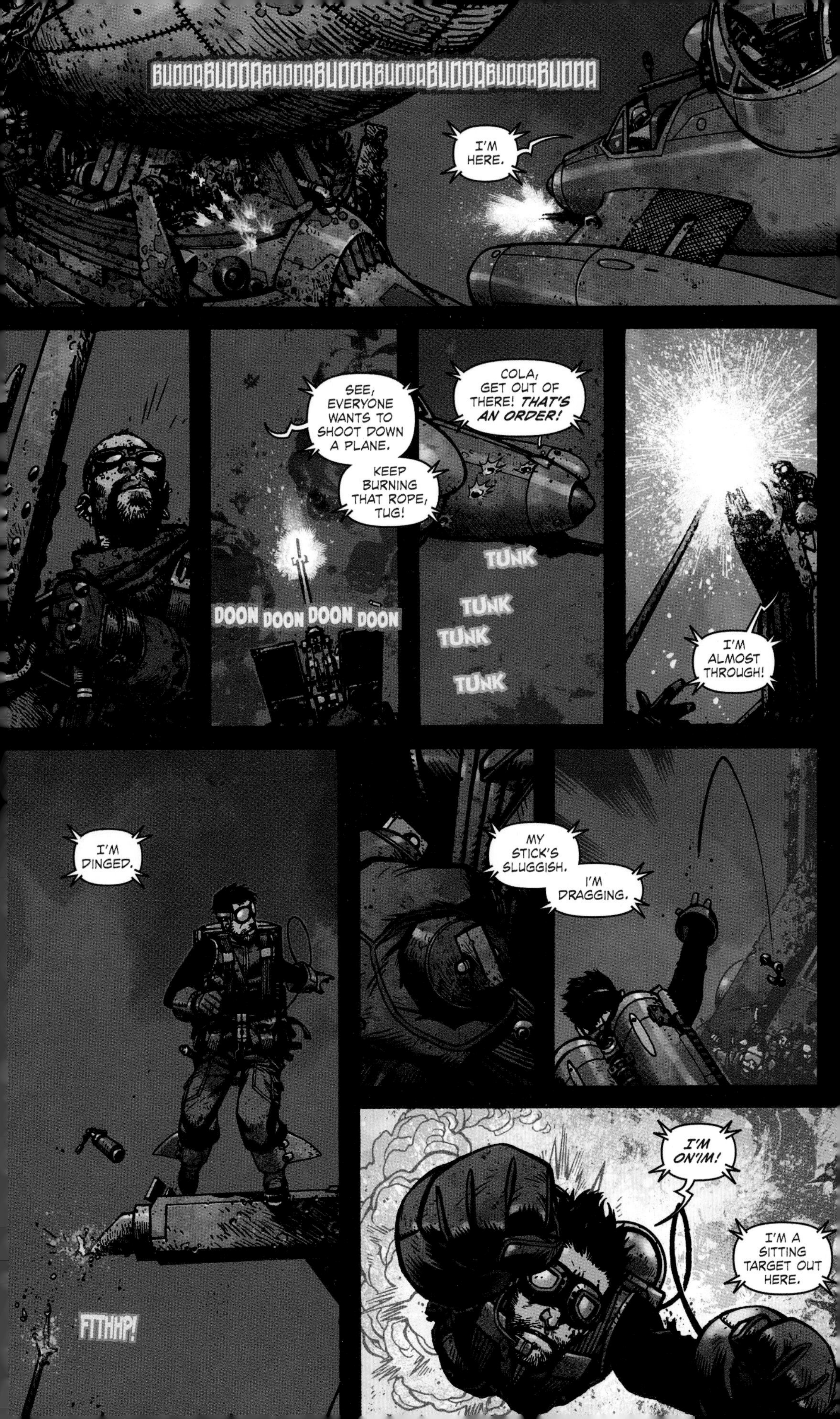
BUDDABUDDABUDDABUDDABUDDABUDDABUDDABUDDA
I'M HERE.
SEE, EVERYONE WANTS TO SHOOT DOWN A PLANE.
KEEP BURNING THAT ROPE, TUG!
DOON DOON DOON DOON
COLA, GET OUT OF THERE! THAT'S AN ORDER!
TUNK
TUNK
TUNK
TUNK
I'M ALMOST THROUGH!
I'M DINGED.
FTTHHP!
MY STICK'S SLUGGISH.
I'M DRAGGING.
I'M ON'IM!
I'M A SITTING TARGET OUT HERE.

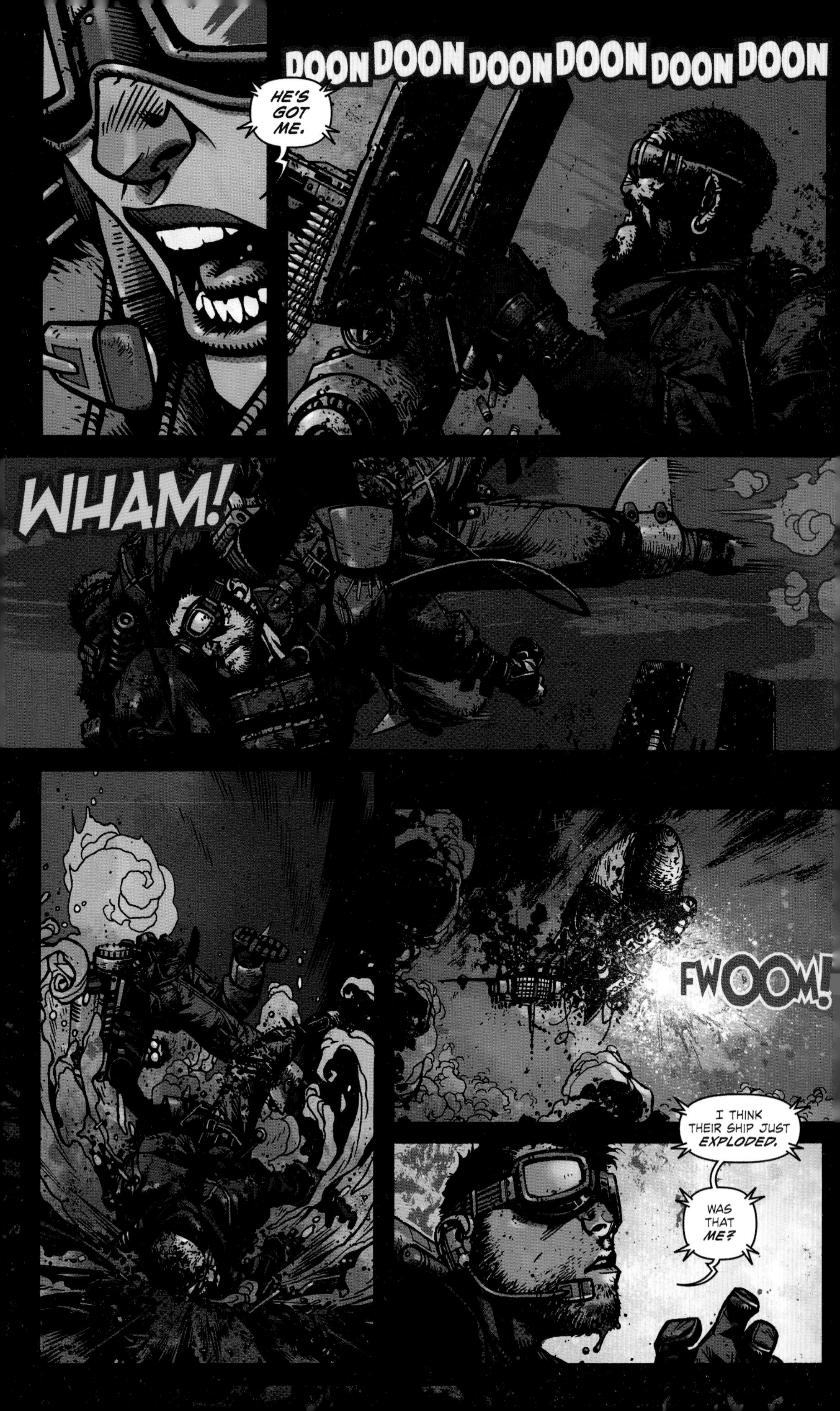
DOON DOON DOON DOON DOON DOON
HE'S GOT ME.
WHAM!
FWOOM!
I THINK THEIR SHIP JUST *EXPLODED.*
WAS THAT *ME?*

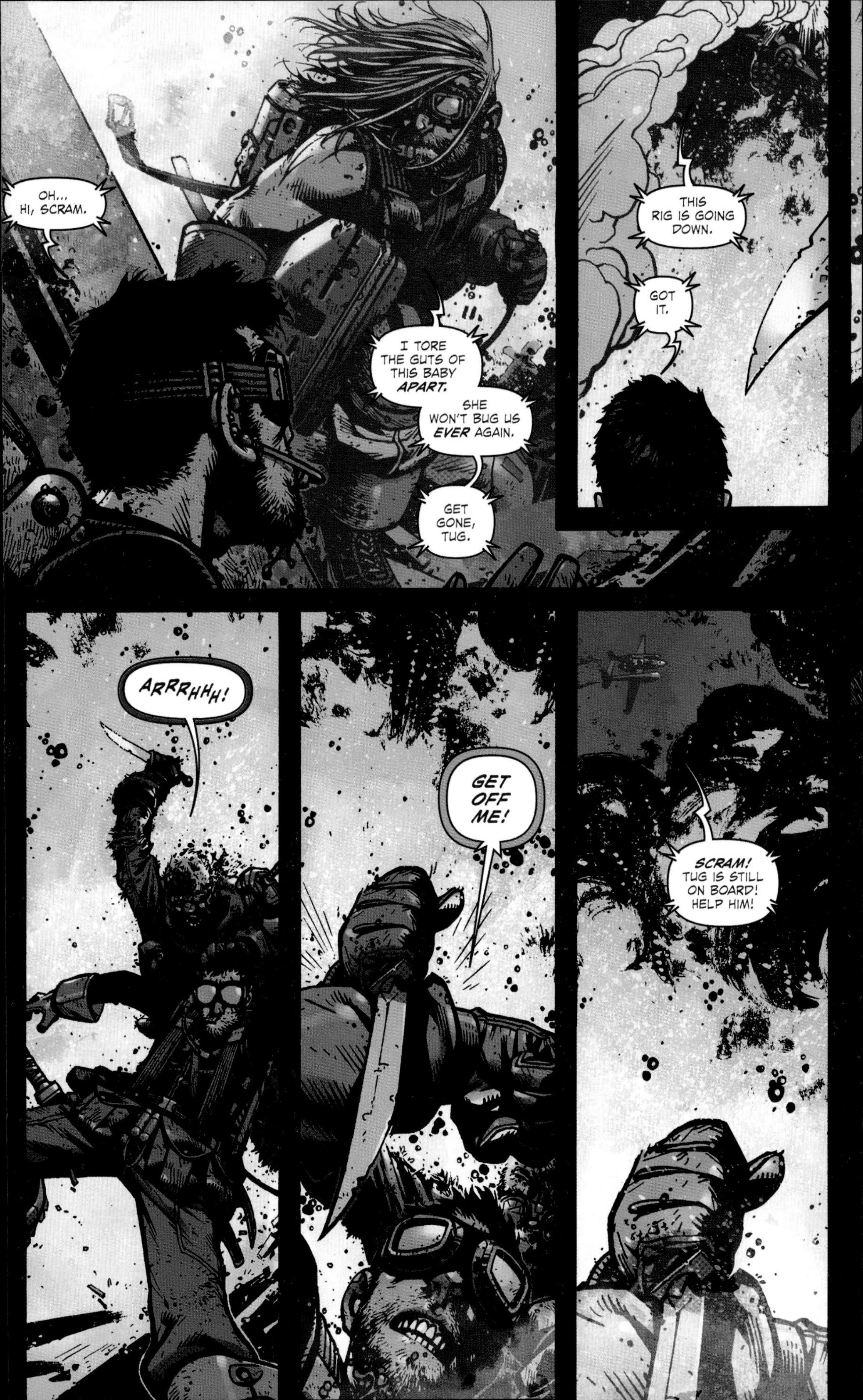
OH... HI, SCRAM.
I TORE THE GUTS OF THIS BABY APART.
SHE WON'T BUG US EVER AGAIN.
GET GONE, TUG.
THIS RIG IS GOING DOWN.
GOT IT.
ARRRHHH!
GET OFF ME!
SCRAM! TUG IS STILL ON BOARD! HELP HIM!

COLA, THIS IS COMMAND. SCRAM IS ALL USED UP.

HE'S ON THE DECK ALREADY.

YOUR PLANE IS SMOKING. I CAN SEE YOU FROM HERE.

DO *NOT* CHASE HIM.

NOT A CHANCE!

I *WON'T* LEAVE HIM, MOM.

DAMMIT!

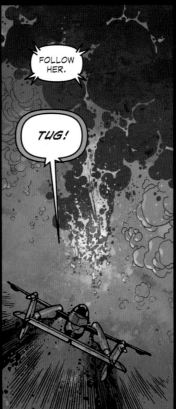

FOLLOW HER.

TUG!

EVERYTHING WE HAVE.

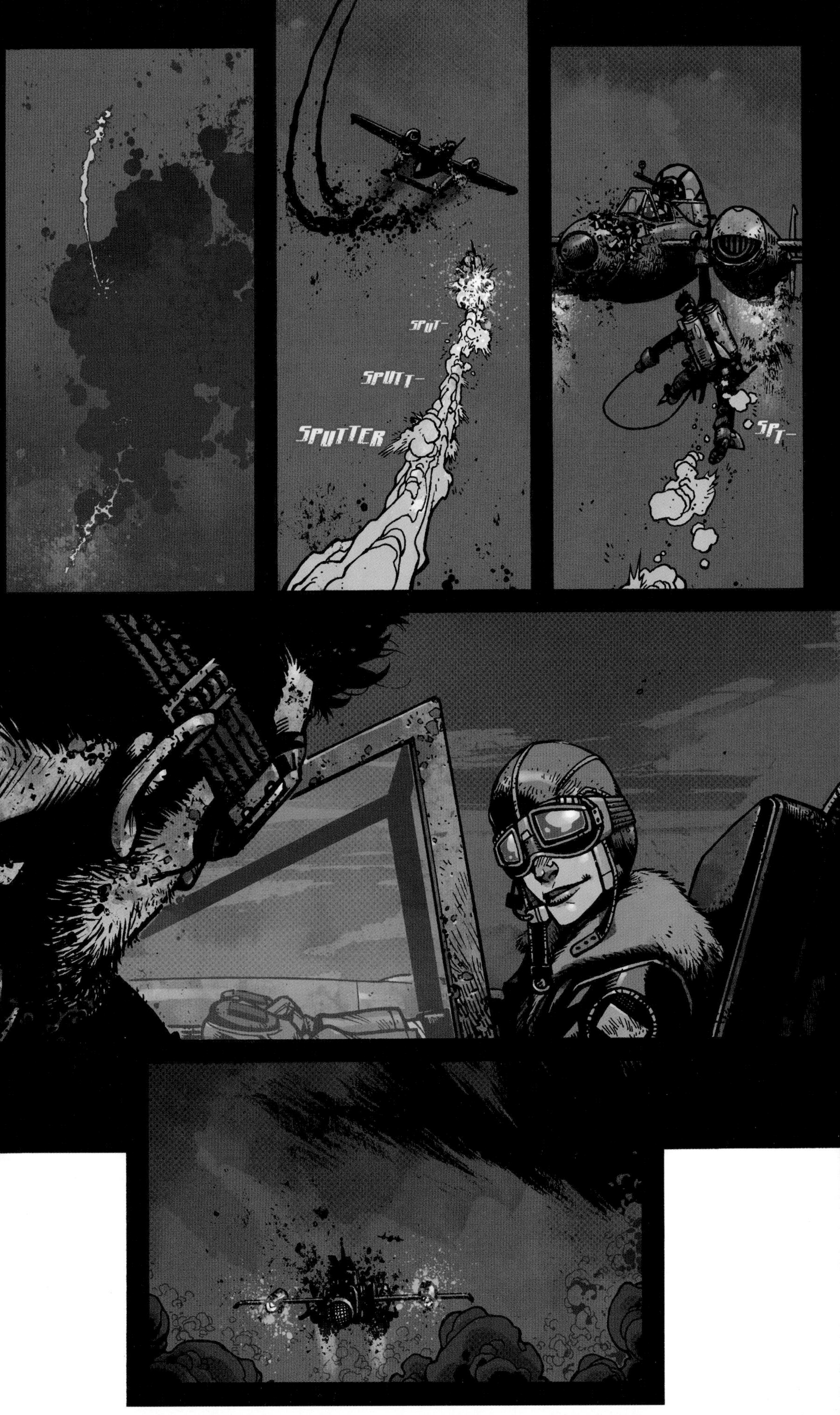
SPUT-
SPUTT-
SPUTTER
SPT-

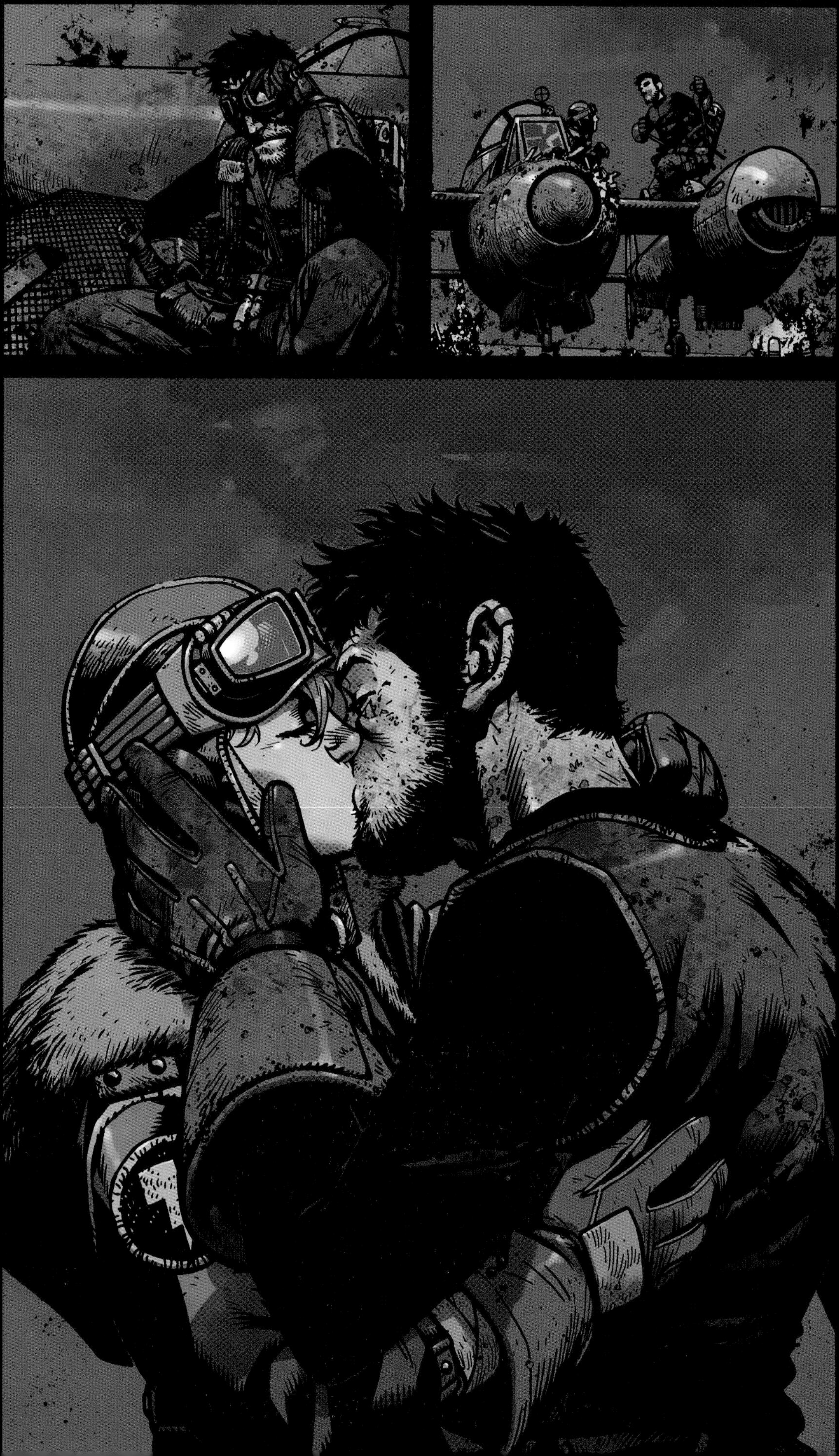

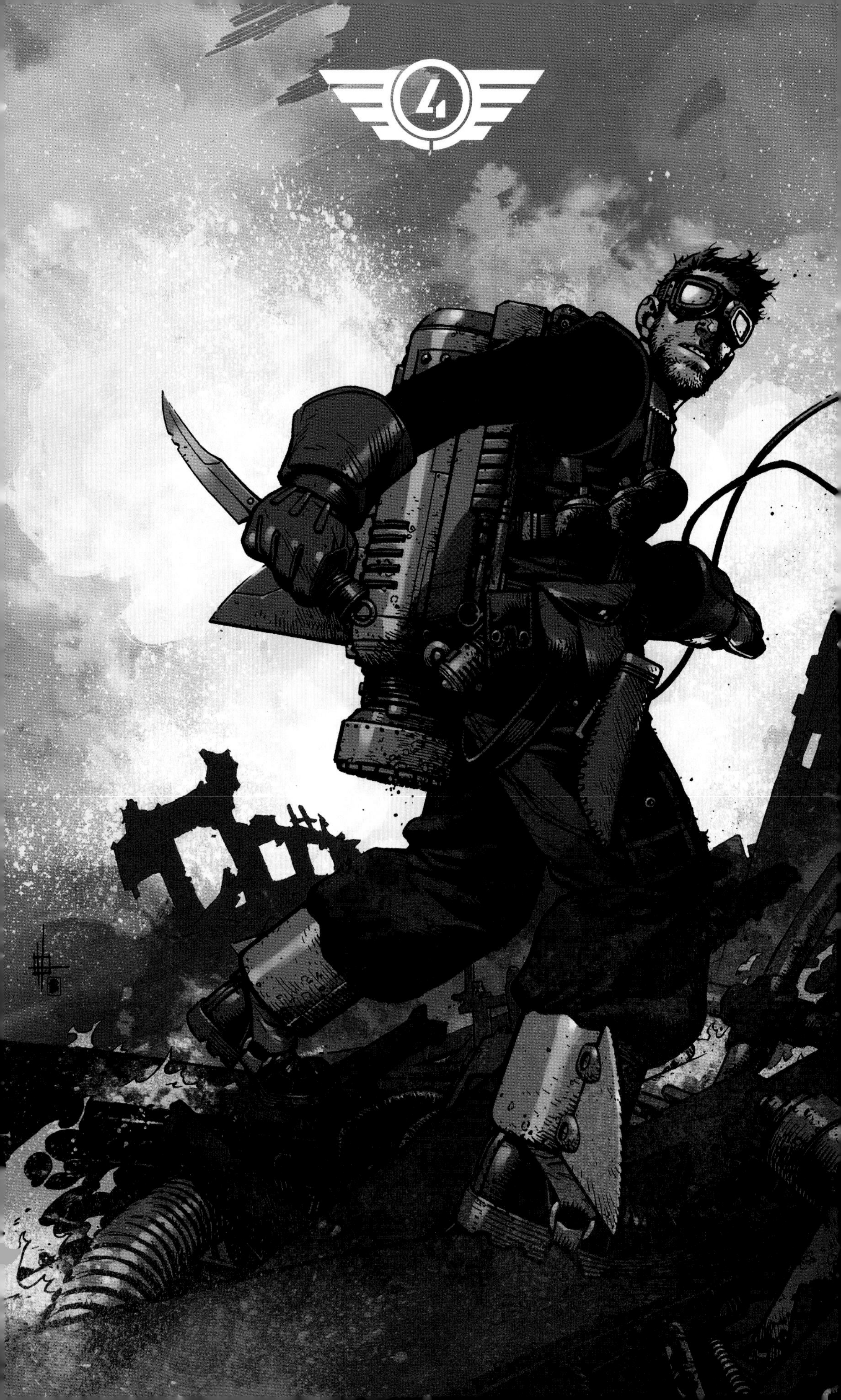
4

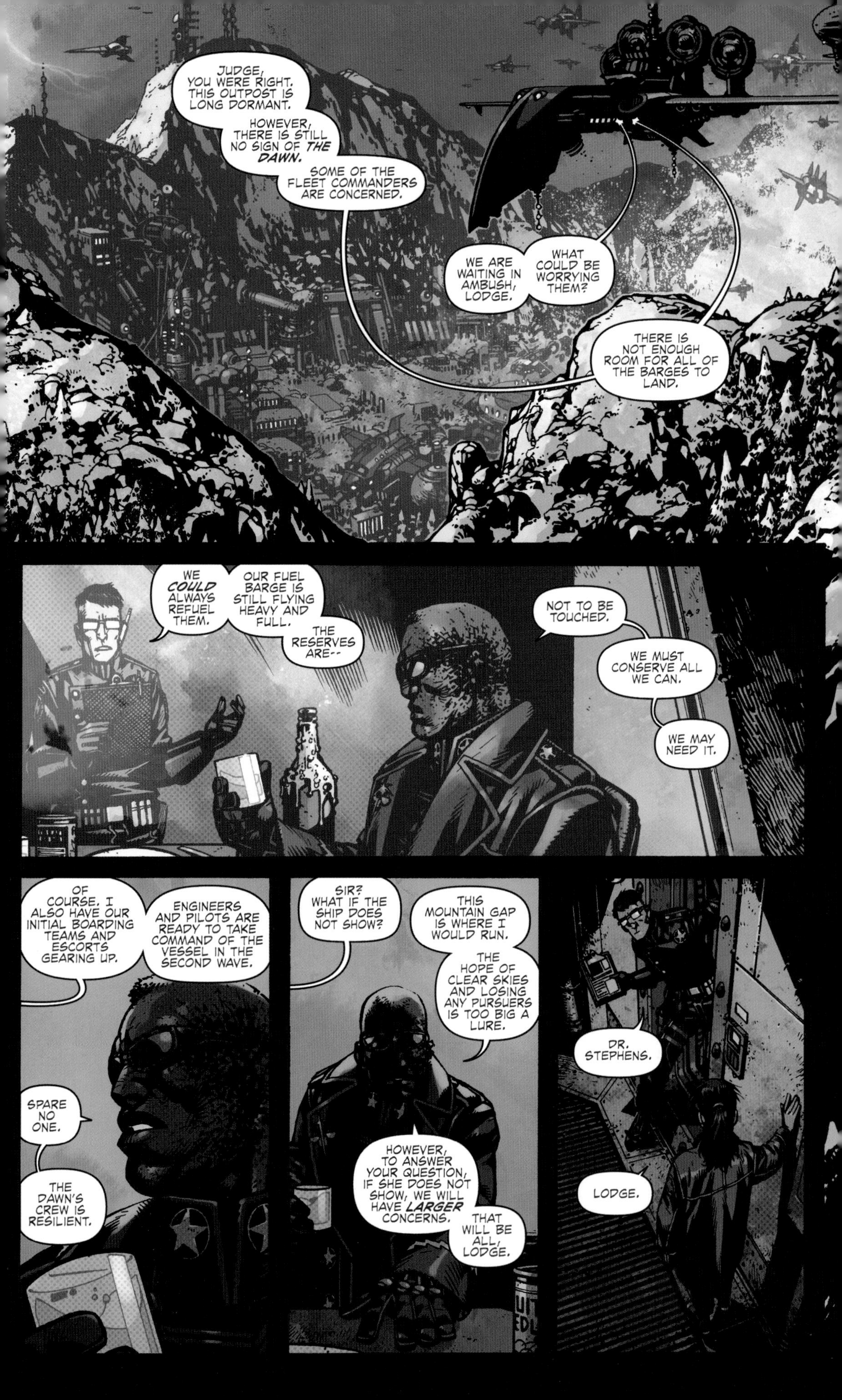
JUDGE, YOU WERE RIGHT. THIS OUTPOST IS LONG DORMANT.
HOWEVER, THERE IS STILL NO SIGN OF *THE DAWN.*
SOME OF THE FLEET COMMANDERS ARE CONCERNED.
WHAT COULD BE WORRYING THEM?
WE ARE WAITING IN AMBUSH, LODGE.
THERE IS NOT ENOUGH ROOM FOR ALL OF THE BARGES TO LAND.
WE *COULD* ALWAYS REFUEL THEM.
OUR FUEL BARGE IS STILL FLYING HEAVY AND FULL.
THE RESERVES ARE--
NOT TO BE TOUCHED.
WE MUST CONSERVE ALL WE CAN.
WE MAY NEED IT.
OF COURSE. I ALSO HAVE OUR INITIAL BOARDING TEAMS AND ESCORTS GEARING UP.
ENGINEERS AND PILOTS ARE READY TO TAKE COMMAND OF THE VESSEL IN THE SECOND WAVE.
SPARE NO ONE.
THE DAWN'S CREW IS RESILIENT.
SIR? WHAT IF THE SHIP DOES NOT SHOW?
THIS MOUNTAIN GAP IS WHERE I WOULD RUN.
THE HOPE OF CLEAR SKIES AND LOSING ANY PURSUERS IS TOO BIG A LURE.
HOWEVER, TO ANSWER YOUR QUESTION, IF SHE DOES NOT SHOW, WE WILL HAVE *LARGER* CONCERNS.
THAT WILL BE ALL, LODGE.
DR. STEPHENS.
LODGE.

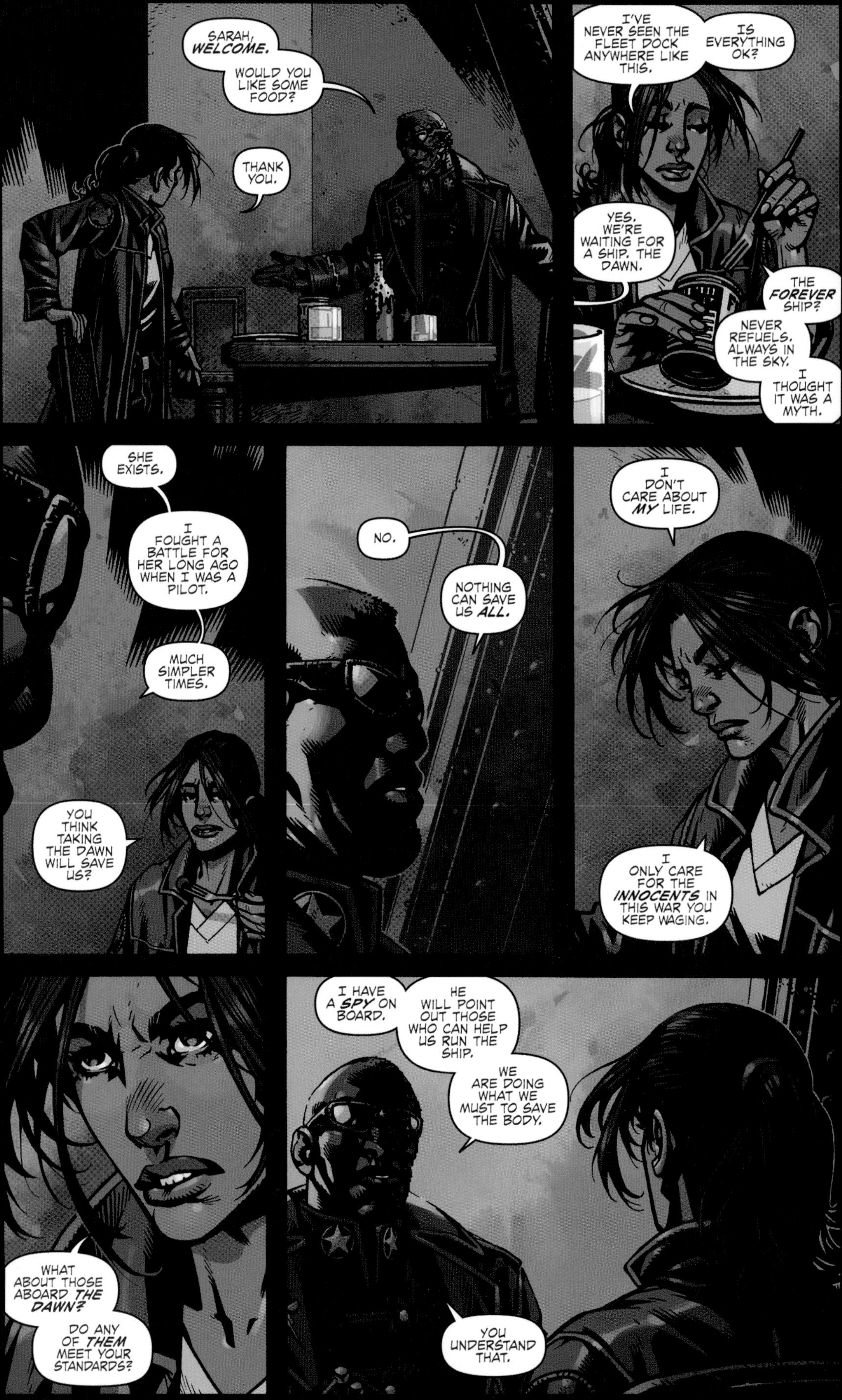
SARAH, WELCOME.
WOULD YOU LIKE SOME FOOD?
THANK YOU.
I'VE NEVER SEEN THE FLEET DOCK ANYWHERE LIKE THIS.
IS EVERYTHING OK?
YES. WE'RE WAITING FOR A SHIP. THE DAWN.
THE FOREVER SHIP?
NEVER REFUELS. ALWAYS IN THE SKY.
I THOUGHT IT WAS A MYTH.
SHE EXISTS.
I FOUGHT A BATTLE FOR HER LONG AGO WHEN I WAS A PILOT.
MUCH SIMPLER TIMES.
YOU THINK TAKING THE DAWN WILL SAVE US?
NO.
NOTHING CAN SAVE US ALL.
I DON'T CARE ABOUT MY LIFE.
I ONLY CARE FOR THE INNOCENTS IN THIS WAR YOU KEEP WAGING.
WHAT ABOUT THOSE ABOARD THE DAWN?
DO ANY OF THEM MEET YOUR STANDARDS?
I HAVE A SPY ON BOARD.
HE WILL POINT OUT THOSE WHO CAN HELP US RUN THE SHIP.
WE ARE DOING WHAT WE MUST TO SAVE THE BODY.
YOU UNDERSTAND THAT.

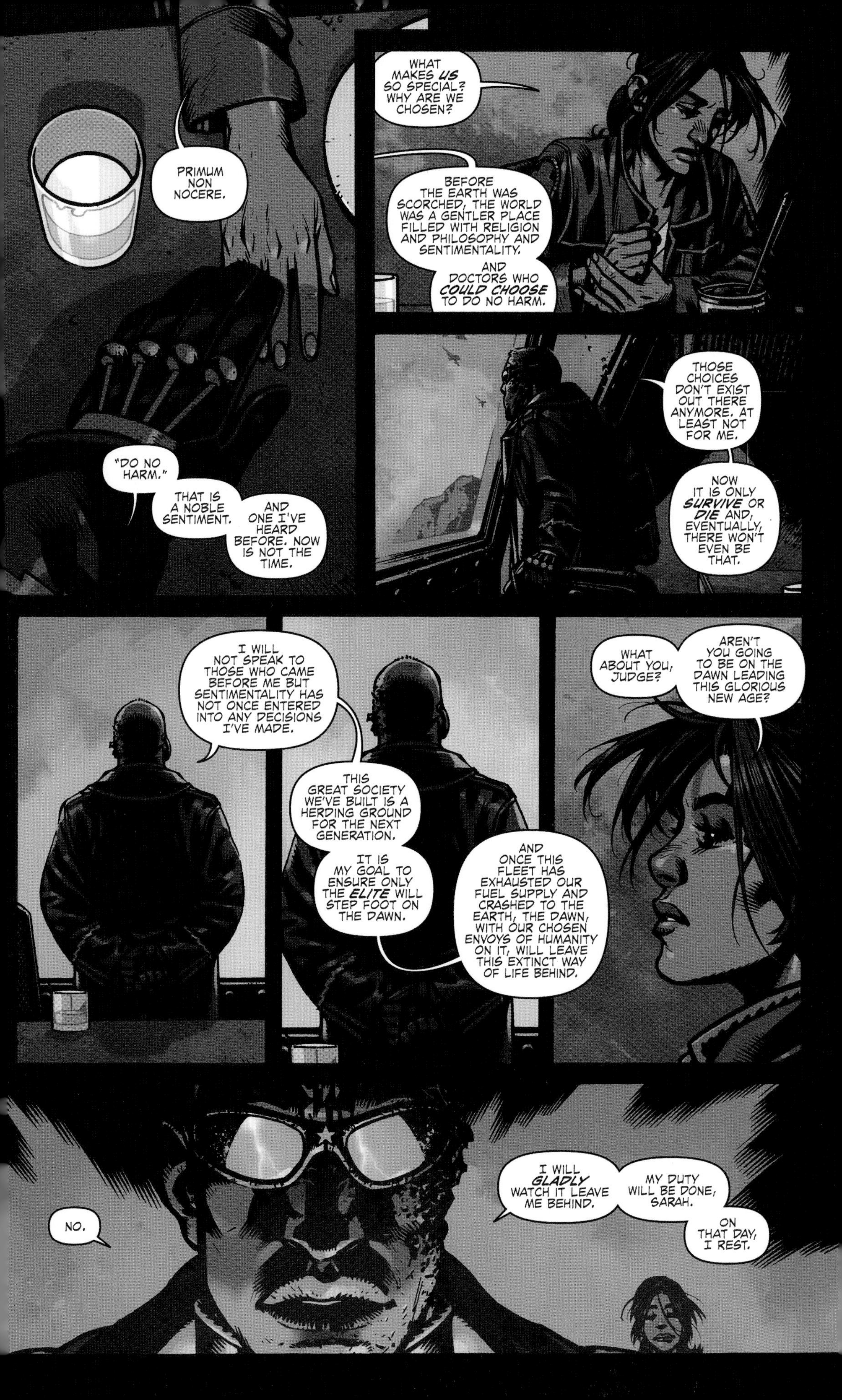
PRIMUM NON NOCERE.
WHAT MAKES US SO SPECIAL? WHY ARE WE CHOSEN?
BEFORE THE EARTH WAS SCORCHED, THE WORLD WAS A GENTLER PLACE FILLED WITH RELIGION AND PHILOSOPHY AND SENTIMENTALITY.
AND DOCTORS WHO COULD CHOOSE TO DO NO HARM.
"DO NO HARM."
THAT IS A NOBLE SENTIMENT.
AND ONE I'VE HEARD BEFORE. NOW IS NOT THE TIME.
THOSE CHOICES DON'T EXIST OUT THERE ANYMORE. AT LEAST NOT FOR ME.
NOW IT IS ONLY SURVIVE OR DIE AND, EVENTUALLY, THERE WON'T EVEN BE THAT.
I WILL NOT SPEAK TO THOSE WHO CAME BEFORE ME BUT SENTIMENTALITY HAS NOT ONCE ENTERED INTO ANY DECISIONS I'VE MADE.
THIS GREAT SOCIETY WE'VE BUILT IS A HERDING GROUND FOR THE NEXT GENERATION.
IT IS MY GOAL TO ENSURE ONLY THE ELITE WILL STEP FOOT ON THE DAWN.
AND ONCE THIS FLEET HAS EXHAUSTED OUR FUEL SUPPLY AND CRASHED TO THE EARTH, THE DAWN, WITH OUR CHOSEN ENVOYS OF HUMANITY ON IT, WILL LEAVE THIS EXTINCT WAY OF LIFE BEHIND.
WHAT ABOUT YOU, JUDGE?
AREN'T YOU GOING TO BE ON THE DAWN LEADING THIS GLORIOUS NEW AGE?
NO.
I WILL GLADLY WATCH IT LEAVE ME BEHIND.
MY DUTY WILL BE DONE, SARAH.
ON THAT DAY, I REST.

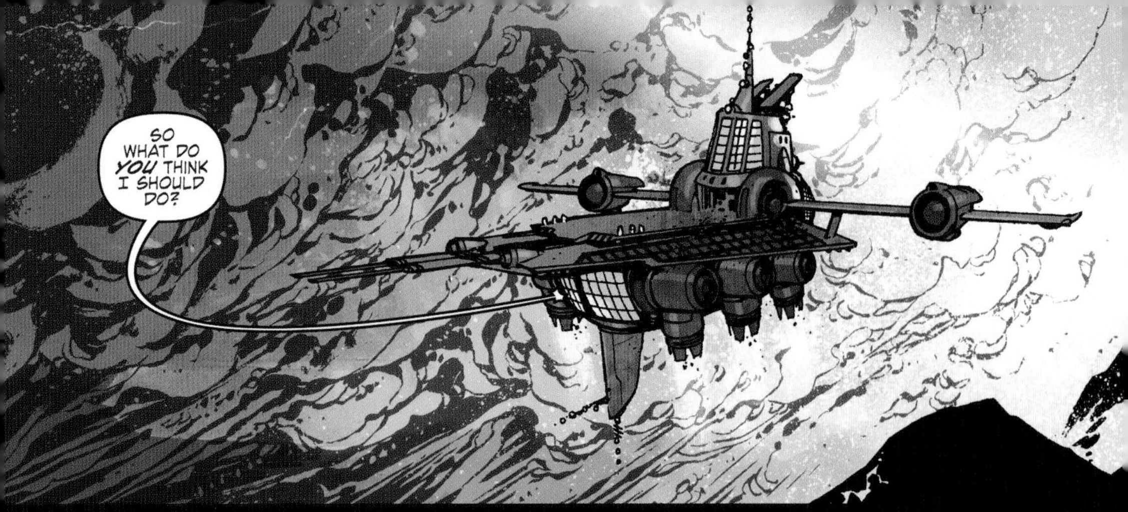
SO WHAT DO *YOU* THINK I SHOULD DO?

CHAPTER FOUR

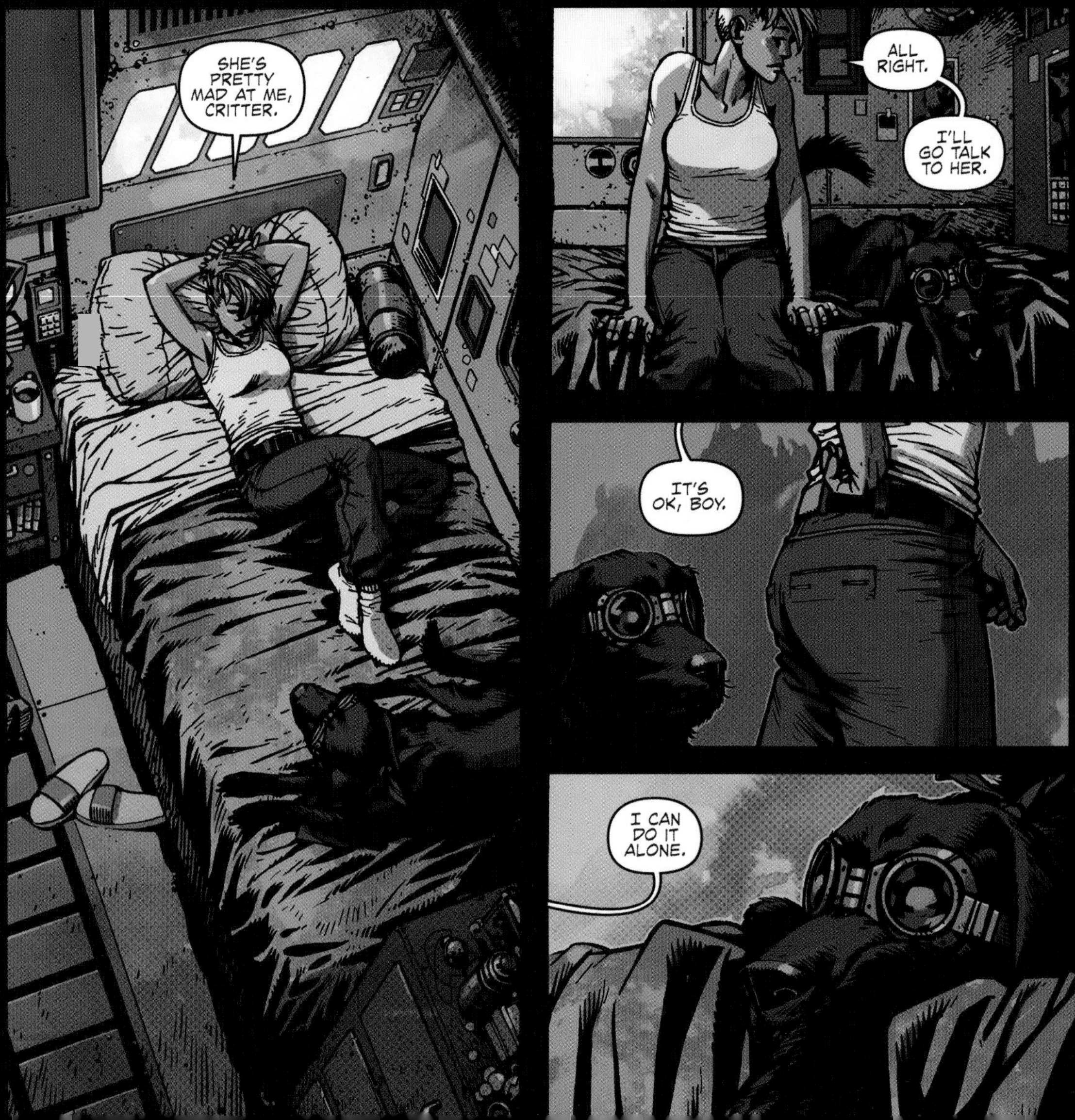
SHE'S PRETTY MAD AT ME, CRITTER.
ALL RIGHT.
I'LL GO TALK TO HER.
IT'S OK, BOY.
I CAN DO IT ALONE.

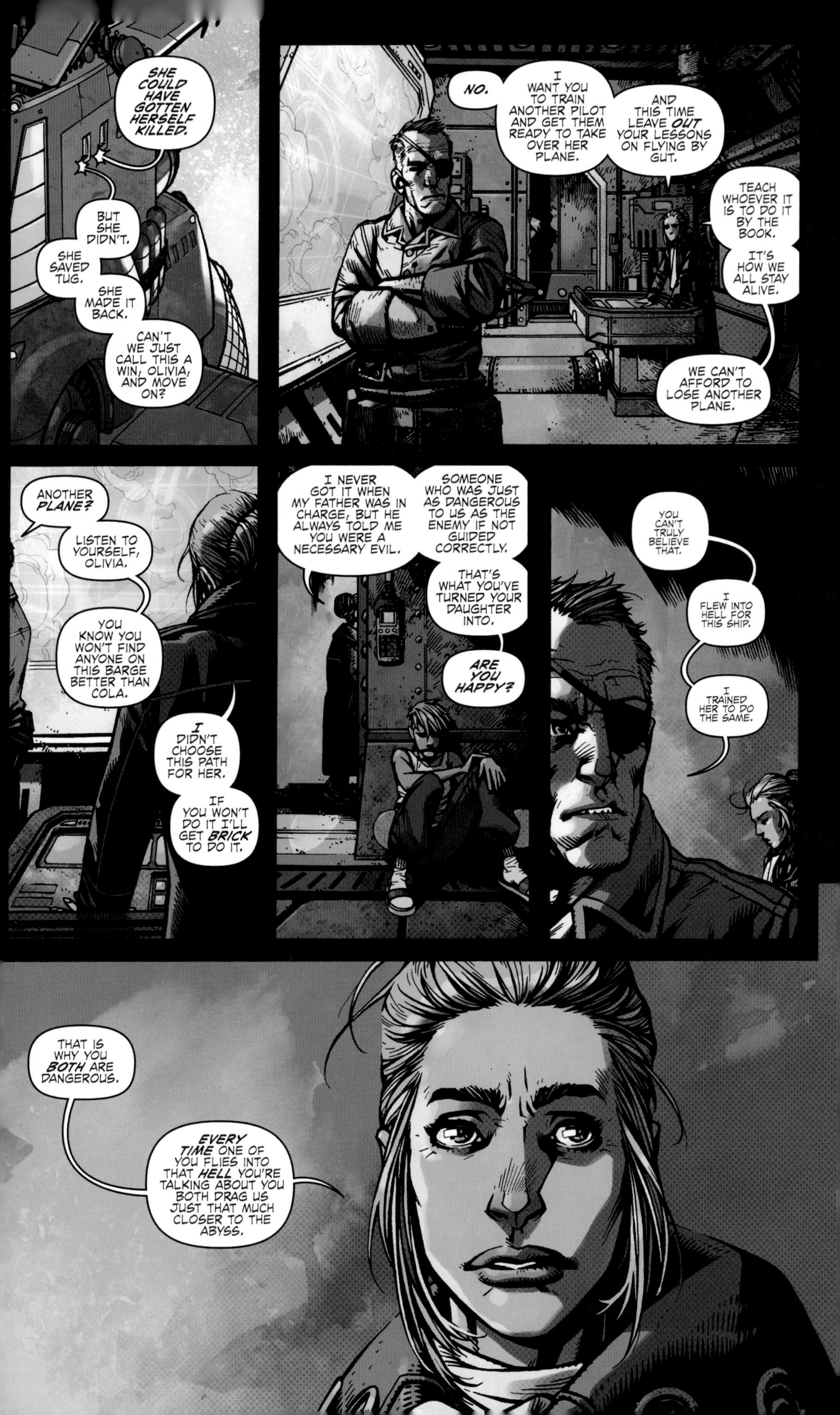
SHE COULD HAVE GOTTEN HERSELF KILLED.
BUT SHE DIDN'T.
SHE SAVED TUG.
SHE MADE IT BACK.
CAN'T WE JUST CALL THIS A WIN, OLIVIA, AND MOVE ON?
NO.
I WANT YOU TO TRAIN ANOTHER PILOT AND GET THEM READY TO TAKE OVER HER PLANE.
AND THIS TIME LEAVE OUT YOUR LESSONS ON FLYING BY GUT.
TEACH WHOEVER IT IS TO DO IT BY THE BOOK.
IT'S HOW WE ALL STAY ALIVE.
WE CAN'T AFFORD TO LOSE ANOTHER PLANE.
ANOTHER PLANE?
LISTEN TO YOURSELF, OLIVIA.
YOU KNOW YOU WON'T FIND ANYONE ON THIS BARGE BETTER THAN COLA.
I DIDN'T CHOOSE THIS PATH FOR HER.
IF YOU WON'T DO IT I'LL GET BRICK TO DO IT.
I NEVER GOT IT WHEN MY FATHER WAS IN CHARGE, BUT HE ALWAYS TOLD ME YOU WERE A NECESSARY EVIL.
SOMEONE WHO WAS JUST AS DANGEROUS TO US AS THE ENEMY IF NOT GUIDED CORRECTLY.
THAT'S WHAT YOU'VE TURNED YOUR DAUGHTER INTO.
ARE YOU HAPPY?
YOU CAN'T TRULY BELIEVE THAT.
I FLEW INTO HELL FOR THIS SHIP.
I TRAINED HER TO DO THE SAME.
THAT IS WHY YOU BOTH ARE DANGEROUS.
EVERY TIME ONE OF YOU FLIES INTO THAT HELL YOU'RE TALKING ABOUT YOU BOTH DRAG US JUST THAT MUCH CLOSER TO THE ABYSS.

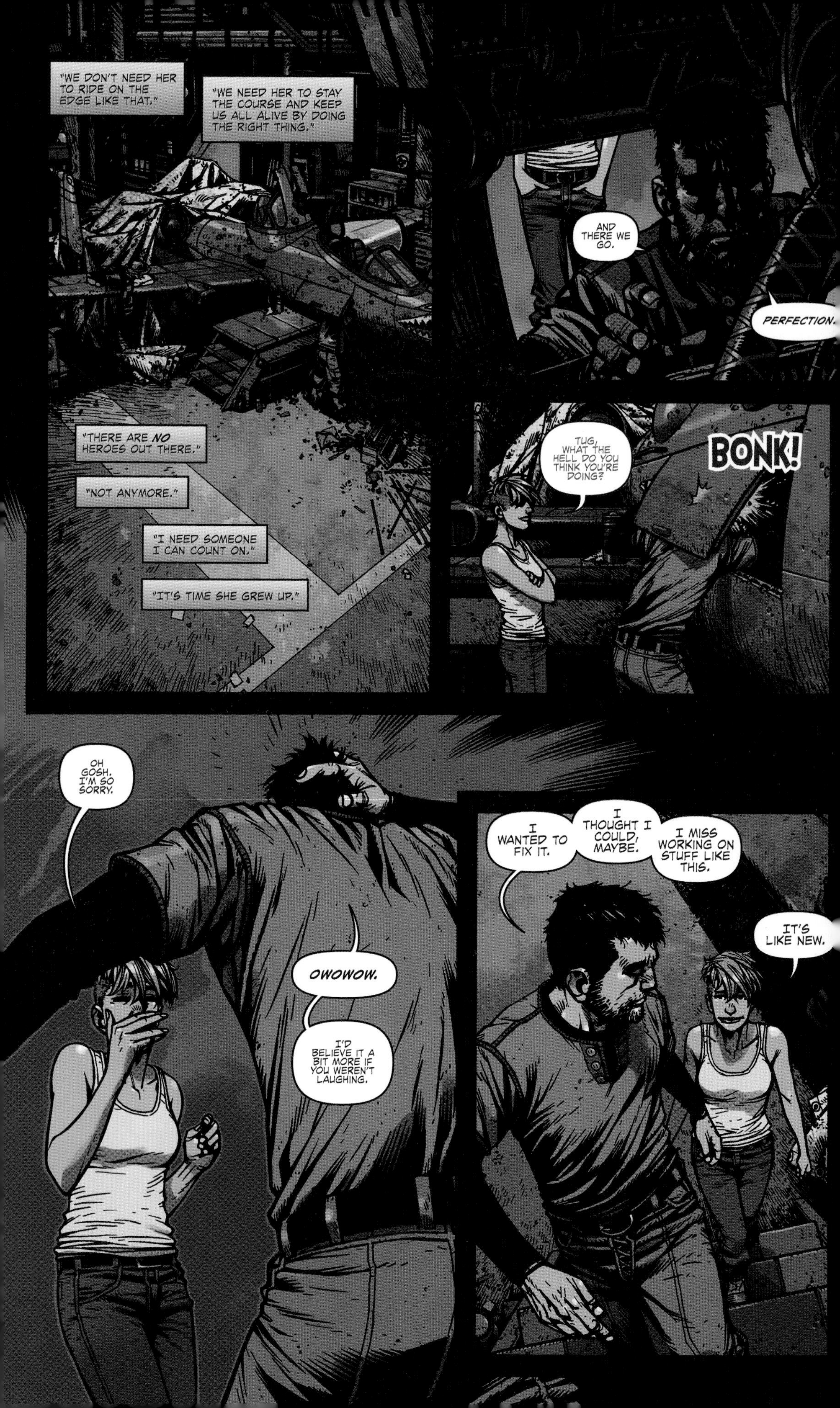
"WE DON'T NEED HER TO RIDE ON THE EDGE LIKE THAT."
"WE NEED HER TO STAY THE COURSE AND KEEP US ALL ALIVE BY DOING THE RIGHT THING."
AND THERE WE GO.
PERFECTION.
"THERE ARE NO HEROES OUT THERE."
"NOT ANYMORE."
"I NEED SOMEONE I CAN COUNT ON."
"IT'S TIME SHE GREW UP."
BONK!
TUG, WHAT THE HELL DO YOU THINK YOU'RE DOING?
OH GOSH. I'M SO SORRY.
OWOWOW.
I'D BELIEVE IT A BIT MORE IF YOU WEREN'T LAUGHING.
I WANTED TO FIX IT.
I THOUGHT I COULD, MAYBE.
I MISS WORKING ON STUFF LIKE THIS.
IT'S LIKE NEW.

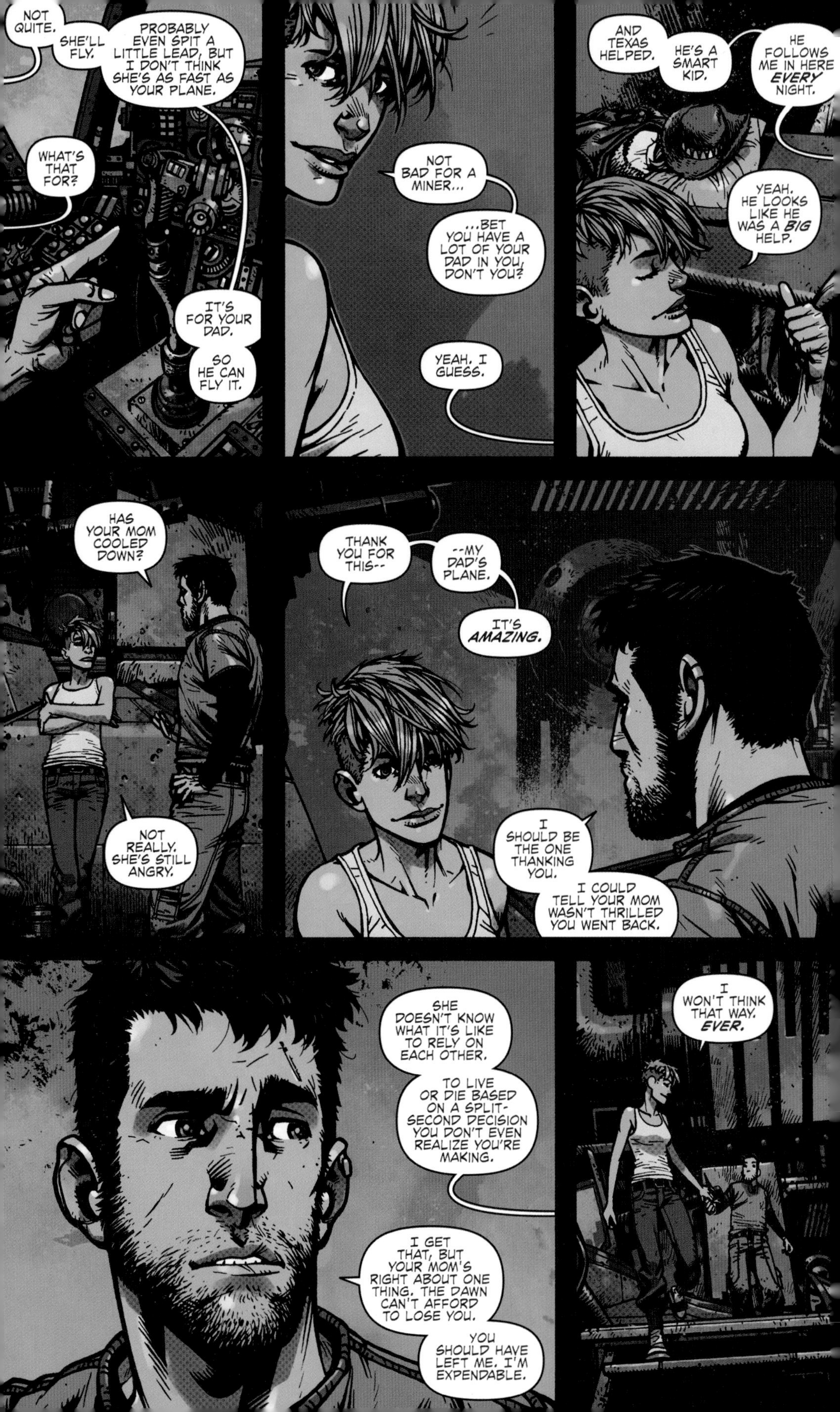
NOT QUITE.
SHE'LL FLY.
PROBABLY EVEN SPIT A LITTLE LEAD, BUT I DON'T THINK SHE'S AS FAST AS YOUR PLANE.
WHAT'S THAT FOR?
IT'S FOR YOUR DAD.
SO HE CAN FLY IT.
NOT BAD FOR A MINER...
...BET YOU HAVE A LOT OF YOUR DAD IN YOU, DON'T YOU?
YEAH. I GUESS.
AND TEXAS HELPED.
HE'S A SMART KID.
HE FOLLOWS ME IN HERE EVERY NIGHT.
YEAH. HE LOOKS LIKE HE WAS A BIG HELP.
HAS YOUR MOM COOLED DOWN?
NOT REALLY. SHE'S STILL ANGRY.
THANK YOU FOR THIS--
--MY DAD'S PLANE.
IT'S AMAZING.
I SHOULD BE THE ONE THANKING YOU.
I COULD TELL YOUR MOM WASN'T THRILLED YOU WENT BACK.
SHE DOESN'T KNOW WHAT IT'S LIKE TO RELY ON EACH OTHER.
TO LIVE OR DIE BASED ON A SPLIT-SECOND DECISION YOU DON'T EVEN REALIZE YOU'RE MAKING.
I GET THAT, BUT YOUR MOM'S RIGHT ABOUT ONE THING. THE DAWN CAN'T AFFORD TO LOSE YOU.
YOU SHOULD HAVE LEFT ME. I'M EXPENDABLE.
I WON'T THINK THAT WAY. EVER.

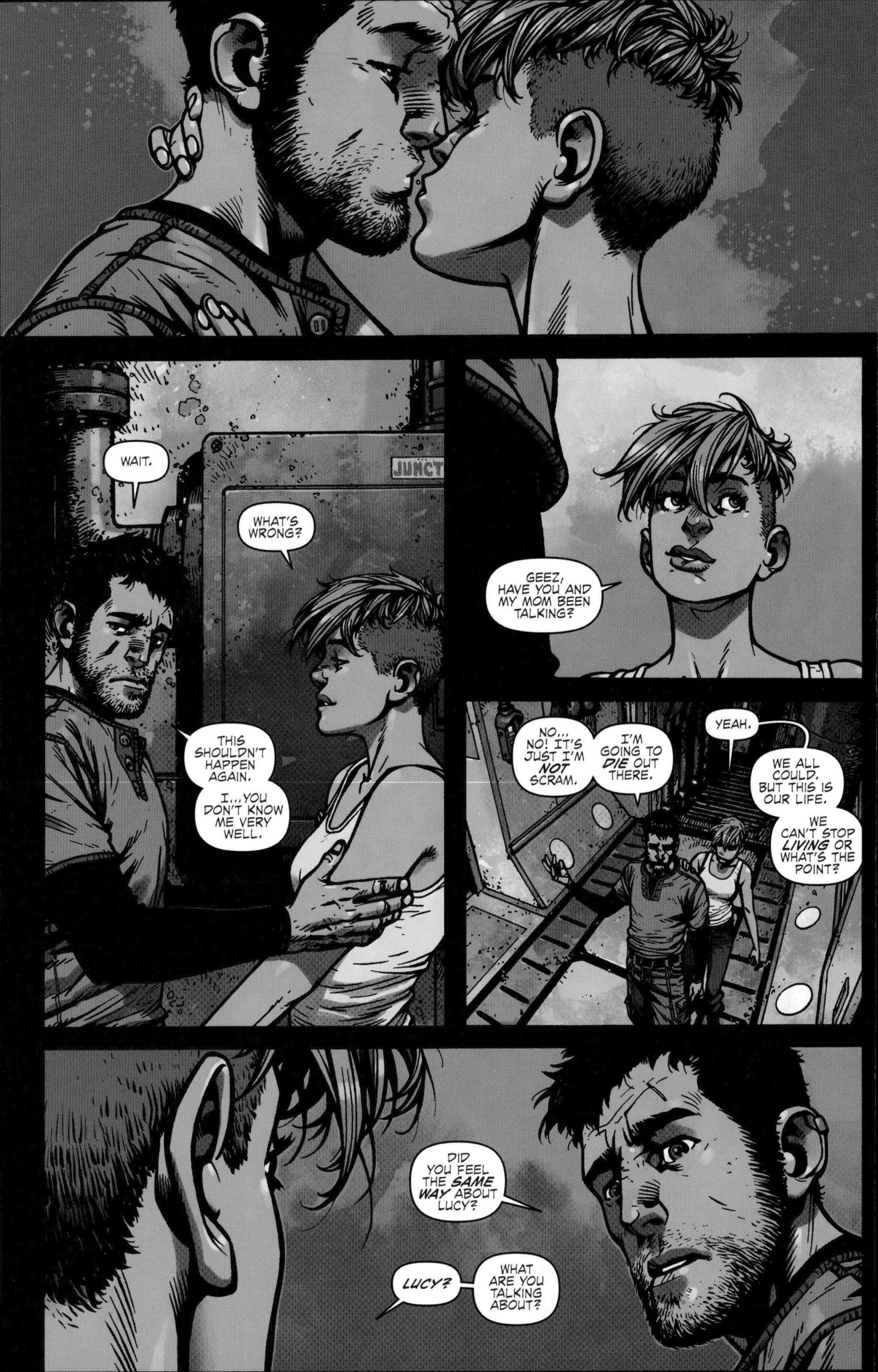
WAIT.
WHAT'S WRONG?
THIS SHOULDN'T HAPPEN AGAIN.
I...YOU DON'T KNOW ME VERY WELL.
GEEZ, HAVE YOU AND MY MOM BEEN TALKING?
NO... NO! IT'S JUST I'M NOT SCRAM.
I'M GOING TO DIE OUT THERE.
YEAH.
WE ALL COULD. BUT THIS IS OUR LIFE.
WE CAN'T STOP LIVING OR WHAT'S THE POINT?
DID YOU FEEL THE SAME WAY ABOUT LUCY?
LUCY?
WHAT ARE YOU TALKING ABOUT?

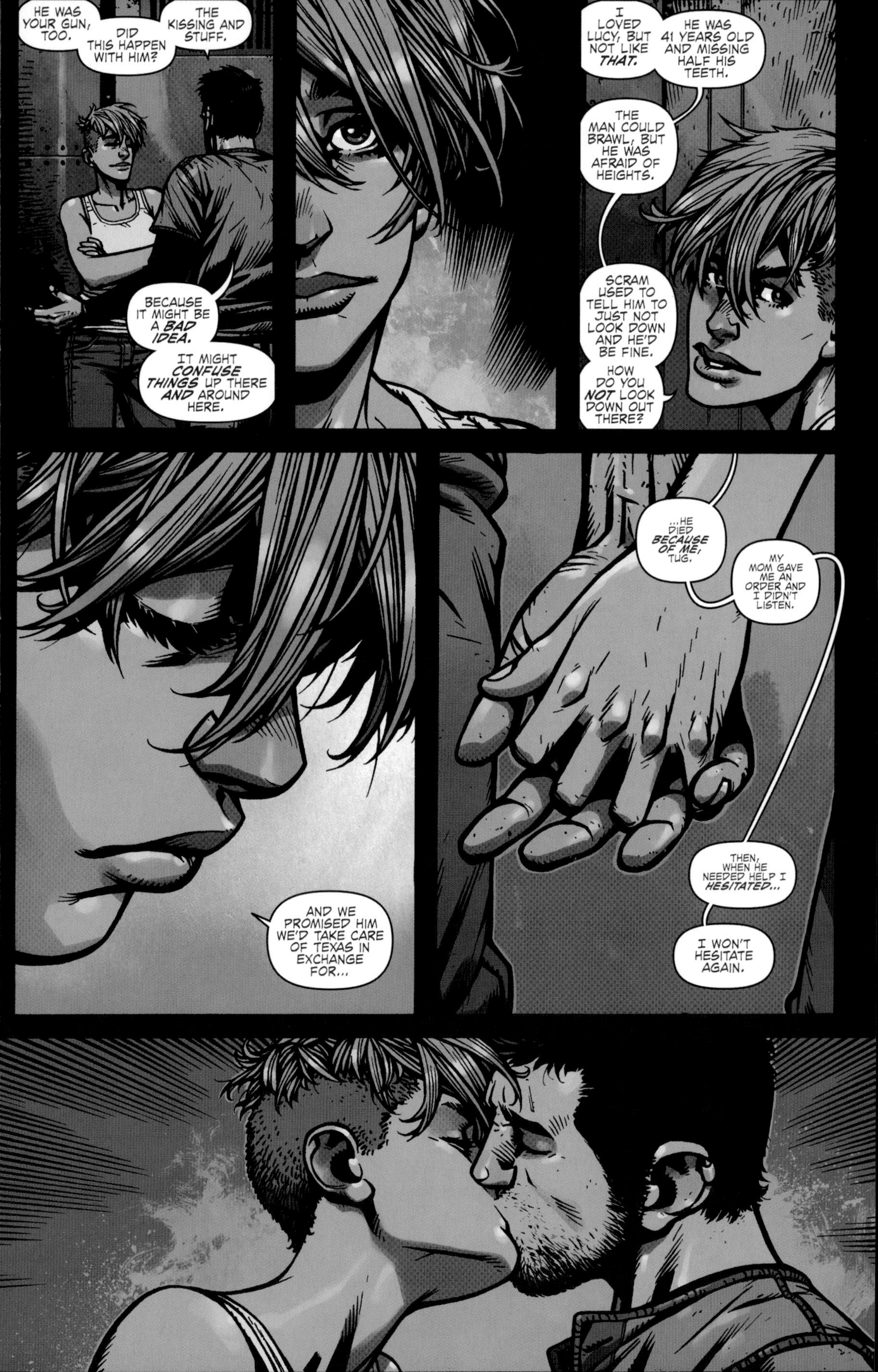
HE WAS YOUR GUN, TOO.
DID THIS HAPPEN WITH HIM?
THE KISSING AND STUFF.
BECAUSE IT MIGHT BE A *BAD IDEA.*
IT MIGHT *CONFUSE THINGS* UP THERE *AND* AROUND HERE.
I LOVED LUCY, BUT NOT LIKE *THAT.*
HE WAS 41 YEARS OLD AND MISSING HALF HIS TEETH.
THE MAN COULD BRAWL, BUT HE WAS AFRAID OF HEIGHTS.
SCRAM USED TO TELL HIM TO JUST NOT LOOK DOWN AND HE'D BE FINE.
HOW DO YOU *NOT* LOOK DOWN OUT THERE?
AND WE PROMISED HIM WE'D TAKE CARE OF TEXAS IN EXCHANGE FOR...
...HE DIED *BECAUSE OF ME,* TUG.
MY MOM GAVE ME AN ORDER AND I DIDN'T LISTEN.
THEN, WHEN HE NEEDED HELP I *HESITATED...*
I WON'T HESITATE AGAIN.

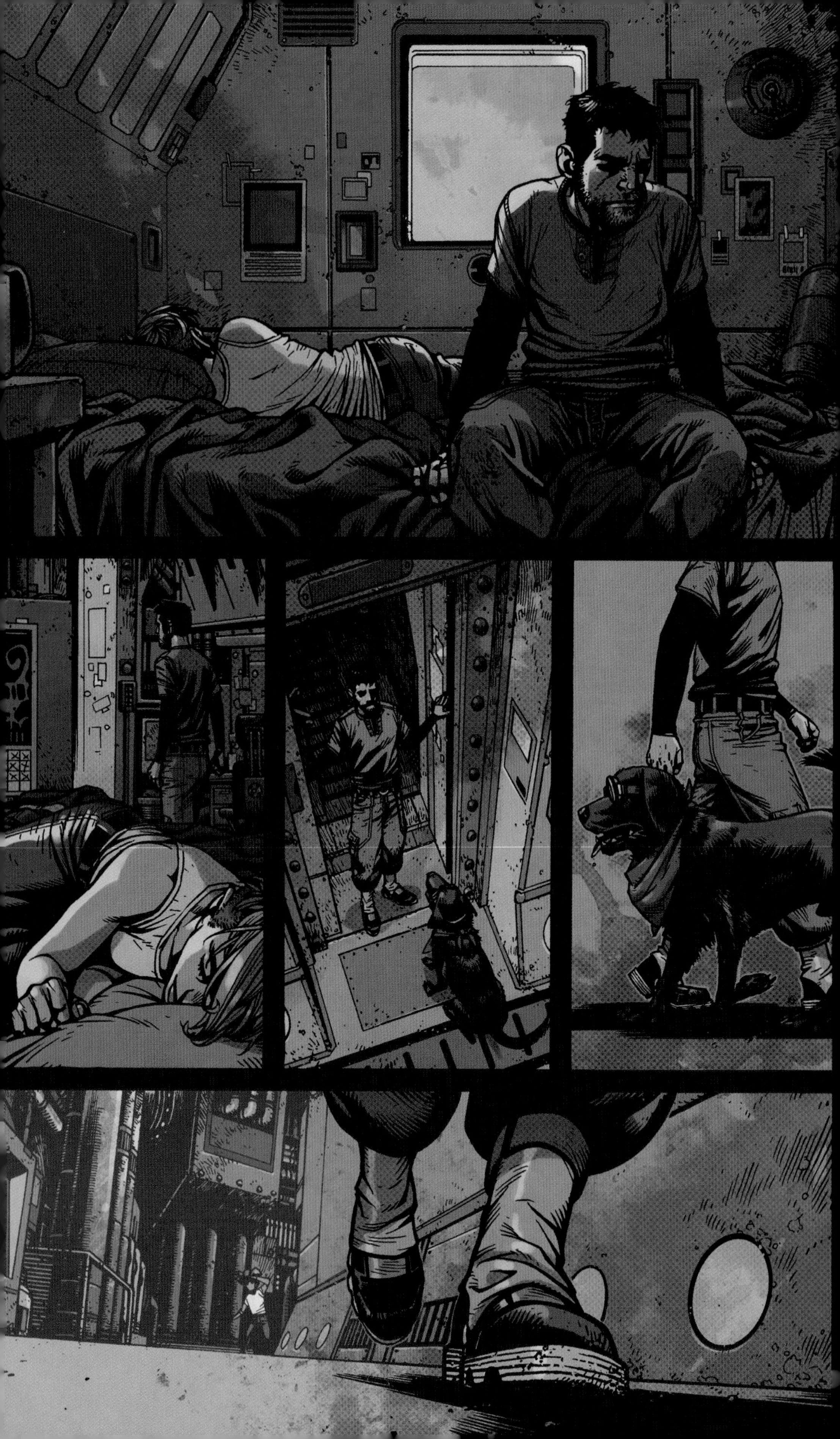

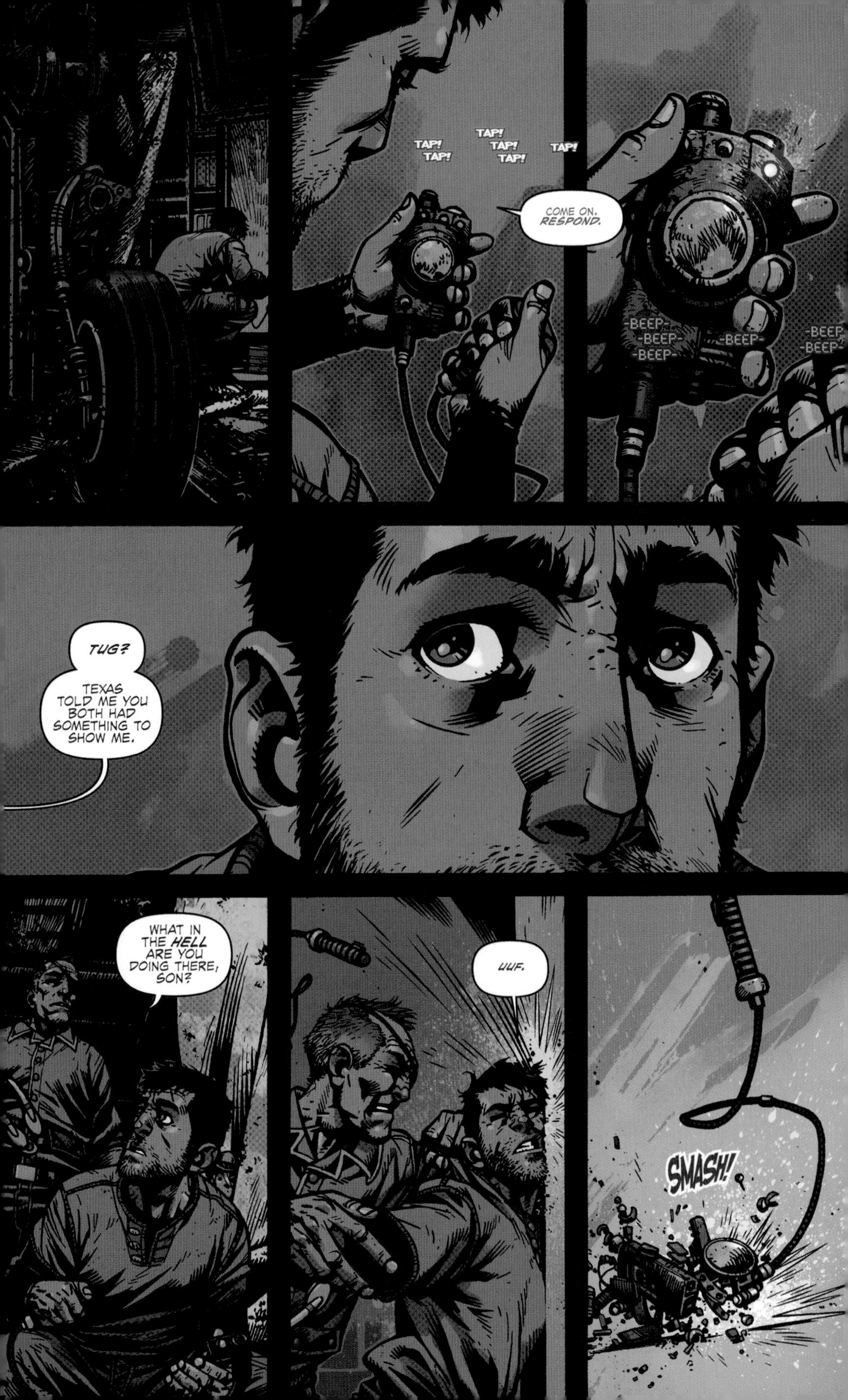
TAP!
TAP!
TAP!
TAP!
TAP!
TAP!
COME ON. RESPOND.
-BEEP- -BEEP- -BEEP-
-BEEP-
-BEEP- -BEEP-
TUG?
TEXAS TOLD ME YOU BOTH HAD SOMETHING TO SHOW ME.
WHAT IN THE HELL ARE YOU DOING THERE, SON?
UUF.
SMASH!

JUDGE, WE RECEIVED A TRANSMISSION FROM OUR AGENT ABOARD THE DAWN.

WHAT DID IT SAY?

TELL HIM.

THE MESSAGE READS, "COURSE HEADING CORRECTION. 123 DEGREES SOUTH AND--" THEN IT STOPPED.

WHERE DID YOU RECEIVE THIS FROM?

IT WAS A DIRECT TRANSMISSION. NO REDIRECT FROM ANY OF OUR COMM BASES.

THEY ARE *CLOSE*.

THEN THEY ARE HEADING THIS WAY.

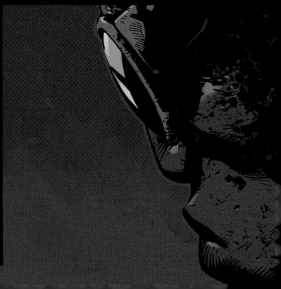

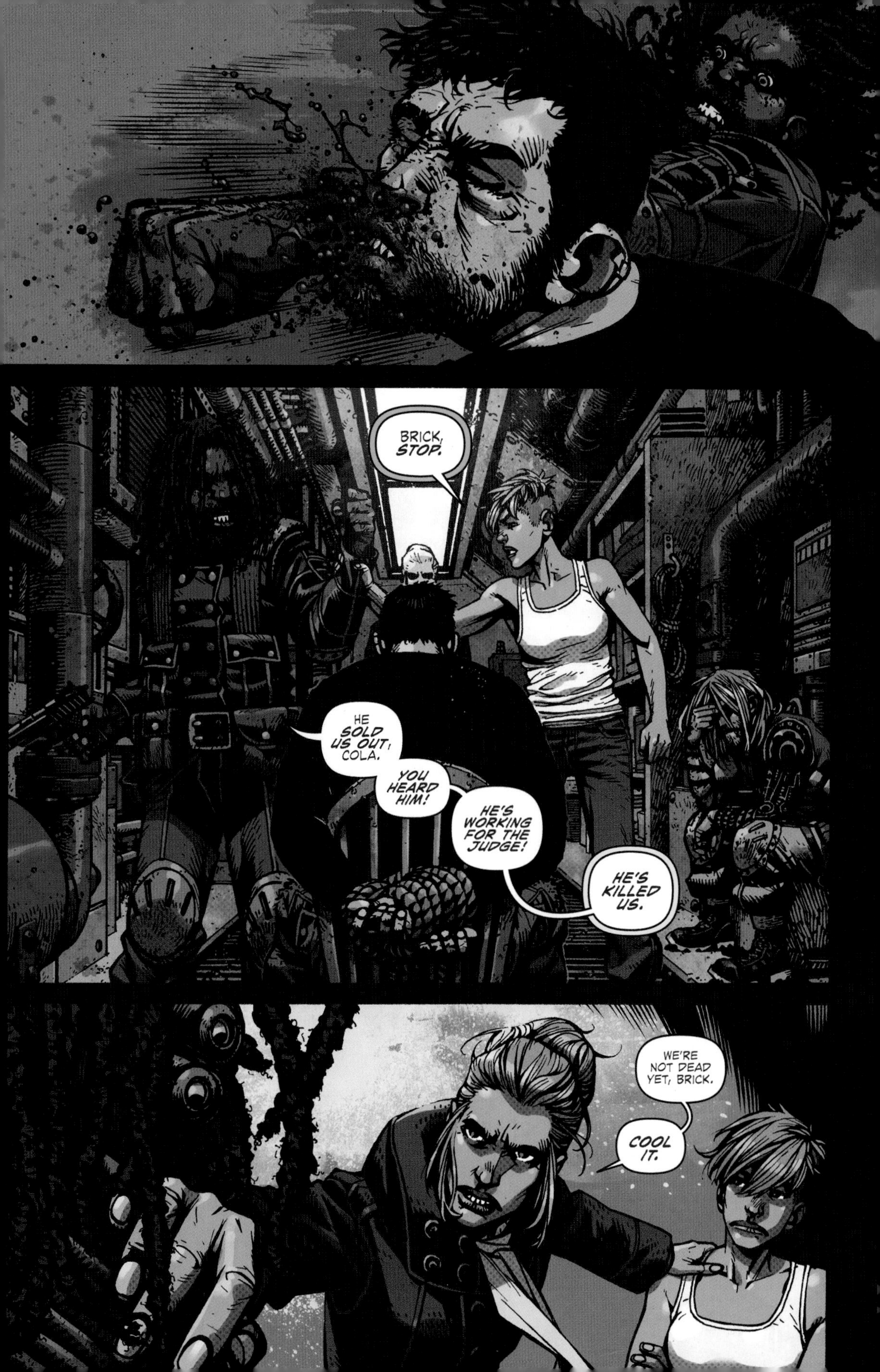
BRICK, STOP.
HE SOLD US OUT, COLA.
YOU HEARD HIM!
HE'S WORKING FOR THE JUDGE!
HE'S KILLED US.
WE'RE NOT DEAD YET, BRICK.
COOL IT.

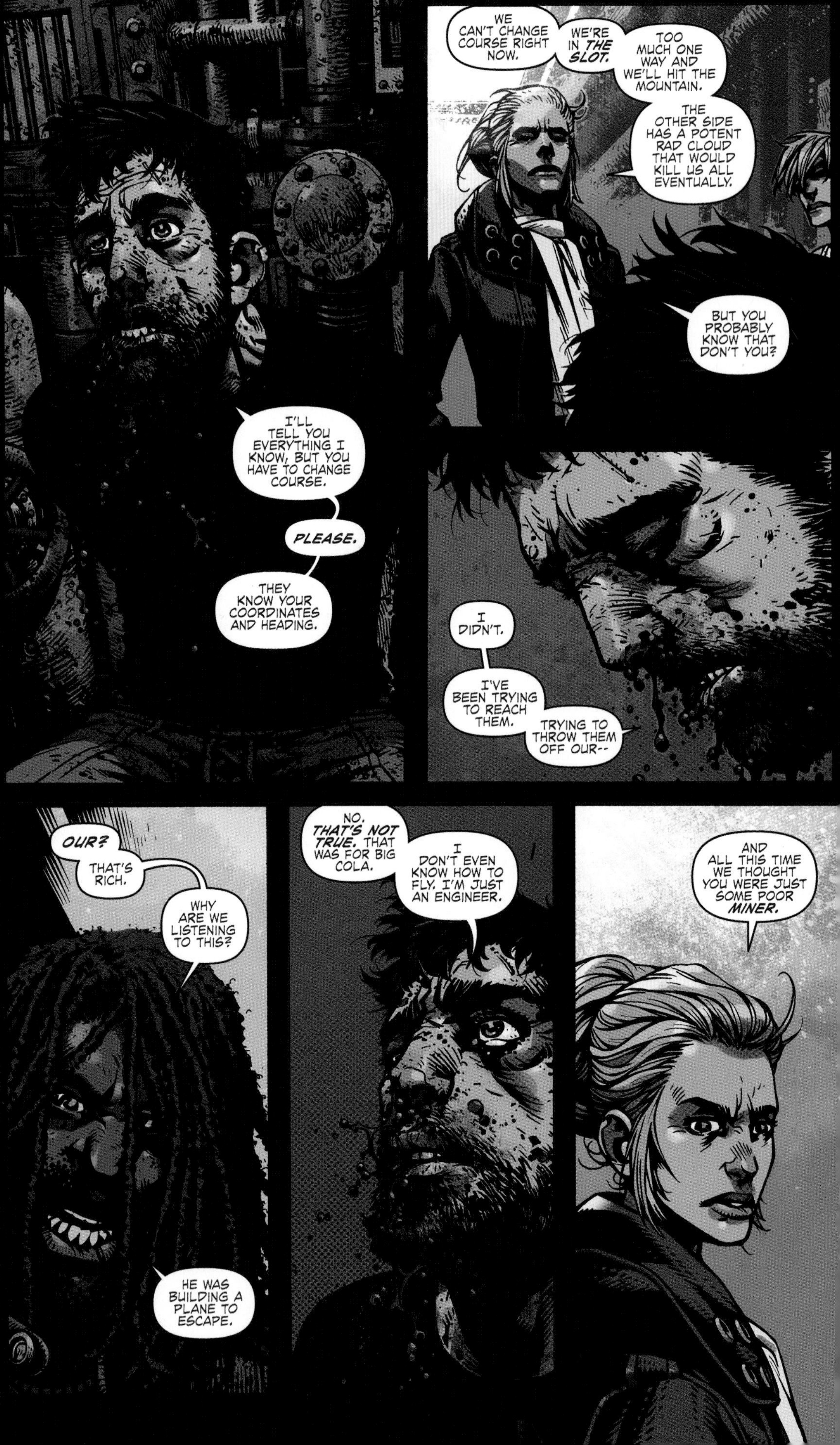
WE CAN'T CHANGE COURSE RIGHT NOW.
WE'RE IN THE SLOT.
TOO MUCH ONE WAY AND WE'LL HIT THE MOUNTAIN.
THE OTHER SIDE HAS A POTENT RAD CLOUD THAT WOULD KILL US ALL EVENTUALLY.
BUT YOU PROBABLY KNOW THAT DON'T YOU?
I'LL TELL YOU EVERYTHING I KNOW, BUT YOU HAVE TO CHANGE COURSE.
PLEASE.
THEY KNOW YOUR COORDINATES AND HEADING.
I DIDN'T.
I'VE BEEN TRYING TO REACH THEM.
TRYING TO THROW THEM OFF OUR--
OUR?
THAT'S RICH.
WHY ARE WE LISTENING TO THIS?
HE WAS BUILDING A PLANE TO ESCAPE.
NO. THAT'S NOT TRUE. THAT WAS FOR BIG COLA.
I DON'T EVEN KNOW HOW TO FLY. I'M JUST AN ENGINEER.
AND ALL THIS TIME WE THOUGHT YOU WERE JUST SOME POOR MINER.

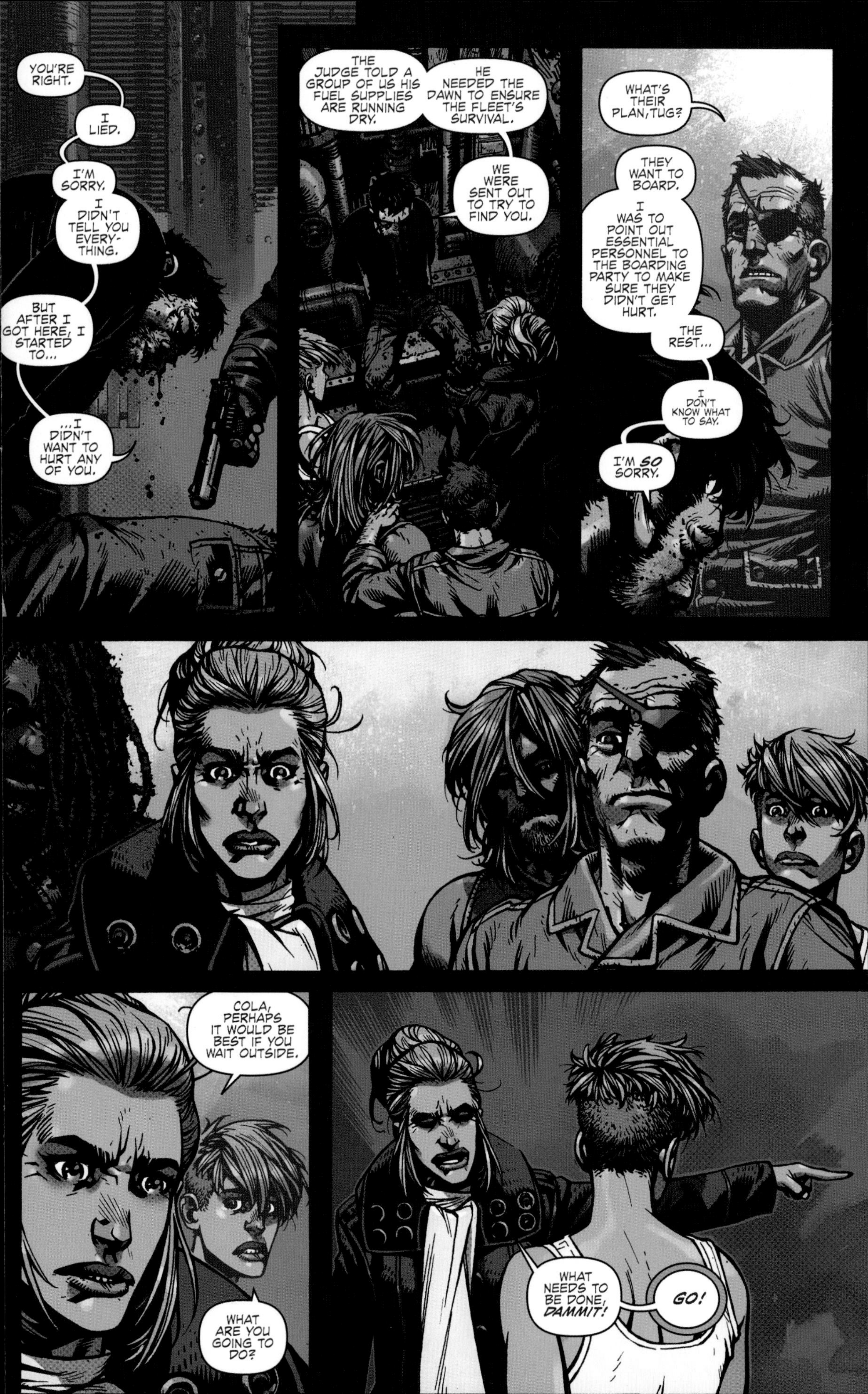
YOU'RE RIGHT.
I LIED.
I'M SORRY.
I DIDN'T TELL YOU EVERY-THING.
BUT AFTER I GOT HERE, I STARTED TO...
...I DIDN'T WANT TO HURT ANY OF YOU.
THE JUDGE TOLD A GROUP OF US HIS FUEL SUPPLIES ARE RUNNING DRY.
HE NEEDED THE DAWN TO ENSURE THE FLEET'S SURVIVAL.
WE WERE SENT OUT TO TRY TO FIND YOU.
WHAT'S THEIR PLAN, TUG?
THEY WANT TO BOARD.
I WAS TO POINT OUT ESSENTIAL PERSONNEL TO THE BOARDING PARTY TO MAKE SURE THEY DIDN'T GET HURT.
THE REST...
I DON'T KNOW WHAT TO SAY.
I'M SO SORRY.
COLA, PERHAPS IT WOULD BE BEST IF YOU WAIT OUTSIDE.
WHAT ARE YOU GOING TO DO?
WHAT NEEDS TO BE DONE, DAMMIT!
GO!

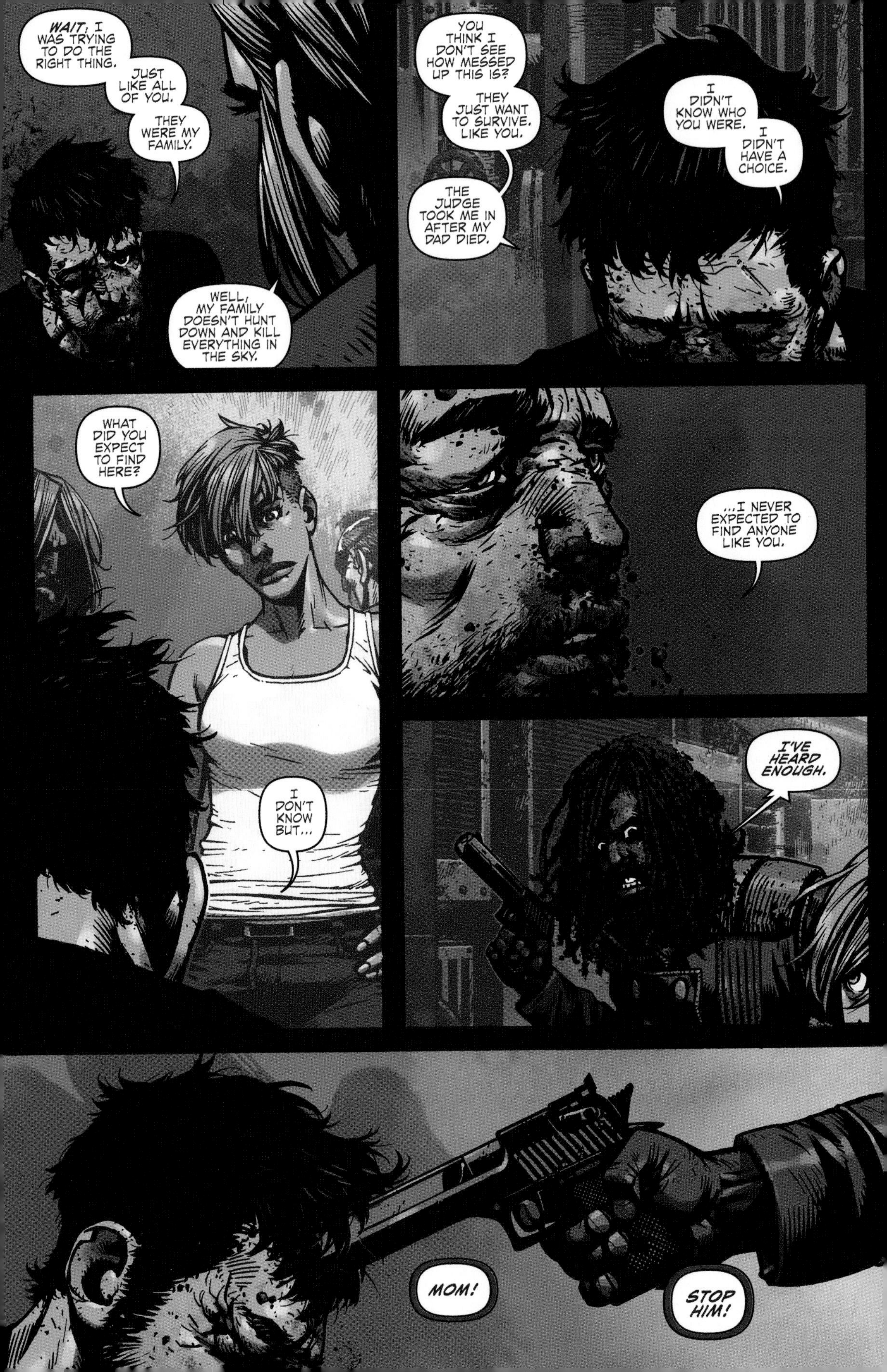
WAIT, I WAS TRYING TO DO THE RIGHT THING.
JUST LIKE ALL OF YOU.
THEY WERE MY FAMILY.
WELL, MY FAMILY DOESN'T HUNT DOWN AND KILL EVERYTHING IN THE SKY.
YOU THINK I DON'T SEE HOW MESSED UP THIS IS?
THEY JUST WANT TO SURVIVE. LIKE YOU.
THE JUDGE TOOK ME IN AFTER MY DAD DIED.
I DIDN'T KNOW WHO YOU WERE.
I DIDN'T HAVE A CHOICE.
WHAT DID YOU EXPECT TO FIND HERE?
I DON'T KNOW BUT...
...I NEVER EXPECTED TO FIND ANYONE LIKE YOU.
I'VE HEARD ENOUGH.
MOM!
STOP HIM!

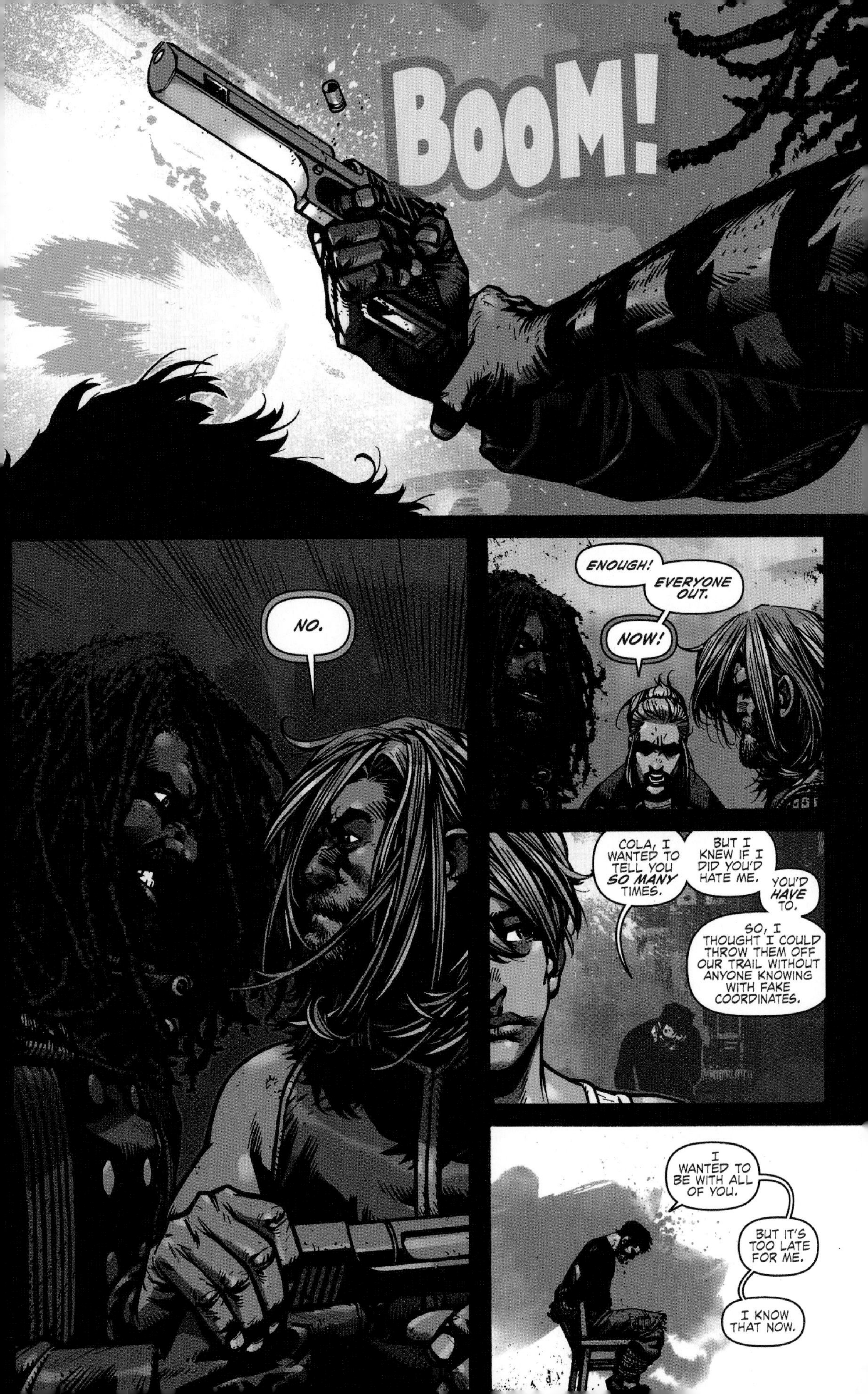
BOOM!
NO.
ENOUGH!
EVERYONE OUT.
NOW!
COLA, I WANTED TO TELL YOU SO MANY TIMES.
BUT I KNEW IF I DID YOU'D HATE ME.
YOU'D HAVE TO.
SO, I THOUGHT I COULD THROW THEM OFF OUR TRAIL WITHOUT ANYONE KNOWING WITH FAKE COORDINATES.
I WANTED TO BE WITH ALL OF YOU.
BUT IT'S TOO LATE FOR ME.
I KNOW THAT NOW.

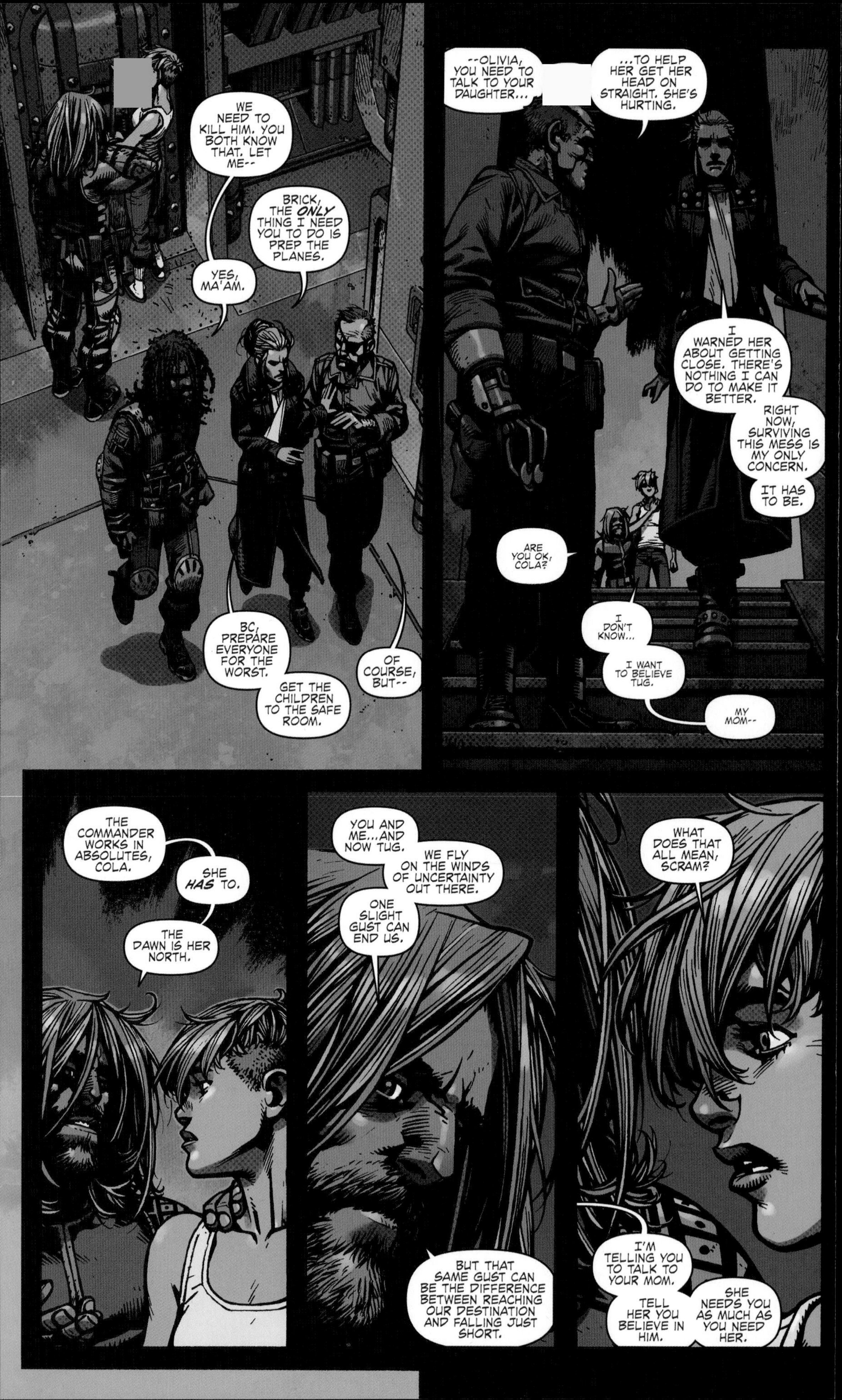
WE NEED TO KILL HIM. YOU BOTH KNOW THAT. LET ME--
BRICK, THE ONLY THING I NEED YOU TO DO IS PREP THE PLANES.
YES, MA'AM.
BC, PREPARE EVERYONE FOR THE WORST.
GET THE CHILDREN TO THE SAFE ROOM.
OF COURSE, BUT--
--OLIVIA, YOU NEED TO TALK TO YOUR DAUGHTER...
...TO HELP HER GET HER HEAD ON STRAIGHT. SHE'S HURTING.
I WARNED HER ABOUT GETTING CLOSE. THERE'S NOTHING I CAN DO TO MAKE IT BETTER.
RIGHT NOW, SURVIVING THIS MESS IS MY ONLY CONCERN.
IT HAS TO BE.
ARE YOU OK, COLA?
I DON'T KNOW...
I WANT TO BELIEVE TUG.
MY MOM--
THE COMMANDER WORKS IN ABSOLUTES, COLA.
SHE HAS TO.
THE DAWN IS HER NORTH.
YOU AND ME...AND NOW TUG.
WE FLY ON THE WINDS OF UNCERTAINTY OUT THERE.
ONE SLIGHT GUST CAN END US.
BUT THAT SAME GUST CAN BE THE DIFFERENCE BETWEEN REACHING OUR DESTINATION AND FALLING JUST SHORT.
WHAT DOES THAT ALL MEAN, SCRAM?
I'M TELLING YOU TO TALK TO YOUR MOM.
TELL HER YOU BELIEVE IN HIM.
SHE NEEDS YOU AS MUCH AS YOU NEED HER.

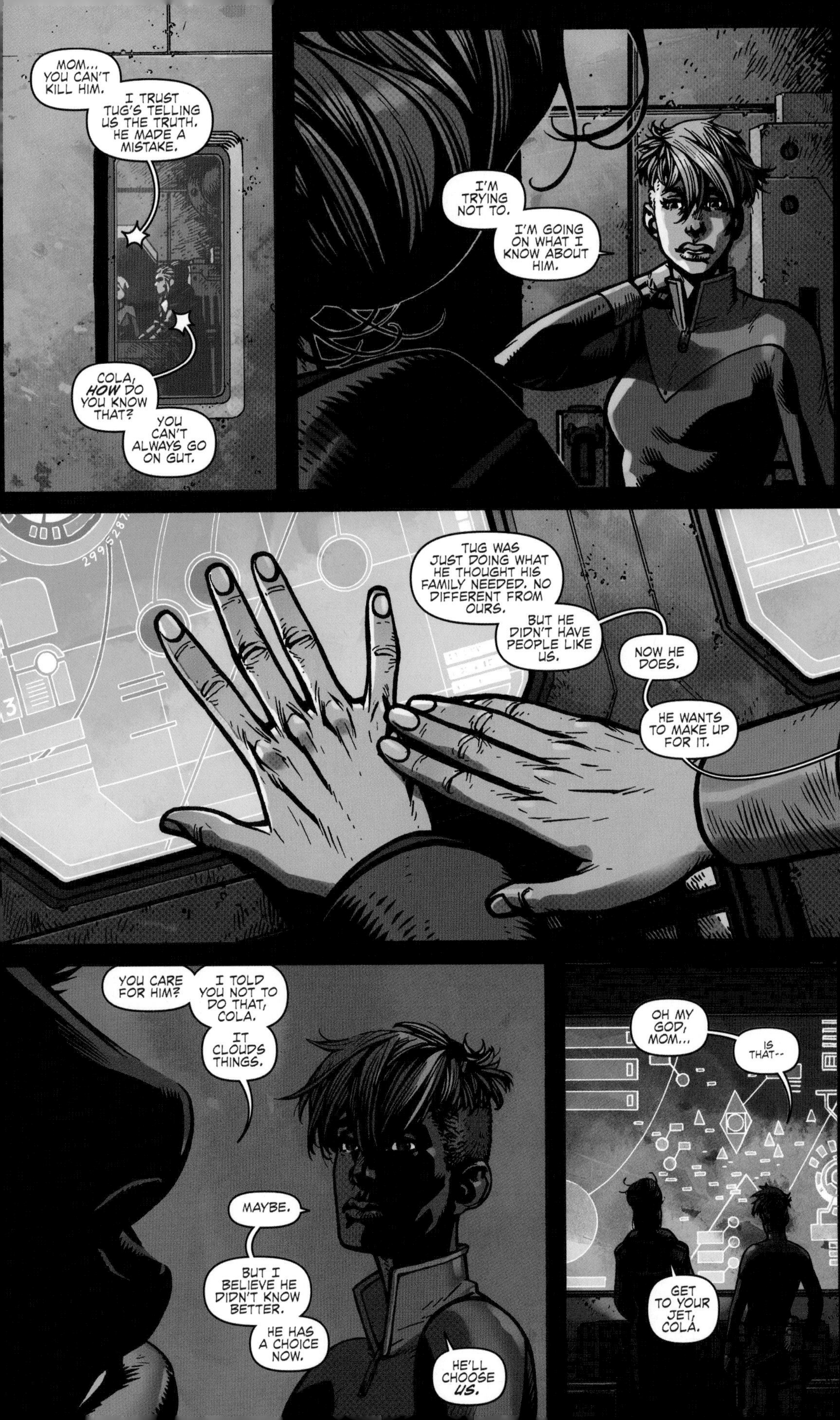
MOM... YOU CAN'T KILL HIM.
I TRUST TUG'S TELLING US THE TRUTH. HE MADE A MISTAKE.
COLA, HOW DO YOU KNOW THAT?
YOU CAN'T ALWAYS GO ON GUT.
I'M TRYING NOT TO.
I'M GOING ON WHAT I KNOW ABOUT HIM.
TUG WAS JUST DOING WHAT HE THOUGHT HIS FAMILY NEEDED. NO DIFFERENT FROM OURS.
BUT HE DIDN'T HAVE PEOPLE LIKE US.
NOW HE DOES.
HE WANTS TO MAKE UP FOR IT.
YOU CARE FOR HIM?
I TOLD YOU NOT TO DO THAT, COLA.
IT CLOUDS THINGS.
MAYBE.
BUT I BELIEVE HE DIDN'T KNOW BETTER.
HE HAS A CHOICE NOW.
HE'LL CHOOSE US.
OH MY GOD, MOM...
IS THAT--
GET TO YOUR JET, COLA.

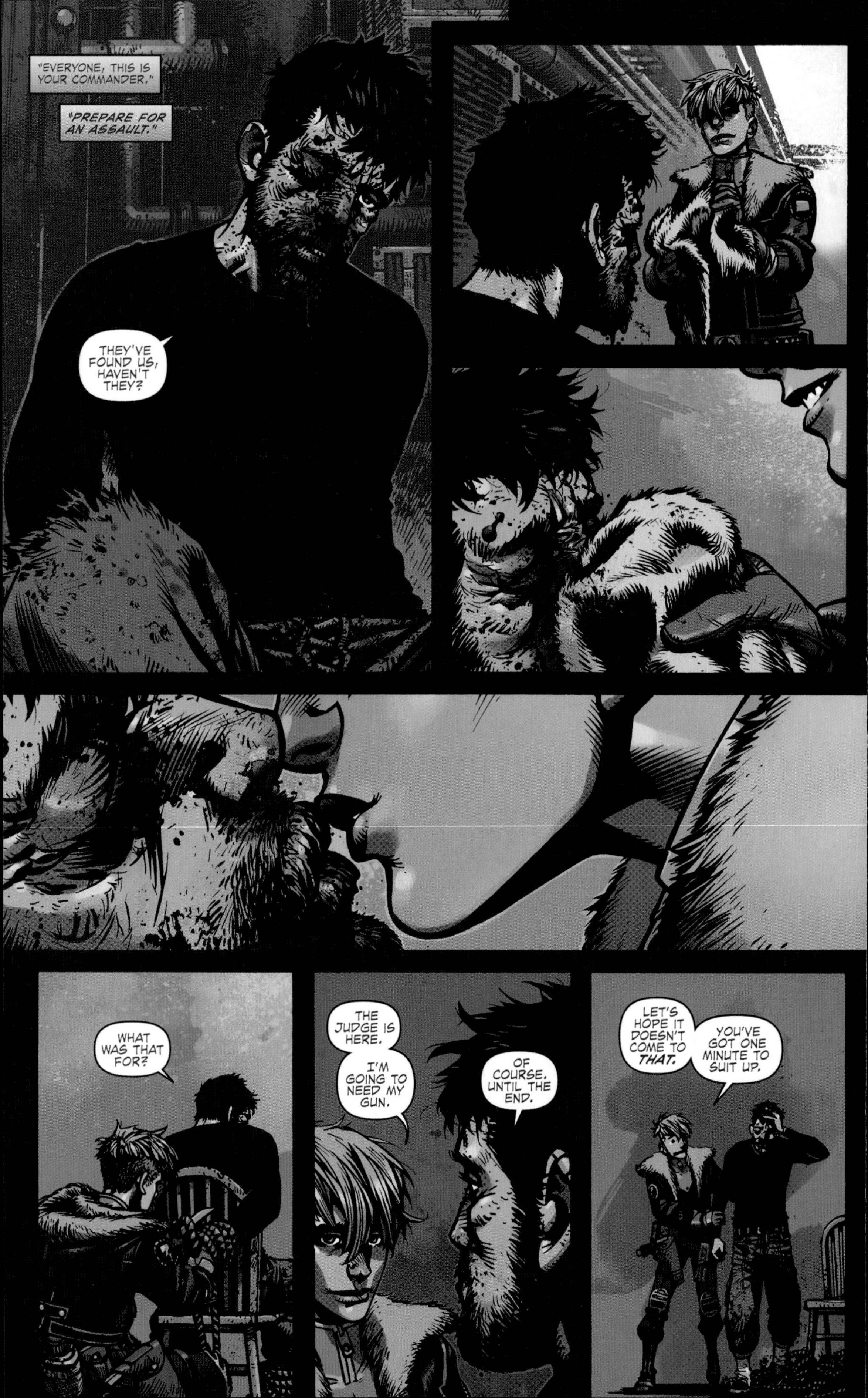
"EVERYONE, THIS IS YOUR COMMANDER."
"PREPARE FOR AN ASSAULT."
THEY'VE FOUND US, HAVEN'T THEY?
WHAT WAS THAT FOR?
THE JUDGE IS HERE.
I'M GOING TO NEED MY GUN.
OF COURSE. UNTIL THE END.
LET'S HOPE IT DOESN'T COME TO THAT.
YOU'VE GOT ONE MINUTE TO SUIT UP.

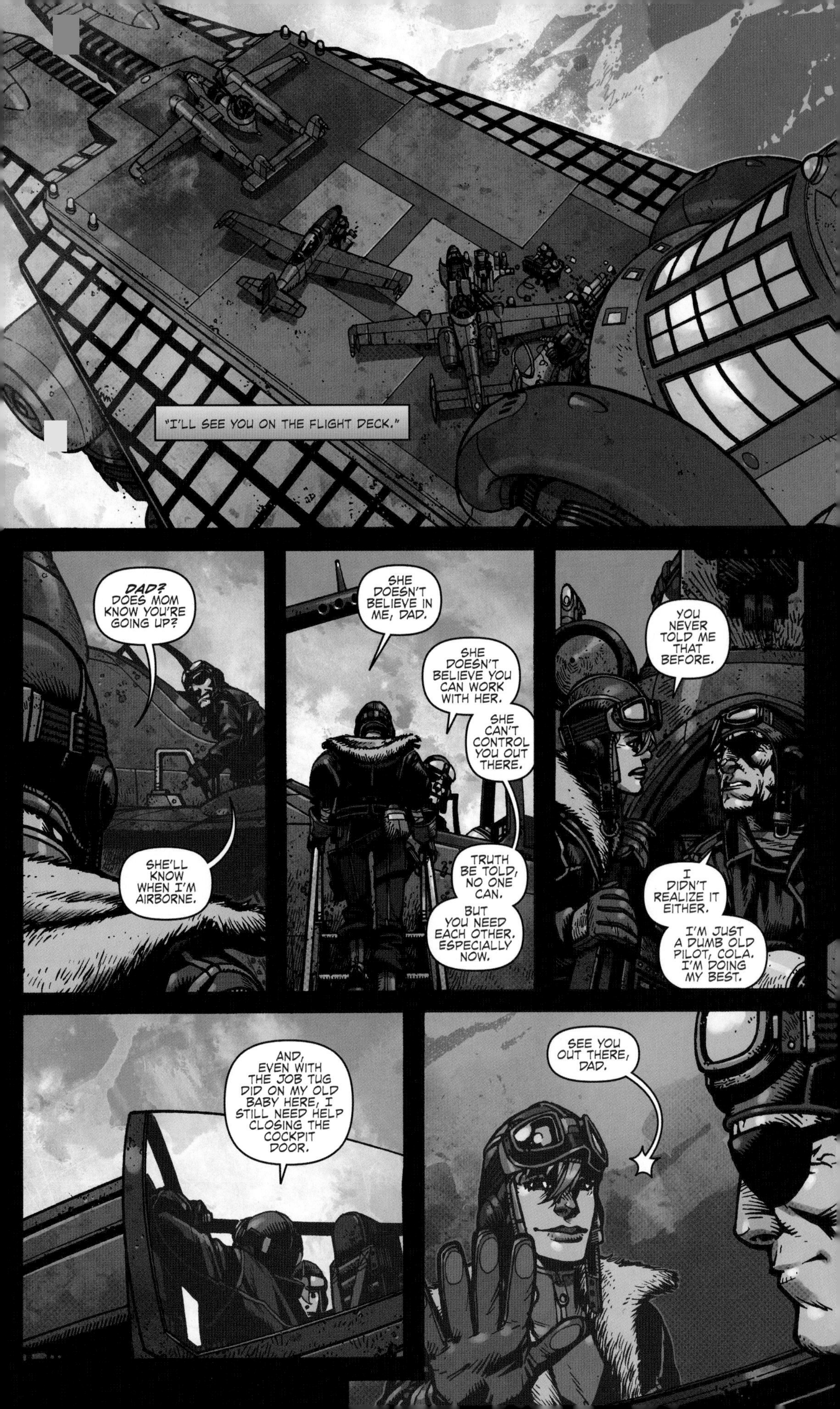
"I'LL SEE YOU ON THE FLIGHT DECK."
DAD? DOES MOM KNOW YOU'RE GOING UP?
SHE'LL KNOW WHEN I'M AIRBORNE.
SHE DOESN'T BELIEVE IN ME, DAD.
SHE DOESN'T BELIEVE YOU CAN WORK WITH HER.
SHE CAN'T CONTROL YOU OUT THERE.
TRUTH BE TOLD, NO ONE CAN.
BUT YOU NEED EACH OTHER. ESPECIALLY NOW.
YOU NEVER TOLD ME THAT BEFORE.
I DIDN'T REALIZE IT EITHER.
I'M JUST A DUMB OLD PILOT, COLA. I'M DOING MY BEST.
AND, EVEN WITH THE JOB TUG DID ON MY OLD BABY HERE, I STILL NEED HELP CLOSING THE COCKPIT DOOR.
SEE YOU OUT THERE, DAD.

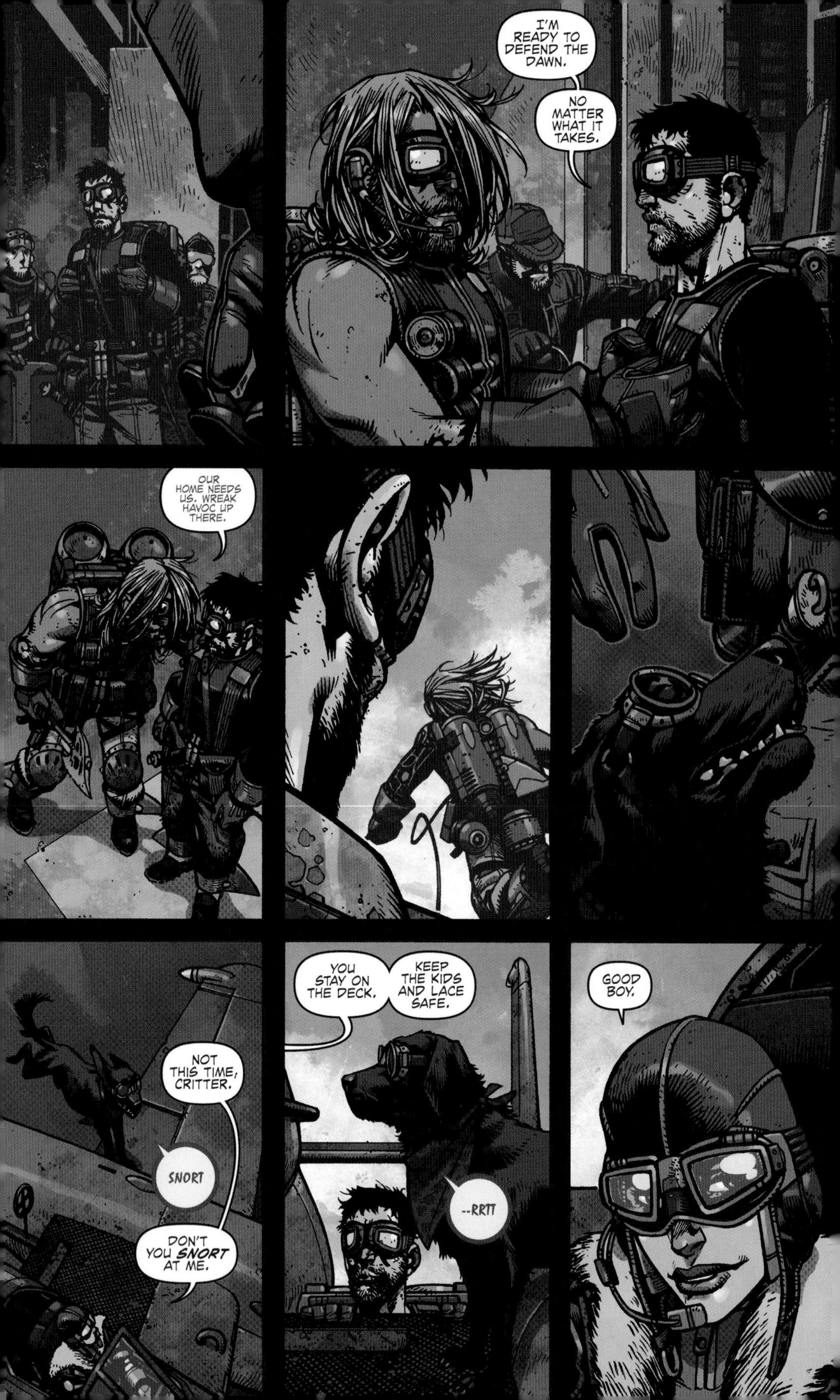

I'M READY TO DEFEND THE DAWN.
NO MATTER WHAT IT TAKES.
OUR HOME NEEDS US. WREAK HAVOC UP THERE.
NOT THIS TIME, CRITTER.
SNORT
DON'T YOU SNORT AT ME.
YOU STAY ON THE DECK.
KEEP THE KIDS AND LACE SAFE.
--RRTT
GOOD BOY.

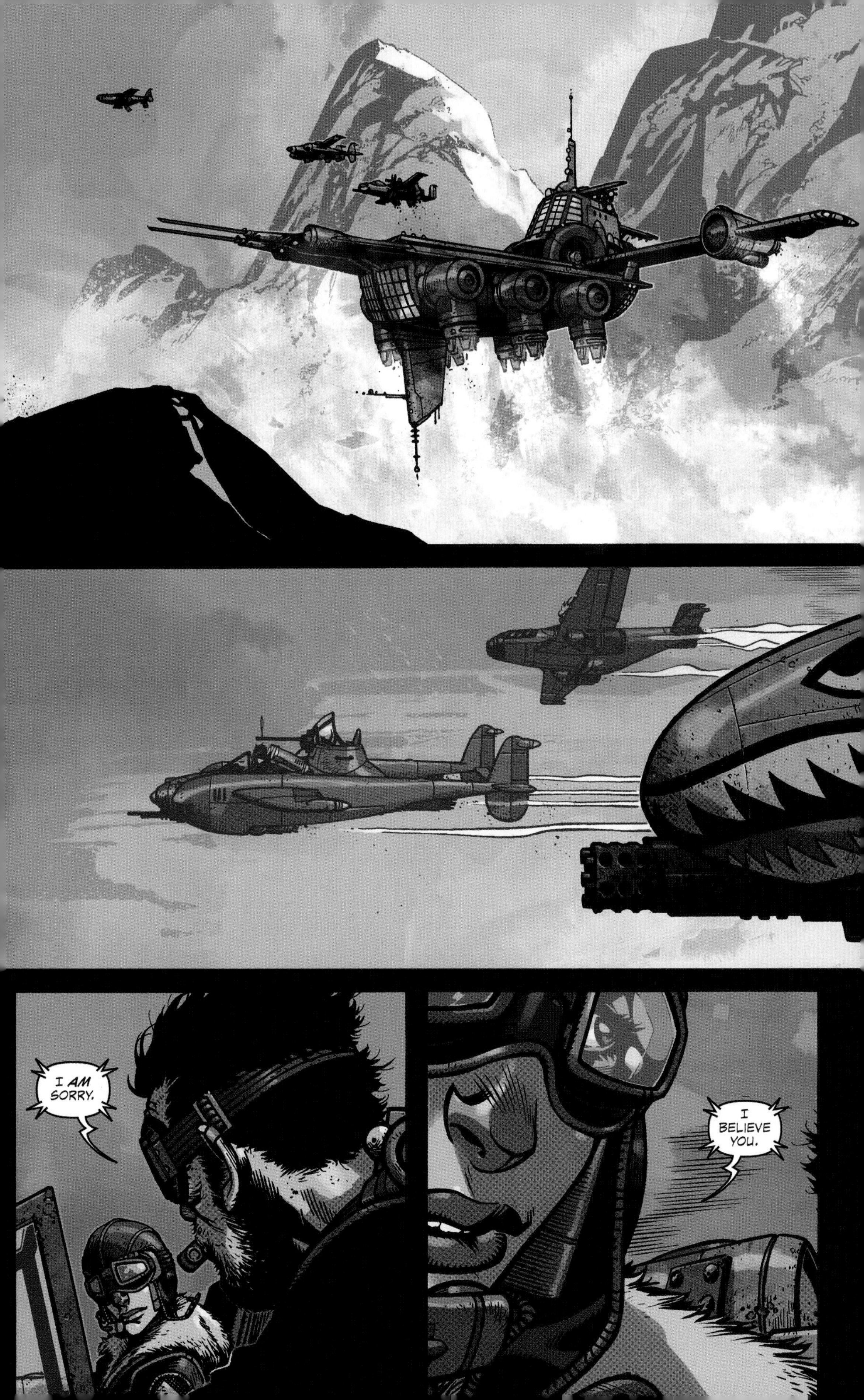
I AM SORRY.
I BELIEVE YOU.

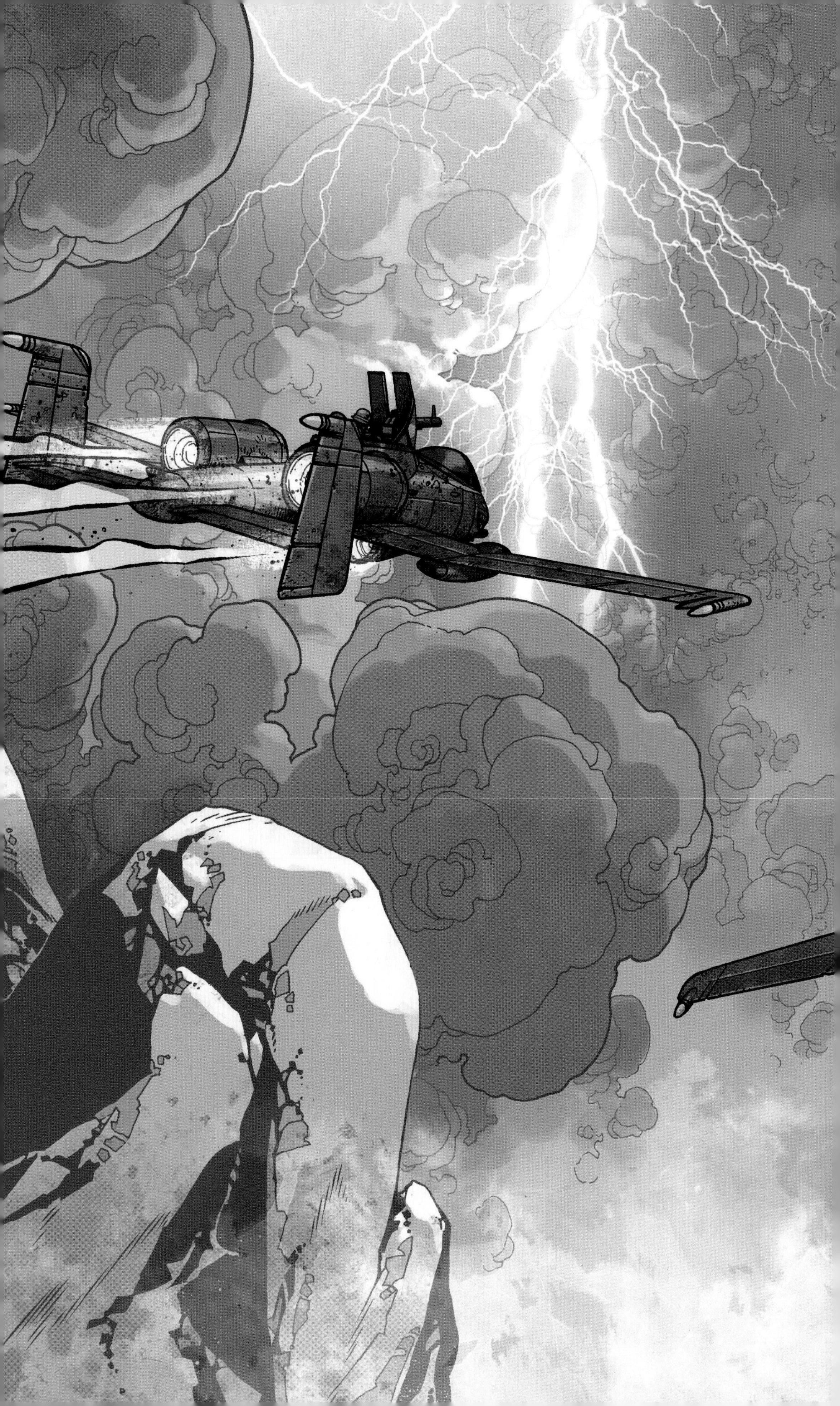

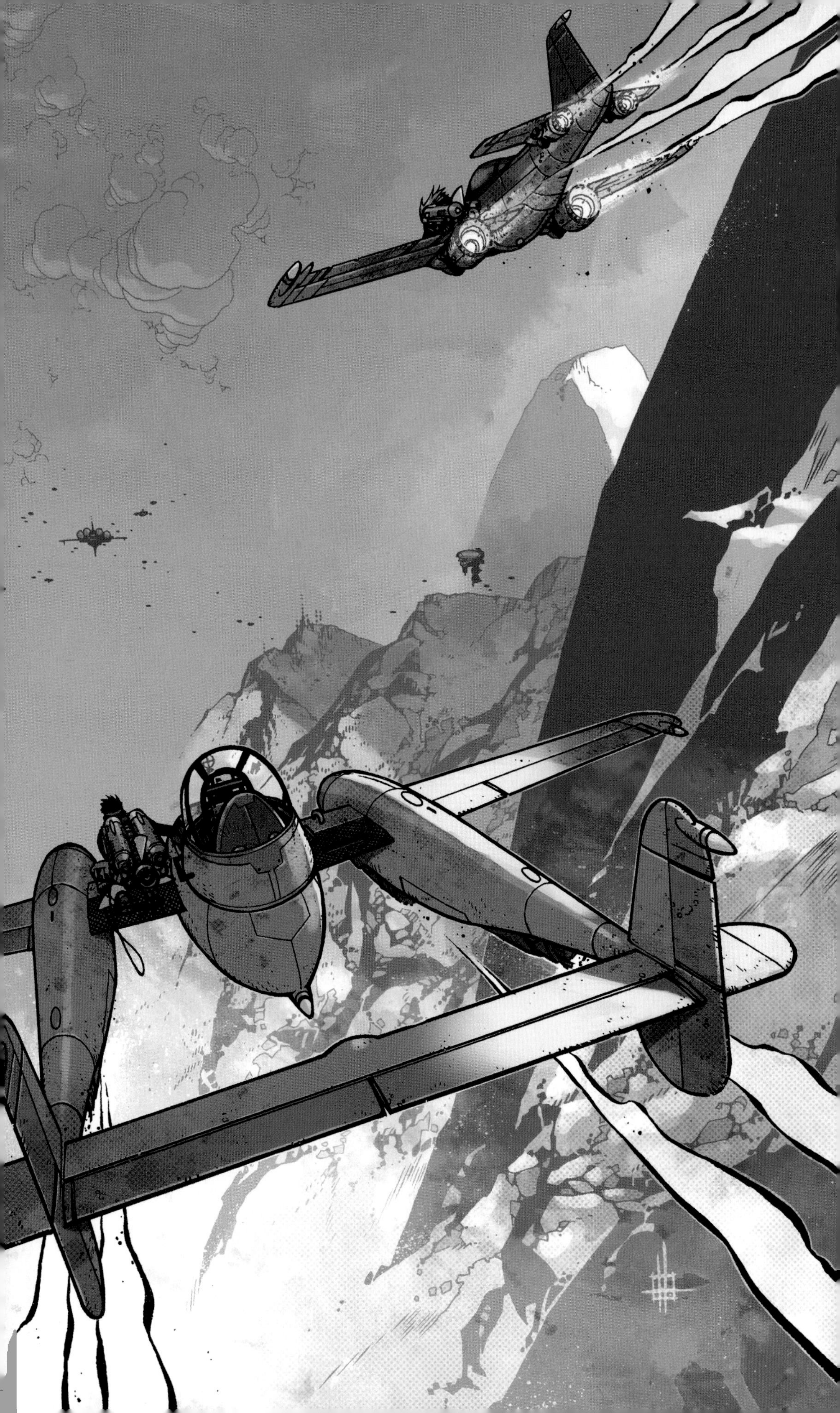

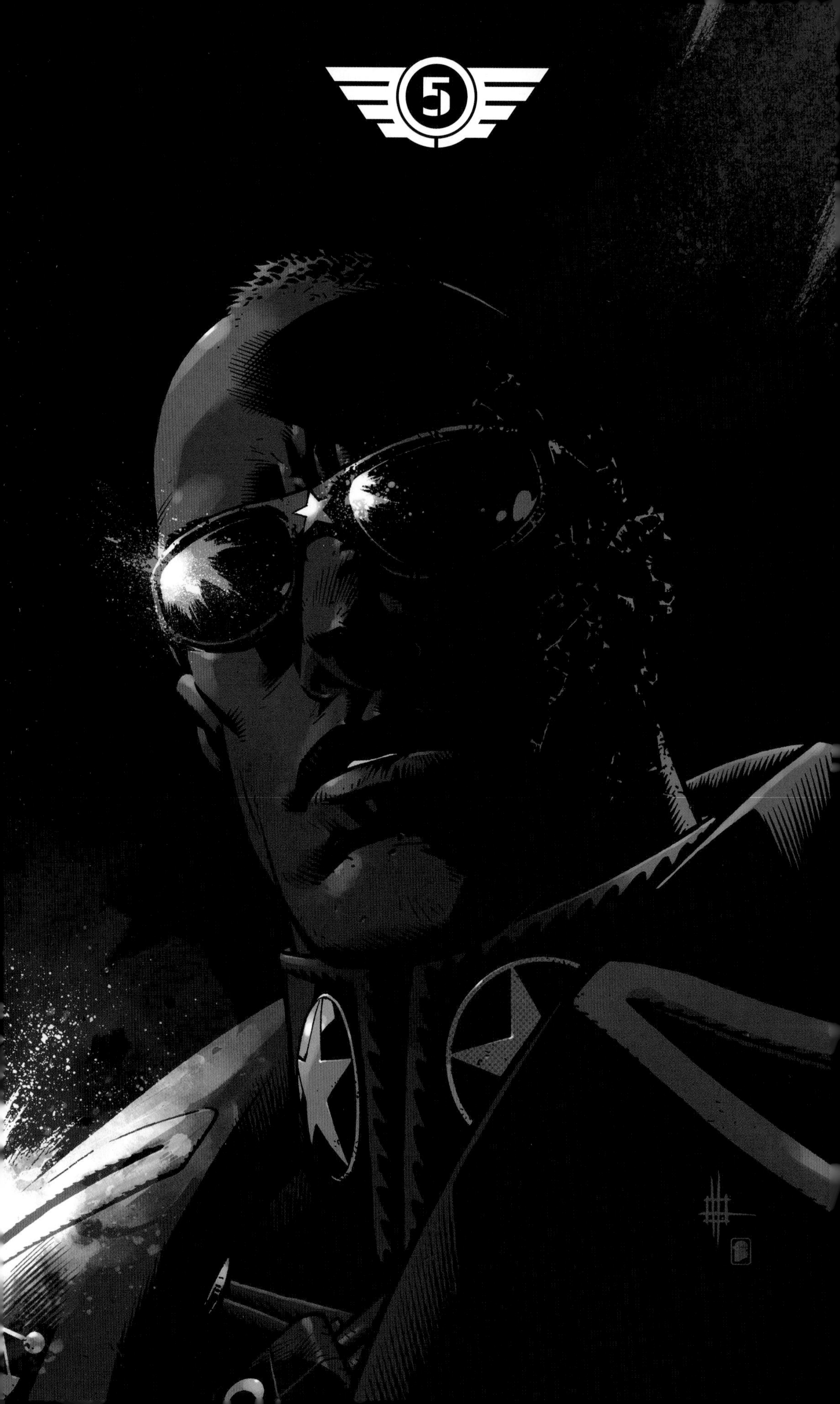

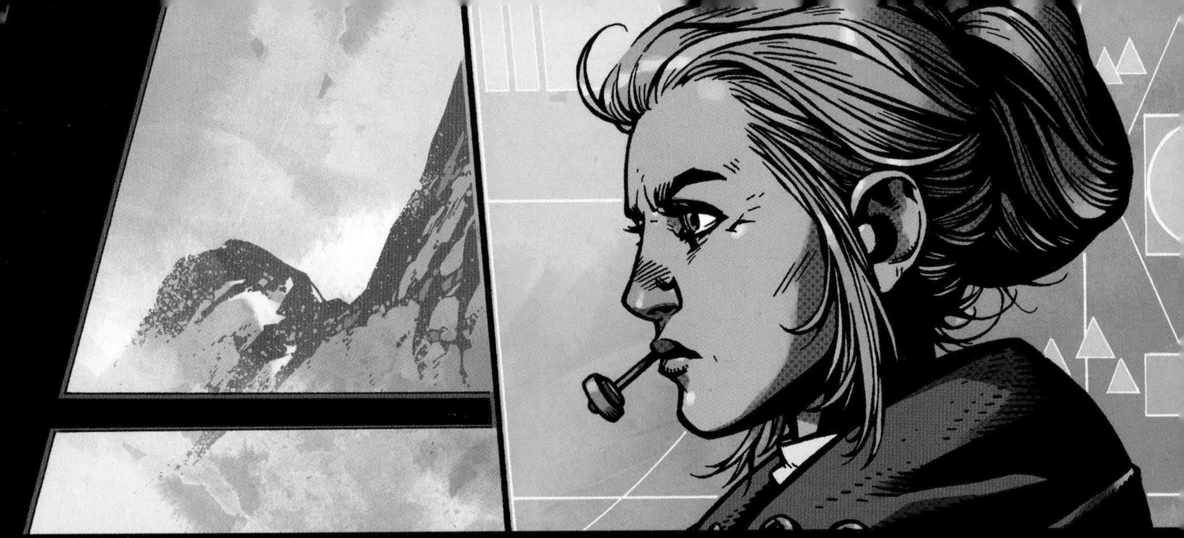

CHAPTER FIVE

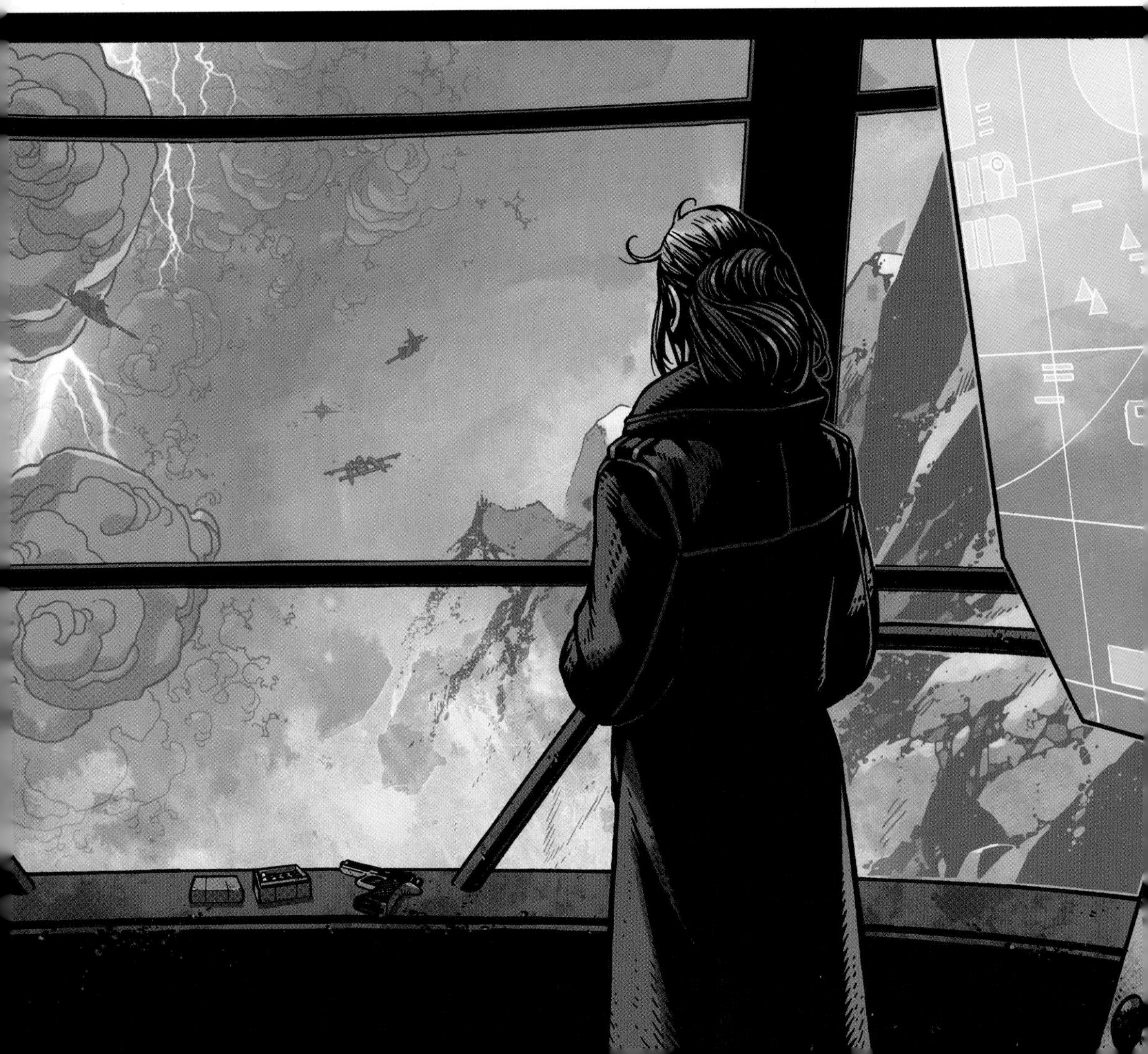

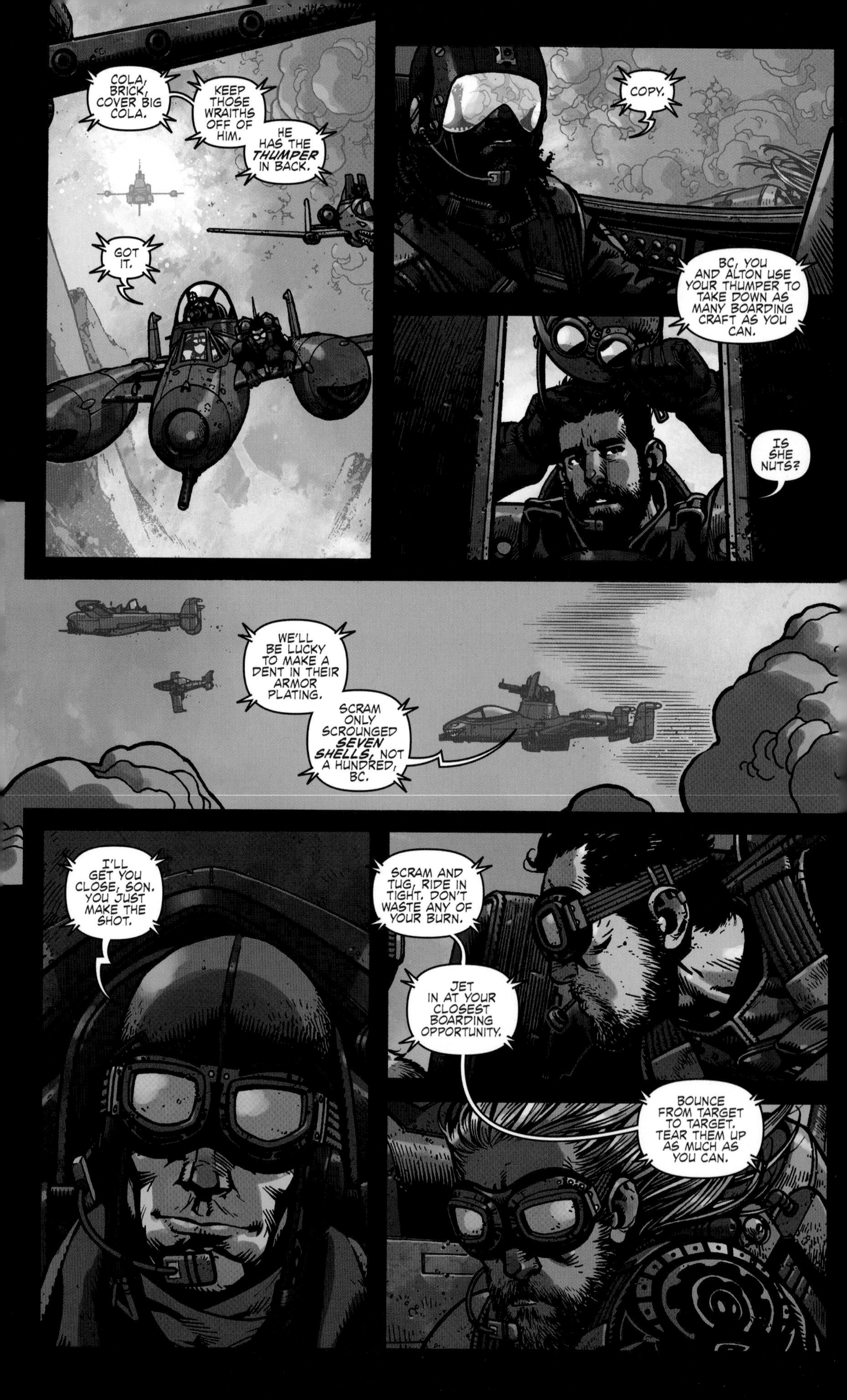
COLA, BRICK, COVER BIG COLA.
KEEP THOSE WRAITHS OFF OF HIM.
HE HAS THE *THUMPER* IN BACK.
GOT IT.
COPY.
BC, YOU AND ALTON USE YOUR THUMPER TO TAKE DOWN AS MANY BOARDING CRAFT AS YOU CAN.
IS SHE NUTS?
WE'LL BE LUCKY TO MAKE A DENT IN THEIR ARMOR PLATING.
SCRAM ONLY SCROUNGED *SEVEN SHELLS,* NOT A HUNDRED, BC.
I'LL GET YOU CLOSE, SON. YOU JUST MAKE THE SHOT.
SCRAM AND TUG, RIDE IN TIGHT. DON'T WASTE ANY OF YOUR BURN.
JET IN AT YOUR CLOSEST BOARDING OPPORTUNITY.
BOUNCE FROM TARGET TO TARGET. TEAR THEM UP AS MUCH AS YOU CAN.

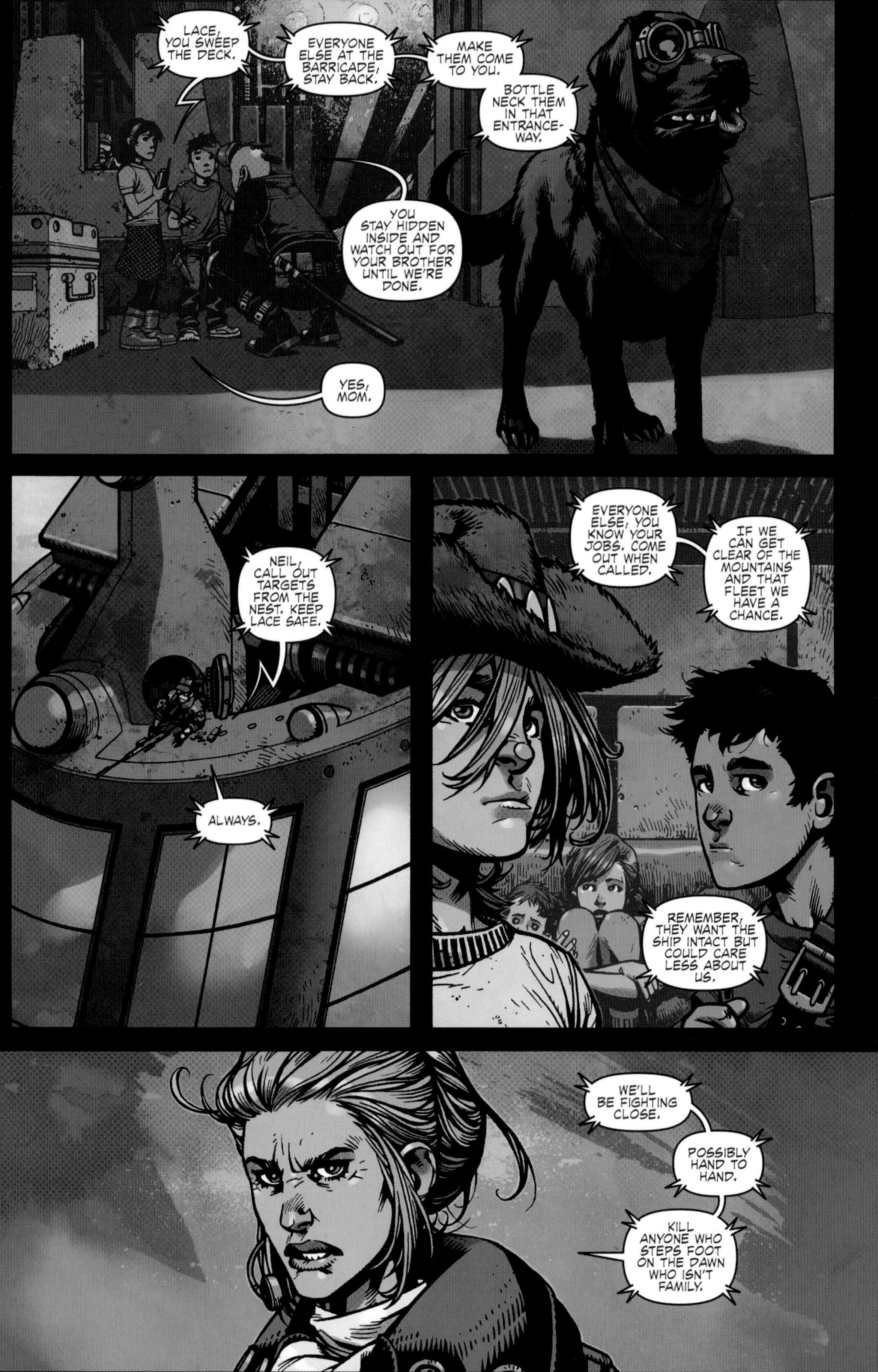
LACE, YOU SWEEP THE DECK.
EVERYONE ELSE AT THE BARRICADE, STAY BACK.
MAKE THEM COME TO YOU.
BOTTLE NECK THEM IN THAT ENTRANCE-WAY.
YOU STAY HIDDEN INSIDE AND WATCH OUT FOR YOUR BROTHER UNTIL WE'RE DONE.
YES, MOM.
NEIL, CALL OUT TARGETS FROM THE NEST. KEEP LACE SAFE.
ALWAYS.
EVERYONE ELSE, YOU KNOW YOUR JOBS. COME OUT WHEN CALLED.
IF WE CAN GET CLEAR OF THE MOUNTAINS AND THAT FLEET WE HAVE A CHANCE.
REMEMBER, THEY WANT THE SHIP INTACT BUT COULD CARE LESS ABOUT US.
WE'LL BE FIGHTING CLOSE.
POSSIBLY HAND TO HAND.
KILL ANYONE WHO STEPS FOOT ON THE DAWN WHO ISN'T FAMILY.

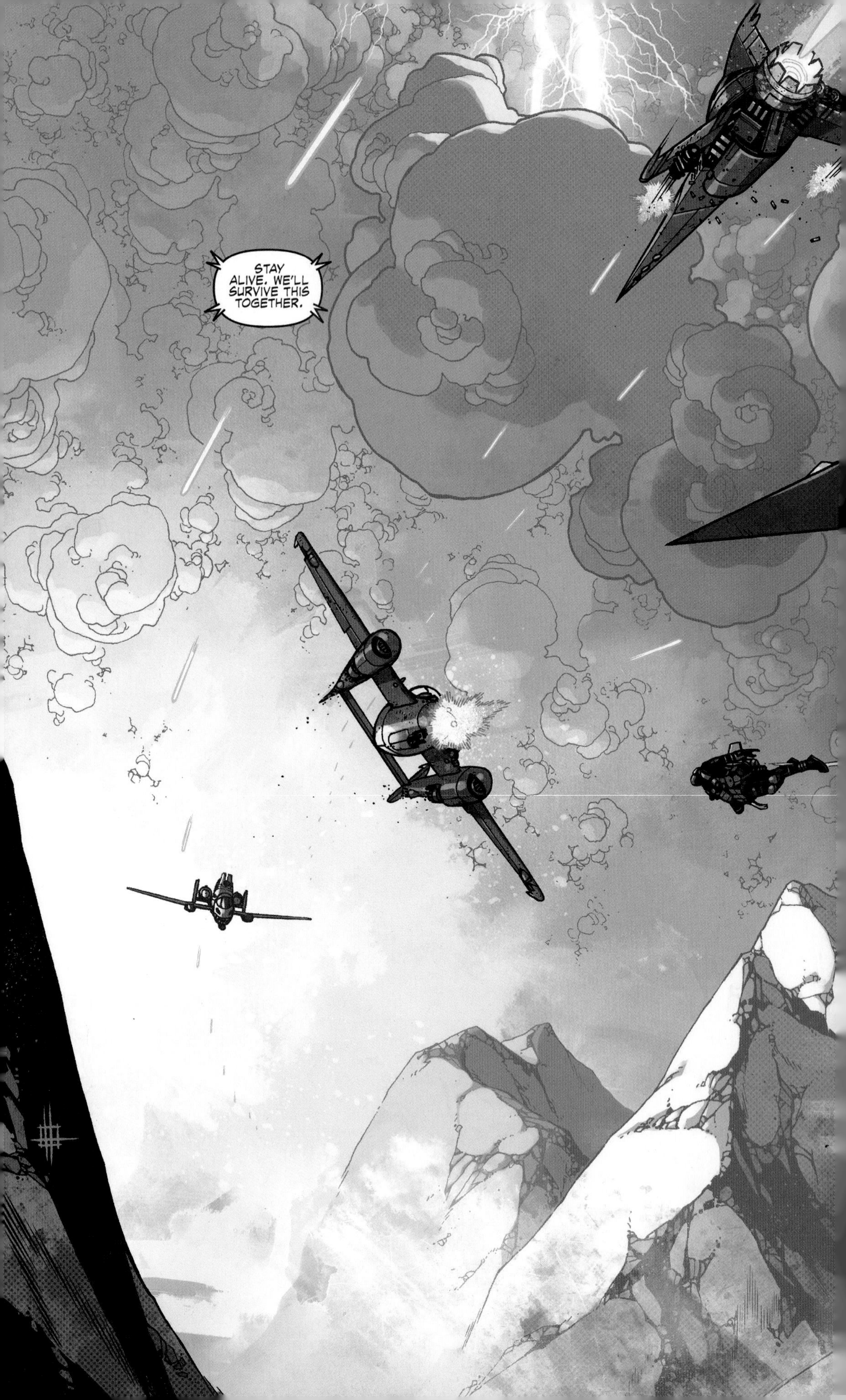
STAY ALIVE. WE'LL SURVIVE THIS TOGETHER.

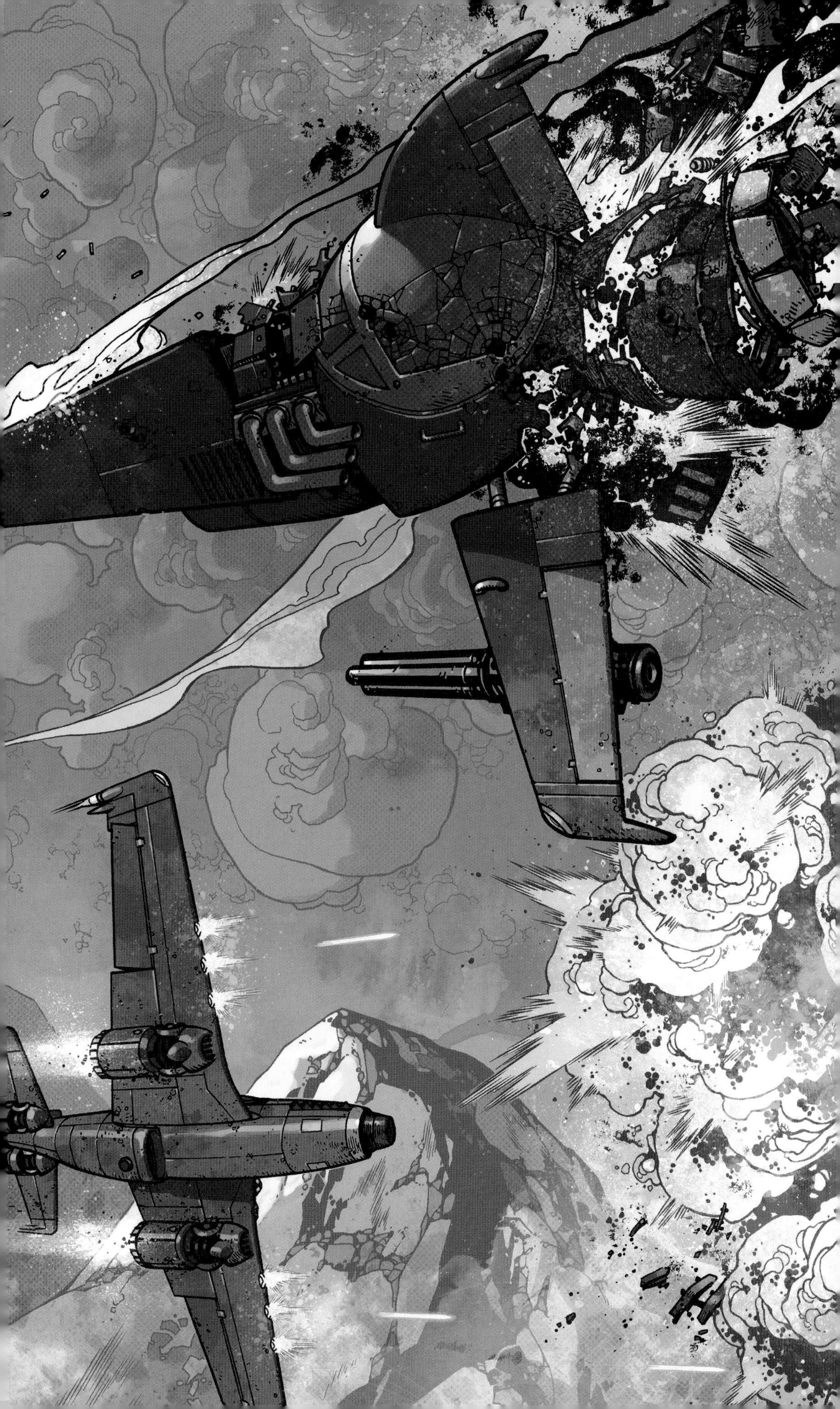

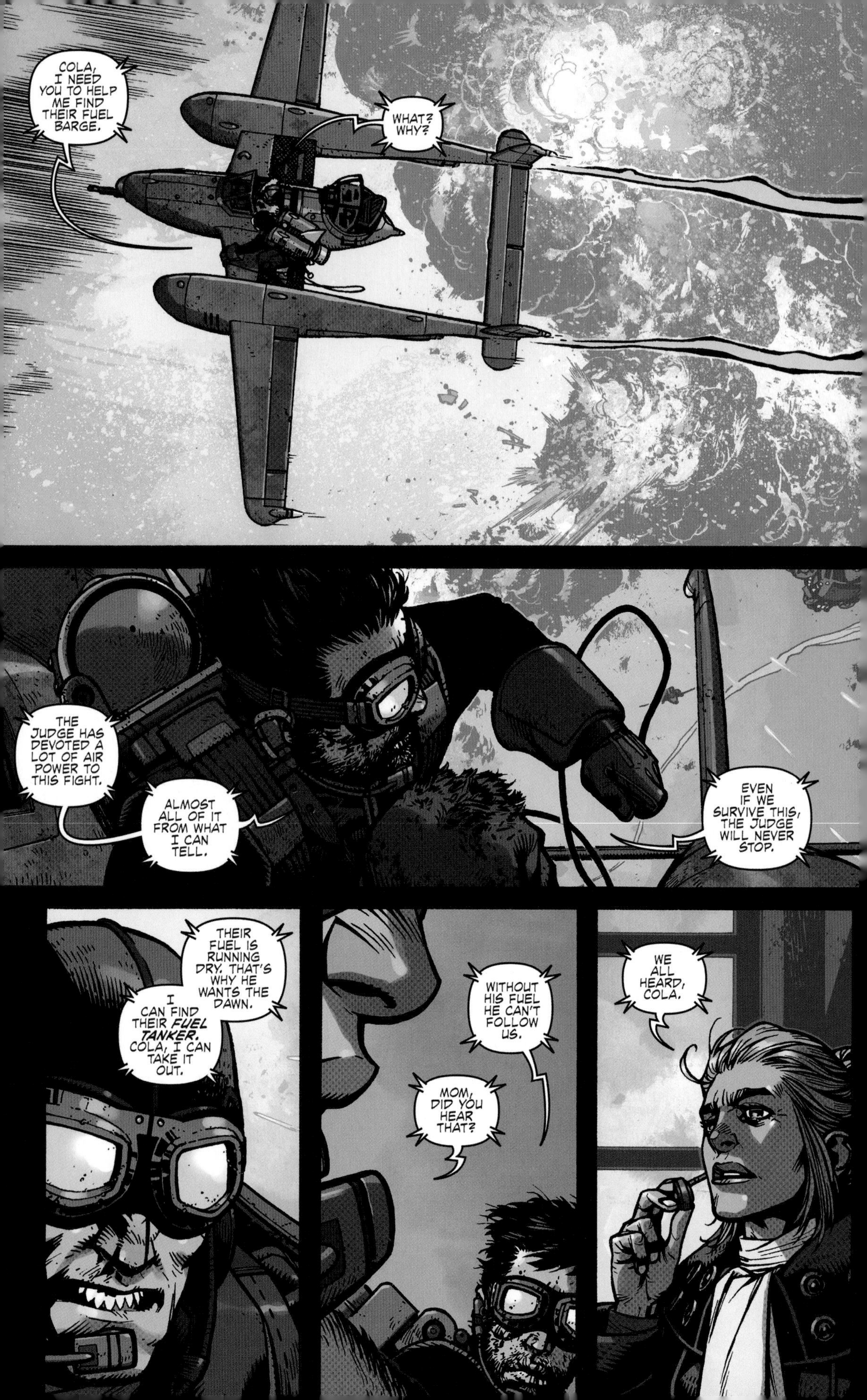
COLA, I NEED YOU TO HELP ME FIND THEIR FUEL BARGE.
WHAT? WHY?
THE JUDGE HAS DEVOTED A LOT OF AIR POWER TO THIS FIGHT.
ALMOST ALL OF IT FROM WHAT I CAN TELL.
EVEN IF WE SURVIVE THIS, THE JUDGE WILL NEVER STOP.
THEIR FUEL IS RUNNING DRY. THAT'S WHY HE WANTS THE DAWN.
I CAN FIND THEIR *FUEL TANKER.* COLA, I CAN TAKE IT OUT.
WITHOUT HIS FUEL HE CAN'T FOLLOW US.
MOM, DID YOU HEAR THAT?
WE ALL HEARD, COLA.

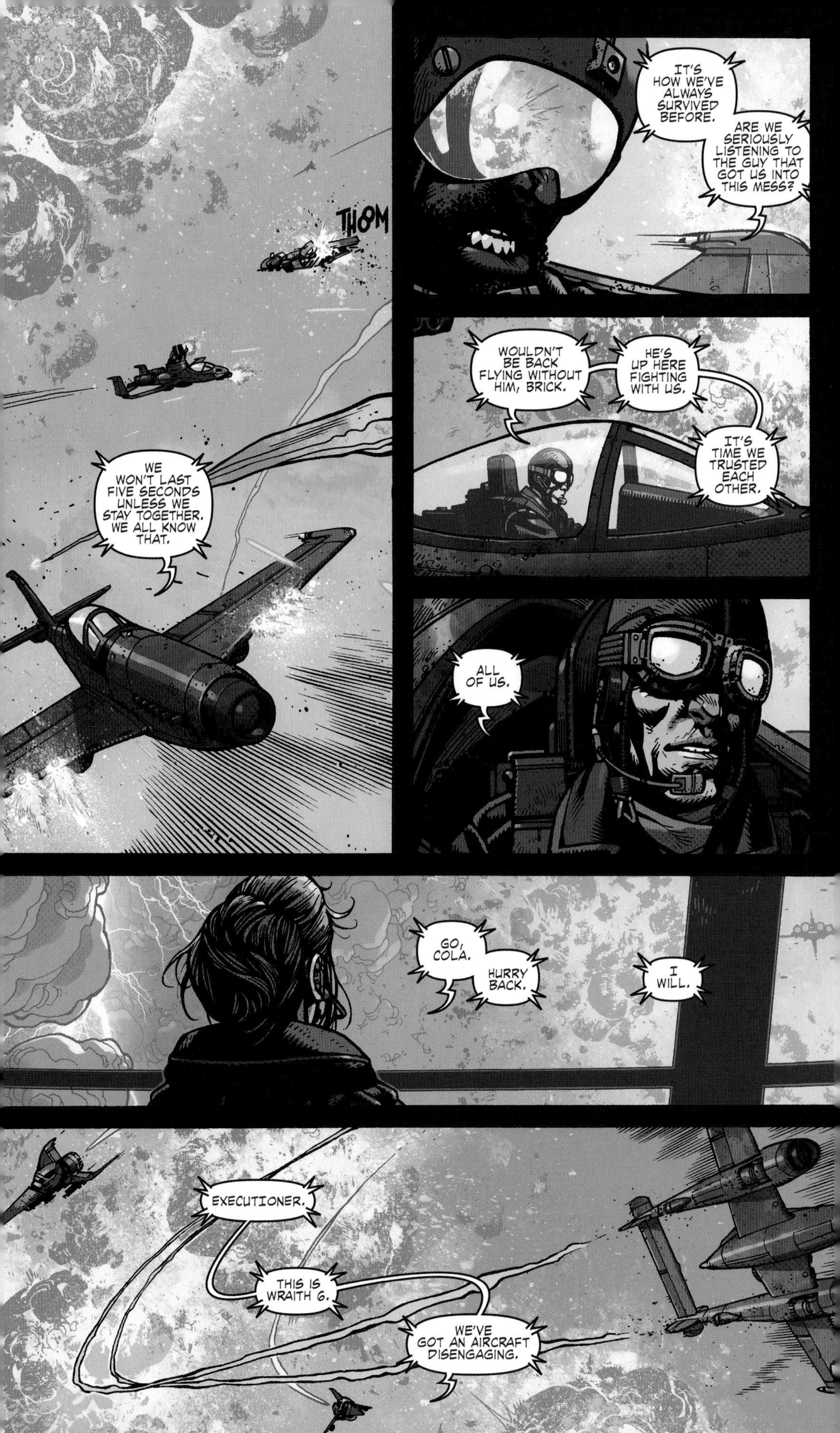
THOOM
WE WON'T LAST FIVE SECONDS UNLESS WE STAY TOGETHER. WE ALL KNOW THAT.
IT'S HOW WE'VE ALWAYS SURVIVED BEFORE.
ARE WE SERIOUSLY LISTENING TO THE GUY THAT GOT US INTO THIS MESS?
WOULDN'T BE BACK FLYING WITHOUT HIM, BRICK.
HE'S UP HERE FIGHTING WITH US.
IT'S TIME WE TRUSTED EACH OTHER.
ALL OF US.
GO, COLA.
HURRY BACK.
I WILL.
EXECUTIONER.
THIS IS WRAITH 6.
WE'VE GOT AN AIRCRAFT DISENGAGING.

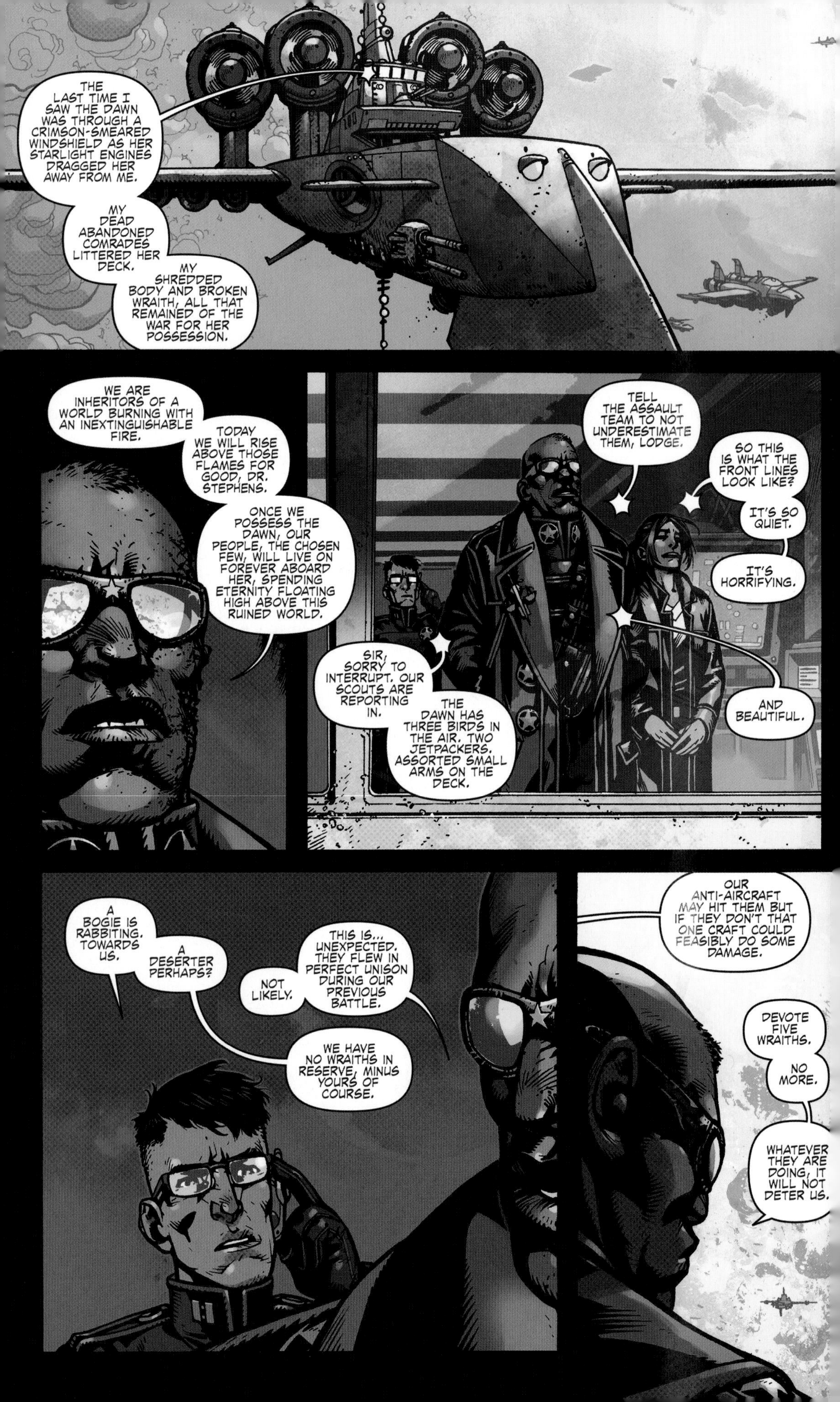
THE LAST TIME I SAW THE DAWN WAS THROUGH A CRIMSON-SMEARED WINDSHIELD AS HER STARLIGHT ENGINES DRAGGED HER AWAY FROM ME.
MY DEAD ABANDONED COMRADES LITTERED HER DECK.
MY SHREDDED BODY AND BROKEN WRAITH, ALL THAT REMAINED OF THE WAR FOR HER POSSESSION.
WE ARE INHERITORS OF A WORLD BURNING WITH AN INEXTINGUISHABLE FIRE.
TODAY WE WILL RISE ABOVE THOSE FLAMES FOR GOOD, DR. STEPHENS.
ONCE WE POSSESS THE DAWN, OUR PEOPLE, THE CHOSEN FEW, WILL LIVE ON FOREVER ABOARD HER, SPENDING ETERNITY FLOATING HIGH ABOVE THIS RUINED WORLD.
TELL THE ASSAULT TEAM TO NOT UNDERESTIMATE THEM, LODGE.
SO THIS IS WHAT THE FRONT LINES LOOK LIKE?
IT'S SO QUIET.
IT'S HORRIFYING.
AND BEAUTIFUL.
SIR, SORRY TO INTERRUPT. OUR SCOUTS ARE REPORTING IN.
THE DAWN HAS THREE BIRDS IN THE AIR. TWO JETPACKERS. ASSORTED SMALL ARMS ON THE DECK.
A BOGIE IS RABBITING. TOWARDS US.
A DESERTER PERHAPS?
NOT LIKELY.
THIS IS... UNEXPECTED. THEY FLEW IN PERFECT UNISON DURING OUR PREVIOUS BATTLE.
WE HAVE NO WRAITHS IN RESERVE, MINUS YOURS OF COURSE.
OUR ANTI-AIRCRAFT MAY HIT THEM BUT IF THEY DON'T THAT ONE CRAFT COULD FEASIBLY DO SOME DAMAGE.
DEVOTE FIVE WRAITHS.
NO MORE.
WHATEVER THEY ARE DOING, IT WILL NOT DETER US.

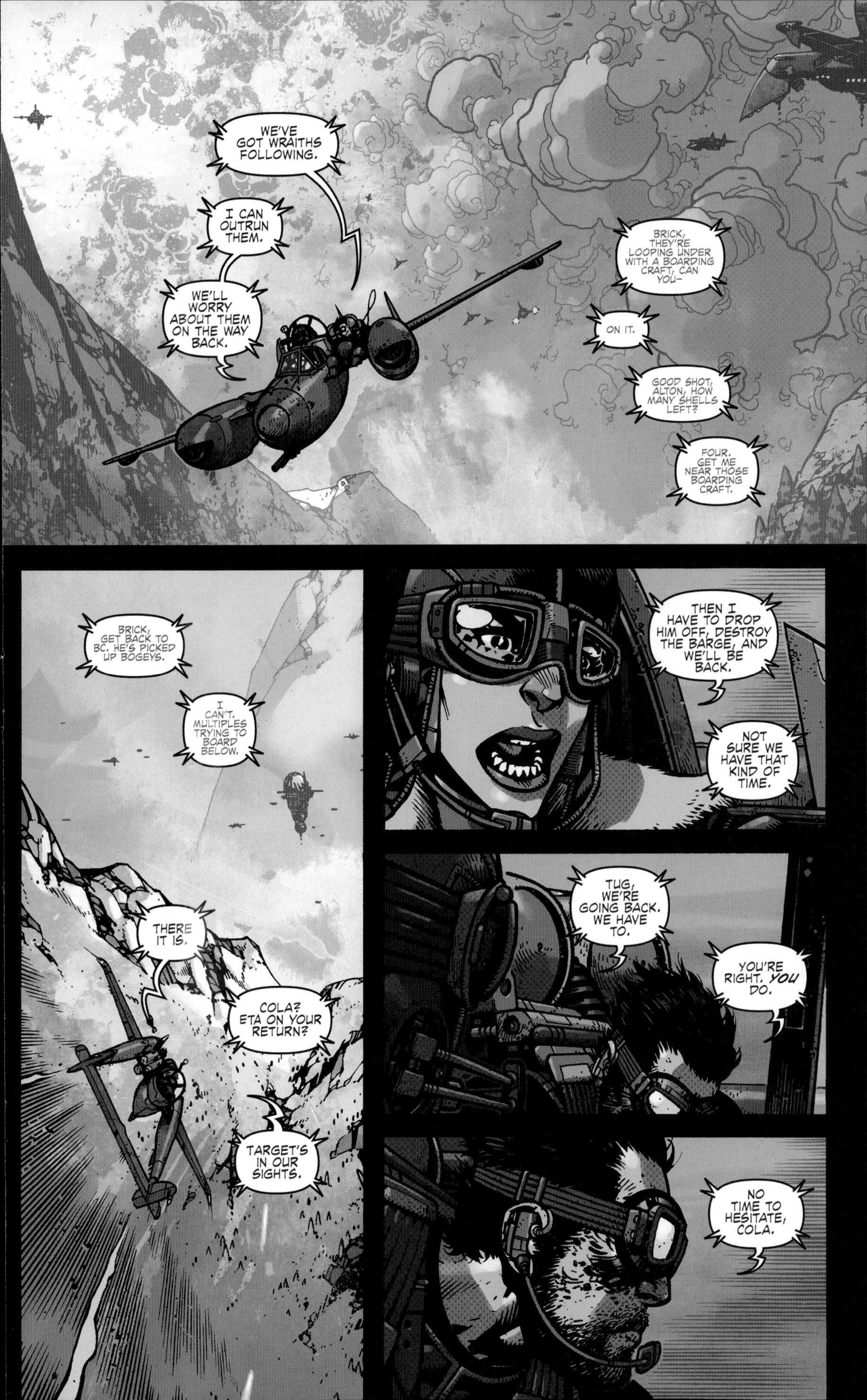
WE'VE GOT WRAITHS FOLLOWING.
I CAN OUTRUN THEM.
WE'LL WORRY ABOUT THEM ON THE WAY BACK.
BRICK, THEY'RE LOOPING UNDER WITH A BOARDING CRAFT, CAN YOU–
ON IT.
GOOD SHOT, ALTON, HOW MANY SHELLS LEFT?
FOUR. GET ME NEAR THOSE BOARDING CRAFT.
BRICK, GET BACK TO BC. HE'S PICKED UP BOGEYS.
I CAN'T. MULTIPLES TRYING TO BOARD BELOW.
THERE IT IS.
COLA? ETA ON YOUR RETURN?
TARGET'S IN OUR SIGHTS.
THEN I HAVE TO DROP HIM OFF, DESTROY THE BARGE, AND WE'LL BE BACK.
NOT SURE WE HAVE THAT KIND OF TIME.
TUG, WE'RE GOING BACK. WE HAVE TO.
YOU'RE RIGHT. *YOU* DO.
NO TIME TO HESITATE, COLA.

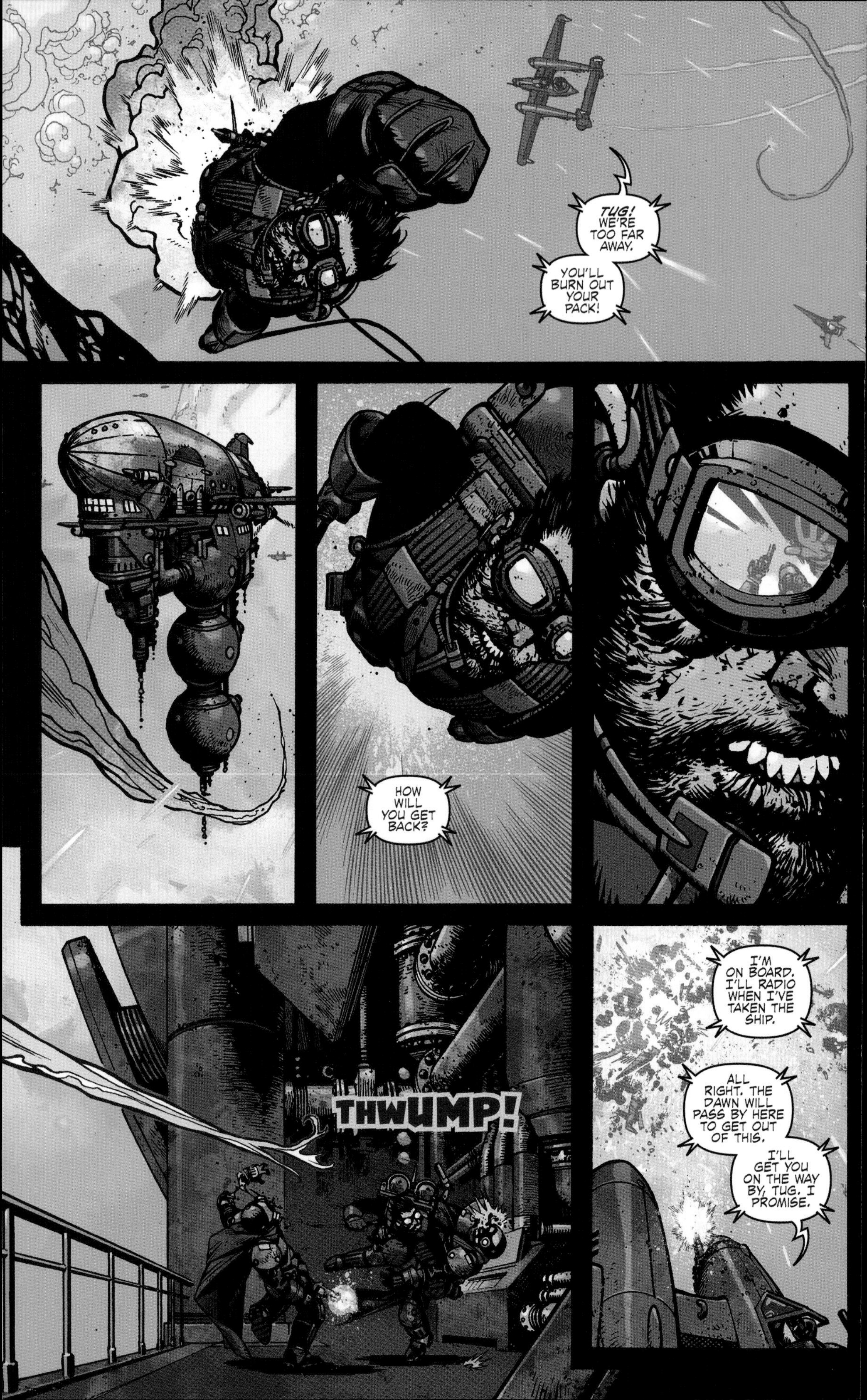
TUG! WE'RE TOO FAR AWAY.
YOU'LL BURN OUT YOUR PACK!
HOW WILL YOU GET BACK?
THWUMP!
I'M ON BOARD. I'LL RADIO WHEN I'VE TAKEN THE SHIP.
ALL RIGHT. THE DAWN WILL PASS BY HERE TO GET OUT OF THIS.
I'LL GET YOU ON THE WAY BY, TUG. I PROMISE.

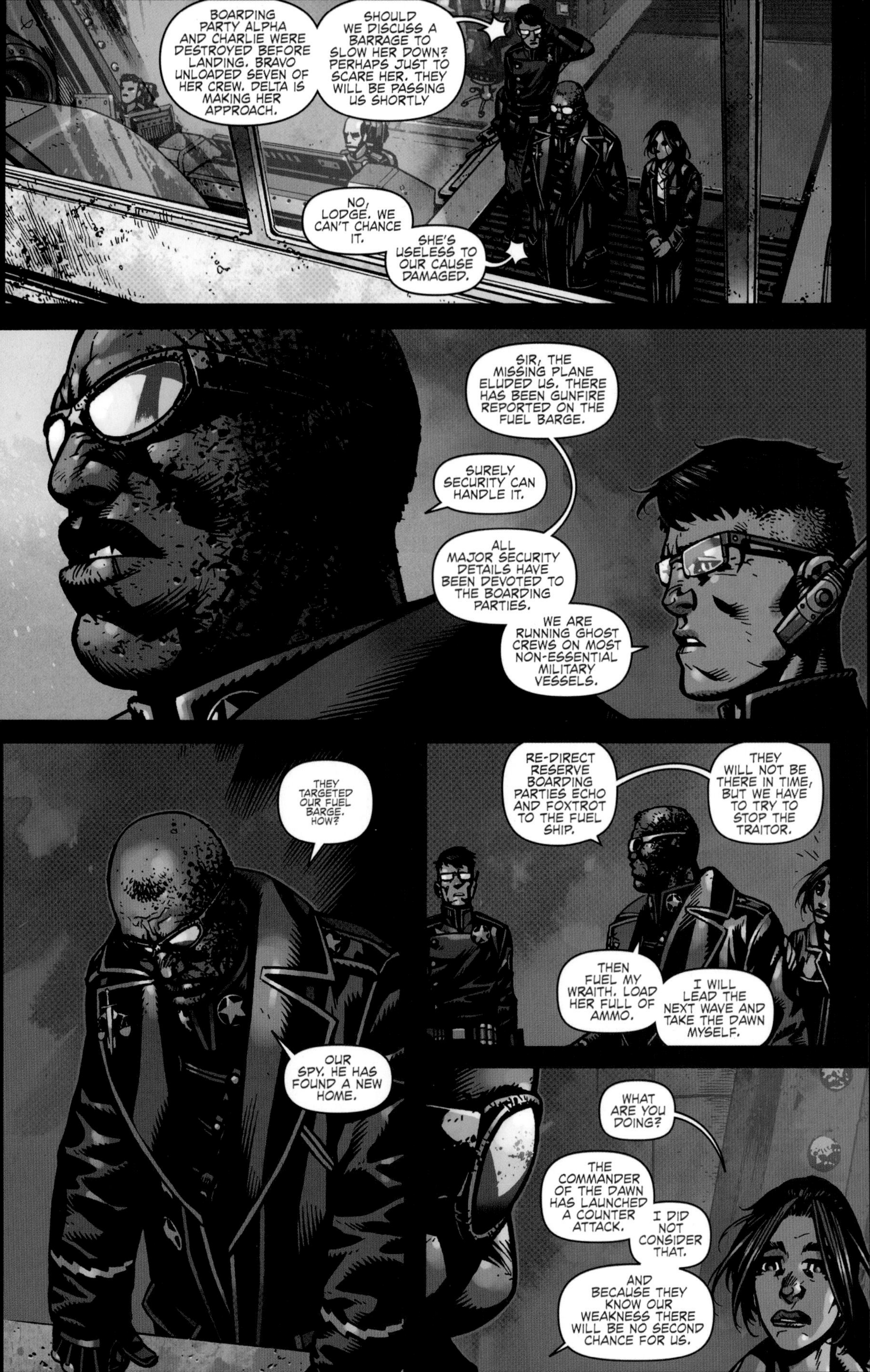
BOARDING PARTY ALPHA AND CHARLIE WERE DESTROYED BEFORE LANDING. BRAVO UNLOADED SEVEN OF HER CREW. DELTA IS MAKING HER APPROACH.
SHOULD WE DISCUSS A BARRAGE TO SLOW HER DOWN? PERHAPS JUST TO SCARE HER. THEY WILL BE PASSING US SHORTLY
NO, LODGE. WE CAN'T CHANCE IT.
SHE'S USELESS TO OUR CAUSE DAMAGED.
SIR, THE MISSING PLANE ELUDED US. THERE HAS BEEN GUNFIRE REPORTED ON THE FUEL BARGE.
SURELY SECURITY CAN HANDLE IT.
ALL MAJOR SECURITY DETAILS HAVE BEEN DEVOTED TO THE BOARDING PARTIES.
WE ARE RUNNING GHOST CREWS ON MOST NON-ESSENTIAL MILITARY VESSELS.
THEY TARGETED OUR FUEL BARGE. HOW?
OUR SPY. HE HAS FOUND A NEW HOME.
RE-DIRECT RESERVE BOARDING PARTIES ECHO AND FOXTROT TO THE FUEL SHIP.
THEY WILL NOT BE THERE IN TIME, BUT WE HAVE TO TRY TO STOP THE TRAITOR.
THEN FUEL MY WRAITH. LOAD HER FULL OF AMMO.
I WILL LEAD THE NEXT WAVE AND TAKE THE DAWN MYSELF.
WHAT ARE YOU DOING?
THE COMMANDER OF THE DAWN HAS LAUNCHED A COUNTER ATTACK.
I DID NOT CONSIDER THAT.
AND BECAUSE THEY KNOW OUR WEAKNESS THERE WILL BE NO SECOND CHANCE FOR US.

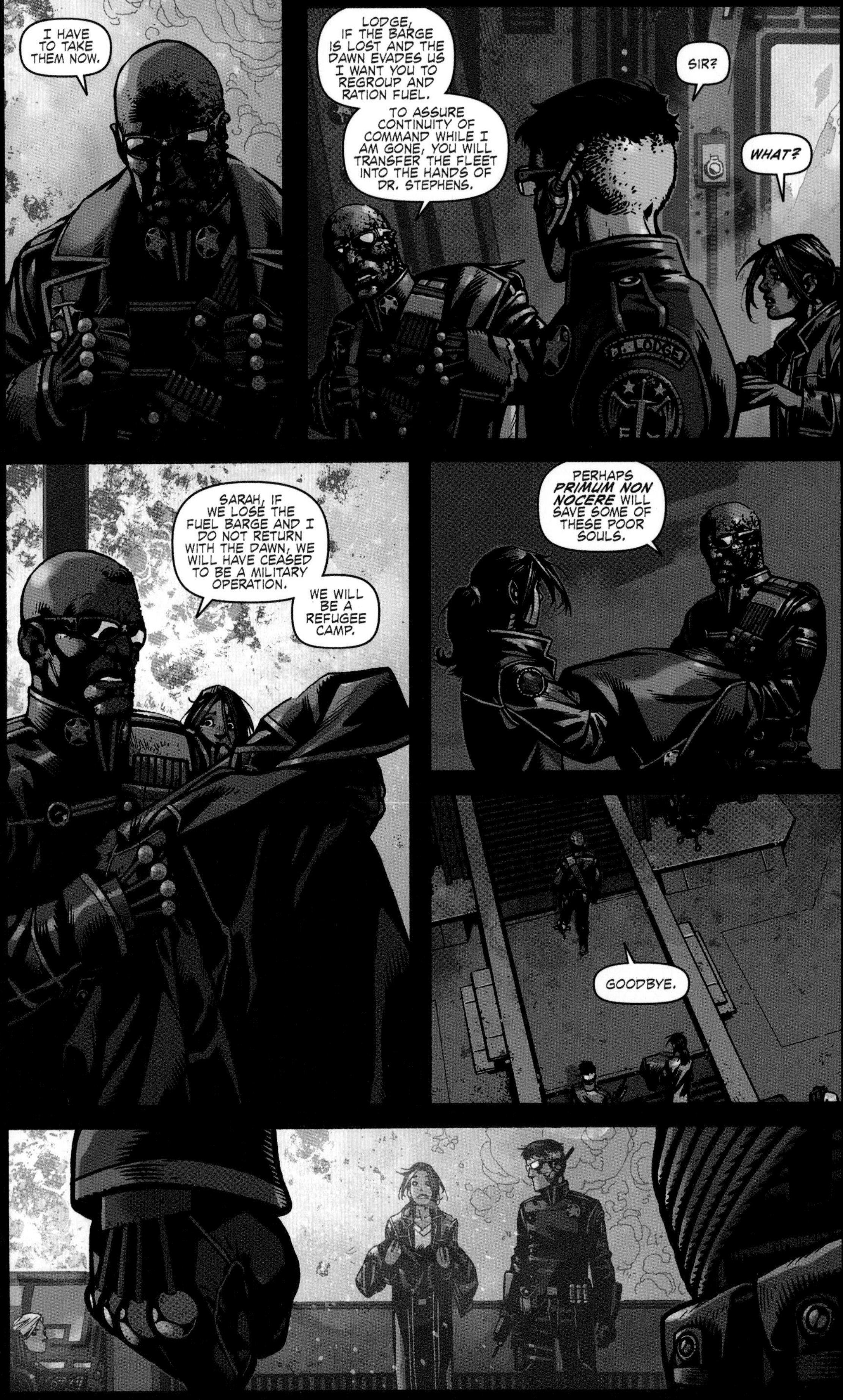
I HAVE TO TAKE THEM NOW.
LODGE, IF THE BARGE IS LOST AND THE DAWN EVADES US I WANT YOU TO REGROUP AND RATION FUEL.
TO ASSURE CONTINUITY OF COMMAND WHILE I AM GONE, YOU WILL TRANSFER THE FLEET INTO THE HANDS OF DR. STEPHENS.
SIR?
WHAT?
LODGE
SARAH, IF WE LOSE THE FUEL BARGE AND I DO NOT RETURN WITH THE DAWN, WE WILL HAVE CEASED TO BE A MILITARY OPERATION.
WE WILL BE A REFUGEE CAMP.
PERHAPS PRIMUM NON NOCERE WILL SAVE SOME OF THESE POOR SOULS.
GOODBYE.

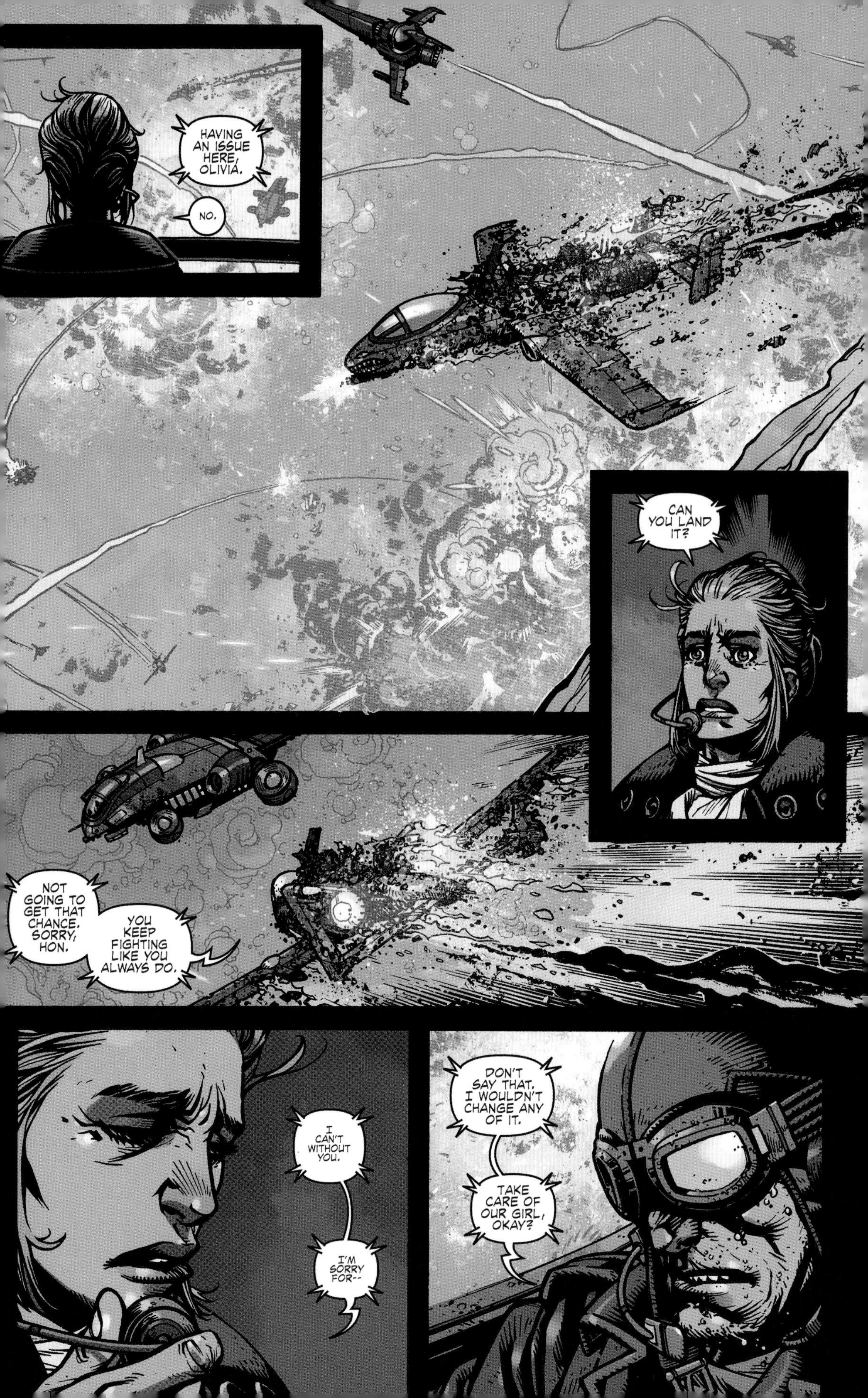
HAVING AN ISSUE HERE, OLIVIA.
NO.
CAN YOU LAND IT?
NOT GOING TO GET THAT CHANCE. SORRY, HON.
YOU KEEP FIGHTING LIKE YOU ALWAYS DO.
I CAN'T WITHOUT YOU.
I'M SORRY FOR--
DON'T SAY THAT. I WOULDN'T CHANGE ANY OF IT.
TAKE CARE OF OUR GIRL, OKAY?

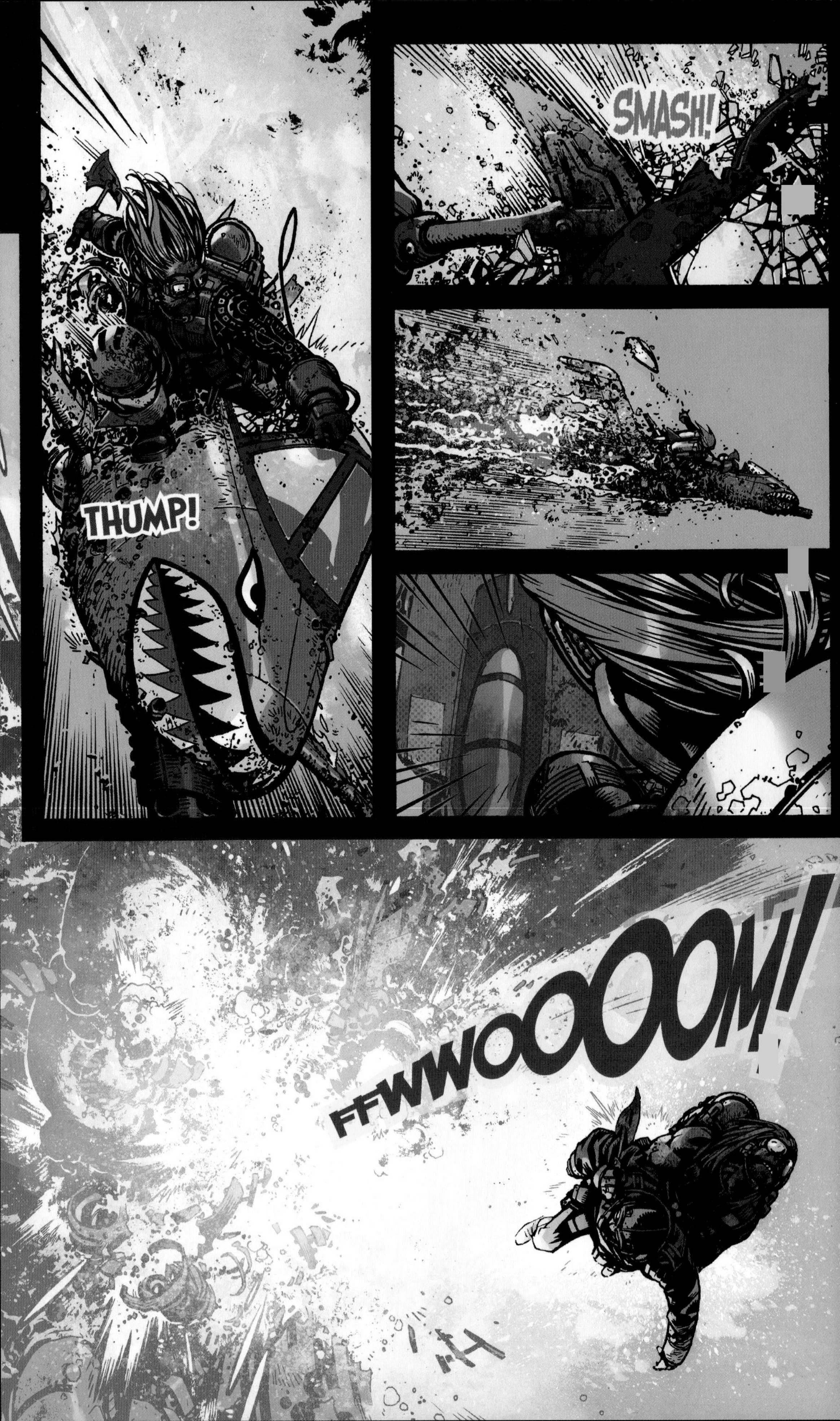
THUMP!
SMASH!
FFWWOOOOM!

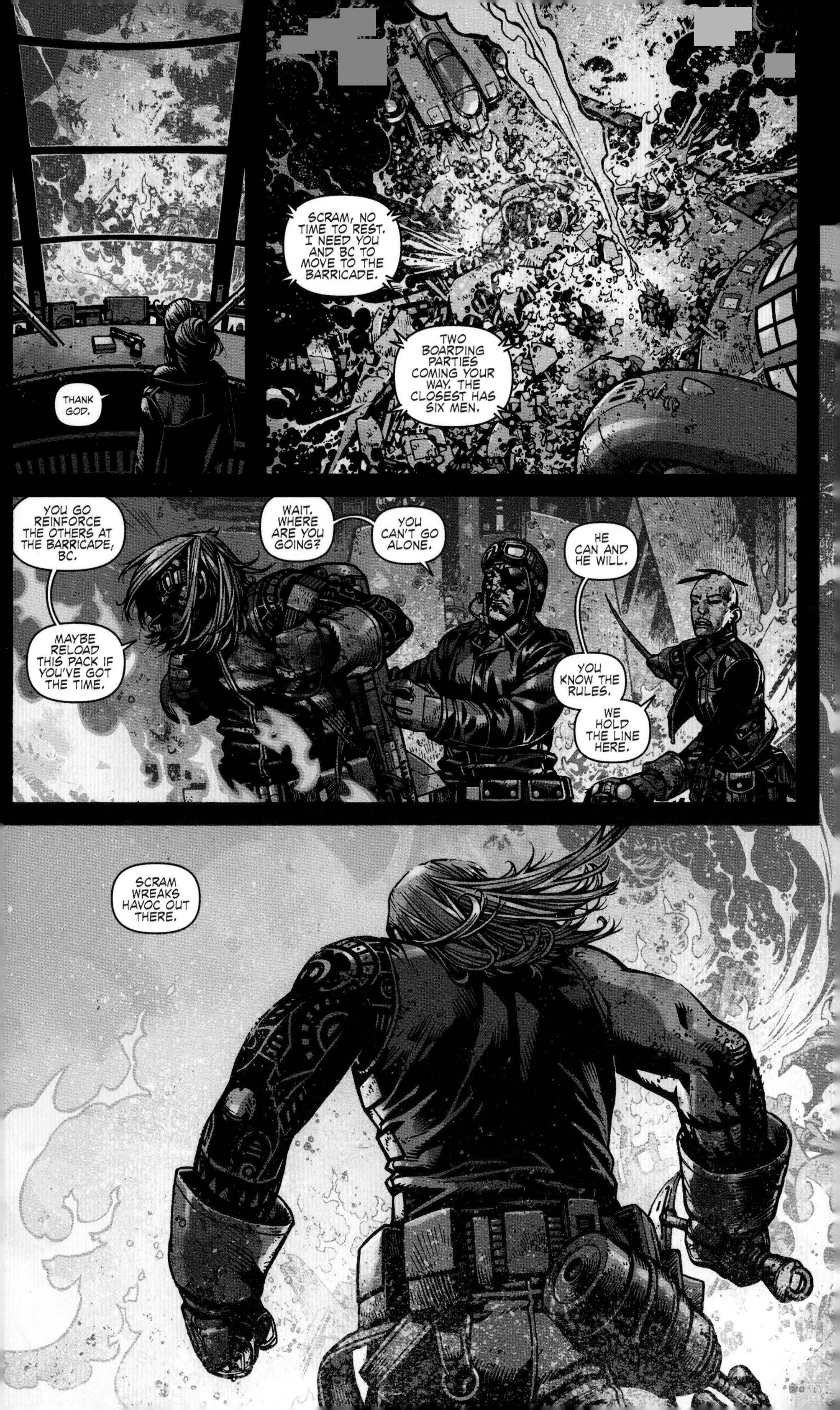
THANK GOD.
SCRAM, NO TIME TO REST. I NEED YOU AND BC TO MOVE TO THE BARRICADE.
TWO BOARDING PARTIES COMING YOUR WAY. THE CLOSEST HAS SIX MEN.
YOU GO REINFORCE THE OTHERS AT THE BARRICADE, BC.
MAYBE RELOAD THIS PACK IF YOU'VE GOT THE TIME.
WAIT. WHERE ARE YOU GOING?
YOU CAN'T GO ALONE.
HE CAN AND HE WILL.
YOU KNOW THE RULES.
WE HOLD THE LINE HERE.
SCRAM WREAKS HAVOC OUT THERE.

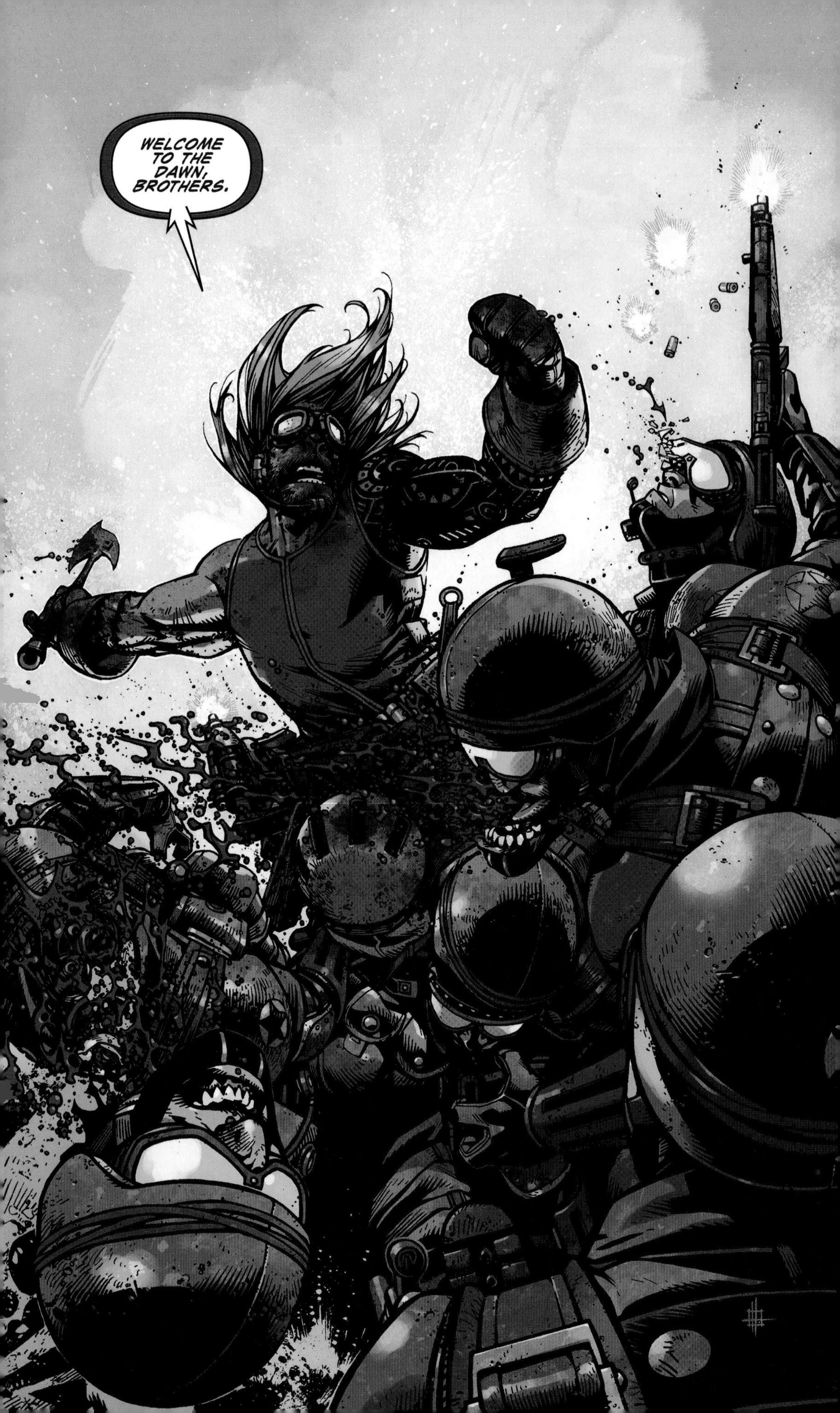
WELCOME TO THE DAWN, BROTHERS.

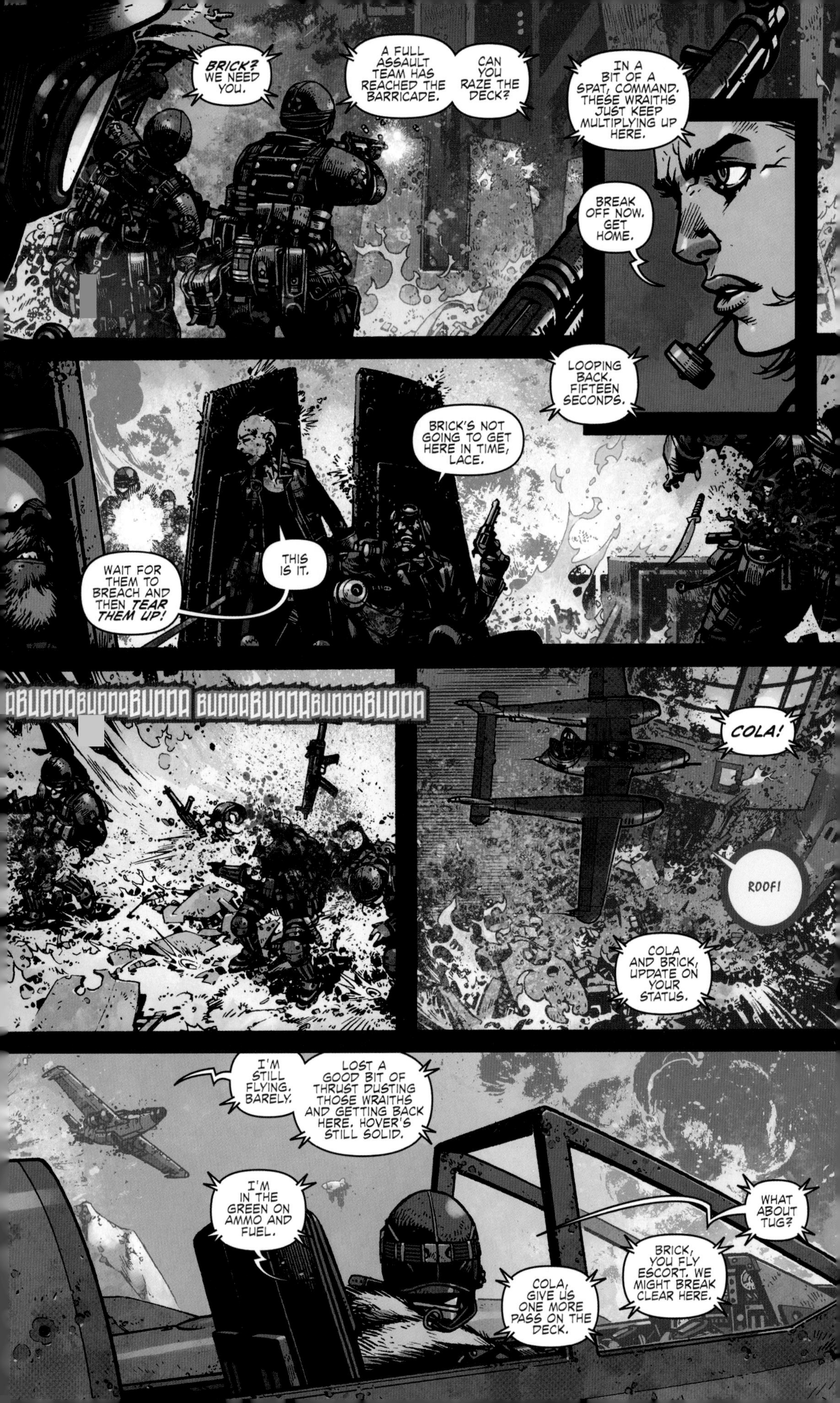
BRICK? WE NEED YOU.
A FULL ASSAULT TEAM HAS REACHED THE BARRICADE.
CAN YOU RAZE THE DECK?
IN A BIT OF A SPAT, COMMAND. THESE WRAITHS JUST KEEP MULTIPLYING UP HERE.
BREAK OFF NOW. GET HOME.
LOOPING BACK. FIFTEEN SECONDS.
BRICK'S NOT GOING TO GET HERE IN TIME, LACE.
THIS IS IT.
WAIT FOR THEM TO BREACH AND THEN TEAR THEM UP!
ABUDDABUDDABUDDA BUDDABUDDABUDDABUDDA
COLA!
ROOF!
COLA AND BRICK, UPDATE ON YOUR STATUS.
I'M STILL FLYING. BARELY.
LOST A GOOD BIT OF THRUST DUSTING THOSE WRAITHS AND GETTING BACK HERE. HOVER'S STILL SOLID.
I'M IN THE GREEN ON AMMO AND FUEL.
WHAT ABOUT TUG?
BRICK, YOU FLY ESCORT. WE MIGHT BREAK CLEAR HERE.
COLA, GIVE US ONE MORE PASS ON THE DECK.

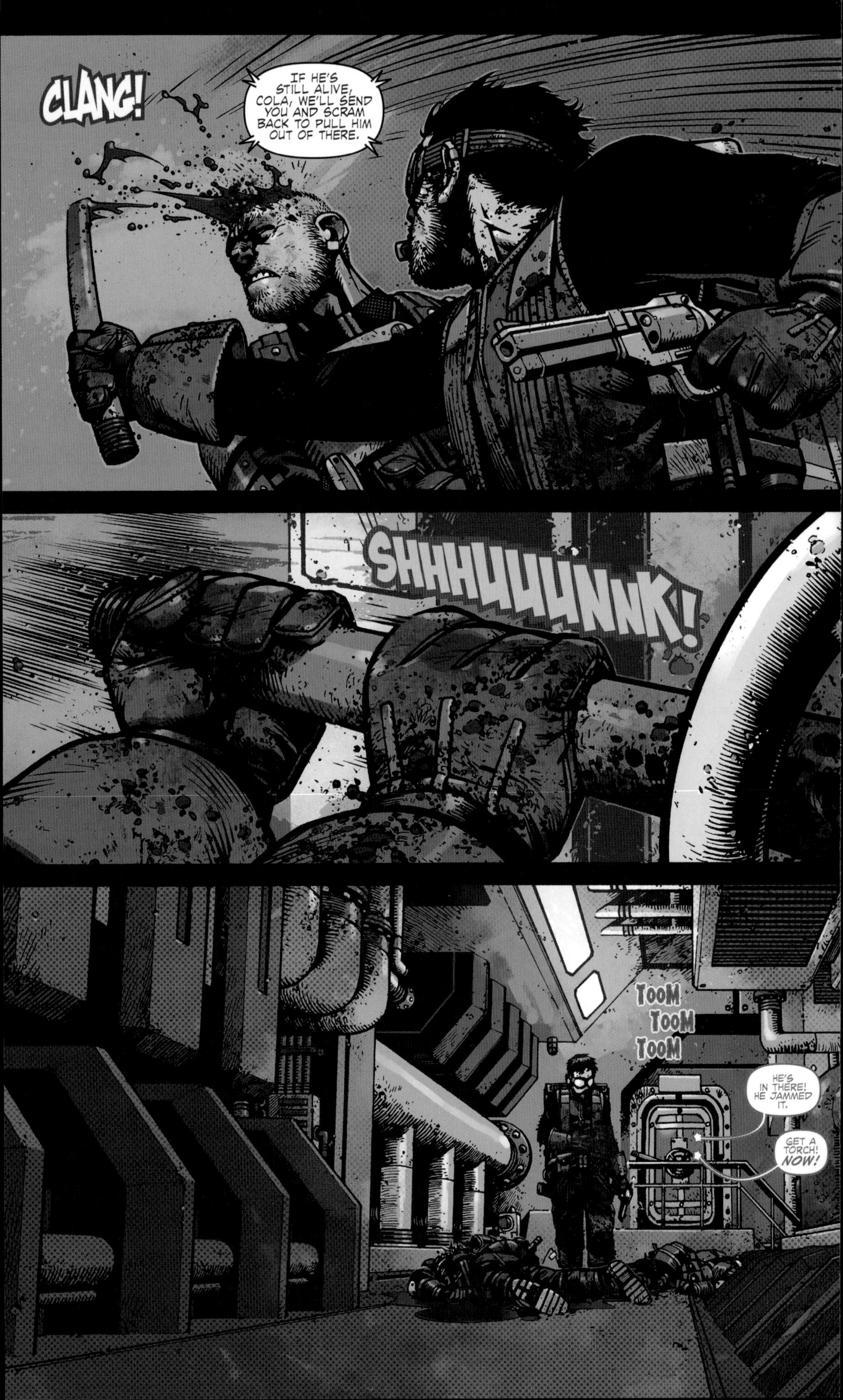
CLANG!
IF HE'S STILL ALIVE, COLA, WE'LL SEND YOU AND SCRAM BACK TO PULL HIM OUT OF THERE.
SHHHUUUUNNK!
TOOM TOOM TOOM
HE'S IN THERE! HE JAMMED IT.
GET A TORCH! NOW!

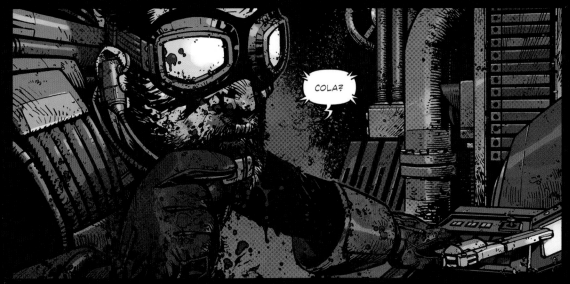

COLA?

ARE YOU OUT THERE?

CAN YOU HEAR ME?

TUG! I'LL COME GET YOU.

NOT GOING TO HAPPEN.

-NNFF-

THEY'RE GOING TO CUT THEIR WAY IN SOON.

JUST ENOUGH.

I HAVE TAKEN THE SHIP.

TELL SCRAM HE WAS RIGHT.

IT *WAS* RIGHTEOUS.

WAIT, TUG. LET ME FIGURE THIS OUT. I CAN SAVE YOU.

NO. YOU'RE ALMOST CLEAR.

AND YOU WOULDN'T MAKE IT BEFORE THEY CUT THEIR WAY IN.

THIS IS MY PART TO FINISH.

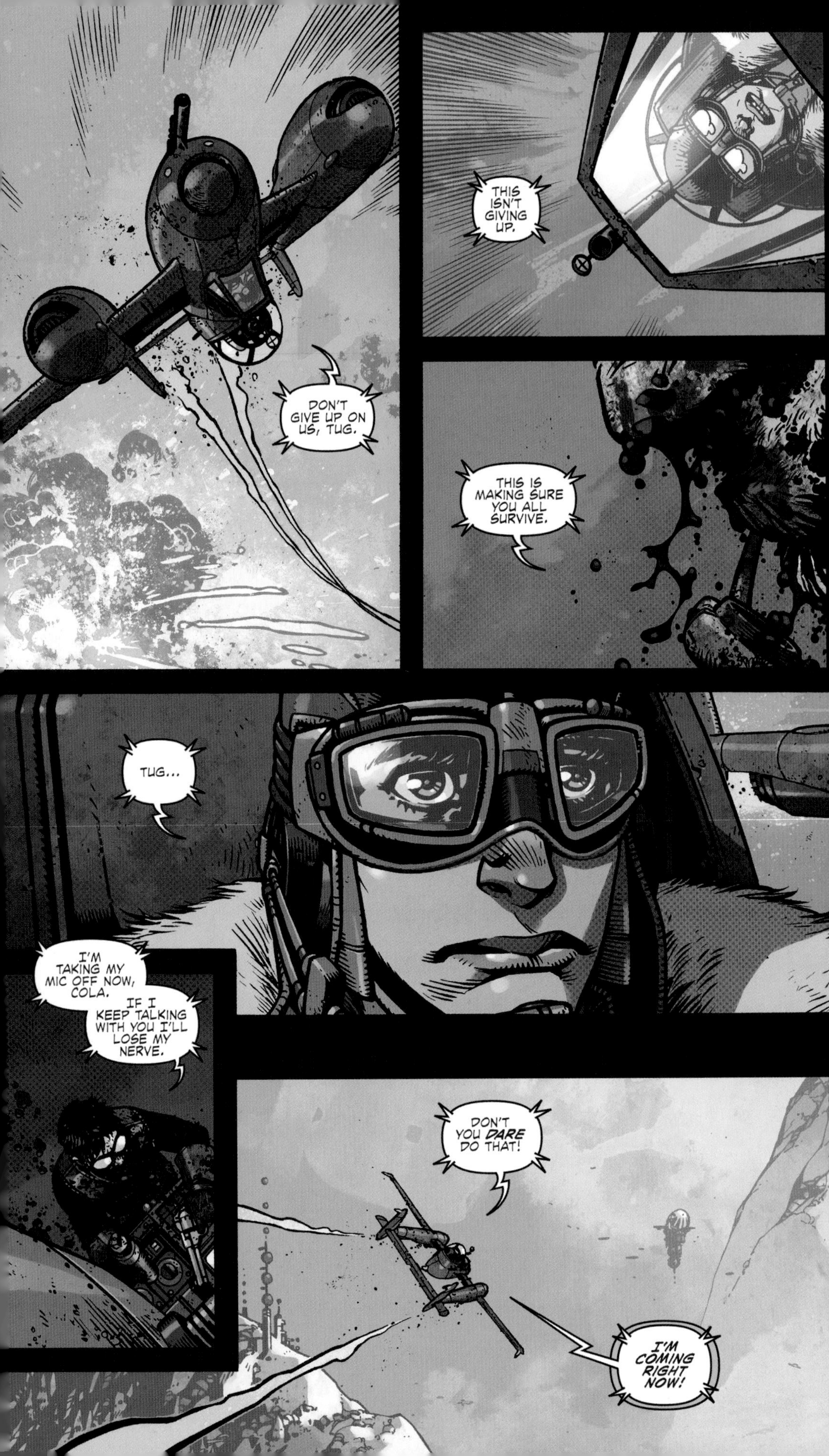

THIS ISN'T GIVING UP.
DON'T GIVE UP ON US, TUG.
THIS IS MAKING SURE YOU ALL SURVIVE.
TUG...
I'M TAKING MY MIC OFF NOW, COLA.
IF I KEEP TALKING WITH YOU I'LL LOSE MY NERVE.
DON'T YOU *DARE* DO THAT!
I'M COMING RIGHT NOW!

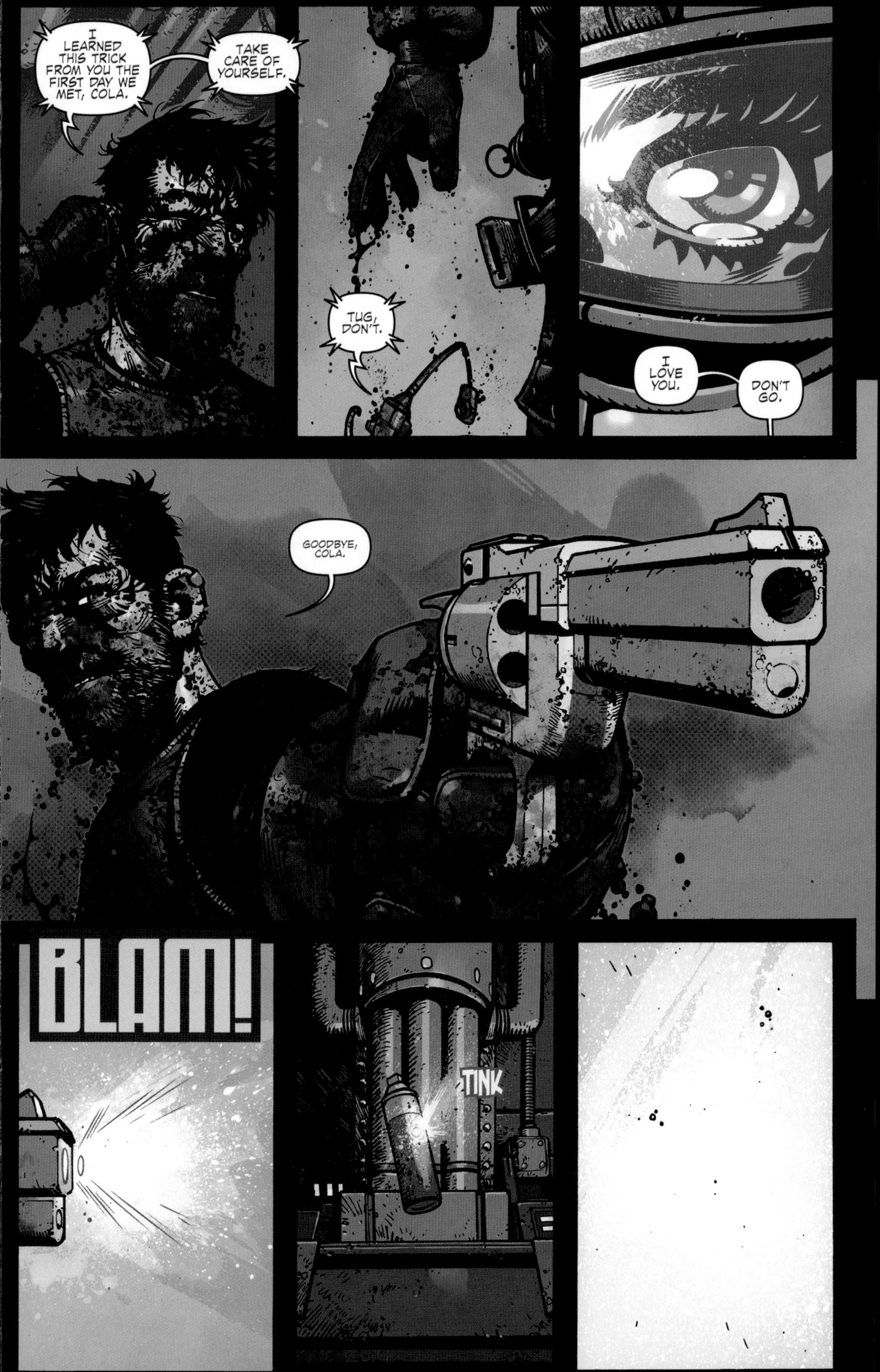
I LEARNED THIS TRICK FROM YOU THE FIRST DAY WE MET, COLA.
TAKE CARE OF YOURSELF.
TUG, DON'T.
I LOVE YOU.
DON'T GO.
GOODBYE, COLA.
BLAM!
TINK

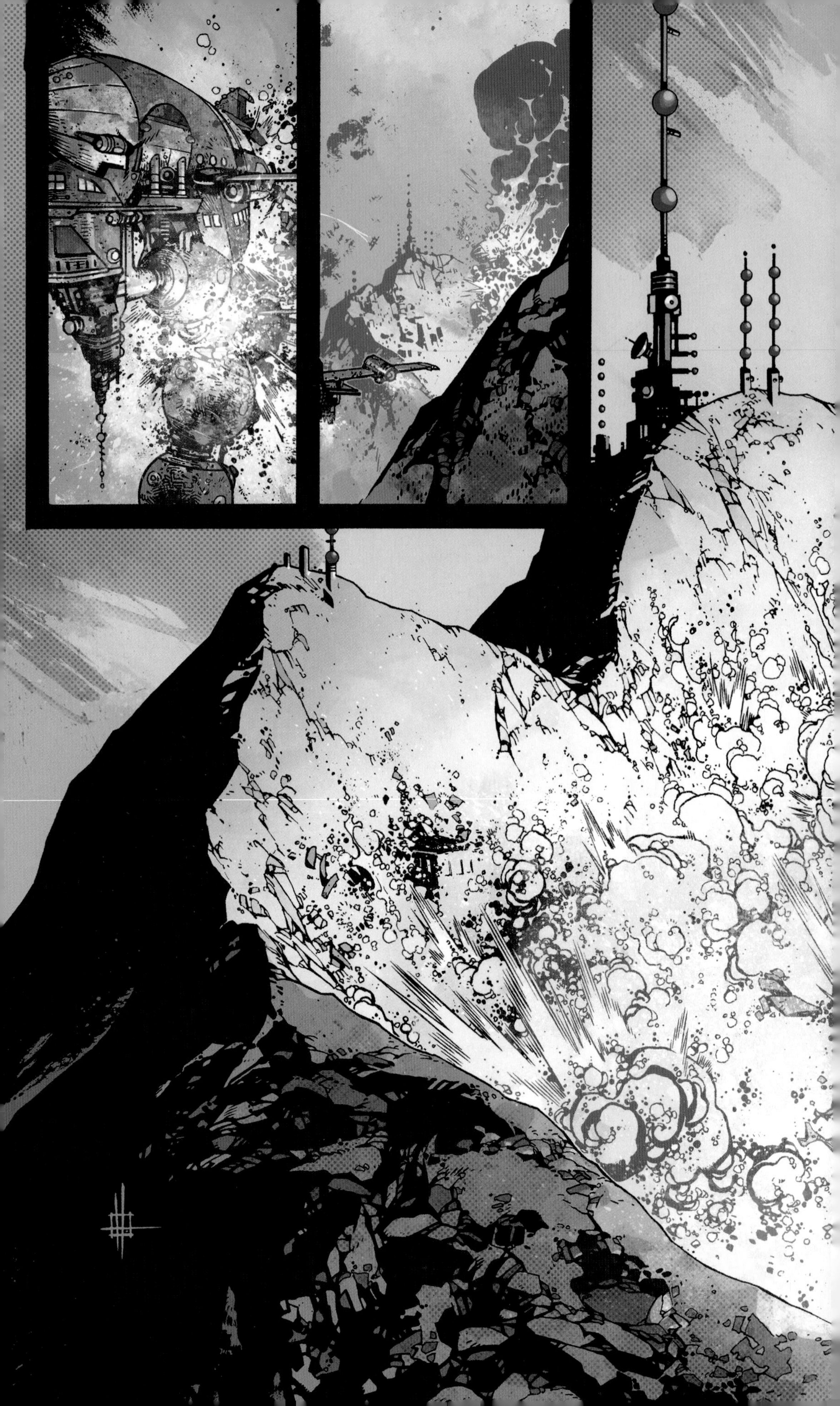

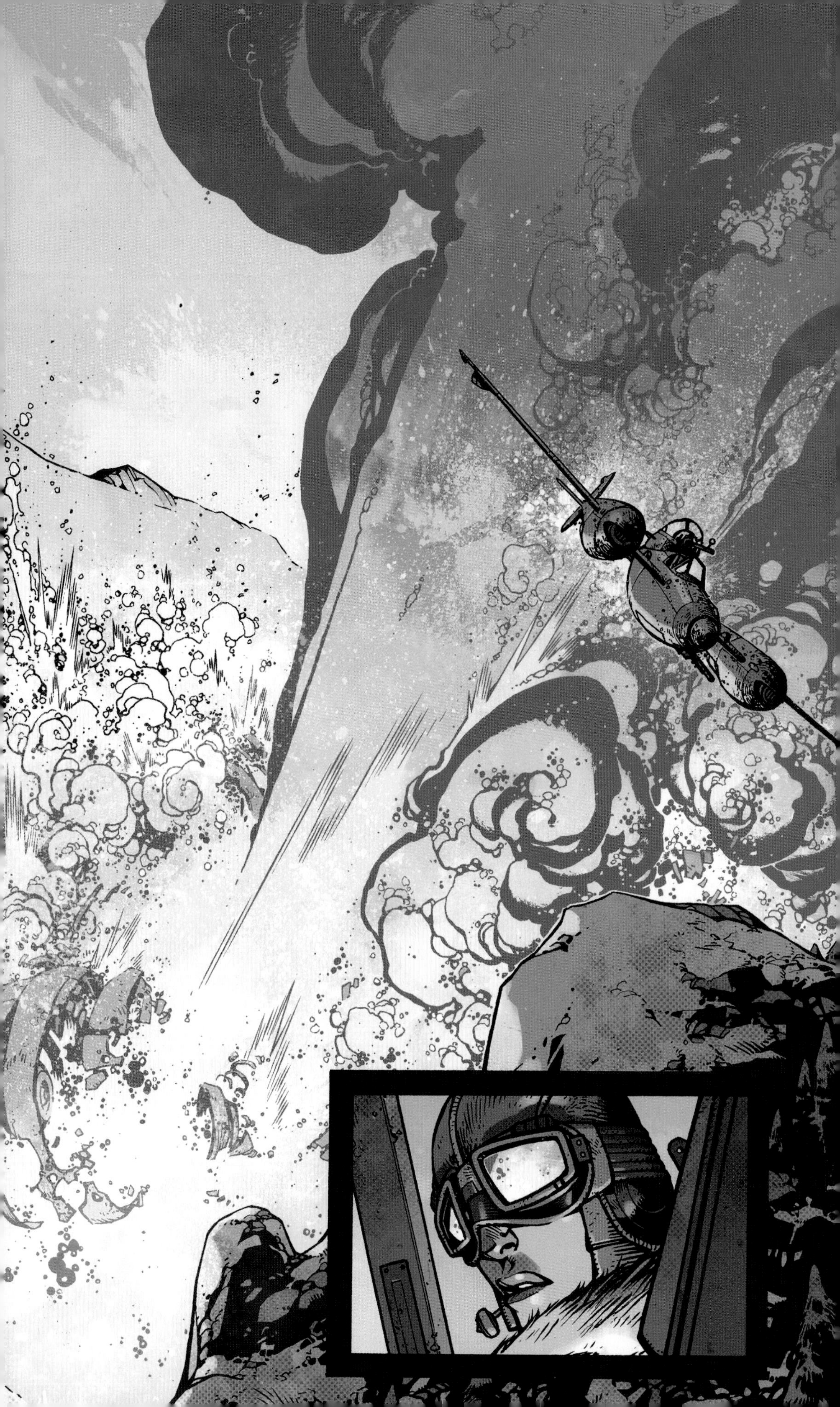

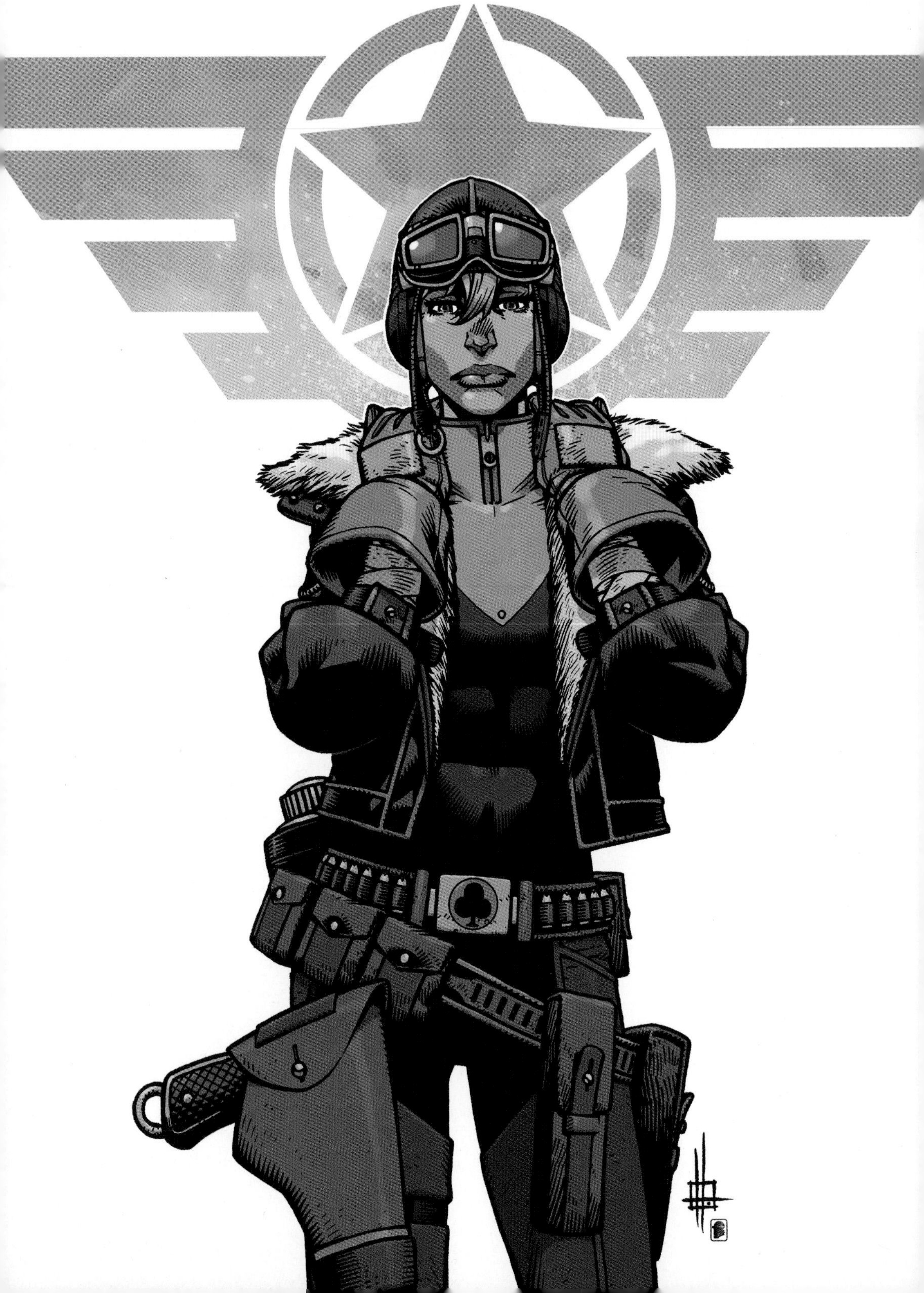

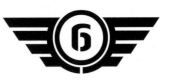

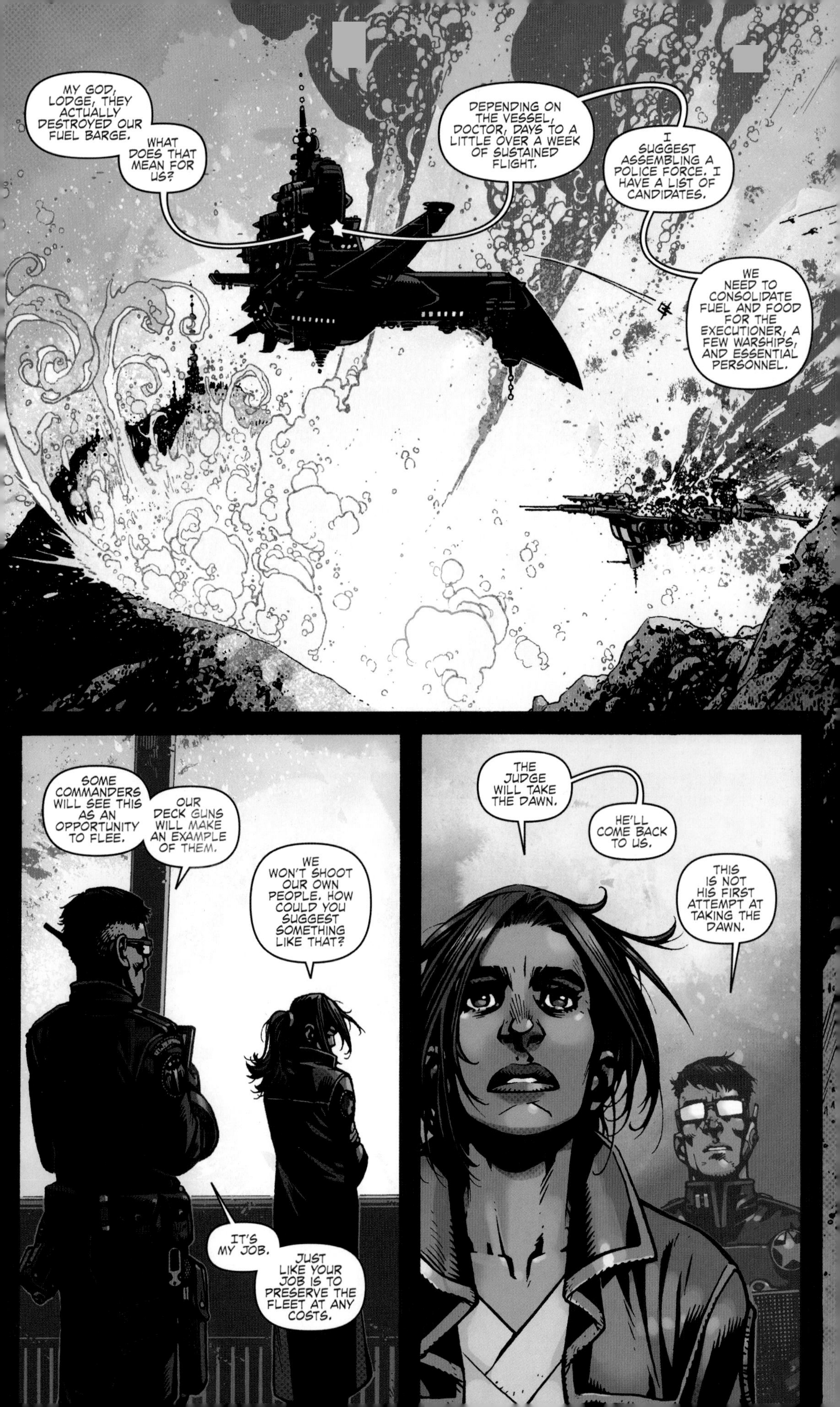

MY GOD, LODGE, THEY ACTUALLY DESTROYED OUR FUEL BARGE.
WHAT DOES THAT MEAN FOR US?
DEPENDING ON THE VESSEL, DOCTOR, DAYS TO A LITTLE OVER A WEEK OF SUSTAINED FLIGHT.
I SUGGEST ASSEMBLING A POLICE FORCE. I HAVE A LIST OF CANDIDATES.
WE NEED TO CONSOLIDATE FUEL AND FOOD FOR THE EXECUTIONER, A FEW WARSHIPS, AND ESSENTIAL PERSONNEL.
SOME COMMANDERS WILL SEE THIS AS AN OPPORTUNITY TO FLEE.
OUR DECK GUNS WILL MAKE AN EXAMPLE OF THEM.
WE WON'T SHOOT OUR OWN PEOPLE. HOW COULD YOU SUGGEST SOMETHING LIKE THAT?
IT'S MY JOB.
JUST LIKE YOUR JOB IS TO PRESERVE THE FLEET AT ANY COSTS.
THE JUDGE WILL TAKE THE DAWN.
HE'LL COME BACK TO US.
THIS IS NOT HIS FIRST ATTEMPT AT TAKING THE DAWN.

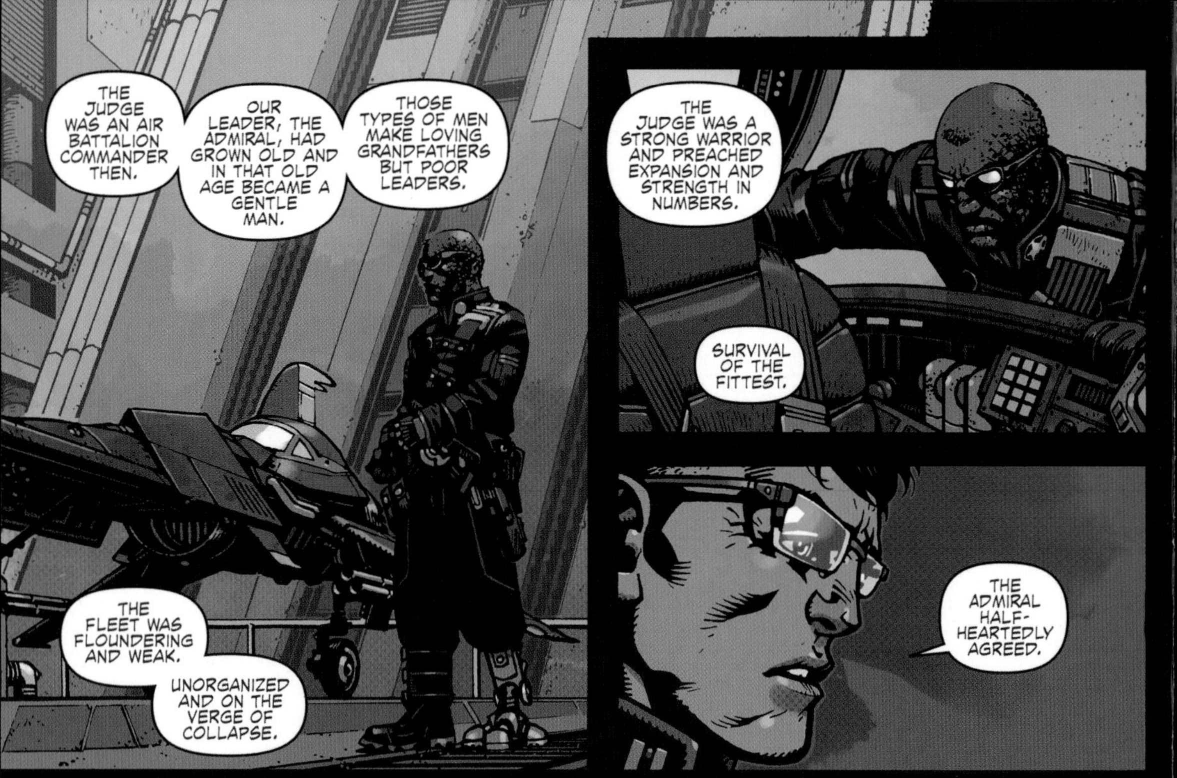
THE JUDGE WAS AN AIR BATTALION COMMANDER THEN.
OUR LEADER, THE ADMIRAL, HAD GROWN OLD AND IN THAT OLD AGE BECAME A GENTLE MAN.
THOSE TYPES OF MEN MAKE LOVING GRANDFATHERS BUT POOR LEADERS.
THE FLEET WAS FLOUNDERING AND WEAK.
UNORGANIZED AND ON THE VERGE OF COLLAPSE.
THE JUDGE WAS A STRONG WARRIOR AND PREACHED EXPANSION AND STRENGTH IN NUMBERS.
SURVIVAL OF THE FITTEST.
THE ADMIRAL HALF-HEARTEDLY AGREED.

CHAPTER SIX

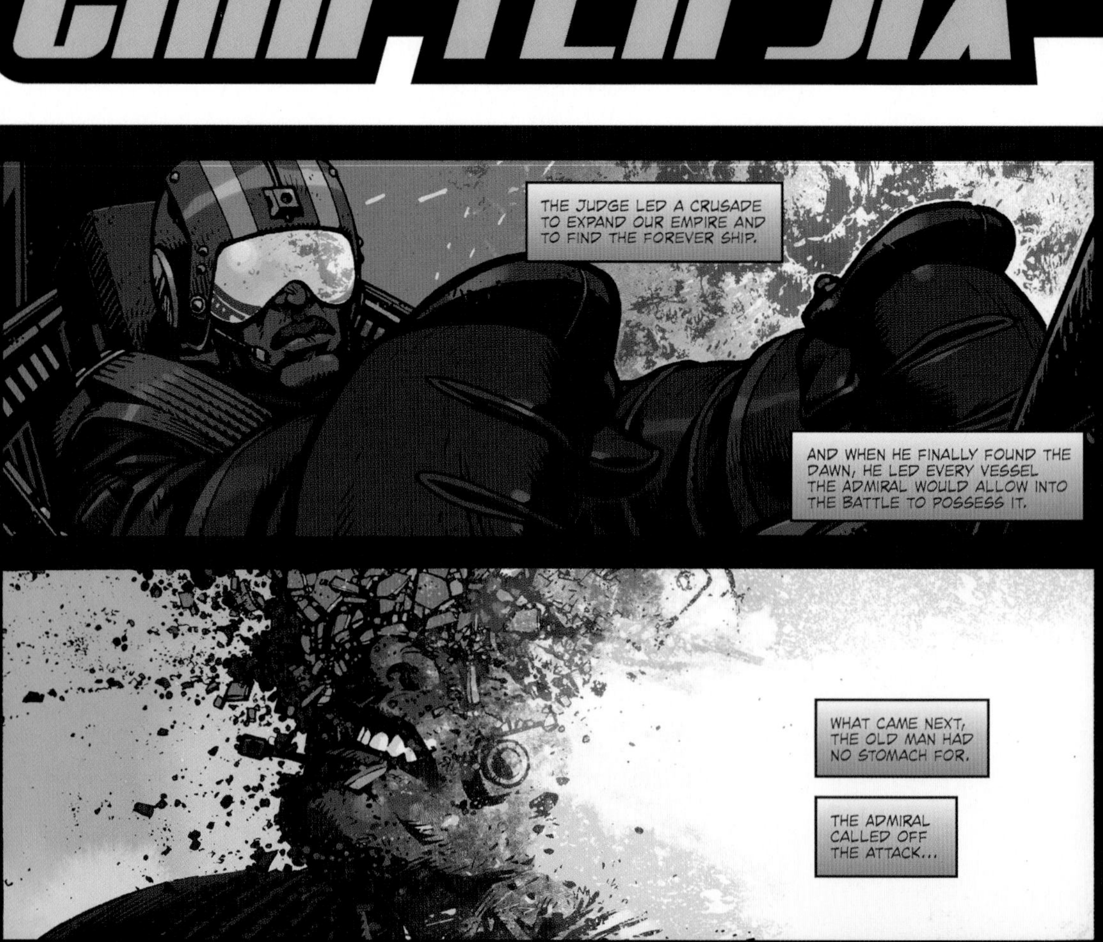
THE JUDGE LED A CRUSADE TO EXPAND OUR EMPIRE AND TO FIND THE FOREVER SHIP.
AND WHEN HE FINALLY FOUND THE DAWN, HE LED EVERY VESSEL THE ADMIRAL WOULD ALLOW INTO THE BATTLE TO POSSESS IT.
WHAT CAME NEXT, THE OLD MAN HAD NO STOMACH FOR.
THE ADMIRAL CALLED OFF THE ATTACK...

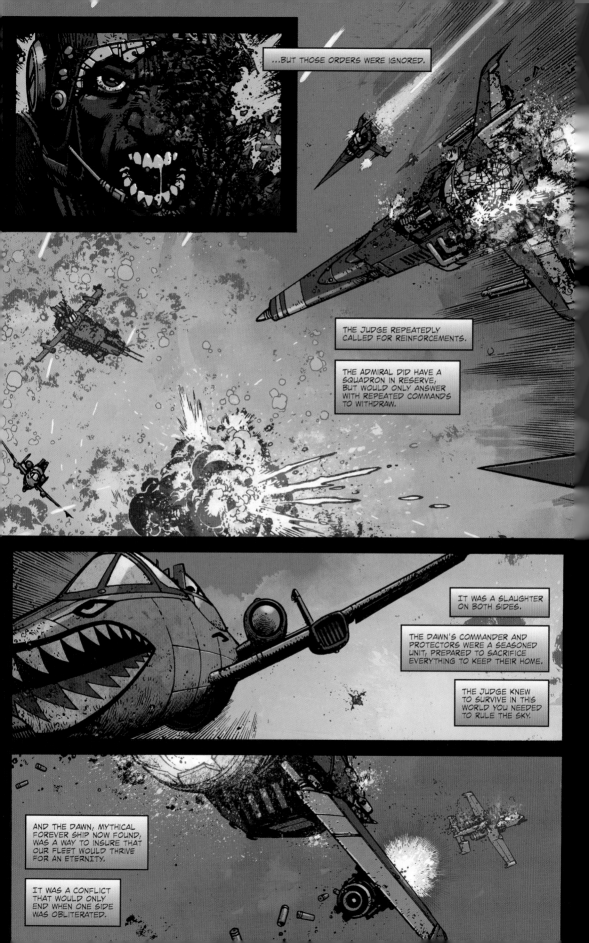

...BUT THOSE ORDERS WERE IGNORED.

THE JUDGE REPEATEDLY CALLED FOR REINFORCEMENTS.

THE ADMIRAL DID HAVE A SQUADRON IN RESERVE, BUT WOULD ONLY ANSWER WITH REPEATED COMMANDS TO WITHDRAW.

IT WAS A SLAUGHTER ON BOTH SIDES.

THE DAWN'S COMMANDER AND PROTECTORS WERE A SEASONED UNIT, PREPARED TO SACRIFICE EVERYTHING TO KEEP THEIR HOME.

THE JUDGE KNEW TO SURVIVE IN THIS WORLD YOU NEEDED TO RULE THE SKY.

AND THE DAWN, MYTHICAL FOREVER SHIP NOW FOUND, WAS A WAY TO INSURE THAT OUR FLEET WOULD THRIVE FOR AN ETERNITY.

IT WAS A CONFLICT THAT WOULD ONLY END WHEN ONE SIDE WAS OBLITERATED.

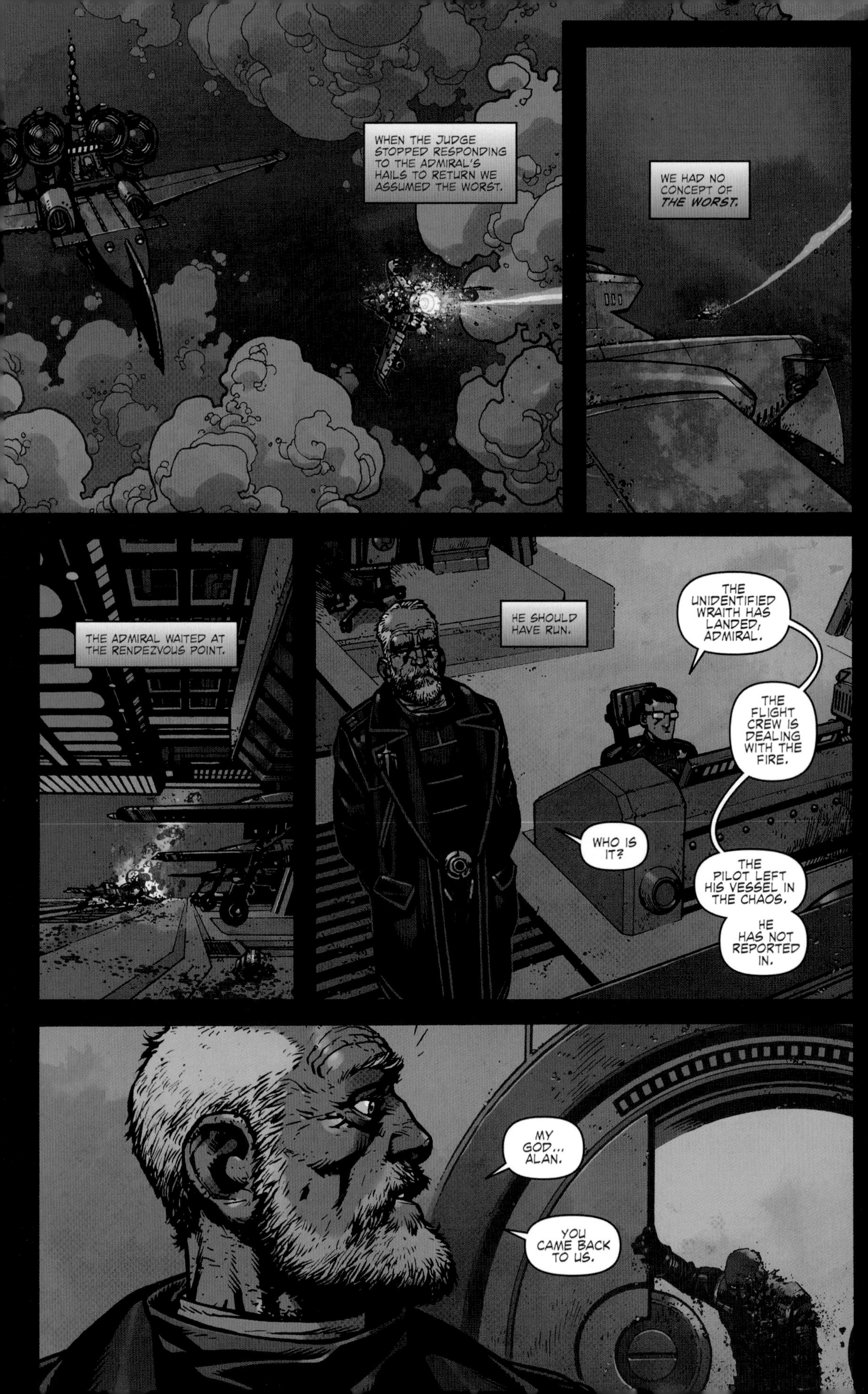
WHEN THE JUDGE STOPPED RESPONDING TO THE ADMIRAL'S HAILS TO RETURN WE ASSUMED THE WORST.
WE HAD NO CONCEPT OF *THE WORST.*
THE ADMIRAL WAITED AT THE RENDEZVOUS POINT.
HE SHOULD HAVE RUN.
THE UNIDENTIFIED WRAITH HAS LANDED, ADMIRAL.
THE FLIGHT CREW IS DEALING WITH THE FIRE.
WHO IS IT?
THE PILOT LEFT HIS VESSEL IN THE CHAOS.
HE HAS NOT REPORTED IN.
MY GOD... ALAN.
YOU CAME BACK TO US.

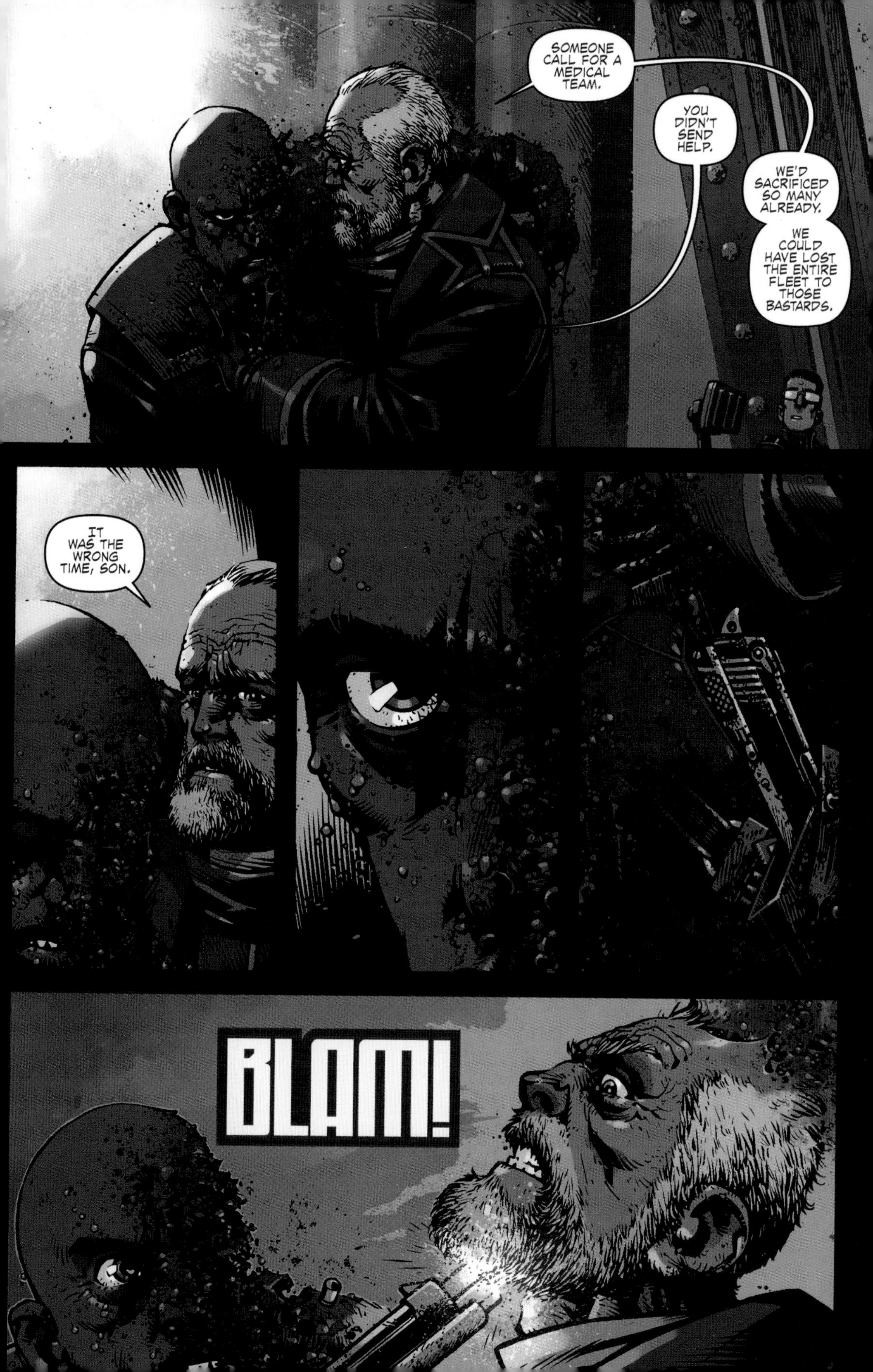
SOMEONE CALL FOR A MEDICAL TEAM.
YOU DIDN'T SEND HELP.
WE'D SACRIFICED SO MANY ALREADY.
WE COULD HAVE LOST THE ENTIRE FLEET TO THOSE BASTARDS.
IT WAS THE WRONG TIME, SON.
BLAM!

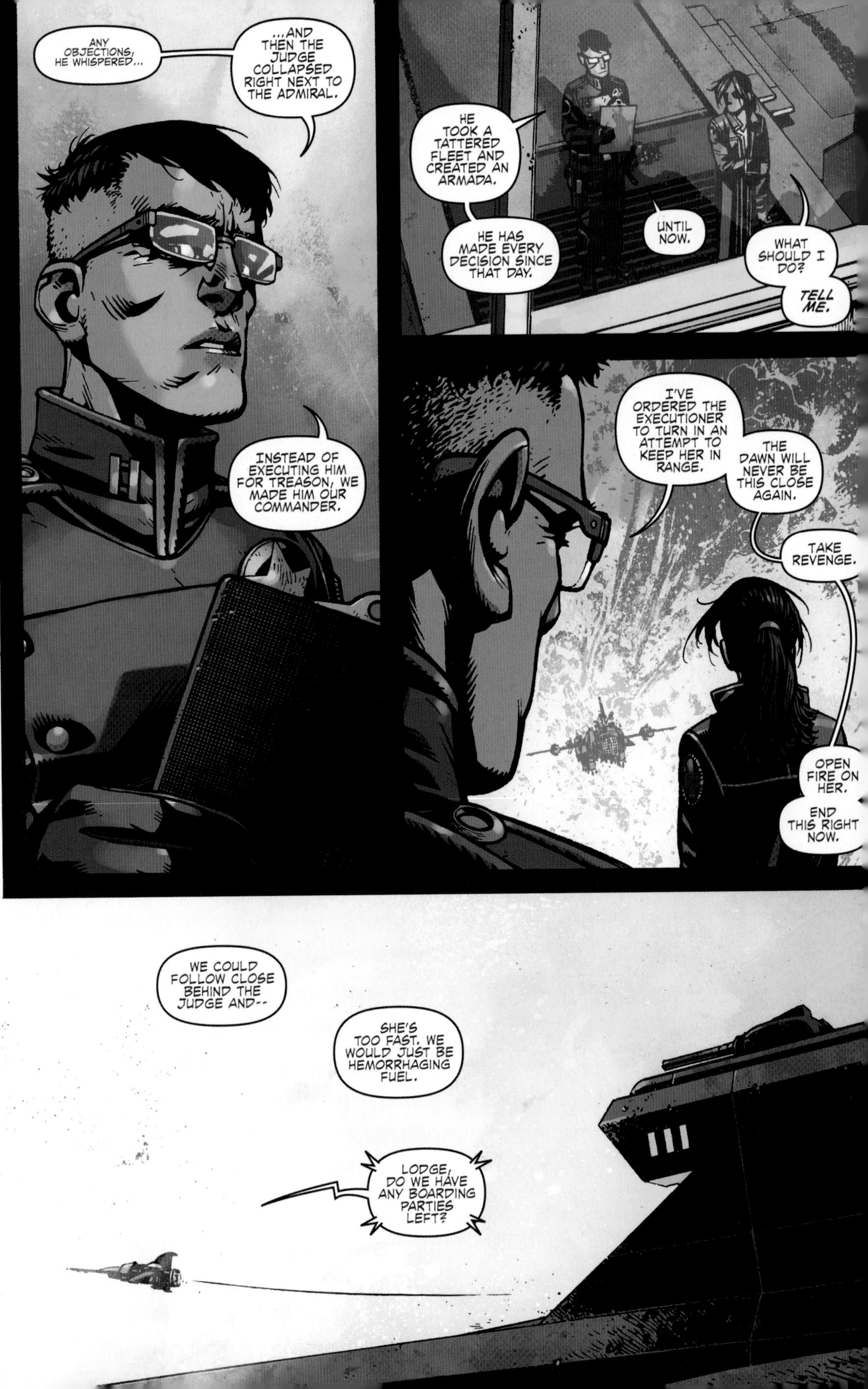
ANY OBJECTIONS, HE WHISPERED...
...AND THEN THE JUDGE COLLAPSED RIGHT NEXT TO THE ADMIRAL.
INSTEAD OF EXECUTING HIM FOR TREASON, WE MADE HIM OUR COMMANDER.
HE TOOK A TATTERED FLEET AND CREATED AN ARMADA.
HE HAS MADE EVERY DECISION SINCE THAT DAY.
UNTIL NOW.
WHAT SHOULD I DO?
TELL ME.
I'VE ORDERED THE EXECUTIONER TO TURN IN AN ATTEMPT TO KEEP HER IN RANGE.
THE DAWN WILL NEVER BE THIS CLOSE AGAIN.
TAKE REVENGE.
OPEN FIRE ON HER.
END THIS RIGHT NOW.
WE COULD FOLLOW CLOSE BEHIND THE JUDGE AND--
SHE'S TOO FAST. WE WOULD JUST BE HEMORRHAGING FUEL.
LODGE, DO WE HAVE ANY BOARDING PARTIES LEFT?

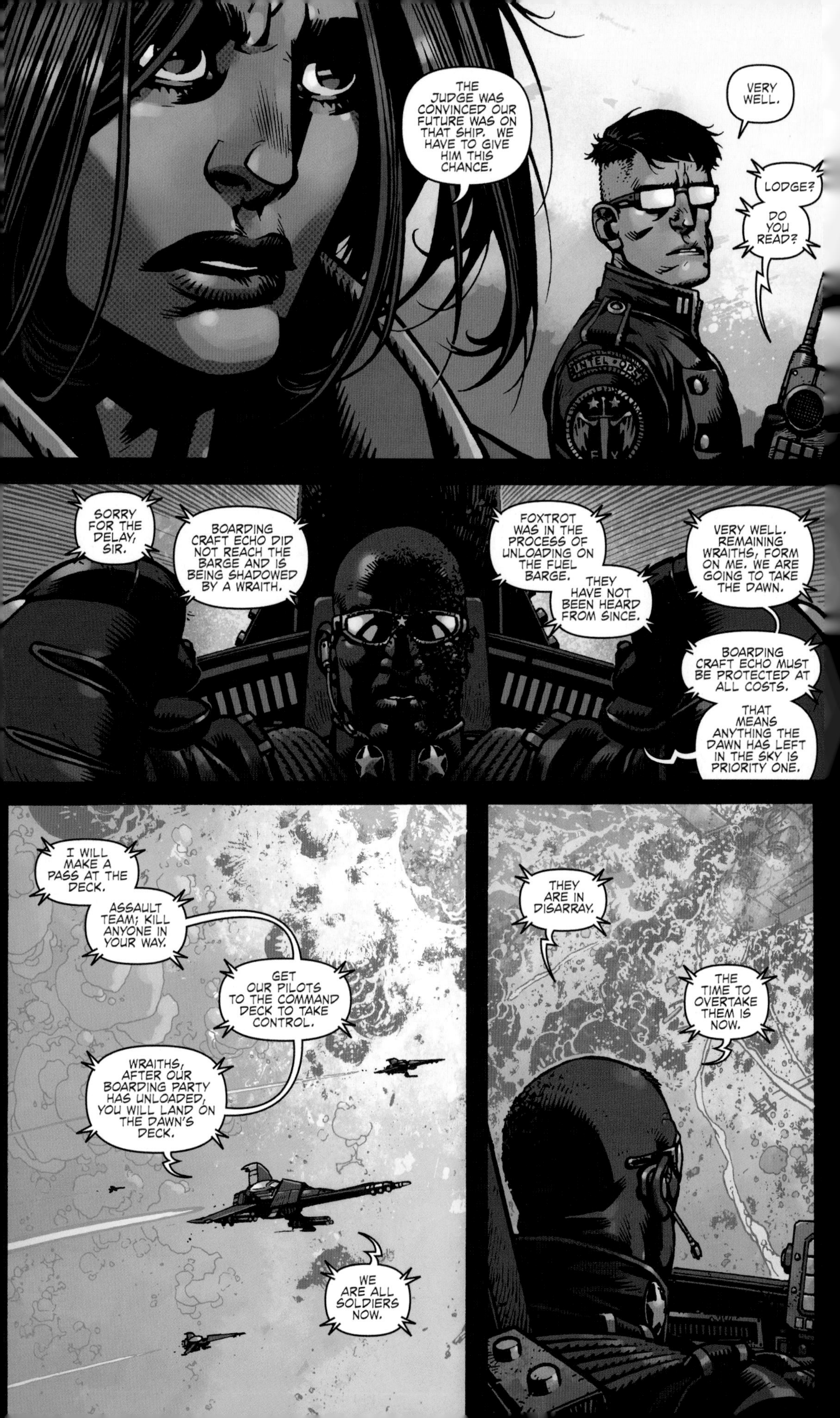
THE JUDGE WAS CONVINCED OUR FUTURE WAS ON THAT SHIP. WE HAVE TO GIVE HIM THIS CHANCE.
VERY WELL.
LODGE?
DO YOU READ?
SORRY FOR THE DELAY, SIR.
BOARDING CRAFT ECHO DID NOT REACH THE BARGE AND IS BEING SHADOWED BY A WRAITH.
FOXTROT WAS IN THE PROCESS OF UNLOADING ON THE FUEL BARGE.
THEY HAVE NOT BEEN HEARD FROM SINCE.
VERY WELL. REMAINING WRAITHS, FORM ON ME. WE ARE GOING TO TAKE THE DAWN.
BOARDING CRAFT ECHO MUST BE PROTECTED AT ALL COSTS.
THAT MEANS ANYTHING THE DAWN HAS LEFT IN THE SKY IS PRIORITY ONE.
I WILL MAKE A PASS AT THE DECK.
ASSAULT TEAM; KILL ANYONE IN YOUR WAY.
GET OUR PILOTS TO THE COMMAND DECK TO TAKE CONTROL.
WRAITHS, AFTER OUR BOARDING PARTY HAS UNLOADED, YOU WILL LAND ON THE DAWN'S DECK.
WE ARE ALL SOLDIERS NOW.
THEY ARE IN DISARRAY.
THE TIME TO OVERTAKE THEM IS NOW.

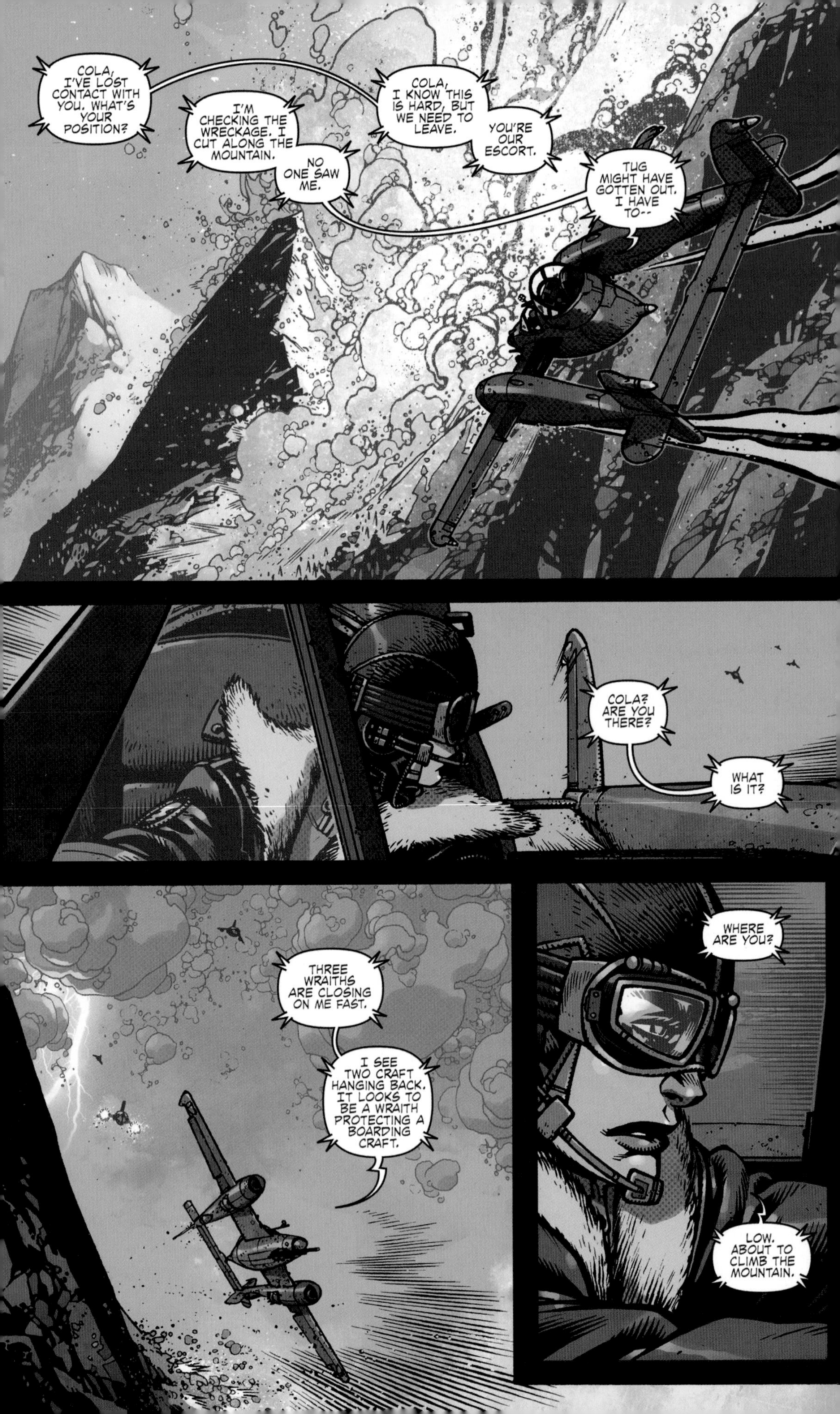

COLA, I'VE LOST CONTACT WITH YOU. WHAT'S YOUR POSITION?
I'M CHECKING THE WRECKAGE. I CUT ALONG THE MOUNTAIN.
NO ONE SAW ME.
COLA, I KNOW THIS IS HARD, BUT WE NEED TO LEAVE.
YOU'RE OUR ESCORT.
TUG MIGHT HAVE GOTTEN OUT. I HAVE TO--
COLA? ARE YOU THERE?
WHAT IS IT?
THREE WRAITHS ARE CLOSING ON ME FAST.
I SEE TWO CRAFT HANGING BACK. IT LOOKS TO BE A WRAITH PROTECTING A BOARDING CRAFT.
WHERE ARE YOU?
LOW. ABOUT TO CLIMB THE MOUNTAIN.

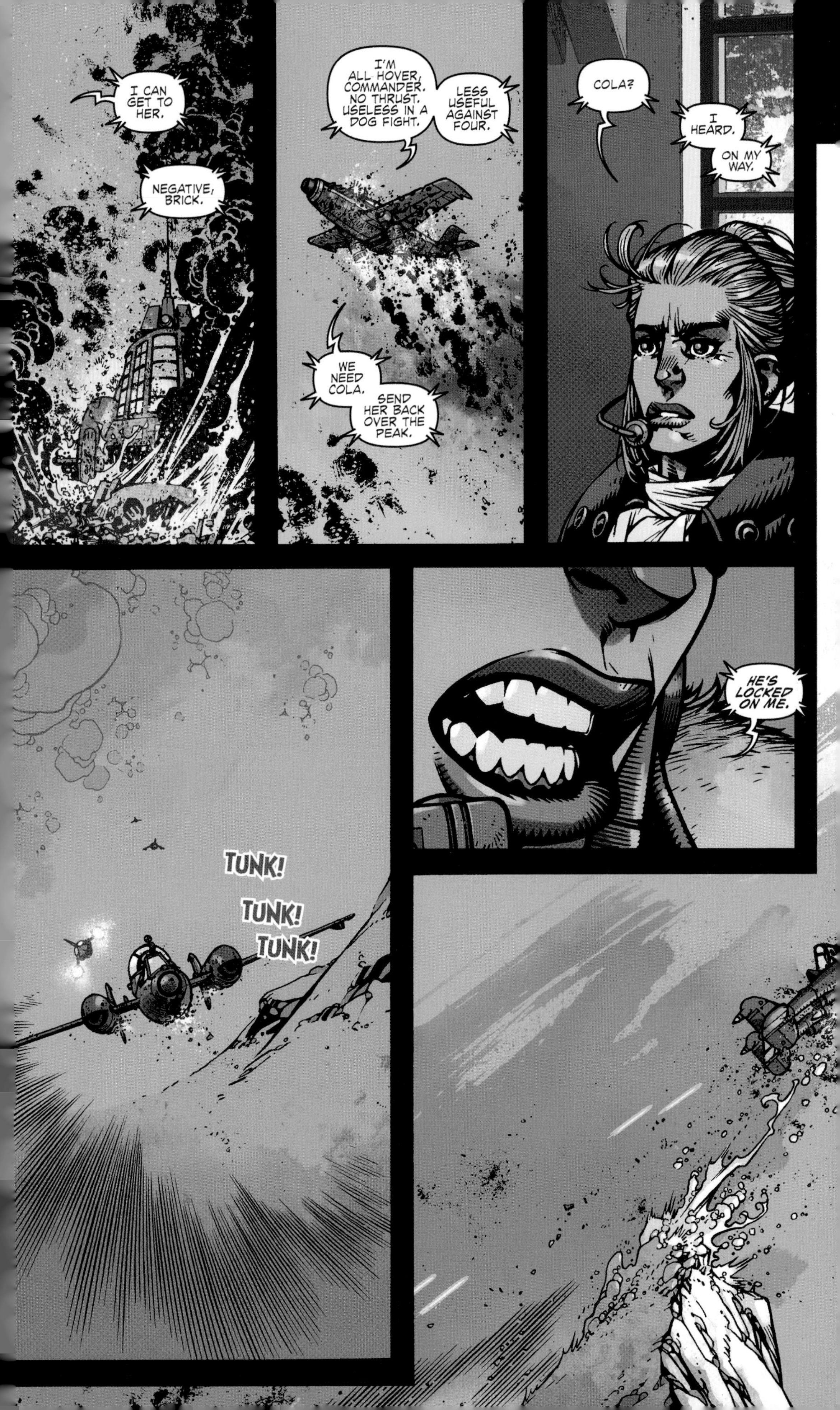
I CAN GET TO HER.
NEGATIVE, BRICK.
I'M ALL HOVER, COMMANDER. NO THRUST. USELESS IN A DOG FIGHT.
LESS USEFUL AGAINST FOUR.
WE NEED COLA.
SEND HER BACK OVER THE PEAK.
COLA?
I HEARD.
ON MY WAY.
HE'S LOCKED ON ME.
TUNK!
TUNK!
TUNK!

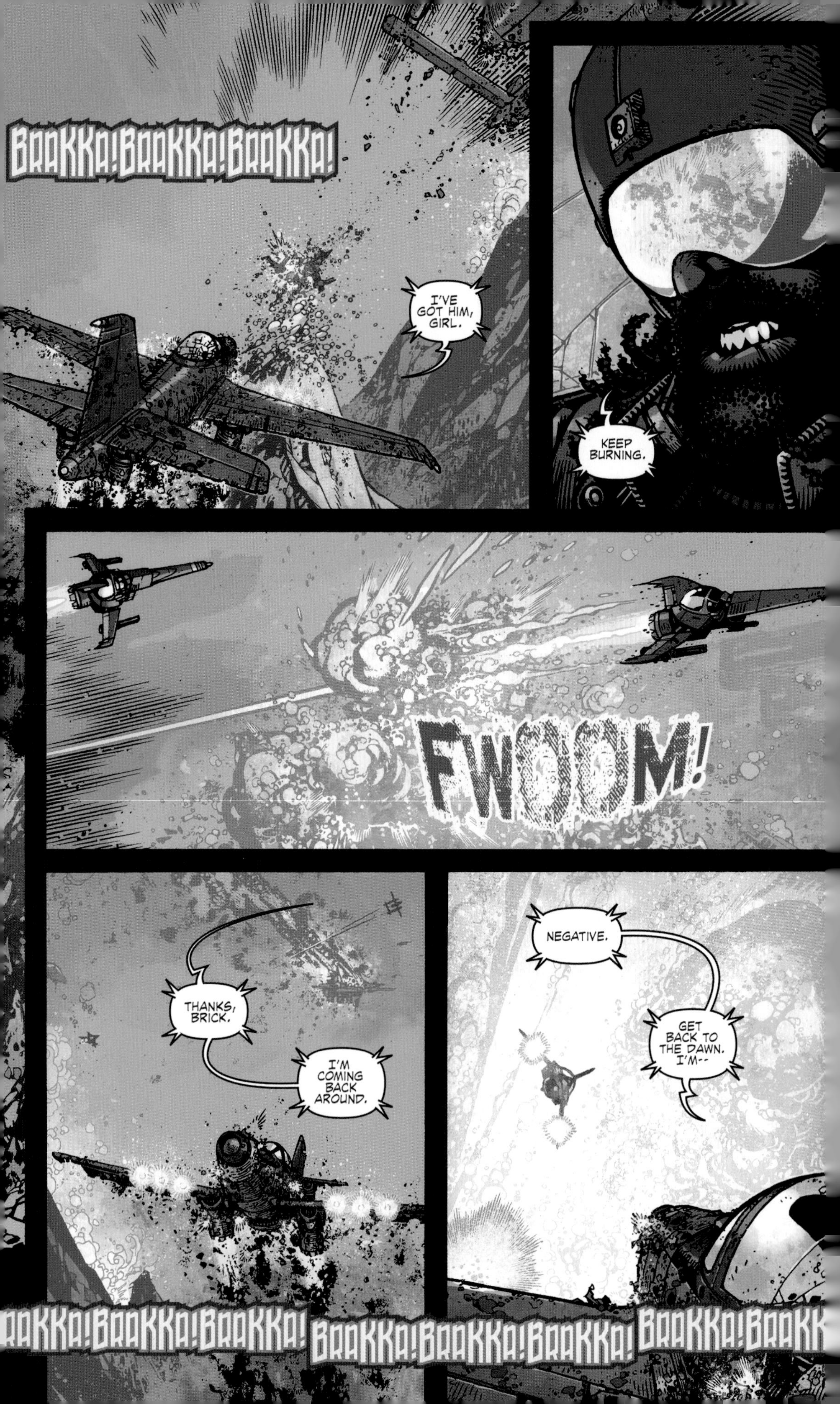
BRAKKA! BRAKKA! BRAKKA!
I'VE GOT HIM, GIRL.
KEEP BURNING.
FWOOM!
THANKS, BRICK.
I'M COMING BACK AROUND.
NEGATIVE.
GET BACK TO THE DAWN. I'M--
RAKKA! BRAKKA! BRAKKA! BRAKKA! BRAKKA! BRAKKA! BRAKKA! BRAKK

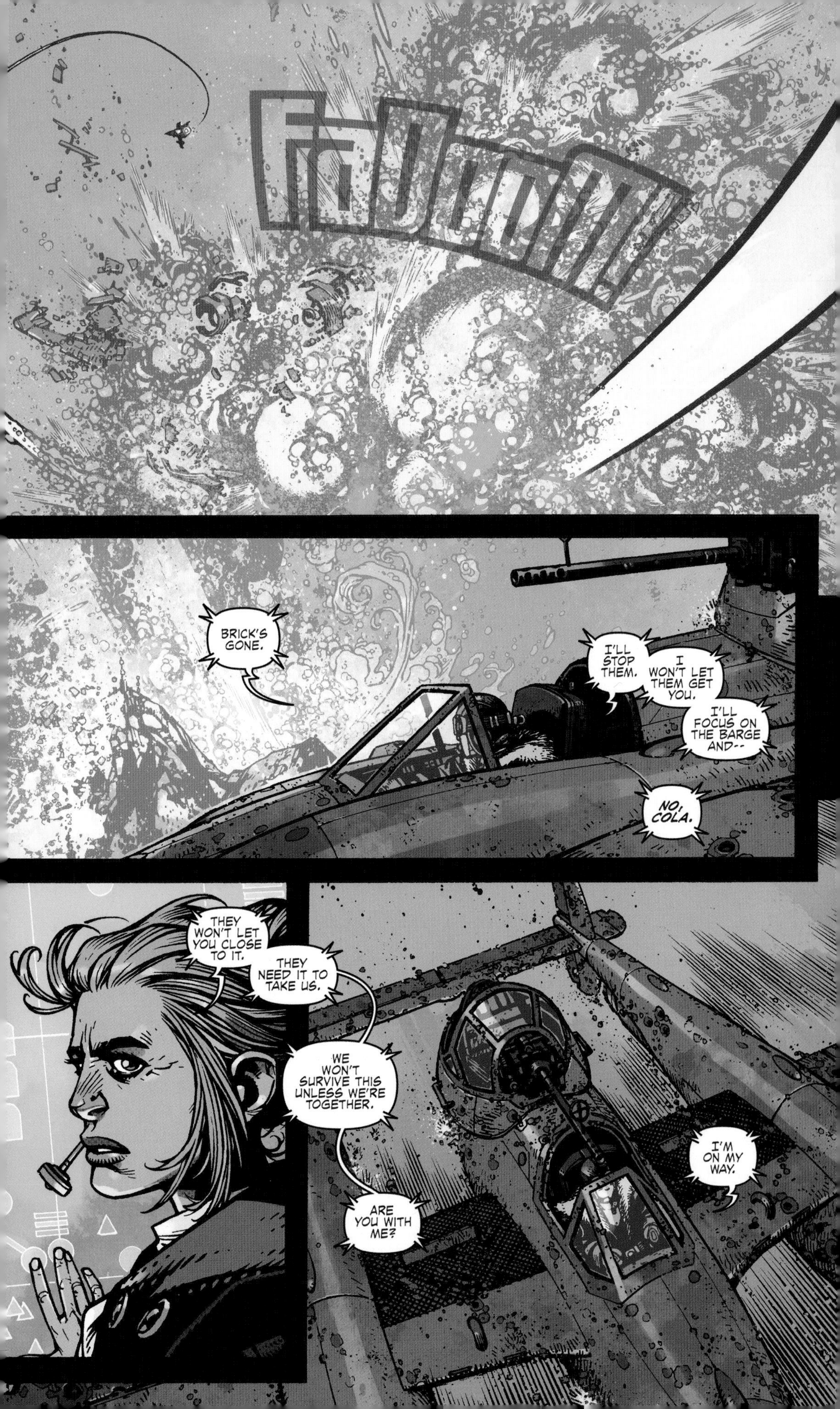
BRICK'S GONE.
I'LL STOP THEM.
I WON'T LET THEM GET YOU.
I'LL FOCUS ON THE BARGE AND--
NO, COLA.
THEY WON'T LET YOU CLOSE TO IT.
THEY NEED IT TO TAKE US.
WE WON'T SURVIVE THIS UNLESS WE'RE TOGETHER.
ARE YOU WITH ME?
I'M ON MY WAY.

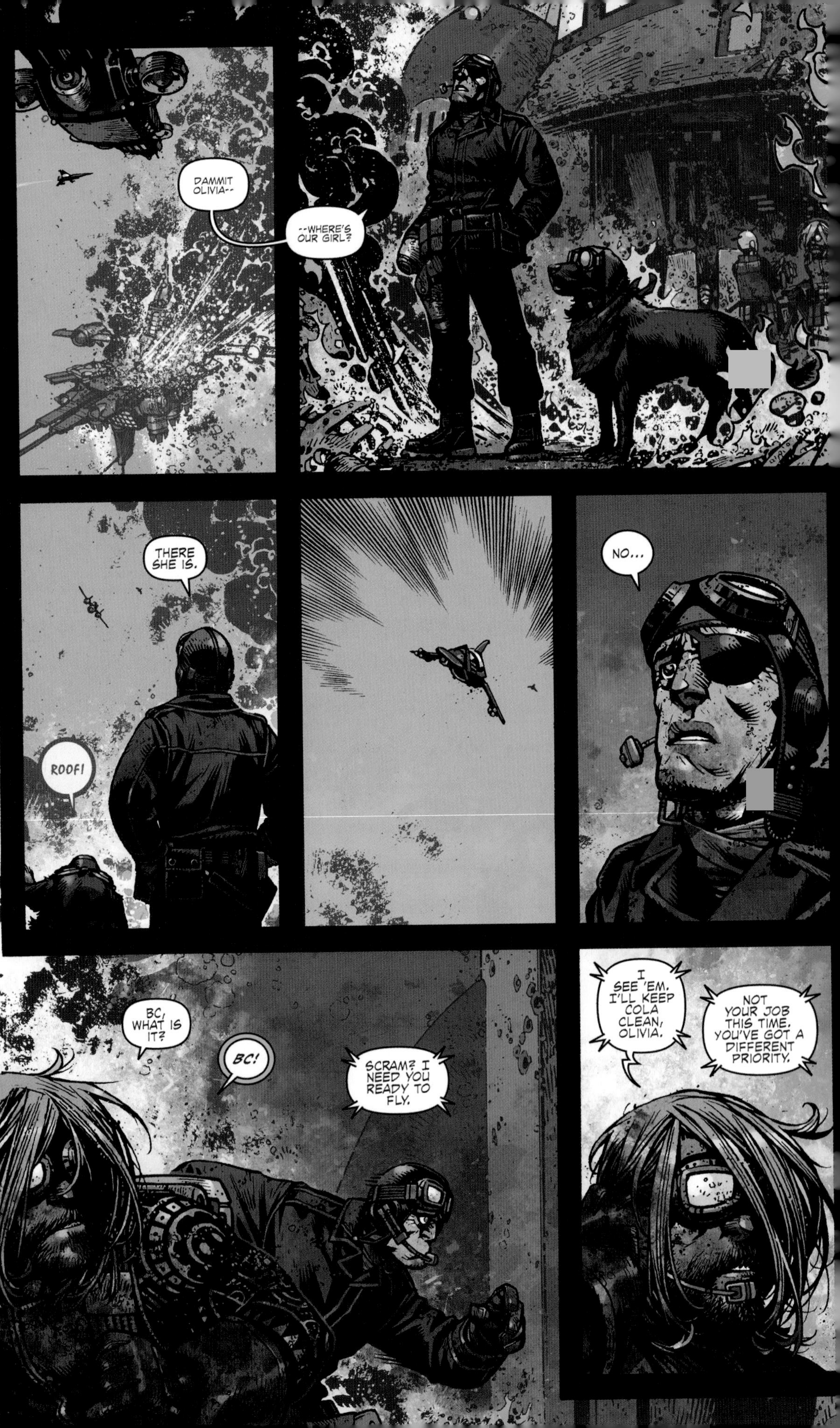

DAMMIT OLIVIA--
--WHERE'S OUR GIRL?
THERE SHE IS.
ROOF!
NO...
BC, WHAT IS IT?
BC!
SCRAM? I NEED YOU READY TO FLY.
I SEE 'EM. I'LL KEEP COLA CLEAN, OLIVIA.
NOT YOUR JOB THIS TIME. YOU'VE GOT A DIFFERENT PRIORITY.

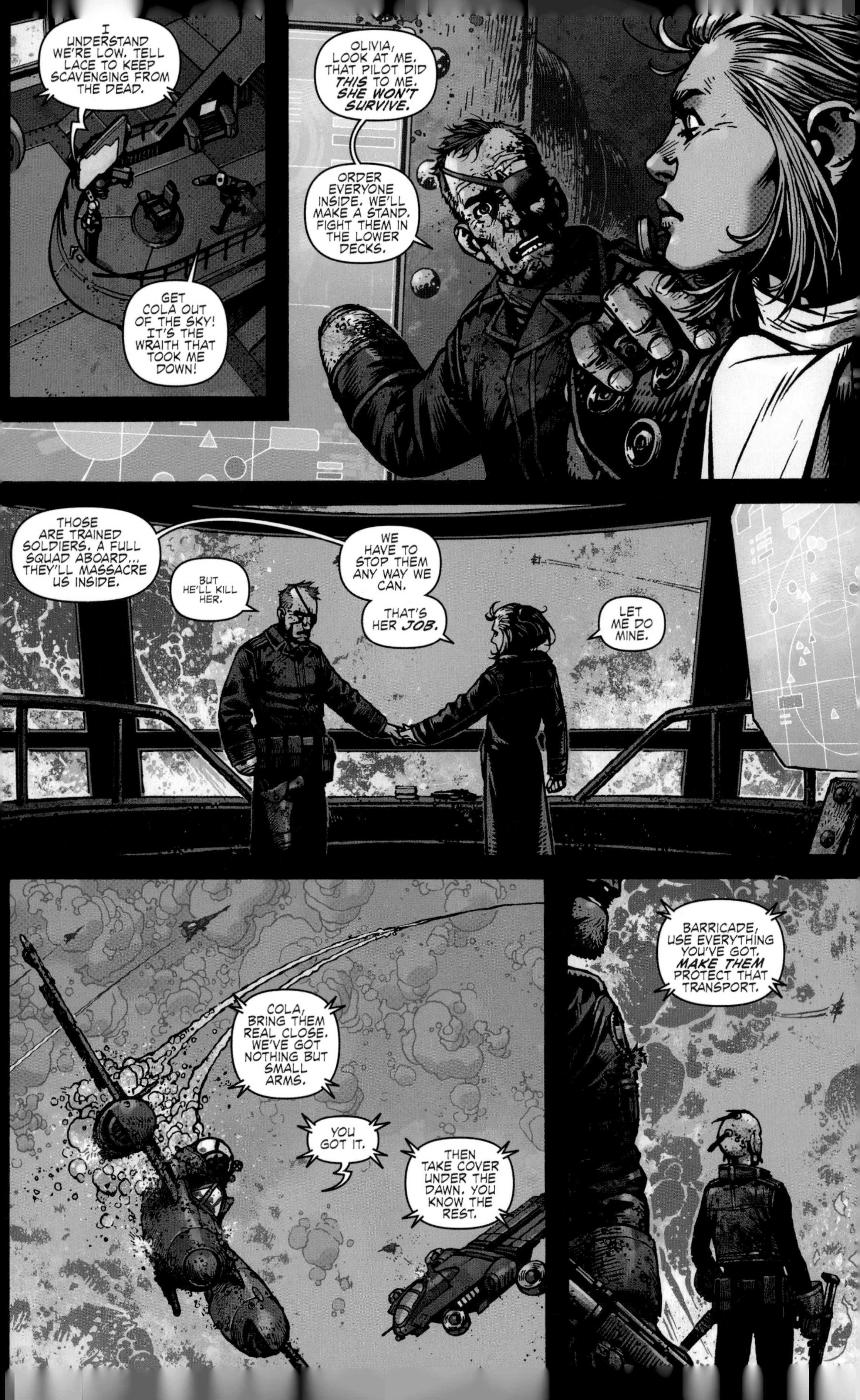
I UNDERSTAND WE'RE LOW. TELL LACE TO KEEP SCAVENGING FROM THE DEAD.
GET COLA OUT OF THE SKY! IT'S THE WRAITH THAT TOOK ME DOWN!
OLIVIA, LOOK AT ME. THAT PILOT DID THIS TO ME. SHE WON'T SURVIVE.
ORDER EVERYONE INSIDE. WE'LL MAKE A STAND. FIGHT THEM IN THE LOWER DECKS.
THOSE ARE TRAINED SOLDIERS. A FULL SQUAD ABOARD... THEY'LL MASSACRE US INSIDE.
WE HAVE TO STOP THEM ANY WAY WE CAN.
BUT HE'LL KILL HER.
THAT'S HER JOB.
LET ME DO MINE.
COLA, BRING THEM REAL CLOSE. WE'VE GOT NOTHING BUT SMALL ARMS.
YOU GOT IT.
THEN TAKE COVER UNDER THE DAWN. YOU KNOW THE REST.
BARRICADE, USE EVERYTHING YOU'VE GOT. MAKE THEM PROTECT THAT TRANSPORT.

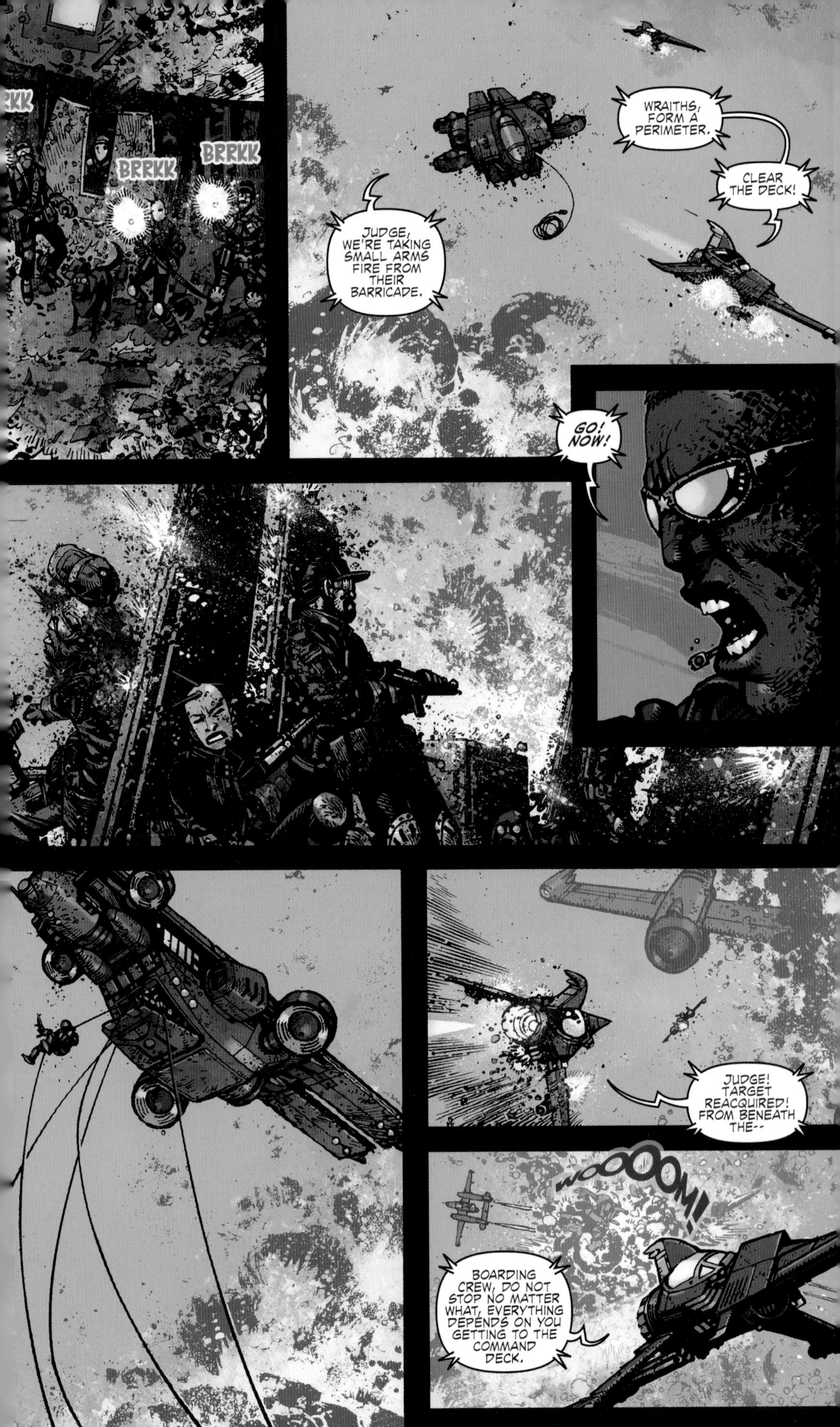
KK
BRRKK
BRRKK
WRAITHS, FORM A PERIMETER.
CLEAR THE DECK!
JUDGE, WE'RE TAKING SMALL ARMS FIRE FROM THEIR BARRICADE.
GO! NOW!
JUDGE! TARGET REACQUIRED! FROM BENEATH THE--
WOOOOM!
BOARDING CREW, DO NOT STOP NO MATTER WHAT, EVERYTHING DEPENDS ON YOU GETTING TO THE COMMAND DECK.

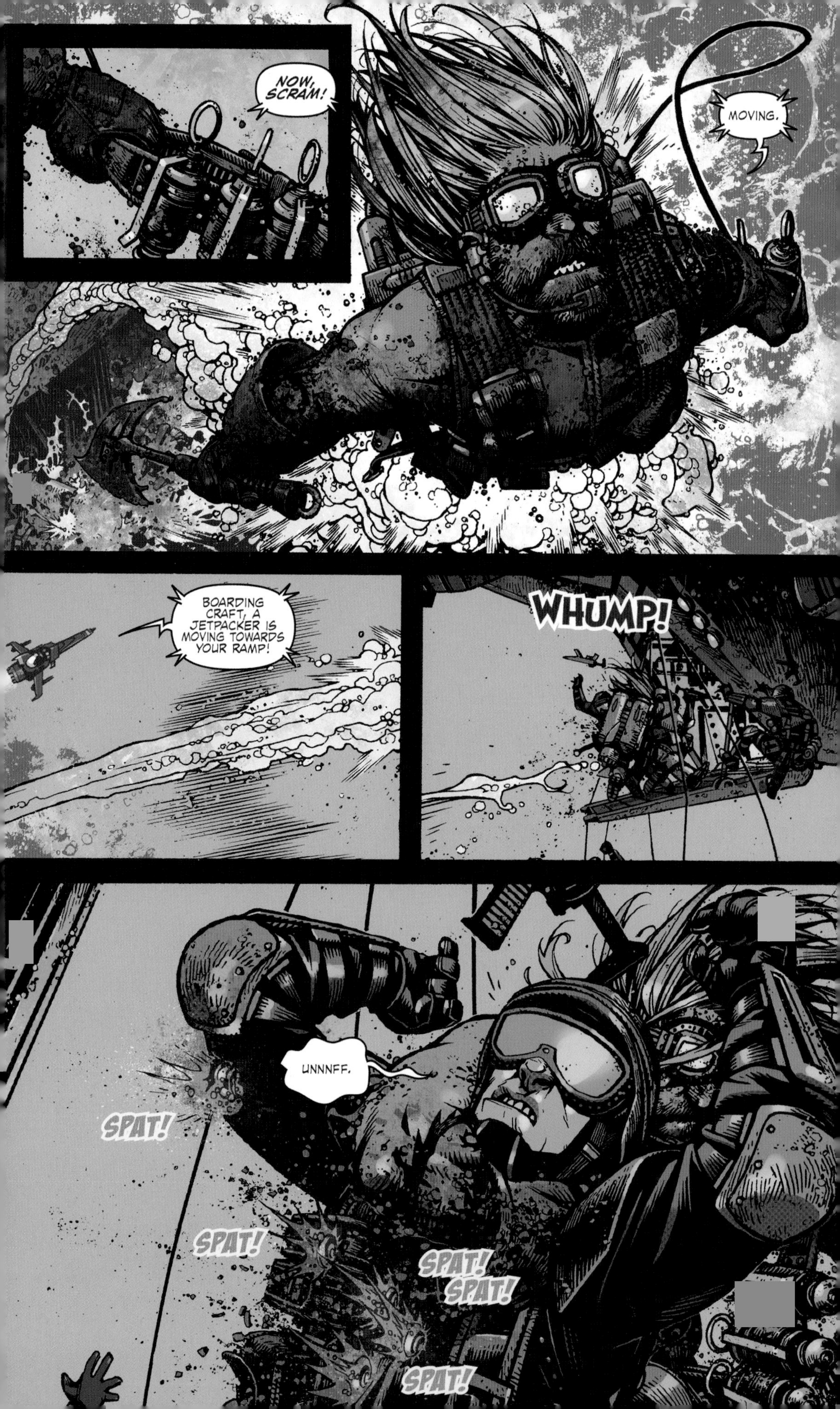
NOW, SCRAM!
MOVING.
BOARDING CRAFT, A JETPACKER IS MOVING TOWARDS YOUR RAMP!
WHUMP!
UNNNFF.
SPAT!
SPAT!
SPAT!
SPAT!
SPAT!

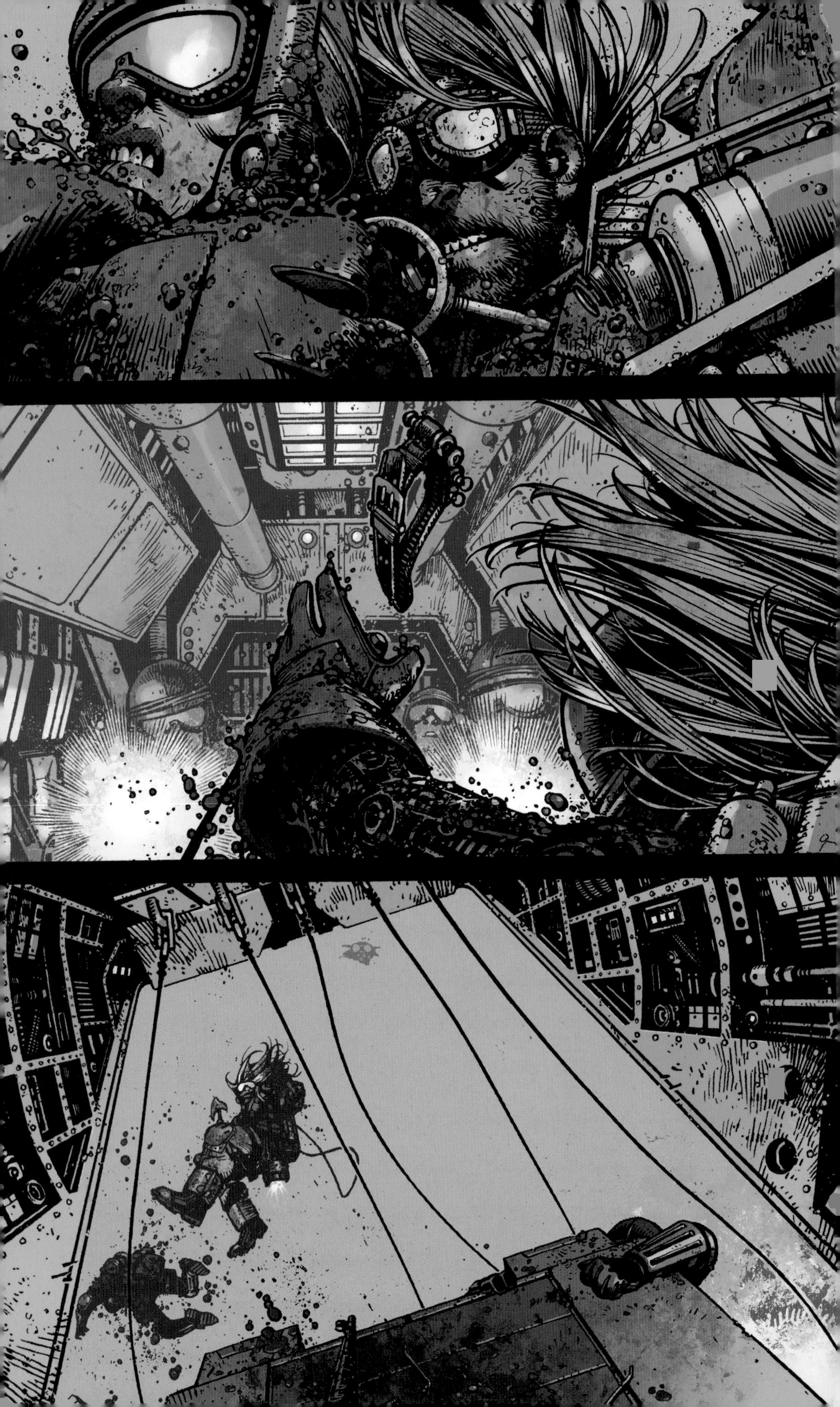

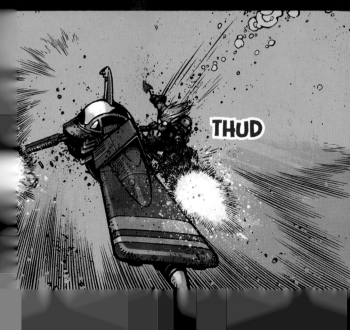

THUD

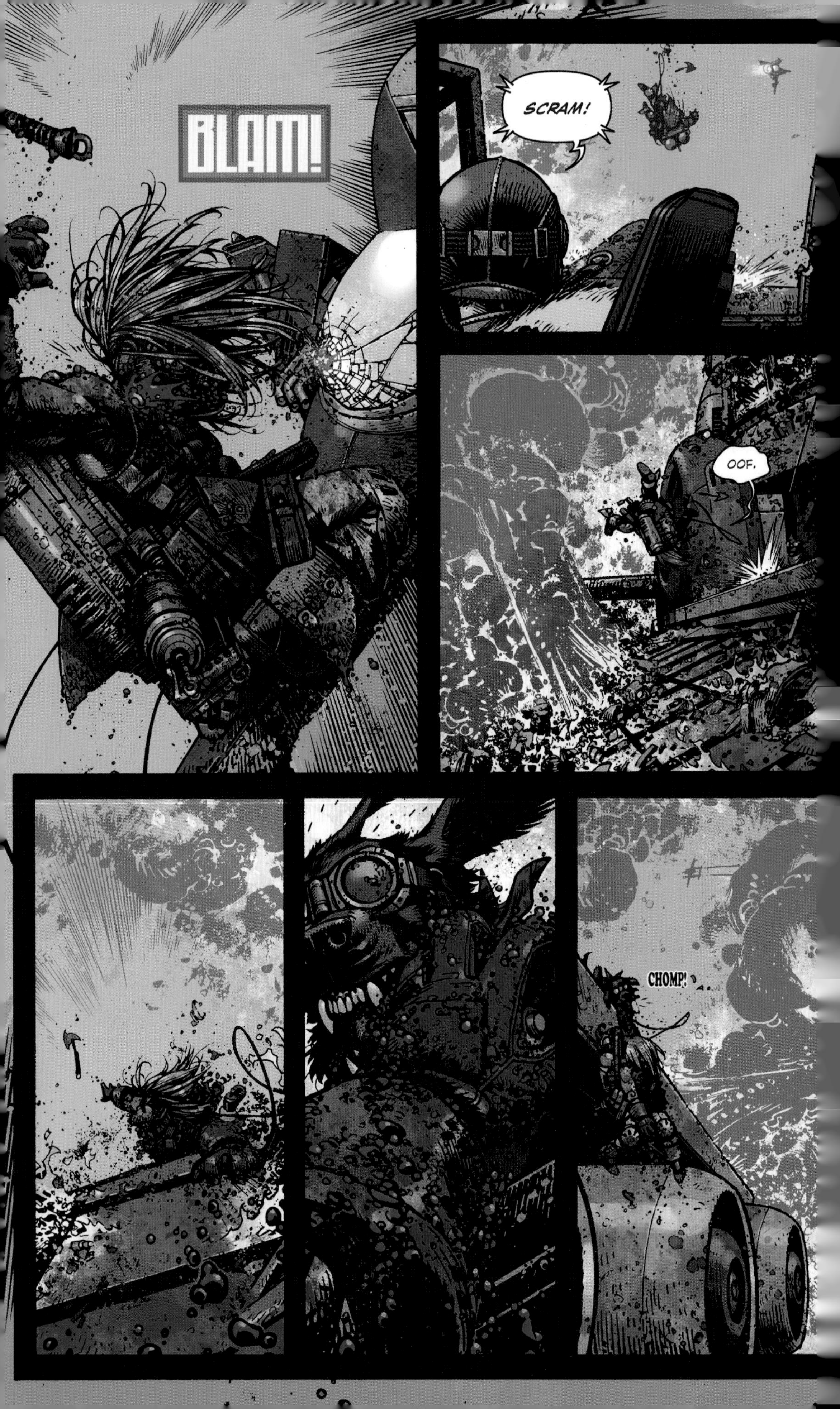
BLAM!
SCRAM!
OOF.
CHOMP!

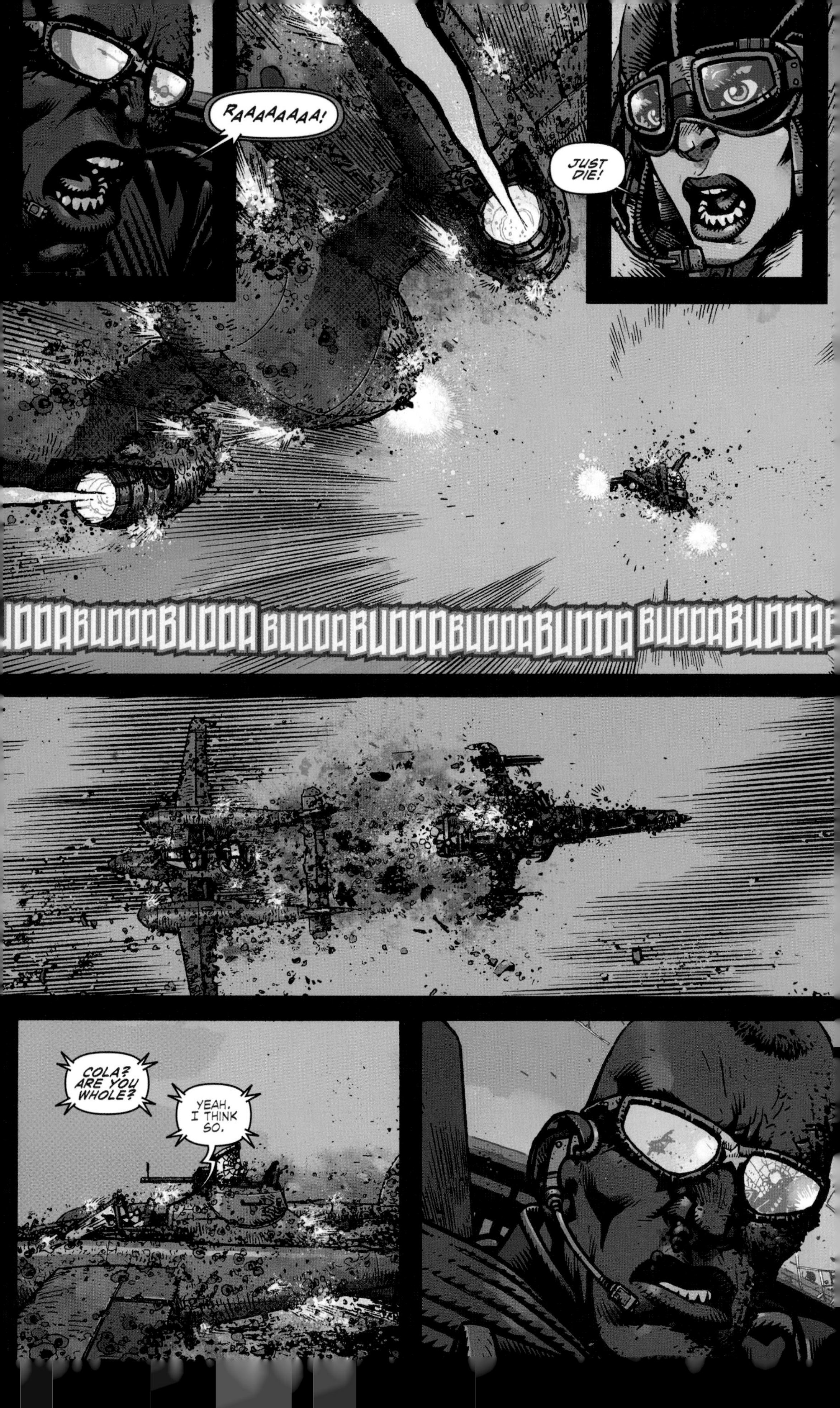
RAAAAAAAA!
JUST DIE!
BUDDABUDDA BUDDABUDDABUDDABUDDA BUDDABUDDA
COLA? ARE YOU WHOLE?
YEAH. I THINK SO.

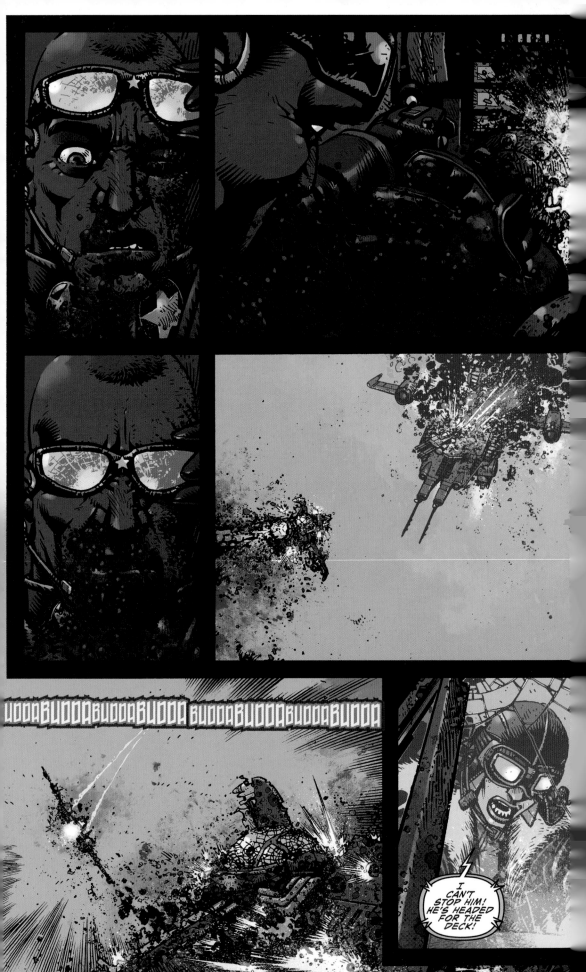

BUDDABUDDABUDDABUDDA BUDDABUDDABUDDABUDDA

I CAN'T STOP HIM! HE'S HEADED FOR THE DECK!

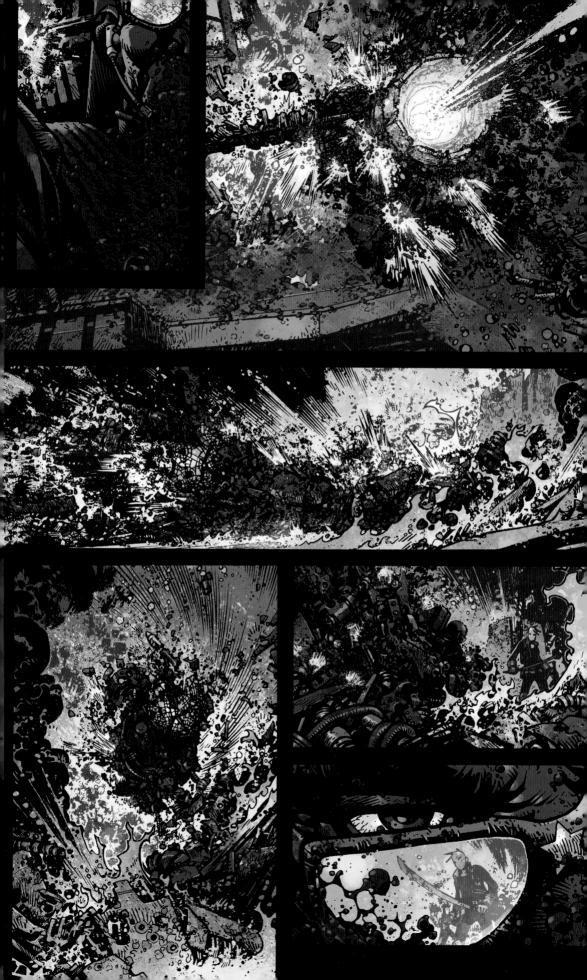

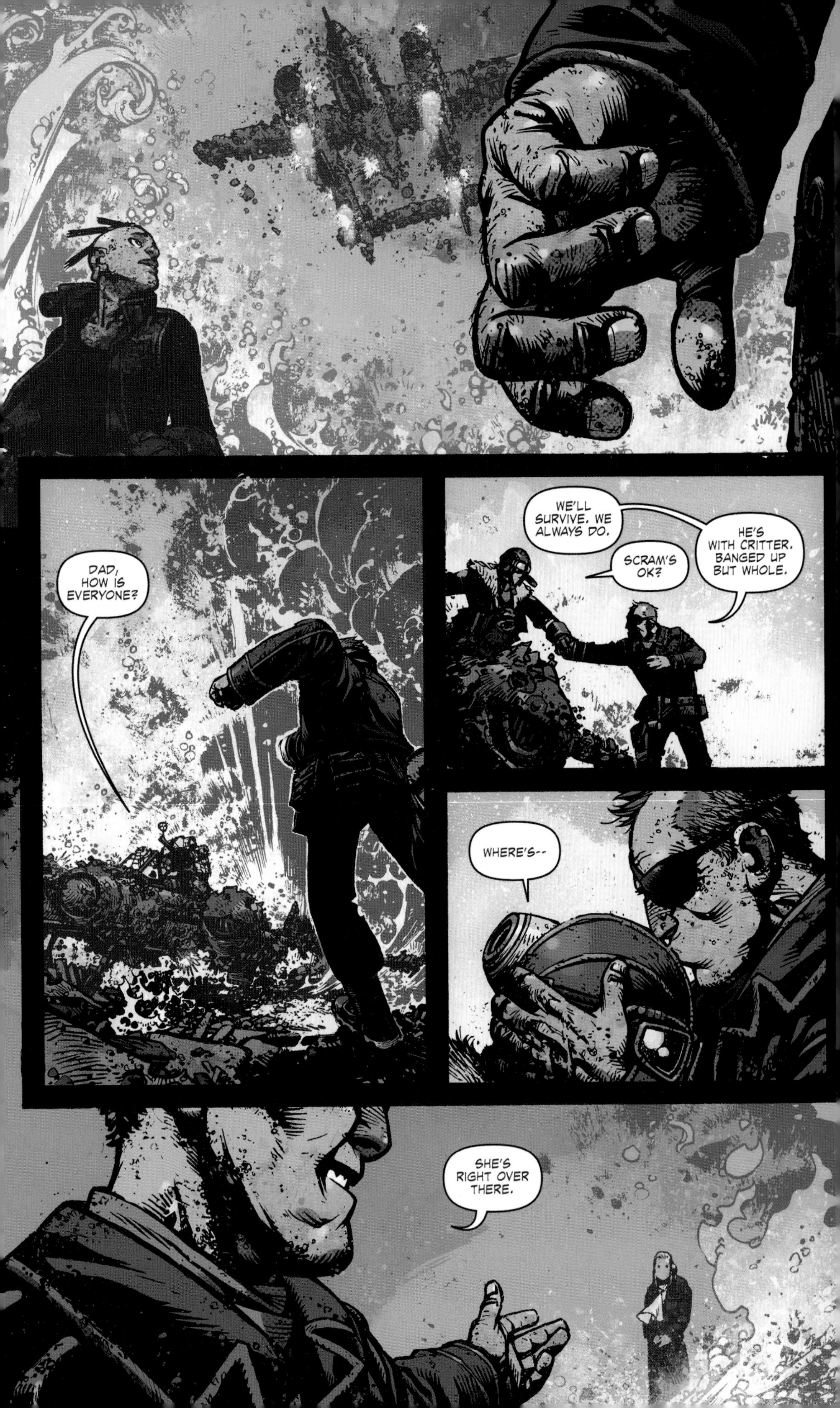
DAD, HOW IS EVERYONE?
WE'LL SURVIVE. WE ALWAYS DO.
SCRAM'S OK?
HE'S WITH CRITTER. BANGED UP BUT WHOLE.
WHERE'S--
SHE'S RIGHT OVER THERE.

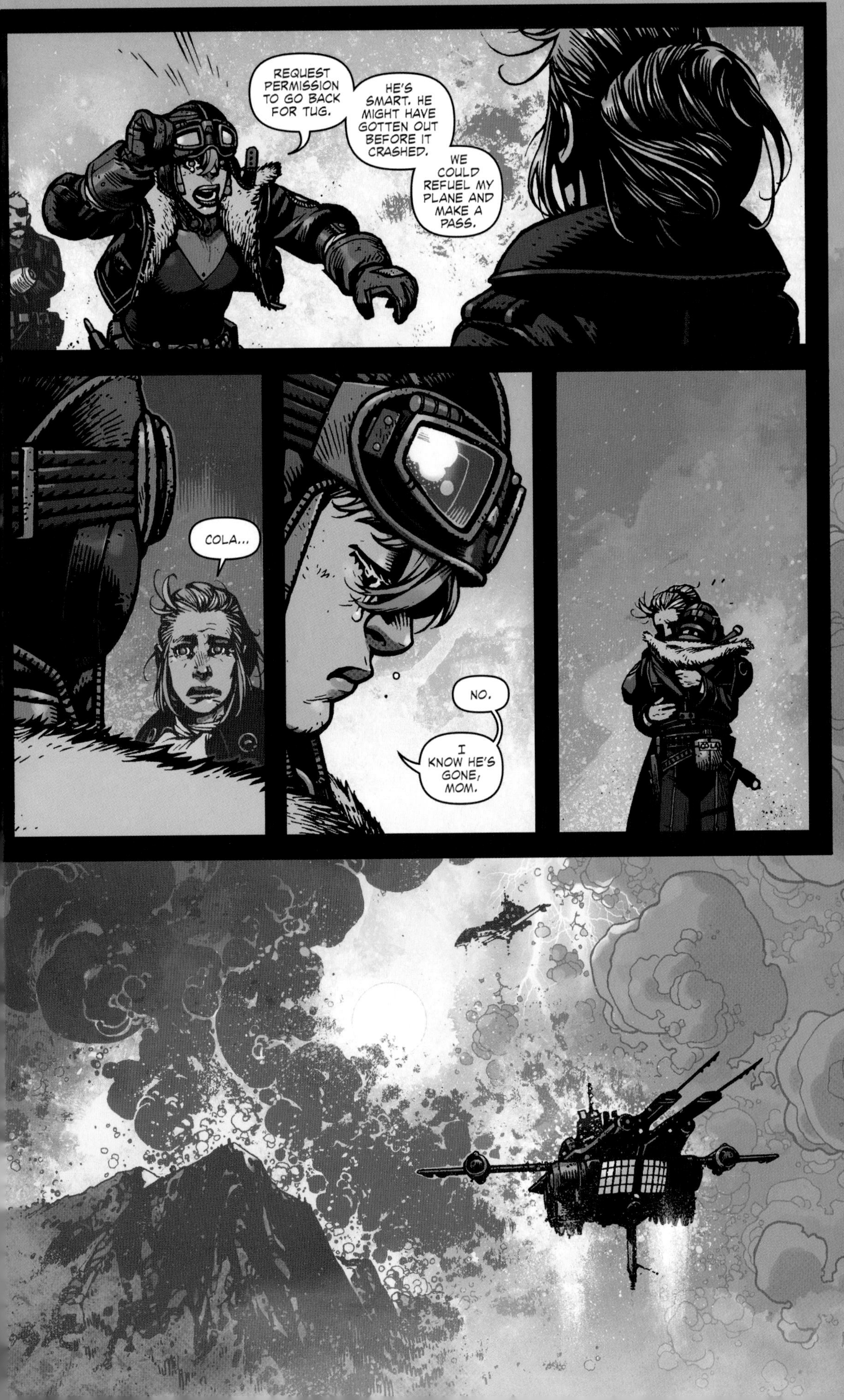
REQUEST PERMISSION TO GO BACK FOR TUG.
HE'S SMART. HE MIGHT HAVE GOTTEN OUT BEFORE IT CRASHED.
WE COULD REFUEL MY PLANE AND MAKE A PASS.
COLA...
NO.
I KNOW HE'S GONE, MOM.

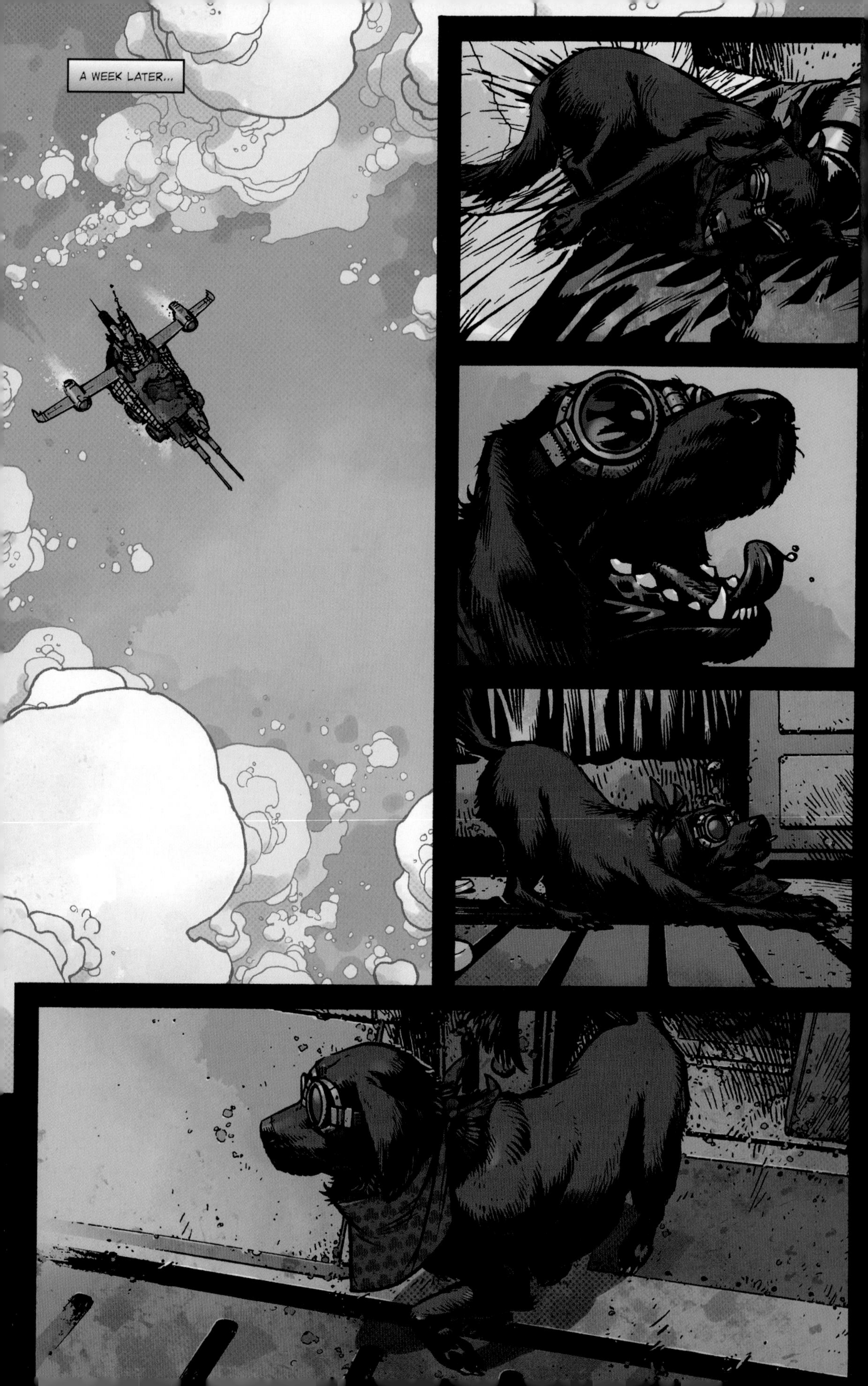
A WEEK LATER...

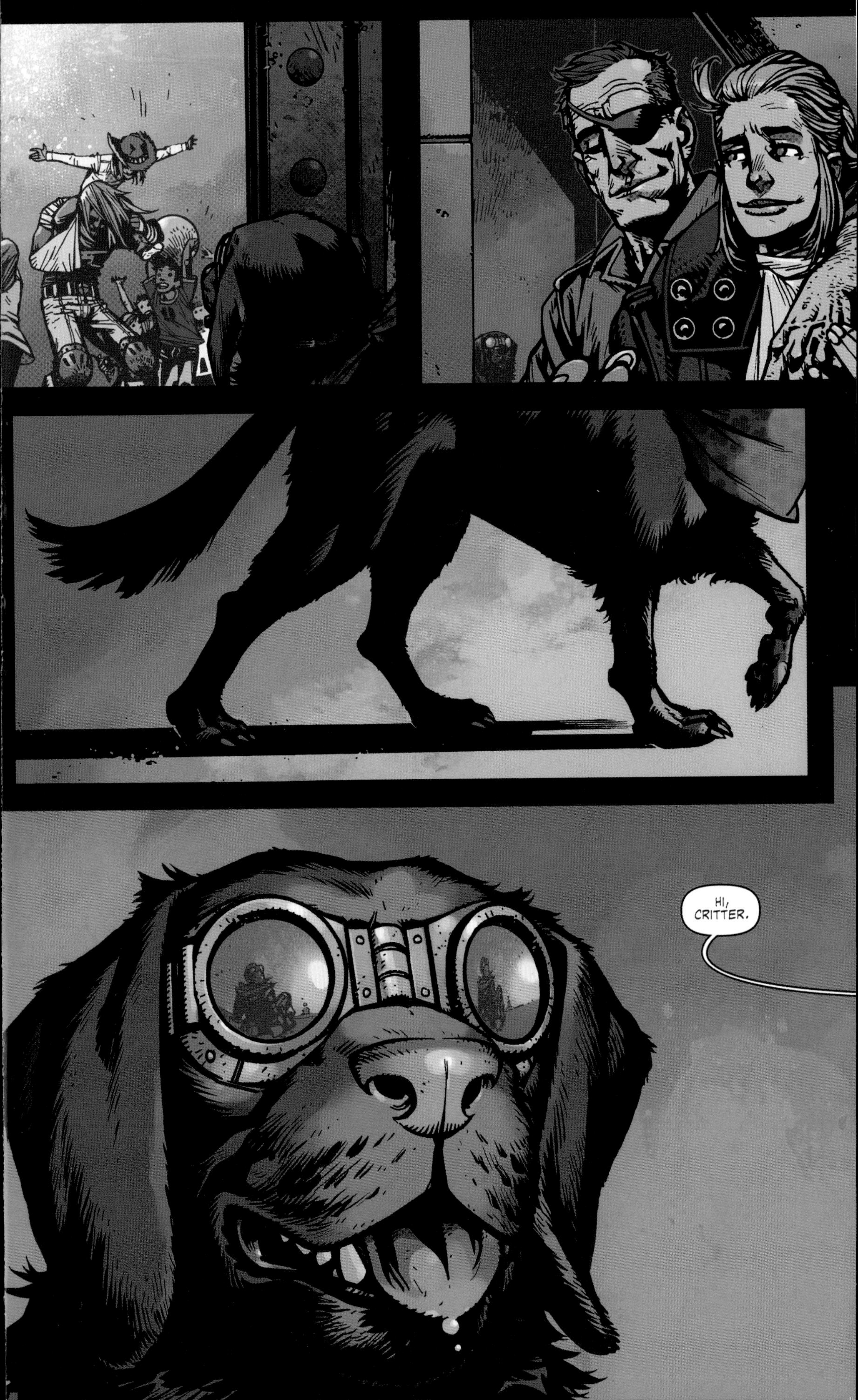
HI, CRITTER.

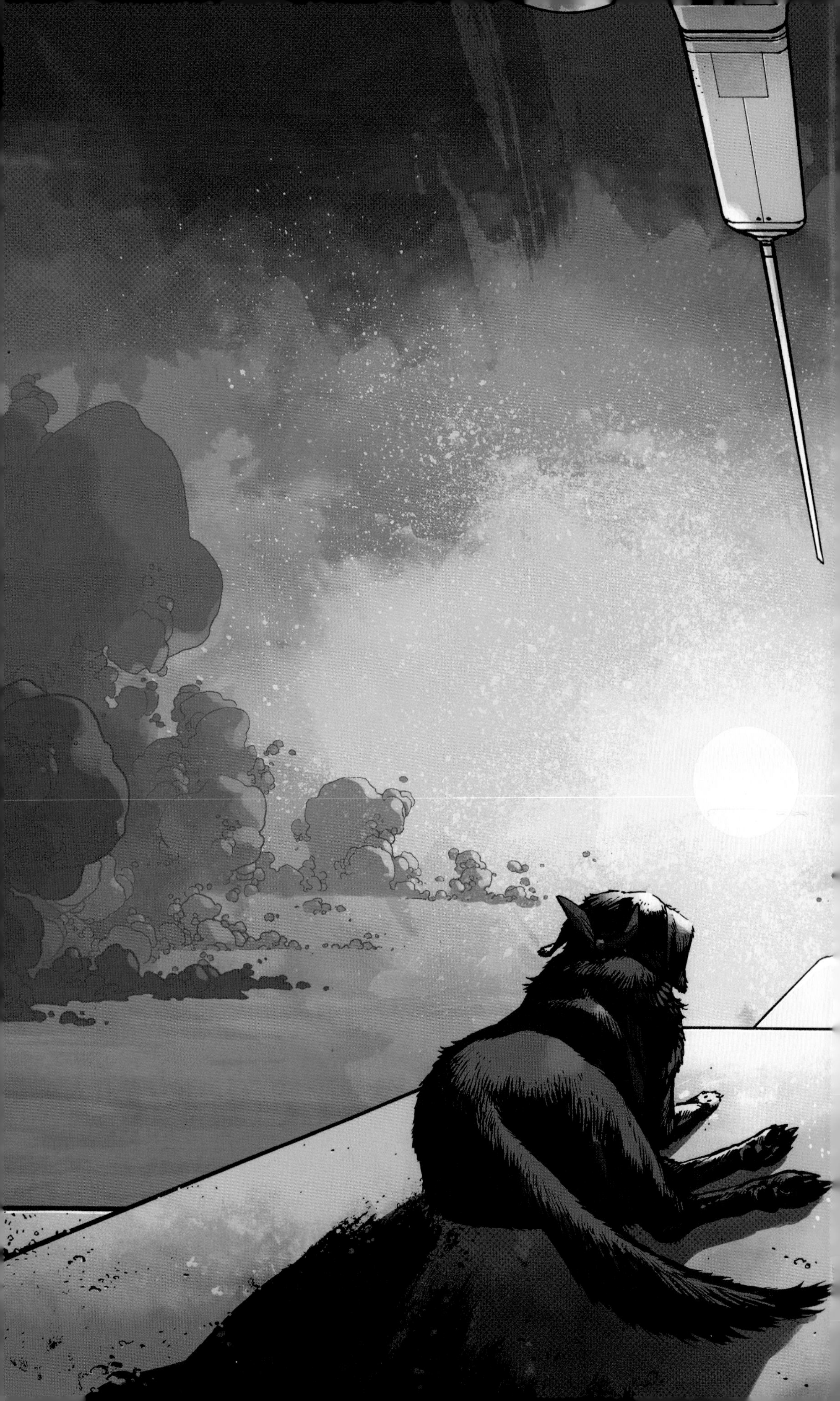

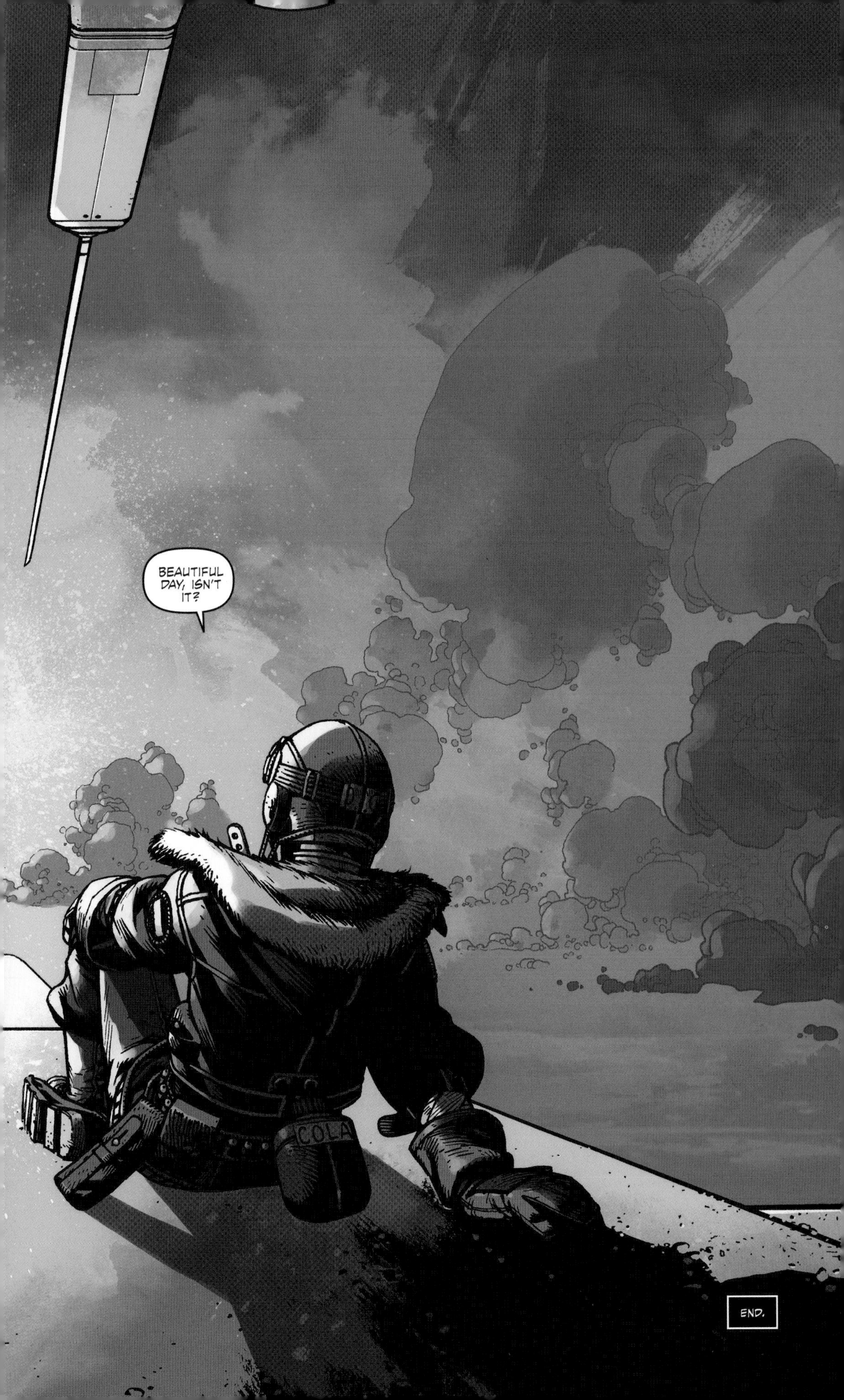
BEAUTIFUL DAY, ISN'T IT?
COLA
END.

GALLERY

PINUPS

NICK RUNGE

PAULIUS ZAKARAUSKAS

JOLYON YATES

DANIEL WARREN JOHNSON

JON ADAMS

COVERS

JENNIFER MEYER

PAULIUS ZAKARAUSKAS

NICK RUNGE

CHARLES PAUL WILSON III

PAULIUS ZAKARAUSKAS

CONCEPT ART

ZACH HOWARD

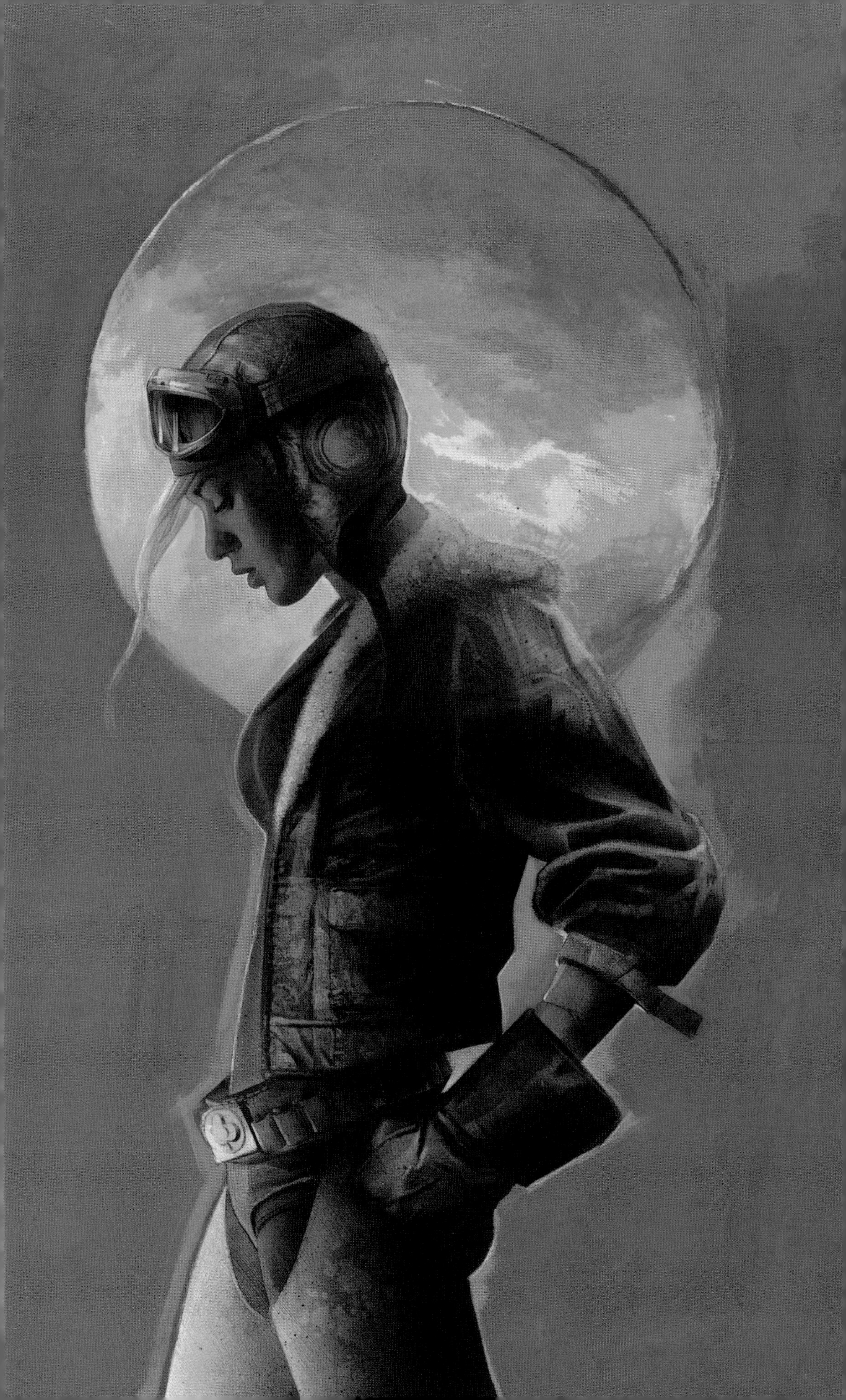

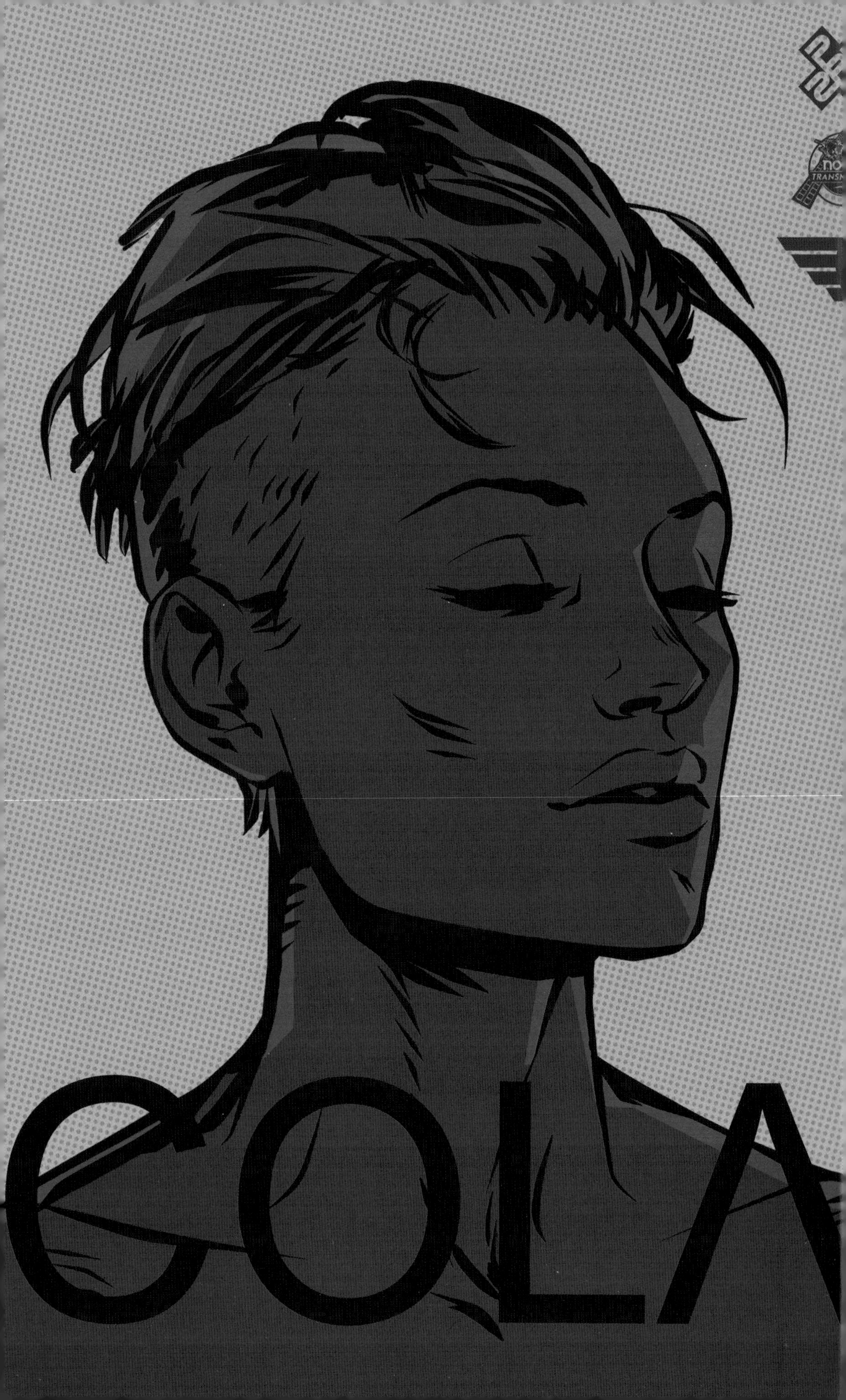
COLA

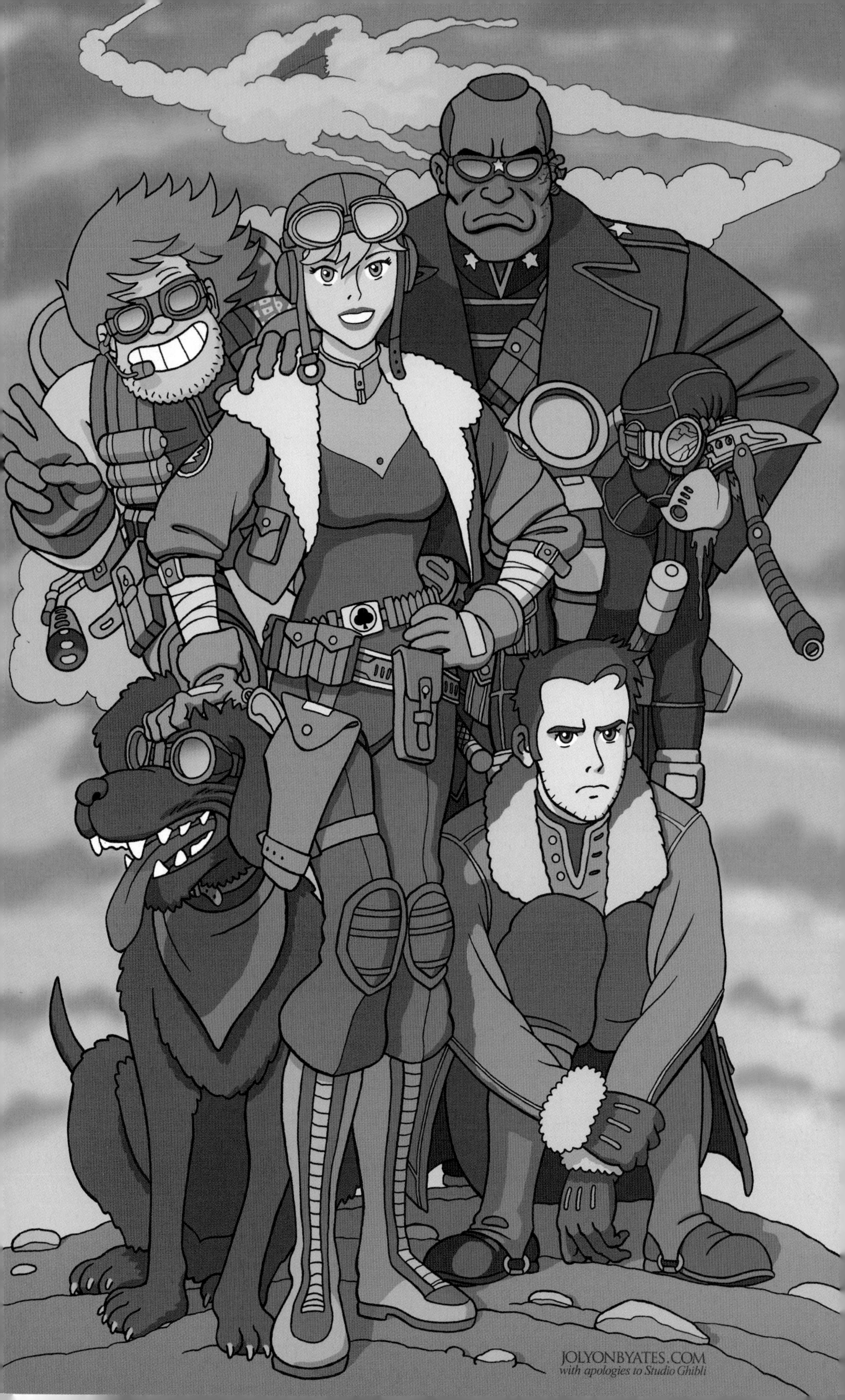
JOLYONBYATES.COM
with apologies to Studio Ghibli

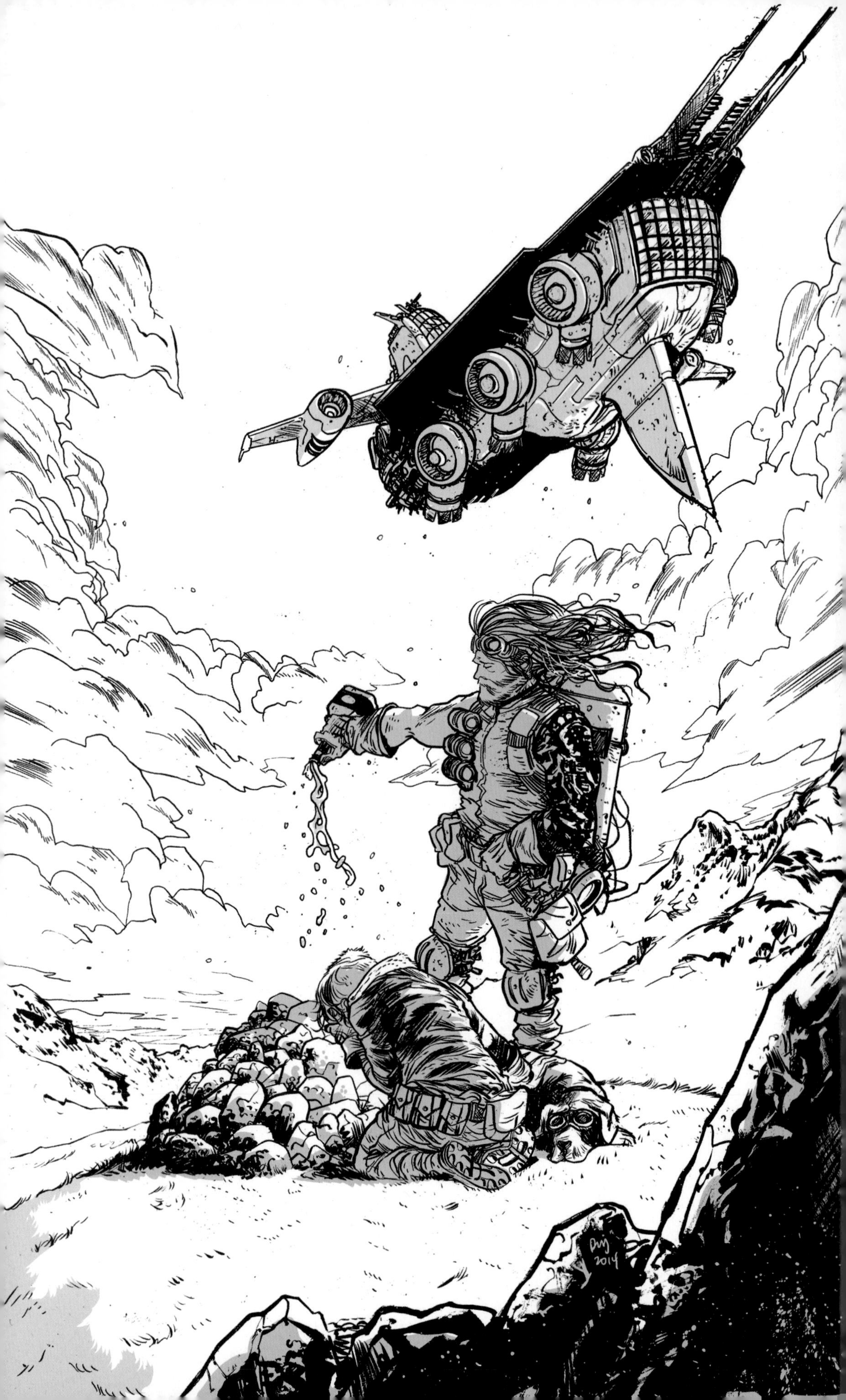

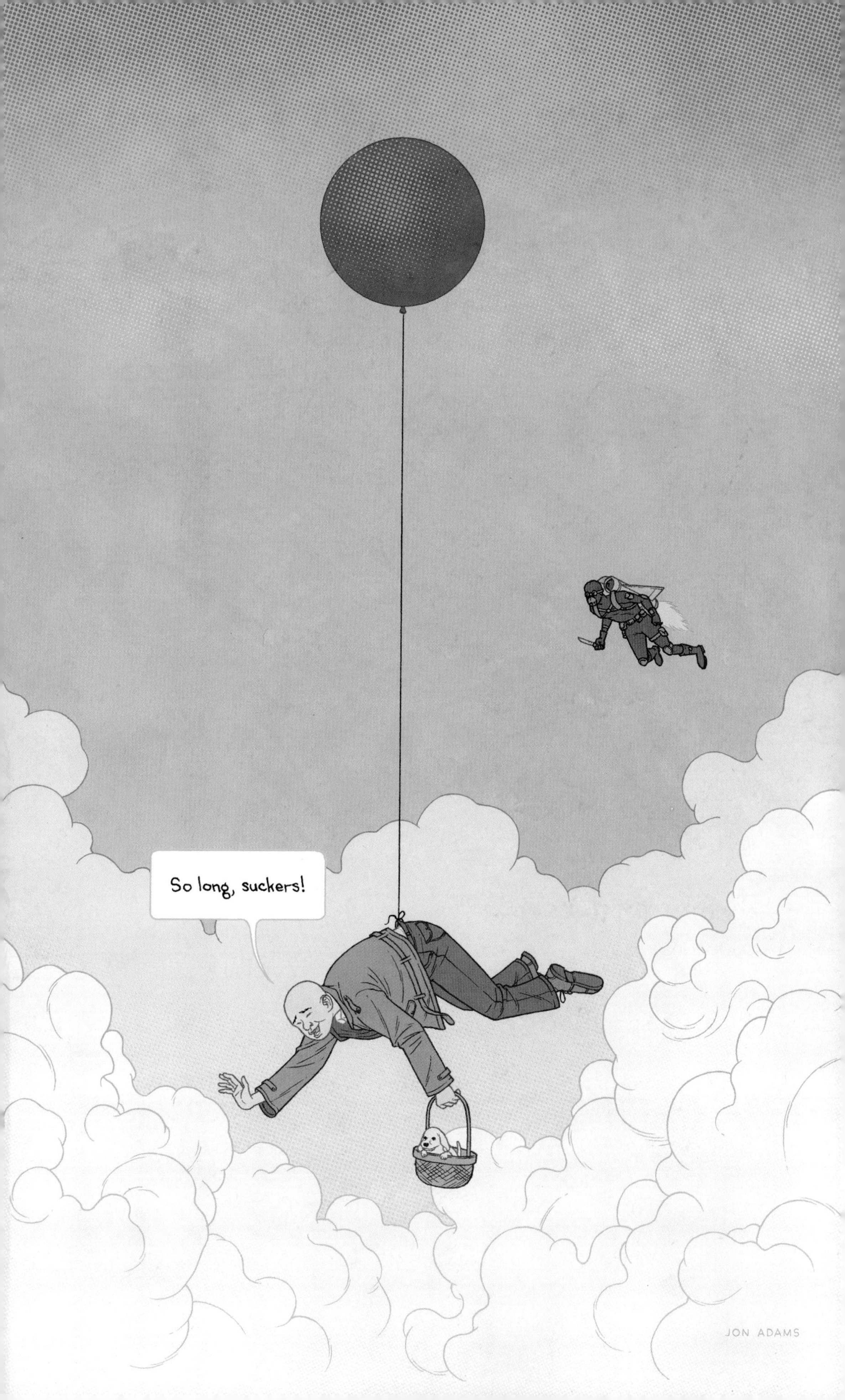
So long, suckers!
JON ADAMS

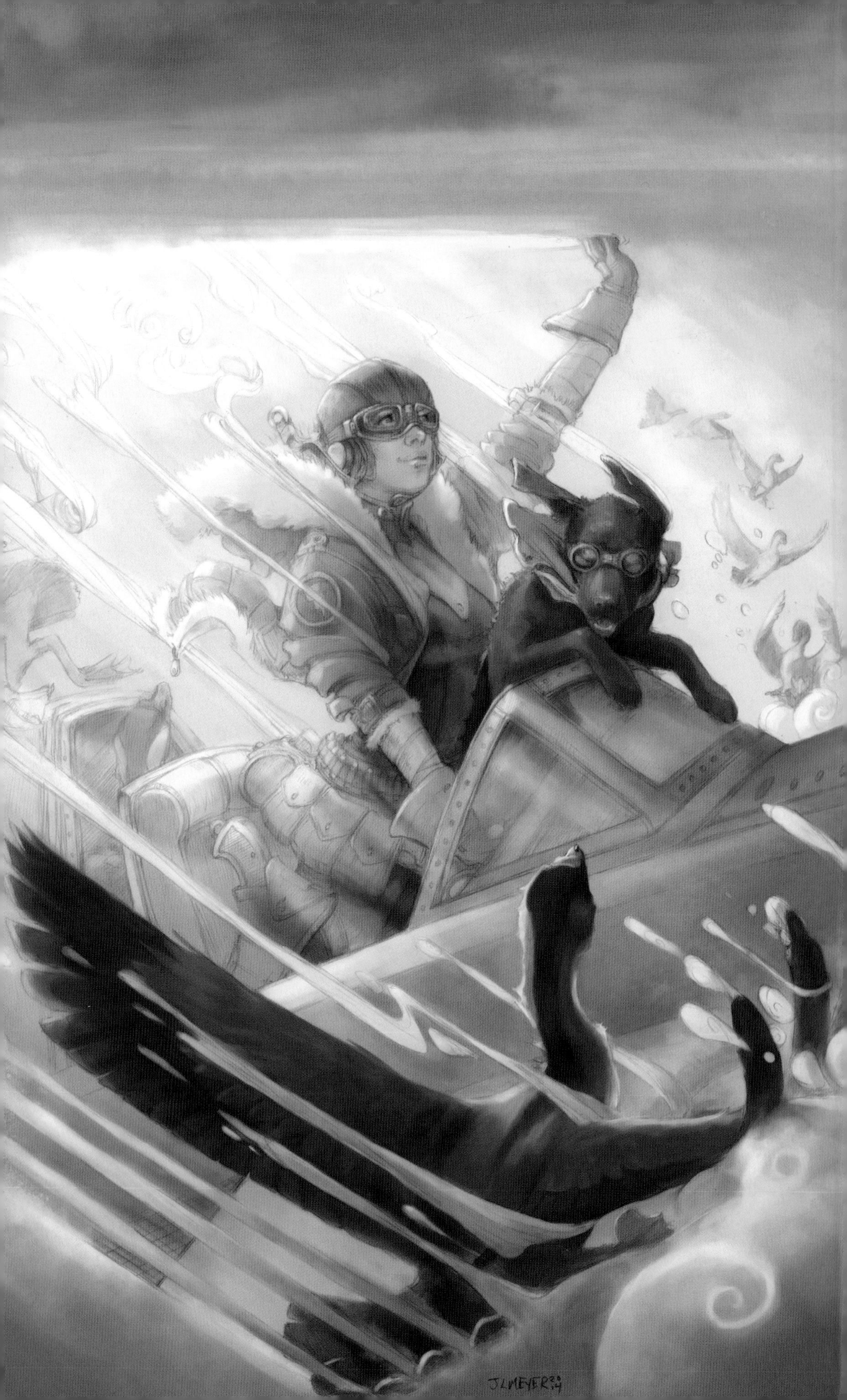
JLMEYER

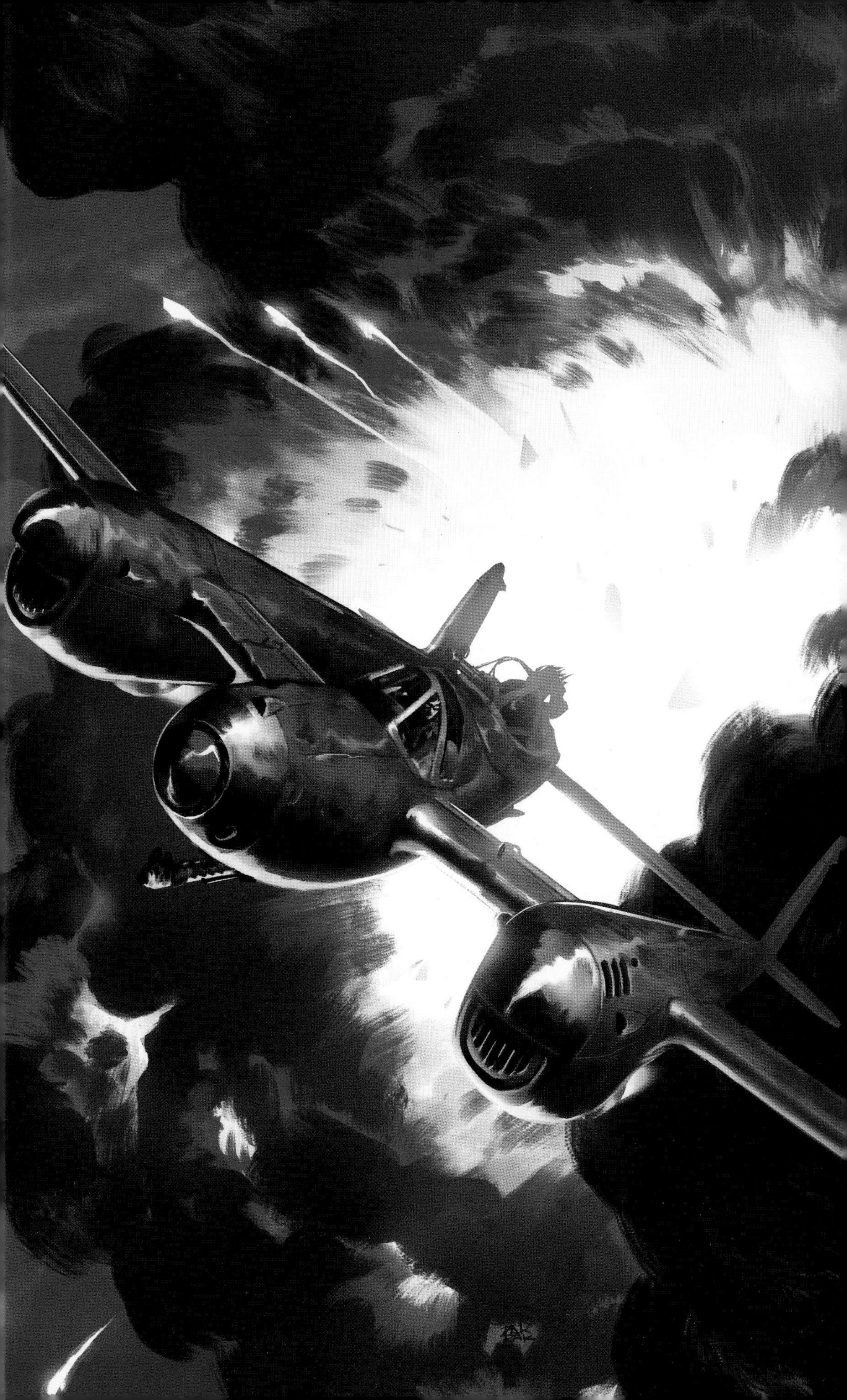

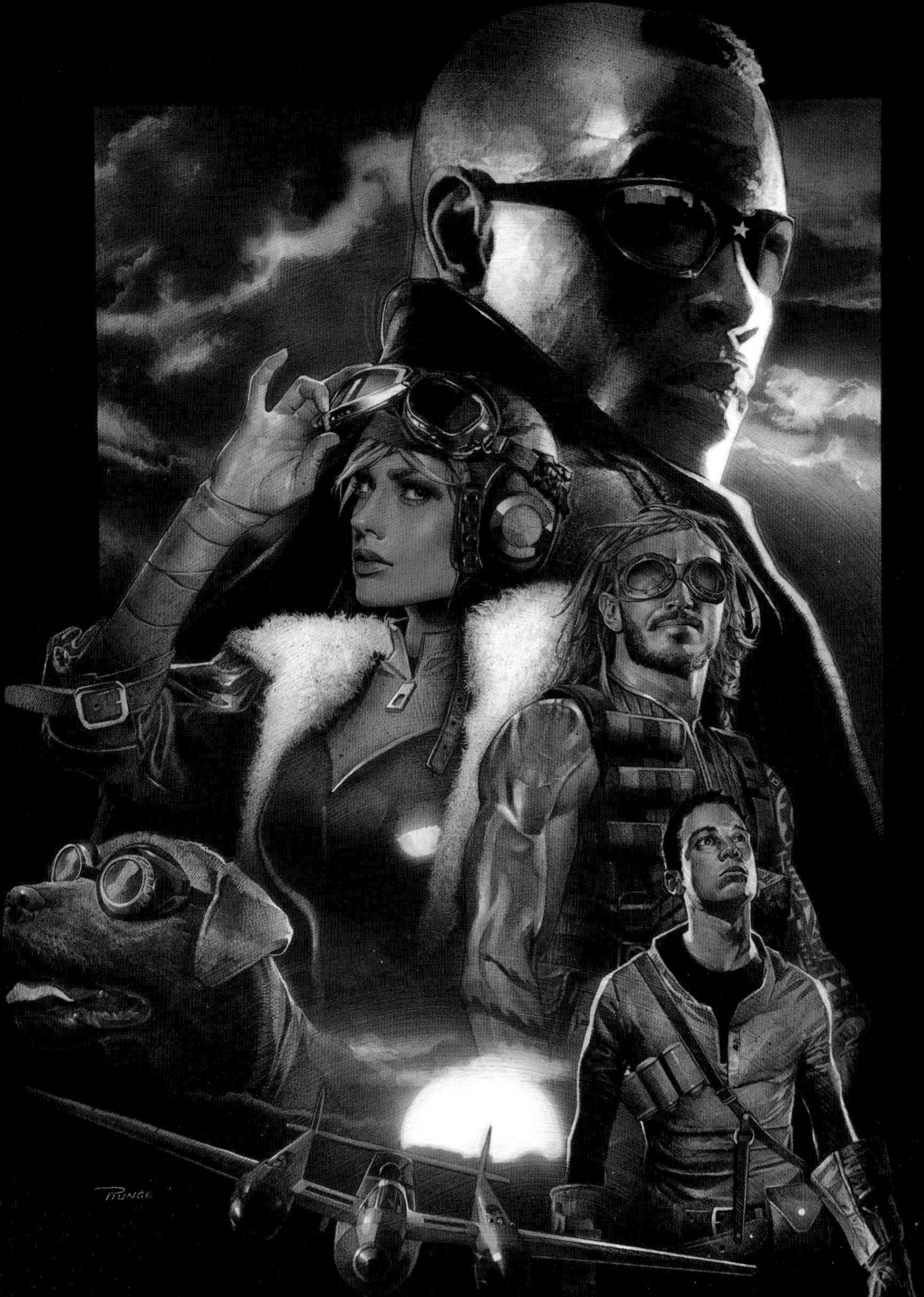
RUNGE

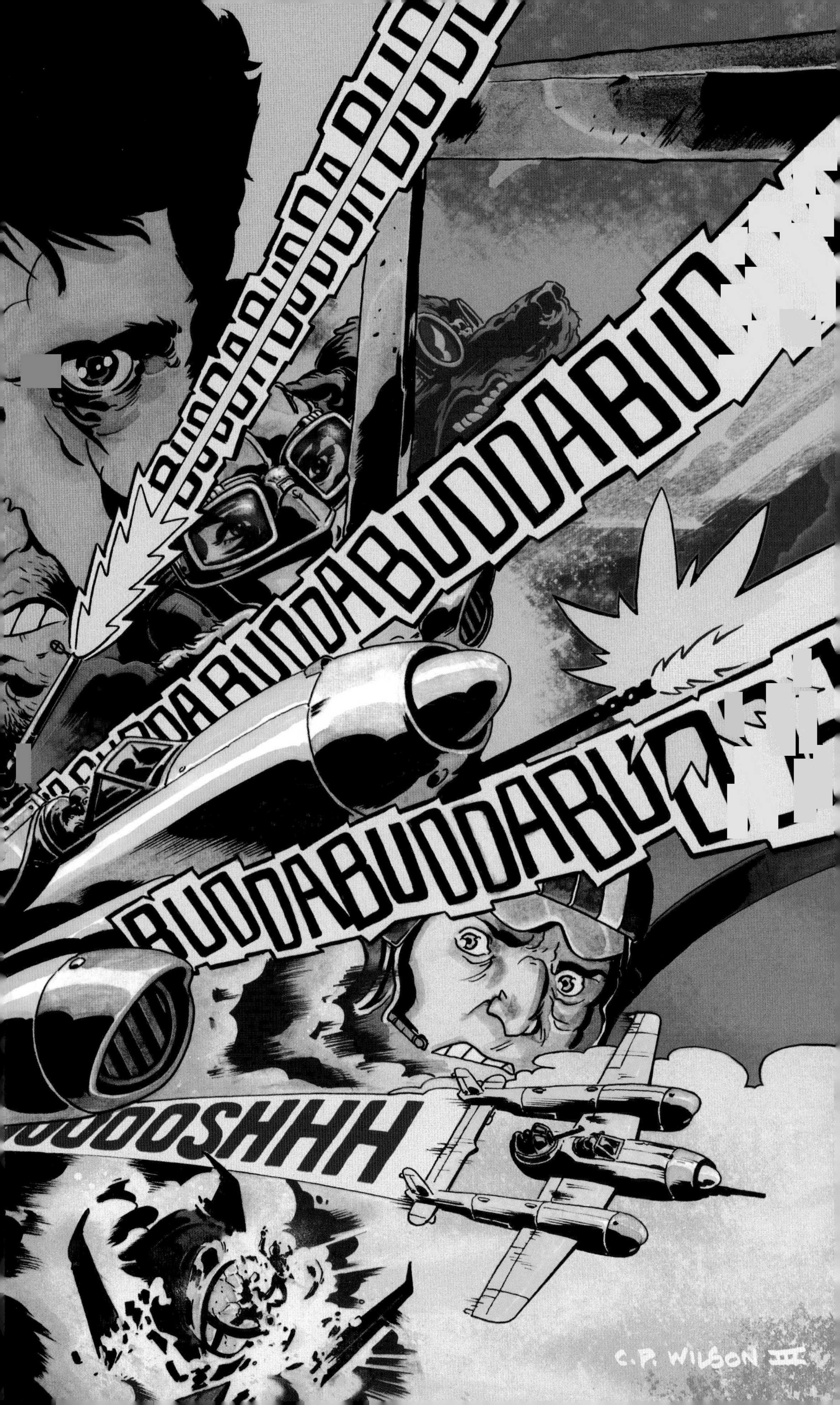
BUDDABUDDABUD
BUDDABUDDABUD
HHHSOOOO
C.P. WILSON III

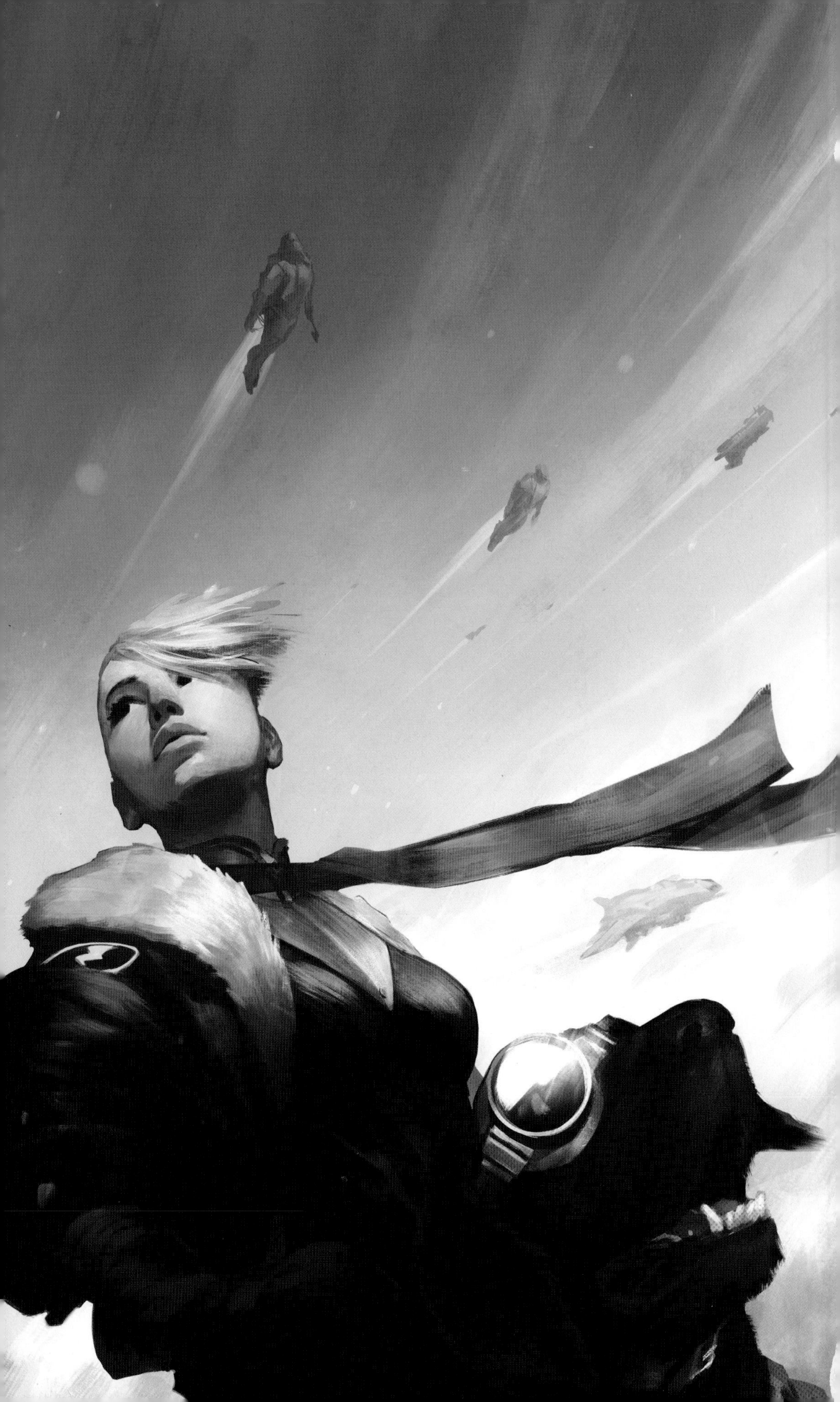

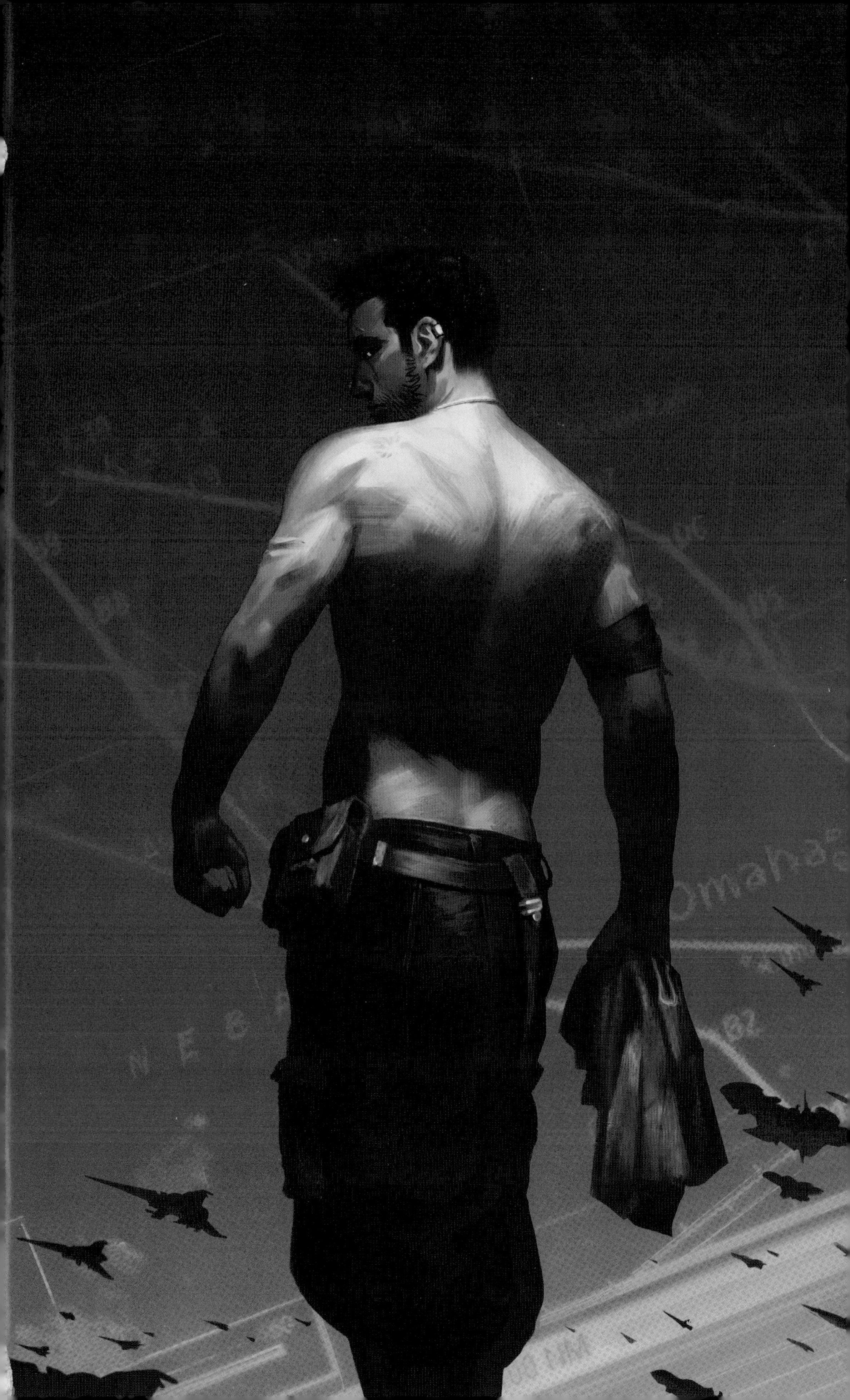

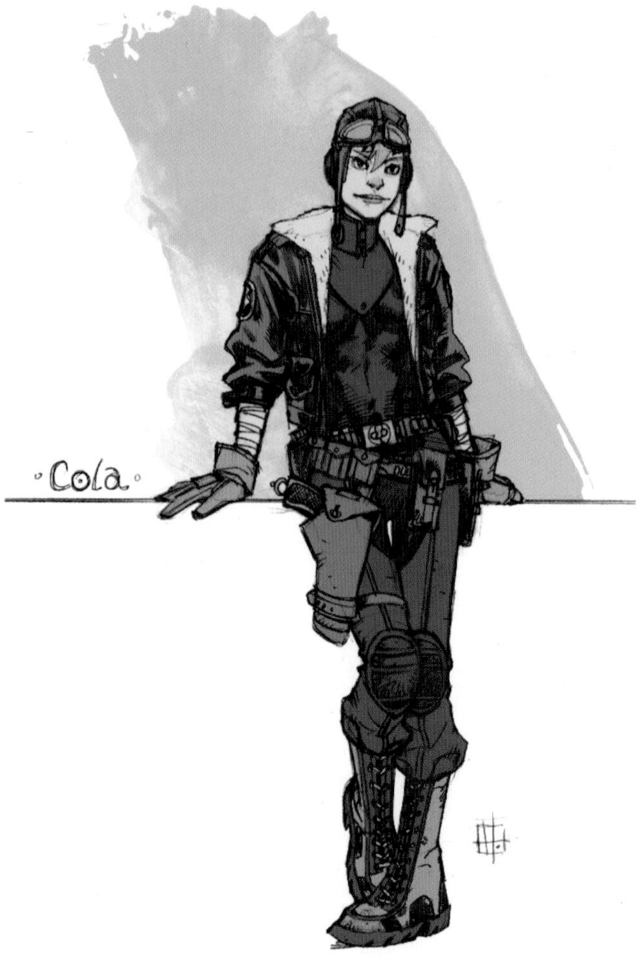
Cola

COLA'S JET

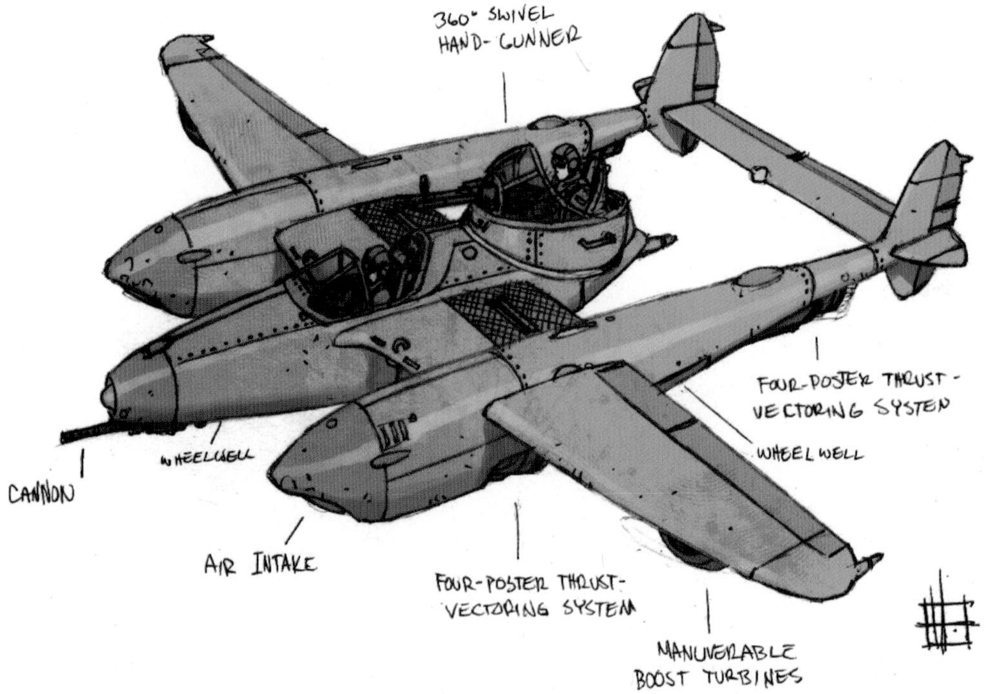
360° SWIVEL HAND-GUNNER
FOUR-POSTER THRUST-VECTORING SYSTEM
WHEEL WELL
WHEELWELL
CANNON
AIR INTAKE
FOUR-POSTER THRUST-VECTORING SYSTEM
MANUVERABLE BOOST TURBINES

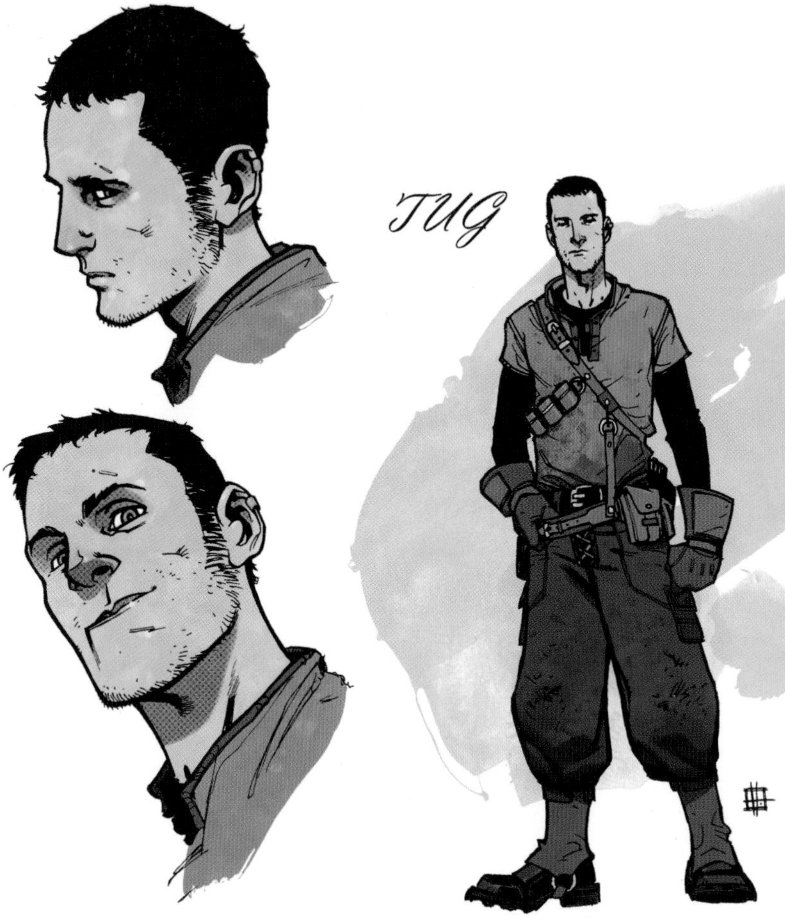
TUG

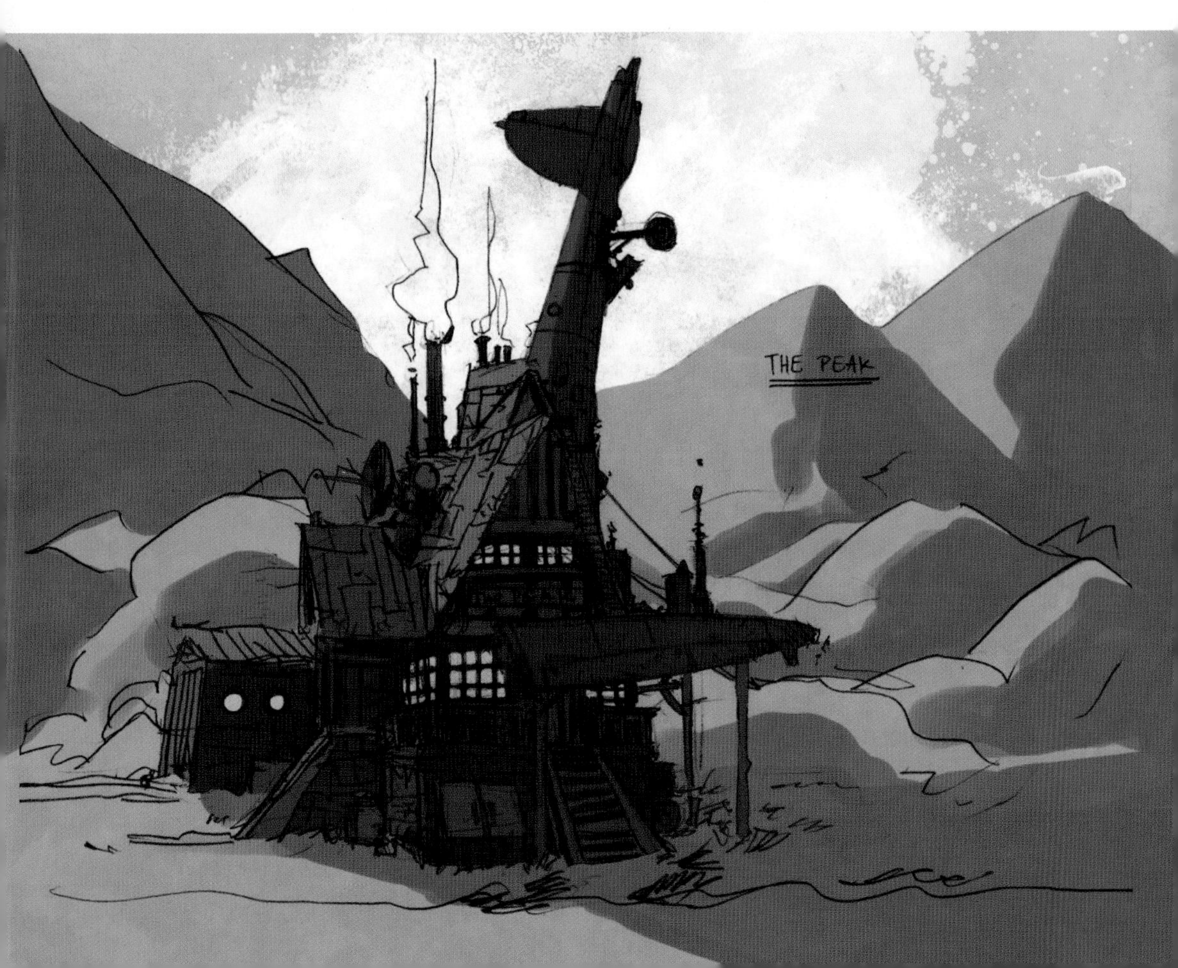
THE PEAK

D U K E

During the making of this book, my beloved model for Critter passed away. Five years ago, my wife and I adopted him from a shelter because he was nine and had little chance of ever finding a home. Shortly after bringing him into our lives, he posed for this wonderful shot of Critter.

Duke was the gentlest creature I have ever met—great or small. He was truly wonderful. I love him and I will miss him horribly. He was a good boy.

- Zach Howard